Discipl Without Distress

135 tools for raising caring, responsible children without
time-out, spanking, punishment, or bribery

by Judy Arnall

Advance Praise For
Discipline Without Distress

"The world is in desperate need of gentle, caring discipline techniques. Judy Arnall has created a wonderful, nurturing guide that all parents can benefit from."
~ Elizabeth Pantley, Author of *The No-Cry Discipline Solution*, *The No-Cry Sleep Solution*, and *The No-Cry Potty Training Solution*

"This book is a very valuable resource for parents of children of all ages. First, Judy Arnall documents the damage that punishment does to the parent-child relationship. Then she offers a wealth of ideas and suggestions for raising children without the use of punishment of any kind. The book deals both with how to prevent problems and conflicts with children and how to handle conflicts once they have occurred. It's especially useful for parents who are P.E.T. graduates. I highly recommend it."
~ Linda Adams, President and CEO of Gordon Training International – P.E.T.

"Many families struggle to create and maintain healthy connection in a fast-paced and technology influenced culture. This book provides a do-able approach for parents who want to provide the highest level of family interaction and support. Arnall's benevolent strategies have worked not only for the hundreds of parents she has guided but also for her five thriving children. Learn the nuts and bolts of raising resilient children. Here's help to 'putting it all together.'"
~ Patricia Morgan, speaker, counsellor and author of *The Light Hearted Approach: 87 Ways to Be an Upbeat Parent* and *Love Her As She Is: Lessons from a Daughter Stolen by Addictions*

"Judy's book is packed with solid information on child discipline from an attachment theory perspective. I particularly appreciated the focus on prevention of misbehavior. The breakdown of typical development by age and stage and how that impacts discipline is particularly helpful. There are good solid tips for parents of children of all ages."
~ Kathy Lynn, Parenting Today

"Judy Arnall's 'Discipline Without Distress' gives parents a kinder, gentler approach to raising well-behaved kids. It's a method both parents and children will appreciate. Every parent should own a copy!"
~ Stephanie Gallagher, author, *The Gallagher Guide to the Baby Years* and editor, Suite 101.com's Healthy Cooking section.

"Parents always prefer to be loving but often don't know how. Arnall's book debunks all the old beliefs about discipline through painful measures such as punishment, consequences or bribes and provides far more effective and kind ways to raise well behaved and thriving children."
~ Naomi Aldort Ph.D. Author, *Raising Our Children, Raising Ourselves*

National Library and Archives Canada Cataloguing in Publication

Arnall, Judy, 1960-

Discipline without distress : 135 tools for raising caring,
responsible children without time-out, spanking, punishment,
or bribery / Judy Arnall

ISBN 0-9780509-0-8
9780978050900

1. Parenting. 2. Child care. 3. Relationships.
4. Child rearing. 5. Self-help.

HQ770.4.A754 2007 649'.64 C2006-906683-3

Published by Professional Parenting Canada, Calgary, Alberta, Canada

jarnall@shaw.ca

www.professionalparenting.ca

First Edition 2007   Second Edition 2008
Third Edition 2010   Fourth Edition 2012

Although the author and publisher have exhaustively researched all sources to
ensure the accuracy and completeness of the information contained in this book,
we assume no responsibility for errors, inaccuracies, omissions, or any other
inconsistency herein. Any slights against people or organizations are
unintentional. Readers are strongly encouraged to use their own judgment in
their parenting decisions.

Editing and Project Management by: Debbie Elicksen,
Freelance Communications, www.freelancepublishing.net

Cover Design and Layout by: Bobbie-Jo Bergner, Mind's Design Studio,
www.mindsdesign.ca

Illustrations by: Heidi Arnall, Christopher Arnall

Printed and Bound in Canada

Dedication

To my loving husband, Peter, thank you for sharing my life and our children. You are my best friend, companion, and love of my life. To my wonderful children, Christopher, Marlin, Heidi, Travis, and Scotty: you have taught me so much as we journey together on life's path. I leave this book for you and my future grandchildren. I hope that it helps make your relationships, your community, and your world a more peaceful place.

I love you very much,

Judy

Acknowledgements

Thank you to the incredible people that helped and supported me in this project. I appreciate your work, encouragement, suggestions, and time. Thanks to my mentor, Patricia Morgan. You have been a constant beacon of light in this writing and parenting journey. Also thanks to my editor, Debbie Elicksen, and my designer, Bobbie-Jo Bergner, who have been a fountain of help. A big thank you to my encouragers, Ellen Percival and the late Sherry Kerr, who gave me the idea of writing a book; my suggestion team, Cathie Pelly, Shari Harding, Mary Simmonds and Cindy Bablitz. Thank you to my first parent educator, Patricia McKeown who opened my eyes to the world of parenting knowledge. Thank you to Dorothy Davis, Suzanne Rosebrugh, and Honey Watts for being my models of respectful relationships. Thank you to my supporters, Celia Osenton, Judith Young, Maureen Dodd, and Jocelyn Churchill for their wonderful teaching ideas, and to Dan Albert who taught me the essentials of people skills. Thank you to my friends who shared their parenting ideas, Corinne Trott, Janice Jernberg, Nancy Heatherington Peirce, Barb Elder, Leslie Barker, Virginia Wilson, Marie McNaughton, Cathy Lockerby, Brenda Henley, Karla Kroeker, Nancy Freiday, Margo Johnson, Donna Joy, Diane Swiatek, Lynnette Parent, Trudi Carol Linklater, Beth Workman, Lisa Rouleau, Lori Pesowski, Val Ritter, Joanne Good, Andrea Pritchard, Susanne Vatne, Gail Geyer, Donna Sharpe, Monica Mullaghan, Megan Roy O-Brien, Carol Harper and Line Valliere. Thank you to my parents John Horvath and Delores Pauli for your support and love, and Sharon Powell, my aunt, who was my model of motherhood in a house full of boys. Of course, much appreciation goes to my wonderful husband, Peter, who has truly been a support and partner in parenting. Thank you to my children, Christopher, Marlin, Heidi, Travis, and Scotty who have provided me with more then enough examples and anecdotes for 10 volumes!

And last, but not least, thank you to the many parents in my seminars and workshops, classes, parent groups, and parenting email lists for your suggestions, anecdotes, and tips. Thank you also to my friends and relatives who are parents, if I missed your name. Your support and resourcefulness astounds me. You are a vast body of knowledge and your expertise is appreciated!

Preface

> A perfect parent is a person with excellent child-rearing
> theories and no actual children.
> ~ Dave Barry, Author

I was an expert in parenting in my 20s. I would look at other people's children having tantrums in restaurants and be thinking, oh; my children will never do that! Then I had my first son. I recounted my expertise the day he accidentally set off the fire alarm in the library when he was two years old. I placed him on the counter to keep him from running out the door and he pushed the red alarm. Just when I had it all figured out, along came my second son. He was a totally different little person. What worked with the first son didn't work very well with the second. Now, I have five children. All have different personalities, temperaments, birth orders, genders, and learning styles. Each child is unique.

Although I was always interested in the psychology of human behavior, not much was as relevant to me in university until I became a parent. I was raised in a strict environment and always thought that teaching children could be done differently. I was convinced that by following the "right" parenting book advice, I would have perfectly behaved children. They would always do everything I asked – and with a smile! However, my children didn't read the same books. They didn't follow their part. If anything, I learned it was impossible to control other human beings without giving up some of the better facets of the relationship.

When my children were young, I searched desperately for parenting advice and read about 226 parenting books looking for the "correct" approach, and especially one approach that fit my style. I preferred a democratic, non-punitive, caring, respectful parenting style. I was committed to building bridges of communication with my children. Many of the books were non-punitive, yet they still advocated time-out, logical consequences, grounding, and other punishment-type corrections of misbehavior. When I tried them on my children, we were each left feeling disconnected, angry, and resentful towards each other. I'm sure other parents didn't find those methods punitive, but I sure did, and more importantly, so did my children. I kept on searching for a better way.

I had three profound influences in my life that heavily affected my parenting philosophy.

First, I was a crisis line phone volunteer for 13 years, and I realized the importance of empathic listening. I believed that people didn't want their problems solved by me. They wanted validation, acceptance, and clarity – all the things I could provide. They could solve their own problems. In parenting, I find the same theory applies. Children need an active parent to hear them, validate them, and provide clarity. They don't always want parents jumping in and doing much of what they can do themselves.

The second influence was my involvement in 12-step programs, fashioned on the model of Alcoholics Anonymous. I discovered that the best way to change and control another person is to accept them as they are and focus on changing yourself first. Be the best model, listener, and problem solver of issues in your own life, and you will not try so hard to control another person's life. Looking at my own shortcomings and building a healthy self-esteem for myself really helped me build my children's healthy self-esteem. I knew that many of their behaviors and actions were not directed at me personally but something they needed to do to grow and become the people they were supposed to be.

Many parents come to my parenting classes bent on changing the children. After a few classes, they start to see the importance of where they are, based on their family history – how the ways they were parented affects how they interact with their own children.

The third influence came when my husband went to work in Peru for two years, leaving me as the sole parent of four children. I wanted to survive without pulling out my hair. I re-read Dr. Thomas Gordon's *Parent Effectiveness Training* (P.E.T.) and took the course. Suddenly, a book that was so foreign to me when my child was two made much more sense years later. People say that when the student is ready, the teacher appears. I think I was just ready to hear it. I put it into action and on a practical daily level; it helped deepen our relationship and our qualities of love, respect, assertiveness, and openness. Although, I had never been a spanker, I used to yell a lot and was surprised to go a whole 24 days without once raising my voice! Even though there was no discipline section in the course, the whole approach is one of non-punishment parenting.

What I liked about the P.E.T. program was its emphasis on two-way communication and how each relationship involved two people, not one. Many books on discipline talk about what the parents should do to the children. Not many address how the children react back. Many children don't follow the prescribed script. Mine certainly didn't. If I gave my child a time-out, she was supposed to say, "I've thought about what I did, Mom, and I'm really sorry about that." Instead, she would say, "I hate you! You're being so unfair!" And then she wouldn't take out the garbage an hour later!

Many parents say that what works with one child, doesn't with another, but I believe that all children respond favorably to being treated respectfully and without punishments, regardless of their temperament, age, gender, and personality. You can raise a loving, caring, responsible child without hurting them or causing you distress. I wish you love, peace, and communication in your parenting from here on!

HOW TO USE THIS BOOK

I have used the terms "he" and "she" intermittently throughout the text to address both genders. This book is heavily based on communication rather than behavior modification, so I have used quotation marks extensively to show you the "words to use."

This book is the culmination of being in the trenches. I've used many of the tools, and the parents in my classes have offered tips that worked for them.

The first half of the book is about the theory behind non-punitive relationship building and provides much needed background information. In this book, I've outlined briefly the widely accepted principles of child development, from classic writings of John Bowlby, and Mary Ainsworth, Jean Piaget, Erik Erikson, Alfred Adler, Rudolph Dreikers, Arnold Gesell, Abraham Maslow, Haim Ginott, and Thomas Gordon.

Some parenting concepts are from modern day writers, Mary Sheedy Kurcinka, Barbara Coloroso, Jane Nelson and Cheryl Erwin, Patricia Morgan, Adele Faber and Elaine Mazlish, Elizabeth Crary, Jean Illsley Clarke, Kathy Lynn, Ann Douglas, Sarah Landy, Pam Levin, T. Berry Brazelton, William Sears, Gordon Neufeld, Alfie Kohn, and many more.

This book has five keys of discipline:
- Teach, not hurt.
- Stay with your "no" and honor your word.
- Look for the need or feeling (NOF) behind the behavior.
- Separate your anger from your discipline.
- Be the person you want them to be.

The second half is about practical tools and tips gathered from hundred of parents. If you are committed to the decision of teaching your child without hurting them, or your relationship, this book will help you deal with the daily challenges in parenting. You really can discipline without causing distress to you or your child. You will have raised honest, caring, responsible children, and your bond will be better then ever!

Table of Contents

Part One:

Why We Need to Change Our Discipline Tools

1

The Purpose of Discipline:
Teach, not hurt

> To get where we want to go with our children, we need to take a longer route, teaching them with our heads and hearts rather than with our hands and belts.
> ~ Penelope Leach, Author

Parenting is the hardest job on earth. In no other profession is control and accomplishment so difficult to come by. Controlling another human being is very much next to impossible; children have their own little minds and feet to follow. The goals, hopes, and dreams we have can only be realized in our minds. They are not guaranteed for our children.

I spanked one of my children only once. The poor first-born children are always the guinea pigs! We parents try many things on them first and find out what works and doesn't. My husband was away working in Russia, and I had three children under the age of four that were not cooperating in getting to bed. I was tired, stressed, and feeling unappreciated by society. When I spanked my son, he was almost four. He responded to me with tears in his eyes, "Mommy, hitting hurts people!" The very same words that I have uttered to him many, many times. Sometimes, I learn more from my children than I teach them.

As parents, we are going to mess up. We won't do every thing right. At some point in time, our children will fess up about us to their partners, their friends, and very likely, their own children. And that's okay. The truth is they're not perfect children. We're not perfect parents. Once we can admit we're not infallible, it makes it okay to make (or to have made) mistakes. All we can do is begin to do things differently – from right now. Anything new we do today will immediately start to make a difference in our parenting and our relationships.

All parents love their children. Every parent who holds a new baby in their arms wants the very best for that baby. However, most parents don't instinctively know how to meet the needs of their children or how to discipline them effectively. If parents consider going for help in learning how to manage their child's behavior, they worry people will think they don't love the child. From the parent whose child is taken away by Social Services to the parent reading the umpteenth book on child-rearing discipline, the common uniting factor is that all parents everywhere, love their children. But by itself, love is not enough. Love doesn't give parents all the information they need to raise, and teach a child. They need assurance that many of their child's annoying behaviors are developmentally appropriate. They need to be given new tools to help them practice and develop different parenting techniques. They need to know there are many right ways to raise a child.

WHAT IS NEW IN PARENTING FOR THE NEW MILLENNIUM?

Two very profound changes in parenting have occurred since we were raised in the 1960s, 1970s, and 1980s.

The first change is due to technology advancement. We now know more about child rearing and child development. We have MRIs (Magnetic Resonance Imaging) that actually see inside the brain and can measure the effect that stress, neglect, bullying, overindulgence, or nurturance has on humans.

The second change is that our children's playground is no longer limited to the park down the street. Thanks to technology and the internet, our children's playground is now bigger than we could ever imagine; it is impossible to control, supervise, or navigate. When our children are three paces ahead of us in using and managing this technology, we lose our ability to supervise them in a traditional way. We can no longer monitor who and where they are interacting. Therefore, it is crucial we build a relationship and keep our lines of communication open and learn new tools of parenting.

The discipline tools in this book are not the tools our parents used. Our children are not living in the same world we grew up in. It's vastly changed. I'm reminded how little power and control I have every time I need to ask my children to help me do some task on the computer. Not yet into their teens, they all had more control over a crucial part of my life! Their knowledge has exceeded mine in many technological areas. This is probably the first generation of children that are more proficient than we are in many critical technological areas, which is a big factor in our culture. We need to change our ways of disciplining our children.

Some other changes in our lifestyle have also changed our parenting:
- More two-income families means less time for extended family and neighborhood communities. Families are more isolated and bear the brunt of child rearing problems and solutions.

- Parents connect with their children through technology. MSN™ (Microsoft Network: a computer information service that provides access to news, email, and the internet), text-messaging, email, webcam, and cell phones have replaced face-to-face time.

- Families have less time together. When they are together, it's often activity-based and goal-oriented, which can add stress to the event.

- Higher incomes and lower numbers of children means a higher standard of living.

- Children spend more time with peers than any other time through history. Daycare, preschool, school, early kindergarten, sleep-away camp and day camp through the summer, and school holidays means a huge amount of time with same-aged peers and less time with nurturing parents.

- Children are smarter than their parents, technology-wise. They can control more areas of family life through technology.

The old punishment tools our parents used on us no longer work with today's children because:

- Spanking is less socially acceptable as a parenting tool.

- Children don't fear parents or authority figures anymore when they know they can get around punishments with technology; so threat of punishment has little impact. If a teenager is grounded, she can still connect with friends through MSN™. Her parents usually don't know.

- Time-out and grounding needs parents to be around to monitor, and parents are short on time and control in order to supervise.

- There is less community support from teachers, other parents, coaches, and authority figures for supporting parent's punishments and general child supervision.

We need new tools that:

- Build communication with our children face-to-face and through technology in order to have an open connecting relationship.

- Help our children solve their problems, as we are not always around to do it for them.

- Build our children's trust in our experience, so they will listen to us.

- Give our children a solid information base on which to make their decisions.

- Build our influence with our children to counteract the heavy peer contact.

It's imperative we build connections with our children that allows them to come to us with their issues, problems, and concerns.

Children need parents who will help them solve problems, not punish them when they are in trouble. That trust is built layer upon layer when children are young, not suddenly when they become teens. When your child has creepy feelings about someone they're talking to on MSN™, you want them to come to you for advice on how to handle it. They have to know it's safe to come to you for help in solving their problems and trust you to not punish them for anything they have done.

Parenting for the long run

When you look at your child now and imagine the teenage years ahead, does the image fill your heart with dread or joy and anticipation? List the qualities you want to see in the relationship between you and your child as a teenager. Parents almostalways answer with the qualities of open communication; shared feelings, thoughts, and values; fun times together; mutual respect; confidence in self; and being approachable when their child has problems.

The next step is determining what behaviors in your child are driving you nuts right now? Make a list.

Compare the two lists. How you deal with the behaviors that are driving you batty today will affect the quality of your relationship in the future. The two lists are tied together. This book will give you the tools to effectively deal with the annoying behaviors while still preserving the relationship goal you want with your future teen.

Some aspects of parenting can disconnect the relationship. One of those aspects is disciplining using punishment. Are you disciplining your children with your long run relationship goals in mind? The tricky part is: how to handle your eight-year old's swearing today but still keep in mind your desire for open communication when he is fourteen. It is possible!

Parenting is relationship building. You are not raising a child; you are raising an adult. Try to start treating your child with the respect you would afford an adult in today's society. The parenting relationship is basically a love relationship. There is no room for punishment in a love relationship that is built upon good communication. Can parents discipline without using punishment? Of course! It takes time, a little bit of skill, and a lot of patience. Any worthwhile relationship takes time.

For respectful discipline to work, children need six things from parents. Just as the foundation of a building must be built on a firm, secure base, for discipline to work, the relationship foundation must be securely in place or actively being worked towards. Many of the six ingredients necessary for building relationships take presence and time. This is not a quick fix of the child but a gradual, mutually satisfying, connection building of the parent-child bond.

SIX INGREDIENTS FOR A CONNECTED PARENTING RELATIONSHIP

Time: Small children need a lot of parent time. When a parent's time is in short supply, you want to spend that time with your child engaged in doing pleasant activities. You don't want to spend the time being mad at each other.

It doesn't have to be quality time, either. Quantity time is much more preferred. Children need parents around as much as possible, to be there for them when they are going through unpleasant times, as well as positive times.

Attention: Recognize that attention is a basic need and children will take whatever you give them. Negative attention, such as yelling, spanking, scolding, moving them to time-out and keeping them there, and positive attention, such as eye contact, talking, and smiling are all forms of attention. Put your limited energy into positive attention.

Guidance: Nobody likes to be corrected; we need to be shown how to improve by someone showing us how in a very kind, positive, and respectful way.

Kindness: It's usually how it's said, not what is said that is most important. Our children need our warmth, caring, and firmness, and we need to remember the three are not mutually exclusive.

Listening: Every human, whether age two or 82, wants to be heard and validated. Not just their words, but their feelings, beliefs, values, and interpretations. When children feel listened to by their parents, they are more likely to return the favor and listen to their parents.

Self care for parents: Good parent-child relationships and good discipline starts with parents who feel good about themselves. Eating, sleeping, having a creative outlet, doing special things for yourself, and taking time to take care of yourself are a huge investment in your parenting.

Why give up punishments?

Children who are not punished have more control over their fate. They are active participants in what happens to them, rather than helpless victims under someone else's control; thus, they feel more empowered. They acquire better social skills, learn problem-solving, and healthy conflict resolution. Fortunately, for parents and siblings, our homes provide a living laboratory to practice problem-solving skills.

Children who are not punished tend to engage in less bullying-type behaviors. They feel empowered; they don't need to gain their power by controlling others. They can practice more respectful ways of communicating because they already feel they have control over their lives.

Children who are not punished tend to have better sibling relationships. Sibling conflicts often begin issue-oriented rather than resentment-oriented. Children, who are taught how to work out their issues between each other, continue to do so, even when parents are not around. If each sibling feels they have been treated fairly, they have less to feel resentful about and have more good feelings toward each other with fewer underground resentments.

Children who are not punished have a more optimistic outlook on the world. Peacefulness is often an ideal they work for in the community and wider world organizations.

Children who are not punished have less "attitude" and defiance towards their parents. The empowerment of speaking up respectfully for their needs, being heard, and working towards common winning solutions furthers communication and good feelings towards parents.

Children have a healthier self-esteem. People with more control over their world feel better about themselves. They believe they matter and feel valued.

Children develop a higher moral internalization. This is the little voice inside that tells them to do the right thing, even if no one is watching. They develop the inner voice of conscience and have more empathy for other's needs and values because their needs have been met.

That being said, punishments work on some children in the short run to temporarily gain compliance. But beware! Punishments shut down communication. Heidi, my daughter, at age 11, told me that spanking children causes them to be scared of their parents. Fear is the control tool of punishments, however, children don't open up to parents they fear. As educator and author John Holt once said, "When we make a child afraid, we stop learning, dead in its tracks."

Children who have an easygoing temperament are easily compliant with just the threat of punishment. It's the same with younger children. As children get older, punishments get harder to enforce because children become more capable of escape and revenge. They fear less as they grow in size.

Often, the children who respond the best to punishment are the ones who need it the least. Then there are older and spirited children. Punishments only serve to make them more rebellious, angry, humiliated, resentful, and revengeful. These are the children who are sent to time-outs, and instead of thinking about their wrong-doing, they are planning ways to get even with you.

How a child feels determines how he behaves. Jane Nelson, author of *Positive Discipline*, posed the question "Where did we get the idea that in order for children to behave better, we need to make them feel worse?"

 A positive approach is always preferable to a negative approach.

Children often react to punishment in the form of rebellion, retaliation, fear, and/or passive resistance. Power struggles are generally about meeting needs: the needs of the parent and the needs of the child. Both aim to get their way. When parents and children are locked in a power struggle, it is important for the parent to stay calm and let go for the moment. They have more experience in self-control and can switch gears easier. Refuse to participate. The time to re-examine the needs of the parents and child causing the power struggle is later, when the emotional temperature in the relationship has gone down. Be sure to address it, though. Don't let it go.

Many children learn how to deal with their future partners from their childhood training ground in love relationships. I believe the divorce rate is so high these days because partners tend to punish their partners, a skill learned from childhood when their parents punished them and they retaliated back. Respect, consideration, and kindness are also learned traits, but they don't have an equal impact when used in the same arena as punishments.

Why do parents keep using punishments?

In times of stress, we parent the way we were parented. Sometimes, we know of no other way. Even when we have learned non-punitive ways to deal with behavior, it's often easier to fall back on what is familiar and what feels comfortable, like an old shoe.

Our culture, which often promotes child-rearing methods that deteriorate the bond of parenting, tends to value punishment as the preferred method of "lesson teaching." We use it in our jail systems, our workplaces, our schools, and our families. Yet, research consistently shows that punishment doesn't prevent or deter bad behavior. It certainly doesn't reform people to do better. If that was the case, our jails would never have repeat offenders.

The belief still exists that children won't behave unless they are made to suffer at least a wee bit. Because the short run effect of this method appears to work only furthers this belief. Children do obey their parents, but studies show that over the long run, they have fewer problem-solving skills, exhibit less confidence, and are generally less satisfied with their lives. Parents can't control what children think, only what they do, and even then, only to a small degree.

Parents find it easier to DO something, than to NOT do something. Therefore, it's easier to take action and scold, punish, threaten, or correct, than it is to ignore misbehavior and gush over positive behavior. Parents understand the theory of not giving negative attention to bad behavior but find it very hard to do, in practice. They may perceive onlookers to judge them badly if they don't do anything.

Punishments tend to meet the parent's needs for control and authority over the children, more than achieving the goal of teaching children better behavior. Punishments tend to assuage a parent's anger by providing retaliation, which relieves that anger. If parents could get a grip on their anger, calm down, and regain control – before they discipline – many would find punishment easier to avoid.

We still mistakenly believe in the philosophy that punishing a misbehaving child restores the moral aura in humanness. Children have to "pay" for their behavior. Without that "payment," children are allowed to get away with murder.

Behavior modification has been so ingrained in our parenting practices, we sometimes forget that people are more complex than how they behave. They have brains for thinking and hearts for feeling. Children can feel many feelings at one time and can't articulate or explain them. They act certain ways because they feel many conflicting needs, not necessarily to get a goal attained. Part of behaviorism is the social learning theory of parenting, which states that children's behavior occurs through imitation of parents. It's interesting to know that in parenting, behavior modification did not originally include punishments, only reinforcements. Even hardcore behavior modification proponents believed punishments have limitations.

I believe the maturation theory has some validity, whereby the role of genetically determined growth patterns and emotional development have a profound effect on the timetable of a child's development. Children do things, not to misbehave, but in order to move through developmental stages that are pre-determined at birth. Parents need to understand what those stages are in order to help children make the best of them and guide them through. Children are not misbehaving. They are doing their developmental job.

How does a parent know if their discipline is respectful teaching or punishment? Ask yourself three questions:

- Would I want it done to me?
- Does it help my child develop valuable life skills?
- Will it build our relationship or harm it?

If you are using time-out, grounding, unrelated consequences, spanking, yelling, and removal of privileges and it's not achieving the permanent type of relationship you want, this may be the time for a new approach.

Parent with your end goal in mind rather than look for immediate results. The long run goals of developing life skills, such as respect, problem-solving, effective communication, empathy, and self-control can be attained faster when punishment is removed from the mix. You can set limits, provide guidance, and correct misbehavior without the use of punishment. Kindness is so much more effective in the long run than the use of force.

Goals of discipline:
1. To teach the child life long character building skills: responsibility, empathy, problem-solving, and self-control.
2. To protect the child.
3. To instill our parental values.
4. To teach the child how to become a healthy, productive adult in society.

The real test of a "well behaved child" is reflected in what the child does when the parents or other authority figures are not with them.

Effective discipline
- Effective discipline never includes punishment. Common examples of punishment are grounding, unrelated consequences, time-out, and threats of any kind. Effective discipline uses real world "cause and effect" learning experiences. Effective discipline teaches and guides children how to think for themselves. It doesn't just force them to obey.
- Effective discipline is proactive. Parents find underlying causes of misbehavior and address those causes, as well as teach future desired behavior. Punishment tends to be reactive and aims to stop behaviors without addressing what should be substituted.
- Discipline connects the parent and child in their relationship. Both parties leave with mutual respect intact and a better understanding of each other and the situation. Punishment tends to disconnect the relationship and infuses anger, misunderstanding, and resentment into the relationship.
- Effective discipline is mutually respectful. "Do unto others as you would have done to you." Although parents have far more experience and knowledge than their children, both parents and child have the same right of having their feelings and dignity equally respected.
- Effective discipline is 90 percent prevention and 10 percent correction. Ten percent correction focuses on problem-solving. When children's needs are met, they seldom need any correction. However, there will be times they

need guidance and direction, and you will need to provide it. Your children will get practiced in consequences, time-outs, grounding, and other punishments from the other people and institutions in their lives. You are the only person with a vested interest and time to teach them how to solve problems, which is what effective discipline is all about.

- Effective discipline is kind, firm, and safe. As Cheryl Erwin, co-author of *Positive Discipline: The First Three Years* states, "Kind to the person and firm to the needs of the situation." Both can be done at the same time. Discipline needs to always be safe, both to parent and child.

- Effective discipline is based on a firm foundation of mutual respect, caring, and love. Without that foundation, children grow to ignore their parents as they get older. You can't raise a child in a dictatorship and expect him to function as an adult in a democracy. Respecting people, meeting their needs, and solving problems is what discipline is about. The home is a child's first training ground.

YOUR ROLE AS A PARENT

Imagine you are the host to a new immigrant. Her name is Amana. She is visiting your country for the first time and knows nothing about your language, customs, social rules, laws, or culture. You greet her at the airport with great celebration. You bring her home, hoping to make her feel comfortable.

Once settled in, she enrolls in school to learn your language. You take her shopping and to the wonderful opportunities your city has to offer. Amana makes a lot of mistakes. She doesn't take her shoes off when entering houses. She forgets to say thank you when shopping. She puts her elbows on the table when eating in restaurants. As her tour guide, you gently tell her the rules and remind her of them when she forgets. Some rules she remembers, but since there is so much to learn, she feels overwhelmed and forgets.

You don't punish her for forgetting. You understand her feelings of being new and learning and patiently help her to remember. You know that she will learn eventually after much practice.

You and Amana are fellow travelers on life's path. You are the native, and she is the newcomer. You both encounter bumpy parts on the path and navigate them together. You treat her with respect and dignity and gently guide her to learn your culture.

The view of parenting in this book is much the same. You are the parent native and your children are the newcomers, like Amana. The newcomers have much to learn, and you have much to teach. Your relationship is mutually respectful.

Parent as protector

Protect the child and give them a sense of trust in the world. Inform children of dangers. Make sure their home and environment is free from danger as much as possible. Parent Educator, Cathie Pelly states, "You protect your child's mind, body, and spirit." You limit what they watch on TV, what they hear from friends, and what they are exposed to in the media. You keep them safe from cars, lack of sleep, and junk food. You protect their spirit by not quashing it but channeling it towards positive outcomes for themselves and you.

Parent as a source of knowledge and experience in a democratic parenting style

In a *democratic* parenting style, you are a guide, coach, mentor, teacher, protector, and facilitator. Today, a parent wields authority based on experience, communication ability, and respect. It is also called the *authoritative*, backbone, or structured parenting style and has the best researched outcomes for children.

An *authoritarian* parent (not to be confused with *authoritative*) in an authoritarian parenting style, would insist that their children obey all rules, always do as they are told, and always respect their elders, no matter how badly the elders treat children. The role of parents would be dictator, albeit benevolent, sole rule-maker, and rule-enforcer. The problem with this parenting style is that you raise a child that doesn't learn how to think for herself. You do not want a blindly obedient child because many adults do not have your child's best interests in mind. It's best to encourage your child to ask "Why?" Do not scold them for questioning established practices. They need to listen to their inner "gut" feeling about directives in their lives, and that will help guide them in today's world.

An *uninvolved* parent style would have the parent ignore most discipline issues due to lack of time, knowledge or effort in trying to address them. An *overindulgent* parenting style would have the parent give in to the child's every whim in order to avoid the child's anger or other intense emotions. Neither of these styles are beneficial for the child.

Parent as an influence

"Can't you control that child?" Many parents dread hearing that phrase as a criticism to their parenting. But how many parents really have control over their children? Perhaps at birth. As children grow, parents lose their ability to control them but they do gain influence over them. Modeling is a 24-hour, 365 day a year way of influencing another person. There is a huge difference between influence and control. Influence grows as the children and relationships do, if that solid foundation of caring, respect, and guidance is maintained. Control is lost as children get more independent, capable, and smart.

Parent as a detective

Help the child learn to control his behavior, sort out his emotions and manage them, and explore his thinking. Help the child learn appropriate and inappropriate behavior, as well as empathy and consideration for others. Use discipline methods that encourage attachment, respectful teaching, and problem-solving, rather than detachment methods such as isolation, physical punishment, humiliation, and consequences.

Children don't really misbehave. They act in inappropriate ways to get their needs met. The job of parents is to meet those needs and teach children how to get them met in socially appropriate ways. Once the underlying needs and feelings of the child are recognized and addressed, the behavior often improves.

So as a parent, you are also a detective. Children are not very adept at expressing their needs. Often, they don't consciously know why they are behaving a certain way. Your role is to figure it out. Generally, all human behavior is trying to reach certain outcomes:

- Attention
- Power and control
- Protection, escape, avoidance
- Acceptance/belonging/affiliation
- Expression of self
- Gratification
- Justice/revenge

All humans behave to acquire these outcomes. Misbehavior is a term we use to apply to children acquiring these outcomes in non-parent approved ways. We never use the term, misbehavior, to apply to adults acting in the same way. We use more positive terms such as assertive, go-getter, and determined. Our job is to teach children how to acquire their needs and communicate them in positive ways rather than negative ways. That's what discipline is all about. We do that by reinforcing the positive ways they get their needs met and substituting the negative ways with more positive ways. Asking a child "why" he does something doesn't help much. Often, he doesn't know. Active Listening helps with the detective work.

Parent as a structure provider

Studies show that the best parenting style is the democratic style, which is warm and demanding. Parents have expectations of children and are nurturing in encouraging those. Parents also provide a natural rhythm to the day. Both adults and children do well with some kind of routine. In our family, we have daily routines, weekly routines, and session routines (fall, winter, and spring). Scheduled meals, chores, sleep times, playtimes, outdoor time, activity time, and learning times provide children with a semblance of structure and stability that all humans require. We are moved by the clock and calendar. A basic structure allows children to plan and feel secure. It can't be too rigid as to not allow for special things. Children may usually go to bed between 8:00 and 8:30, but if there is a meteor shower at 10:00, then it's okay to have them stay up for it. Likewise, I know many families that don't need to get up in the morning and have their children stay up until midnight. For them, it's routine. That's okay as long as everyone is getting sleep. A family's schedule must work for that family.

Parents as a limit and rule making facilitator and negotiator

Do children need limits? Yes they do. However, they need PURPOSEFUL limits. Not limits for the sake of learning to be restricted but real limits that have a job: to protect a child's body, mind, and spirit. If a child balks against the limit, then parents need to help problem-solve with the child so the limit meets the needs of parents and child at the same time.

Think of three writing instruments: a permanent marker, a washable marker, and a pencil. Now think of all the rules in your house. Are they made by you, both you and the kids, or just the kids? An ideal mix of the democratic parenting style is 10/80/10.

Ten percent of the rules and limits are made only by the parent. They are the permanent marker rules. In our house, these are rules about not hitting, safety rules, and mutual respect. These are non-negotiable and applied to everyone in our house: friends, neighbors, relatives, kids, and parents.

The 80 percent of rules are washable marker rules. They were set up and given input by children and parents and had to work for everybody. Anyone could bring them up for discussion and change them at a family conference. Of course, the younger children didn't really question them until they were older, but if the younger children had an issue, we would talk and see what else could be changed. The only thing that was necessary was the rules had to work for everybody.

Most of the washable marker rules are discussed and solved with both parents and children negotiating:
- Bedtimes and meal times
- Chores
- Care of pets
- Homework and education issues
- Use of recreation equipment and time spent on them
- Allowances
- Privileges
- All logistics of living together

The final 10 percent are pencil rules, which are created by the children. They can be changed anytime by the children, and everyone should abide by them. They do not affect safety, mutual respect, or our core values.

Parent as needs provider

Children have various levels of needs and require parents to help direct them to meet those needs. Food, water, sleep, safety, emotional release, attention, and stimulation are just a few. Encourage exploration and curiosity of his environment within a web of safety. Provide age-appropriate stimulation for intelligence and creativity.

Create joyful memories, rituals, and celebrations of family life to give children a sense of belonging, attachment, and fun.

Let children know when you leave and when you will be back. Avoid threatening phrases that the child will be left behind, as it can foster insecurity. Trust is built when goodbye rituals are established and by making the child feel as comfortable as possible about the goodbye. For a child that has difficulty when separated, consider leaving him as little as possible until he can developmentally handle it.

Try to be as predictable and positive as possible in reacting to the child's behavior. Predictability provides security. Children and adults look for patterns in the world and learn to expect them. When children feel that they can predict patterns, they feel more secure, capable, and a sense of mastery over their environment.

Parent as nurturer

Children need parents who are warm, attentive, empathetic and loving. It's the difference between just putting a bandage on a wound when a child cuts their finger and adding a kiss when the bandage goes on. Provide a source of comfort and nurturing when the child is distressed.

Children often feel afraid, lonely, angry, upset, ill, hurt, or jealous. A nurturing parent will name the feeling, comfort the child with soft words, hugs, and holding, and spend time helping the child sort out their intense feelings. This does not have a time limit and may occur day or night as needed.

ABOUT MUTUAL RESPECT

Respect (Wiktionary definition)
1. To have respect for.
2. To have regard for the rights of others.
3. To consent to abide by an agreement.

Respect (Oxford Dictionary definition)

Regard with deference, esteem, or honor. Avoid degrading, insulting, or injuring. Treat with consideration.

In parenting classes, mutual respect is the cornerstone of parenting theories and philosophies. However, many people do not realize what it means. Mutual respect between parent and child is basically about the Golden Rule: do unto others as you would have them do unto you. So don't do anything to your children that you wouldn't want done to yourself. Many parents object. Since when do we start treating children as grown-ups? Don't we know better than they? They are children, and we are the parent, and yes, we should treat them differently. Or should we? Yes and no.

Children are equal to parents in some ways. Their feelings, dignity, and sense of self worth are equally as important to them as adults. In the workplace – just because the boss has more knowledge and experience doesn't mean she can call you names, berate you in front of the client, or hit you for not getting your work out on time, nor can she wash your mouth out with soap if you swear on the job. Your feelings, dignity, and sense of self worth as an employee are equally as valuable as hers and must be mutually respected. Therefore, children have the right to feel all their feelings, to have their bodies' dignity respected, and are entitled to expect to be treated worthily.

Mutual Respect   To treat others the way you want to be treated.

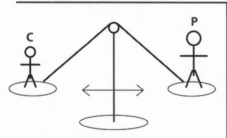 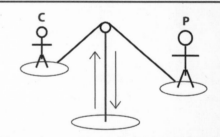

Needs, Feelings, Dignity, Equal | **Experience, Knowledge, Not Equal**

Read the following entry and answer the question following it:

I Lost It Today

I feel bad for losing it today. She was just so naughty. I had to spank her.
I remember the day she came to live with us. So small, so fragile, and so very feisty.
Dressed in a little pink dress, with her wispy, curly blonde hair.

It was a bad week, this week. She took her diaper off and peed all over herself.
One more mess for me to clean up.

She tried to pour a drink and spilled it all over the floor.
Another mess to clean up.
Broken glass and milky liquid, pooling on the floor, mixed in with my tears of exhaustion,
Trying to run a home, work a job, pay the bills, and take care of her.
I feel guilty for spanking her again. She is so demanding of my time.

She won't eat, she won't sleep, and she won't listen.
She does the same misbehaviors over and over again. Will she remember my words this time?
I have to be concerned for her safety. I have to spank her for her own good.

Sometimes I think she is purposefully trying to annoy me. When I yell at her, she just shows her defiance. She looks at me with that attitude in her eyes. She is often a cranky, little lady. Sometimes, she even spits at me! After all I have done for her. I can't let her get spoiled.

It's the endless destruction of our home and things that bother me the most.
She can't be that clumsy all the time. Surely, she could take more care where she goes. I feel helpless for spanking her. I don't know what else to do. She is so helpless. She can't call anyone for help, and she can't escape the house. She is so dependent on me.

How old is the person in the story? Now read the rest of the passage.

I shouldn't hit her. She's 89. She's my mother, but she drives me to it. Why should I feel so guilty? After all, she did it to me.
When she was more powerful, and I was the helpless one…

Up until the last paragraph, most people think the little girl is a toddler. Look at the language terms we use with young children: naughty, spank, demanding, misbehavior, defiance, cranky, spoiled, clumsy. All adjectives we use with young children. The adult versions would be: negative, hit, persistent, inappropriate behavior, assertiveness, tired, gets needs met, out of sync. It changes our perceptions. Somehow the adult terms are more forgiving or understandable of the behavior, just because of the age difference.

 Children are people too!   ~ Louise Porter, Author

At what age do children deserve to be treated with mutual respect? Mutual respect begins at birth. How many parents leave their babies crying for hours and wouldn't even think about leaving a stranger crying in a store. How many parents send their upset toddlers to time-out, yet wouldn't tell an upset boss, "Go to your office for 45 minutes (one minute per year of age) and don't call me back until you've calmed down!" Perhaps we need to think of the ways we treat our children versus how we treat others. Mutual respect is not limited to adults only. It helps to model the behavior you want to see. If you want to be treated with respect, be respectful.

Mutual respect differs in the way we thought of respect 30 years ago. Back then, the respect of elders was expected, not earned. Respect of children was not the same. Children respected parents and adults because they were authority figures to them and generally had more knowledge and were a bigger size.

Things have changed. Respect is now changed. Now, an adult acquires authority based on their knowledge, experience, and open communication, as well as being mutually respectful to children. Respect is not fear based, but communication based.

Parent Authority

30 Years Ago

Elder Respect
(AGE)
Size
Fear

Now

Knowledge
Experience
Open Communication
Mutual Respect

THE DISCIPLINE CONTINUUM

Many parents waver between two ends of the discipline continuum. Either they are too strict and punish because they have had enough and let things slide too often. Or they do nothing because they are stressed, tired, and short of time . . . and the time they do have they don't want to waste on negative interactions and power struggles. Or they just don't have the words or actions to handle things and don't know what to do. So they turn their heads. In the middle of these two ends is where a kind, firm, respectful approach fits, one that meets both parent and child's needs with kindness.

Some parents spend more time with the first approach, some with the third approach, and most with oscillating between the two approaches, which can cause the most damage to children. Oscillating between two extremes doesn't provide children with the predictability they need to feel secure. Not knowing how a parent will react most of the time; ignoring a behavior today that wasn't ignored yesterday or flying off the handle because a behavior is not tolerated today, can be quite unsettling to children. They need a firm, kind, and predictable approach most of the time.

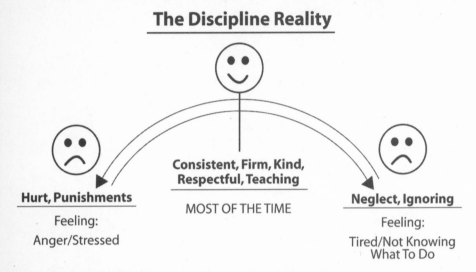

The Discipline Reality

Consistent, Firm, Kind, Respectful, Teaching

MOST OF THE TIME

Hurt, Punishments
Feeling:
Anger/Stressed

Neglect, Ignoring
Feeling:
Tired/Not Knowing What To Do

Do your methods connect your relationship or disconnect it?

Most parenting strategies work better when there is a strong emotional connection between the parent and the child.

In my classes, I ask parents to write down their favorite or most often used discipline technique on a sticky. Then I draw a line on a flip chart and write "connect" or "disconnect" on either side. I ask parents what the technique on the sticky does to the relationship. Connect or disconnect it? It doesn't matter if it works or not to gain compliance, but how does it leave the parents and children feeling toward each other and toward their relationship? Try it here. Write down your favorite discipline method on a sticky and stick it under either "connects the relationship" or "disconnects the relationship."

Discipline connects the relationship
- Provides guidance.
- Enhances communication.
- Is prevention focussed.
- Problem-solving occurs.
- Empathic learning is occuring.

Punishment disconnects the relationship
- Hurt that a more powerful person does to a less powerful one, in order to gain a change in behavior.
- Forced compliance.

Discipline connects the relationship	Punishment disconnects the relationship
• Leaves good feelings of belonging and connection intact. • Teaches fairness, responsibility, and life skills. • Preserves understanding. • Respects both parent and child.	• Anger is present; misguided learning is occurring. • Passive aggression/rebellion is forming. • Revenge breaks down communication. • Child and adult feel misunderstood. • Respects the parent, but not the child.

If you are debating whether your discipline is respectful or not, measure it against this: would I do this to my partner? My neighbor? My friend? My relative? Our children are still students in learning how to be adults. Treat them with the same respect as you would when they become adults. Our children will soon become our neighbors, friends, relatives, and parents themselves. This doesn't mean you give them adult privileges. It means that you value their dignity and feelings as much as the other people in your life.

Short run goals:
- I want to stop that behavior now.
- I want to teach a lesson to prevent the behavior from happening again.
- I want to make the child obey.
- I want to stop the unpleasant expression of feelings in the child's reaction: anger, tears, tantrums, and sulking because it causes me discomfort.

Long run goals:
- I'm teaching my child to feel capable and confident in his abilities.
- I'm teaching my child that he belongs in our family, community, and culture.
- I'm teaching my child that he is valued for who he is and what he does.
- I'm helping my child to be responsible and accountable for his actions.
- I'm teaching my child to learn how to solve problems in the real world.

When people say that their methods "work," what they really mean is they work to stop a certain behavior in the short run. Their children obey unquestionably. Many discipline methods will do that: punitive and non-punitive. What parents don't realize is that some of their methods don't necessarily work in the long run goals of their parenting: goals that achieve a caring bond, open communication, trust, honesty, and respect, in the relationship and responsibility in the child, especially in the teen years.

Pat, a mom on an online parenting discussion group says, "It's been a l-o-n-g time since I was a teen, but I can still clearly recall those feelings of anger, resentment, and hostility toward authority; and I was a 'good' teen – an excellent student, never in any real trouble. But I did skip school just to 'show them,' vandalized school property, acted like a jerk at the coffee shop with my friends, hung around downtown being as much of a nuisance as I could, smoked on school property because it was a cool way to break the rules, drank when I was underage, and vandalized a hated teacher's house on Halloween night. And I was one of the 'good' ones."

A mom in my class once said, "It's funny how parents hate some qualities in children but want those same qualities when their children are adults."

- They hate having determined, focused children but want their adult children to find their own path.

- They hate having curious "into everything" children but want their adult children to find life long learning.

- They hate having strong willed "having to question everything" children but want their adult children to trust their instincts and stick to their guns.

- They hate having pushy children that have an inner fire but want their adult children to be assertive and possess initiative.

- They hate having children that are dependent but want their adult children to care for them when they are dependent.

> Rather than focus on your child's obedience as a gauge of how well you parent, focus on the quality of your relationship with your child.

Results of short run goals

Does your child do as you or your partner asks 80 percent of the time without arguing, whining, or sulking?

A "yes" or "no" answer is irrelevant. The answer to this question depends on your child's age, temperament, personality, and emotional state. Children are still acting like, well, children. They make mistakes, learn how people and things work, and are not perfectly behaved half the time. For a child under five, a 40 percent "yes" answer is age-appropriate.

Results of long run goals

You will know your parenting is working if you can answer "yes" to most of these questions, most of the time. Keep in mind that children gain these characteristics as they age. There will be more "yes" answers for older children than for younger children. If your relationship with your teenager is an honest, open, communication-based one, by age 13, your teen will have a lot of these characteristics. You don't start parenting teenagers when they are teens. You start when they are very young.

- Does your child come to you to ask questions about sex, drugs, alcohol, peers, and life, at least once a week?
- Does your child listen to how you feel? Does your child care about how you feel? Does your child change his behavior because of how you feel, without the use of threats, punishments, or bribes?
- Does your child listen to your opinions, values, and beliefs with understanding?
- Does your child resolve conflicts with other children, including siblings, with respect, fairness, and a solution that is win-win for everyone?
- Does your child talk out conflicts with you with respect and a focus for finding solutions for everyone?
- Does your child know they can come to you for help for any reason, any time?
- Does your child share problems, anger, jealousy, joy, excitement, and most of his feelings with you?
- Is your child honest with you?
- Is your child happy to be himself?
- Does your child have friends that are kind and respectful to him?
- Is your child responsible to other people, teachers, employers, and volunteer commitments?
- Does your child show empathy and concern for other people's plight?
- Does your child value your family and feel that he belongs?
- Does your child come to you for comfort if he is upset, sick, or hurt?
- Is your child free to express all his emotions in your presence, and do you validate them?
- Does your child listen to his "gut feeling" about adults' interest and follow what his intuition tells him, rather than blindly obey any adult?
- Does your child do the right thing, even when no one is watching?
- Does your child help other people without being told to do so?
- Does your child listen to your teaching and try to implement it even when you are not present?
- Does your child learn from mistakes and still feel good about himself?
- Does your child believe in himself?
- Is he optimistic about other people, the world, and the impact he can have?
- Does he drop risky behaviors after an initial experimentation?
- Does your child find more than one solution to any problem?
- Does your child assert his needs to others?
- Does your child have the appropriate manners, language, and social skills for the occasion or situation he is in?
- Does your child obey the law, even when no one is watching?
- Does your child know unwritten social norms and obey them, even when no one is watching?

- Does your child learn appropriate life skills and academic skills, as per his age?
- Does your child enjoy spending time with you, even when with peers?
- Does your child speak to you with respect, including no backtalk or attitude?
- Does your child respect others property, your property, and the environment?
- Does your child pitch in with household tasks and chores without being asked?
- Does your child occasionally do things to please you without being asked?

Rather than looking at what you are doing as a parent, what do you see in your children? What do you need to work on or where do you need to make changes? Some people say you can't see how your children turn out until they are grown up, have a job, and are married. I disagree. Children send you various progress reports in different ways! Take an evaluation every year or so and see where changes are in order. Work on a small change at a time. Too many at once, the shotgun approach, can be very discouraging for the child and parent.

We must get over the old way of thinking that in order to make children do better, we must make them feel bad. Just like adults, children who feel encouraged want to do better.

~ Elliott Barker, Psychiatrist

One mom in my class wondered if she handled a discipline issue right. She and her 10-year-old daughter agreed that the daughter would not buy popcorn at the movie, and when Mom left to go to the bathroom, the daughter asked the dad to go with her and buy popcorn. When the mom came back, she was furious. She was determined to punish her daughter for deliberately defying her, but instead, she went for a walk and used a calm-down technique called hissing vocally. It helped her deal with her anger. After the movie, in a calm moment, she told the daughter in an "I-statement" how disappointed she was in her breaking their agreement. The daughter listened and didn't say anything. After telling the daughter how she felt, the mother walked away. No punishment. No hurting the daughter to teach her a lesson. The next week, the mom asked if she did the right thing in not disciplining her daughter. I assured the mom she was disciplining the daughter. She was not punishing, but she was teaching her daughter in a respectful way that the daughter did not make a good choice. I'm sure the daughter heard the message more deeply than if she was in a state of anger from being grounded or punished.

Punishments up the ante into power struggles, while encouragement raises everyone to an uplifting connection.

Let's say that you have a child who is hitting his sibling. You tell him politely to stop.

He continues bugging the sibling.
You yell at him to stop, NOW!
He continues bugging the sibling.
You threaten him with a time-out if he doesn't stop now.
He continues bugging the sibling.
You move him against his will to the time-out spot.
He won't stay there and continues to taunt the sibling.
You move him back to the time-out spot and add minutes to the time-out.
He comes out before time is up and won't stay there.
You threaten to spank him.
He continues bugging the sibling.
You spank him.
He yells, screams, and hits the sibling again.
You spank him many times and harder.
He yells, screams, and hits you.

Now what? What do you do? Up the ante and keep hitting him? You are now engaged in a full-blown power struggle. What do you do when the child is only four? What do you do when the child is 10? What do you do when the child is 15?

What if, after the second sentence, you figure out that what your perpetrator really needs is attention and decide to not give it negatively? What can you do instead?

You can change your actions and try a new encouraging approach. Instead of increasing the negative punishment, you take a U-turn and recognize the need or feeling (NOF) underneath the behavior and address that.

You can tell the child you realize you haven't spent enough time with him lately and would he like to play a 10-minute board game or read a book with you? This would nip the attention need in the bud and prevent more sibling fighting.

You could separate them both. Take the one who appears to be a victim away to help you with a task, but keep in mind, you need to spend more time with the perpetrator also. Both actions are non-punitive and solve the problem with encouragement, not punishment.

If the parents are the ship on the ocean and the iceberg is the child, above the surface is the child's behavior – the only part parents tend to see. What they need to do is to get into the little parent submarine and look underneath the part of the iceberg that's hidden under water. There they will find the NOF: the need or feeling that is driving and producing the behavior. When the NOF is addressed, the behavior will be taken care of automatically. If the NOF is not addressed, the behavior will continue.

Attachment parenting discipline

About 50 years ago, a British psychologist named John Bowlby first used the term "attachment" in describing the special bond between a child and the parents or caregivers. He said each new baby needs a special adult in his life to protect, nurture, and comfort him. The loving care provided gives the child a sense of trust in people, that they will meet his needs and let him know he is valued, loved, and the world is a safe, predictable place.

Any nurturing parent, sibling, relative, or caregiver can be an attachment person. Anybody can respond to a baby when he is happy and gurgling. The best way to build this relationship is in responding to baby's distress when he is sick, upset, or hurt. By picking up the baby and cuddling, rocking, and soothing him when he is sick, upset, or hurt shows the baby he has someone to meet his needs and respond to him. The same applies to older children.

Therefore, the core of developing attachment is to respond to the child on their schedule, when they need it, and to respond in the same consistent, nurturing way, most of the time.

In the 1980s, a U.S. physician named Dr. William Sears coined a term called "attachment parenting" that refers to a specific set of behaviors that most people associate with the attachment theory. These behaviors may or may not include child-led weaning from breastfeeding, co-sleeping, carrying the baby most of the time, eating organic food, etc. However, it's important to remember that forming an attachment with a baby is not necessarily associated with any one behavior but rather an underlying philosophy, commitment, belief, and value that the parent will meet the baby's needs for nurturing and love on the baby's schedule, not according to whatever any other "expert" decrees.

Attachment parenting is child-centered parenting. It's about making the baby the expert of what he needs. If a baby hates being cramped in a sling, the parent responding to the baby's needs by not putting him in one, is strengthening those attachment bonds. If the baby hates co-sleeping and prefers the roominess of a crib, then respecting his preferences is attachment parenting. It's a philosophy of getting behind the eyes and brain of a child and trying to see things from their perspective. It's parenting with empathy, kindness, and nurturing guidance.

Many attachment parents struggle with discipline. Most parents do not wish to hurt their child through punishment but recognize the need for teaching clear boundaries and a sense of structure and limits for their children. Since many parents do not have role models from their parents of loving discipline, it can be hard to judge what discipline is appropriate to an attachment parenting philosophy. The goal of attachment discipline is to teach and protect our children through the tools outlined in this book. Every tool is designed to enhance attachment and build the relationship.

The attachment bond doesn't end when babies stop breastfeeding, co-sleeping, and grow out of toddlerhood. Attachment parenting can exist well into the teen years and beyond because it's mostly an emotional connection in the later years, rather then a physical one as in the early years.

HONOR VERSUS CONSISTENCY

Honor in parentng is important. Honor is meaning what you say and saying what you mean. You must remain true to your words or choose your words very carefully before they pop out! Follow up your words and promises with actions. Honor is a necessary part of parenting. Honor is different from consistency.

Consistency is trying to make things equal, all the time, with everyone, everywhere. This is impossible to do in relationships.

 Parents can't be consistent in tasks they find unpleasant, and punishment is unpleasant.

We are human beings with fluctuating feelings, opinions, beliefs, and situations, and consistency is difficult to achieve, especially in parenting. Punishment is even harder because you have to be very consistent for it to work – at least 95 percent of the time. That's what happens when you rely on time-out, grounding, spanking, and consequences for discipline. People are usually not consistent with things they hate doing. Ask anyone who hates exercising but signed up for a gym membership (to force themselves to work out on a regular and consistent basis) if they felt that they got their monies worth. Probably not. Who cleans their toilet religiously every week? Not many people, I would bet! Punishing children under the name of discipline is unpleasant work for parents. So they are not consistent with punishment, even though most parenting books recommend its necessity. On the other hand, negotiating and problem-solving doesn't require consistency. It's flexible and workable to every relationship and families' needs.

> The only thing in parenting where you have to be absolutely consistent is giving your child love, attention, nurturing, and warmth. In other words, unconditional love. That kind of consistency is easy to provide. Most parents can do that naturally or learn how to do it.

This is an extreme example, but it illustrates how we are not the same people every day of the year. Imagine you came home from work and noticed your 10-year-old spilled his plate of lasagna all over your white Berber carpet. You're livid! Or are you? Imagine you had 14 hours of sleep and won the lottery. Are you livid? Chances are good you would probably say, "That's okay. No problem."

Now, imagine your 10-year-old has spilled the lasagna and you have had two hours of sleep the night before and just lost your job. How would you react to the lasagna?

Differently, I'll bet. But to your child, it's the same behavior he just did. Your reaction was different, depending on what happened in your day. So consistency is very difficult. It's better to be honest and say, "Look son, I'm having a bad day and could you clean up that mess please?"

Tell your children how you are feeling. Even three years olds know that things are done differently in different homes and with different people.

The difference between a behavior and a judgment
Behaviors are specific, tangible actions that we can see, hear, touch, or smell; whereas judgments are opinions and beliefs about the behaviors. When speaking to a child about their actions, make it sure it's about specific descriptive behaviors, rather than general judgments.

Specific behaviors

Specific behaviors are those actions that you could take a picture of or record on a tape recorder or video camera. They are objective, non-judgmental, specific, and not subject to anyone's opinion. They are easy to describe. Therefore, they are difficult to deny.

Behaviors	Judgments
1. Running in the room.	1. Unruly behavior.
2. Interrupting others while speaking.	2. Disrespecting others.
3. Saying "you're an idiot".	3. Rude and taunting.
4. Swinging plastic rods at other children.	4. Threatening other children.
5. Standing on the counter.	5. Bad behavior.
6. Knocking over signs.	6. Careless actions.
7. Throwing balls at children.	7. Angry outbursts.
8. Throwing equipment up in the air and letting it smash to the floor.	8. Disrespecting equipment.
9. Saying to the instructor, "You can't make me do that!:	9. Talking back to instructors.
10. Jumping up and down wildly and screaming in a high pitched voice.	10. Throwing temper tantrums.

Judgments

The corresponding judgments of the above behaviors are very subjective and can be argued. What unruly behavior looks like to one person can look very different to another. What is rude for one is not necessarily rude for another. It's a big mistake to assume that all people think alike or interpret actions the same. They don't.

If the behavior bothers the parent, it's called "misbehavior." If it doesn't bother the parents, it's just called "normal behavior."

Make a list of a) behaviors you like, and b) behaviors you don't like.

Start by working on one of each. Express appreciation for the liked behavior at least once a day. Then look at the disliked behavior and decide what tool to use from the lists in section two. Remember to avoid the "shotgun" approach. Work on one behavior at a time and not a whole bunch of them together. A slow, steady approach will have more impact.

THE GOLDEN RULES ABOUT RULES

1. Rules must work for the individual person and the unique situation.

When I became a parent, I read more than 196 parenting books. I discovered most books promote the concept of parental consistency. Rules have to be set and strictly enforced, regardless if they don't quite fit, because otherwise, children would get confused. Children want limits. Parents must provide them, whether they are useful for the family or not. Parents must never waiver. What I found confusing was the aspect of parenting that required consistency. I came to the conclusion that books usually meant that punishments and dealing with discipline matters needed the most consistency rather than rule enforcement.

However, in reality, life is not consistent. To deny that is to look at parenting with naivety and unreasonableness. Let's look at rule making. It's hard to argue that rules are not required in the home, community, or country. Without rules, people would not know what to expect. They're necessary for safety and health reasons. Sometimes, they are unwritten and unstated. Sometimes, they are clearly written, spoken, and demonstrated. The success of rules, meaning that they are acknowledged and abided by, depends on two important factors. WHO is making the rules and for WHAT purpose?

2. Family rules must be made by everyone affected by them.

It's a well known fact that people tend to abide by rules more when they have had a part in making them. This is called the Participatory Rule Theory. People have a vested interest in carrying them out and making them work if the rules respect their needs, and they have had input. Children are no different. Of course, you must keep age appropriateness in mind. A two-year-old has a hard time creating rules. A four-year-old could come up with some if prodded, and a seven-year-old would definitely be able to brainstorm rule creation with a parent.

For example, we have seven people in our house with different needs, interests, and moods. I've tried to establish ground rules and then found myself breaking them just as much as the children.

We have a white berber carpet in the playroom. (Don't ask me why I was insane enough to get a white carpet.) One of my rules was NO FOOD IN THE PLAYROOM. I soon found myself serving the children dry crackers or cereal in the playroom, while they were watching cartoons because it helped us all get out the door faster when we needed to go somewhere. Then, I decided to change the rule to NO WET FOOD IN THE PLAYROOM. However, the toddler had her juice in a spill proof cup, and as hard as she tried not to spill, she would get liquid on the carpet. The rule changed to WET FOOD ALLOWED ONLY IF NONE WAS

SPILLED, which worked until the babysitter was not as careful monitoring spillage as I was. The rule changed to WET FOOD NOT ALLOWED IF BABYSITTER OR DAD IS HOME. Eventually, the rule changed daily, depending on what the food was and who was eating it and how tolerant I was feeling that day if mishaps occurred. I was making all the rules, not anyone else.

One day while I was trying to explain the rule variations to the children, they asked, "What EXACTLY is the food rule in the playroom?" The rules had changed daily but not my underlying NEED, which was to keep the white carpet somewhat clean. This was only one issue of many in our family. It occurred to me that parenting is not a consistent endeavor. I was desperately trying to come up with a rule that would cover every circumstance and every person in the family. This was impossible to do.

The P.E.T. program teaches that all our children's behavior falls into two basic categories: acceptable to us and unacceptable to us. Spaghetti on the rug is unacceptable. Dried crackers on the rug were acceptable because they are easy to vacuum up. In addition, the acceptance level we feel towards our children's behavior is dependent on three factors: The parent, the environment, and the child. First, let's look at the *parent*. How I feel about food on the rug is dependent on how tired I am that day, how stressed I am, and how elated I am. On a day that everything is wonderful and going well, I could probably even handle lasagna spills. On a day that I am sick with the flu, a few cracker crumbs would send me to the madhouse. Secondly, the *environment* is a factor: spaghetti spilled on the patio outside is less of a problem than spaghetti on the rug. And lastly, the particular *child* is a factor: I am much more forgiving of a two-year-old spilling food because she is learning eating skills, than I am of an eight-year-old who was carelessly watching his video game more than where his fork was going.

The division of acceptable behavior and unacceptable behavior to us is altered every hour, every day, and every minute, just as circumstances, moods, and priorities change. For the example of FOOD IN THE PLAYROOM, we all came to the conclusion that it's important to judge each incident on its own merit. So rule consistency went out the window. The food rule's purpose had to fill all our needs and be acceptable to everyone. My need was to keep my white Berber carpet clean. My children's need was to avoid missing their favorite shows during meal time. That was what we had to work around. Each day, we negotiate what can and can't be eaten in the playroom. Everyone agrees to a rule that we negotiate food choices eaten in the family room. The food rule had to work for each person involved and the situation.

Will the children have too much control?

Some parents hesitate to allow their children too much input, control, and decision making. They may state the children can have some input into the discussion, but the parents make the final decision and rules. This seldom considers the child's needs. A power struggle might ensue. Of course, decisions and rule-making is an age-appropriate idea. A two-year-old will not make too many rules. A nine-year-old certainly can. Consider the following chart of parent control and influence.

Parent Involvement

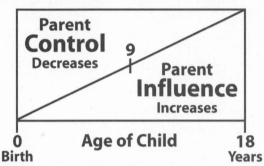

When a baby is born, the parents make 100 percent of the decisions, rules, and decides what the baby eats, where she goes, or what she wears. By age two, a child gains some control over what she wears or eats, but the parent still has the majority of control. Of course, all parents have no control over four things: eating, sleeping, toileting, and learning. Those are all within a child's domain. But everything else is up in the air. A nine-year-old is becoming more adaptable, mobile, and independent and can decide more things for herself and make more rules. By aged 18, a parent has lost pretty much all control over a child.

At what age should a parent seek input into a rule from a child? Usually, when the child is ignoring, rebelling against, or balking against a rule. That's a first indication the rule doesn't meet everyone's needs and may require reworking.

3. Family rules must have a specific purpose or meet a specific need and not be created just to exercise authority.

Children don't need arbitrary limits to feel secure. Children really want to feel accepted. They will frequently go along with a parent-imposed limit or rule in order to gain the parent's acceptance. This doesn't mean children want limits or rules. Actually, they would prefer complete freedom from them. That's why so many power struggles erupt over rules. However, children recognize the need for rules, and they can see the purpose behind it. What is truly important and what children really need is to know what exactly their parent's expectations and needs are. And children need to express their needs and expectations, too. These change daily. The problem with parent-imposed rules is they so often do not take into account the child's needs. Negotiation, discussion, and problem-solving does.

If there are occasional exceptions to the rules, can children adapt to the inconsistency? Of course! They know every subtlest detail of difference in rules between their house and their friends' houses, the difference between Mom's needs and Dad's needs, and the difference between church expectations and playground expectations. They know and accept that you must wear a seatbelt in a car but don't have to on a city bus, school bus, or even a taxi. Knowing the specific expectations of each situation make a person more secure than knowing the general rule that tries to cover all situations and breaks down because of inconsistency. My children know I need my carpet to stay clean. They now make better choices to meet that need. That's what growing up is all about – making good choices in differing circumstances.

4. Rules are made to be broken.

Parents don't feel consistent from day to day, hour to hour, and minute to minute. That's okay. It's being human. Sometimes, the rules need to be broken and that's okay too. Give up the guilt.

Don't worry about being flexible about rules some of the time. What matters more is if the rule is serving the family rather than the family serving the rule. We all need some consistency, but when we let it control our relationships, then we need to look at its feasibility. Is it still working for us? For our children? Does it meet everyone's needs?

> If your family follows your rules MOST of the time, that's great.
> Try to follow rules for young children under 10. Young children need predictability. Older children can appreciate different viewpoints, feelings, and reactions due to circumstances.

Older children are cognitively able to see the gray areas around rules, beyond the black and white and are more open to negotiating. However, that being said, people are generally creatures of habits and routines. As creatures of habits, I watch in amusement as parents tend to sit in exactly the same seat each week in the parenting class. They will settle into a habit unconsciously when it meets a need. Therefore, rules that meet needs will be easier to unconsciously follow.

Life is about change and inconsistency – about having different feelings, moods, and needs from one day to the next. No parent or child should feel guilty about being human. In all parenting, try to be consistently warm, kind, and nurturing most of the time, but be honest about how you feel. If you have a headache and can't smile, that's okay. Tell the child. Even young children understand.

If you have children that are constantly breaking the rules, it might be a clue to you that the rule is no longer working or serving the needs of everyone who must abide by the rule. Negotiation and problem-solving is in order. It doesn't have to be done on the spot, but may need to be addressed at the next family conference. As one of my children said, "We don't have discipline problems in our house. We have conflicts that need to be negotiated."

5. Parents need to follow the rules too.

Credibility is enhanced when everyone follows the rule! It helps to have posted lists of all your major ones. Use pictures if you have young children.

6. Routines, traditions, rituals, and habits build security in children and adults much more so than rules.

Children love routines because they know that something follows something, and they can predict it. They also love traditions. Even teens hold their parents to holiday traditions because they value them, and the traditions make them feel secure. Some of us have a going-to-work routine. We drive on auto pilot and get to work without even thinking about it. It gives us security.

7. Treat each child differently according to their unique needs and capabilities.

In each family, every child is different in temperament, age, gender, personality, needs, and strengths. The same rules and limits do not apply across the board to every child in the family. I've seen families where the eight-year-old has to go to bed earlier than the 10 year old, even though the eight-year-old is fresher with less sleep, because letting him stay up "wouldn't be fair." The bedtime rule was being used as a 'privilege' rather than a rule meeting needs.

Because each child in the birth order has a different parent, we can't be very consistent there either. The first-born child is our guinea pig. We are much too cautious, anxious, and uptight to be the same parent as we would to our third child, when we are more confident, relaxed, and knowledgeable about stages and tend to let more things go because of those factors. Most third-born children have fewer rules than first-borns.

Rules that concern issues between only one child and the parents should be negotiated as such, and not with the whole family. Remember to look at rules that meet the child and parent's needs.

If you've made a rule that isn't working for all concerned, don't be afraid to change it. Simple tell the child or family member, "This rule isn't working for me. My needs are not getting met. What can we do instead?" Every family member should be free to open up a rule for discussion at the next family conference.

Negotiation, rules that meet needs, and problem-solving allows us to live together harmoniously. Where do your family rules need tweaking? Are they meeting everyone's needs?

THE GOLDEN RULES ABOUT PARENTING WITH A PARTNER

Look at the following behaviors and the circumstances you are in. How would you and your parenting partner react differently in each case?

Your child makes you breakfast in bed but leaves the kitchen in a mess. You are feeling tired from being up all night with the baby. Your partner just woke up from sleeping 12 hours straight.

Your child wants you to play a game with him. You have just returned from driving to eight stores looking for an item that none of them carried. Your partner just finished finding a store that carries the item, and it's on sale for 80 percent off.

Who is feeling good about your child's behavior?

1. Striving for a united front is difficult.

I would bet money that each parent would react very differently to the same behavior. So why do we expect parents to present a united front to their children? Do both parents have the exact same feelings, stresses, expectations, and parenting style? No. Parents are not consistent with each other, nor can they honestly present a united front to their children.

2. Children can handle different ways of doing things.

My son was two years old and learned that when he shopped with Daddy, he had to stay in the cart and sit in the little basket. But when he shopped with Mommy, he could hang off the cart and run around. He never attempted to get out with Daddy, and always tried with Mommy!

If any parent has ever tried to explain to their child the different voice tones expected in different environments, they would know that children can handle different expectations. Church voices, playground voices, inside voices, and naptime voices all have different volumes. Children can tell the difference and don't get confused when different environments call for a different standard of behavior. They learn they can run on the playground and not at church. They can jump on Grandma's sofa because Grandma lets them, but not at home. They have to clean up the toys at daycare but don't have to at Daddy's house, and sometimes have to at Mommy's house. Don't worry that they can become confused. They don't. We have to give them more credit than that.

3. It's okay to agree to disagree.

Many parent books state that both parents must present a united front to children. Not true! It's better to create an "equal team." It's all right to disagree on how things should be handled.

There are many, many right ways to parent and a few wrong ways. Opposing parents can discuss issues and identify the absolutely non-negotiable ones in private and then present their agreed upon ones to the children. Ideally, this is what should take place. However, what really happens is that one parent usually doesn't agree but will go along to present the united front to the children. The children can sense this and know there is some wiggle room or space to work on Mom or Dad, whoever is the easier one. Children are not dumb. They know when one parent is not being totally honest. It's better for all concerned if both parents are honest with their feelings and viewpoints, but support the one parent who feels the strongest about the issue. The parent that feels the strongest will deal with it. Who is this more important for? Who has the stronger feelings about the issue?

4. The partner in the trenches should make the daily decisions about their child.

One thing to keep in mind is that unless a person spends 14 hours a day with a child, they rarely have the insight to know what it entails to parent that long. People who are idealists are those that spend little time with children: partners at work, friends, relatives, doctors, and parenting experts that tell you the shoulds. Unfortunately, they are not around to hear you say "no" 20 times in a day and only hear the one "yes" you wearily espouse at the end of the day. They think you are being too permissive. When dealing with children for long hours, you have to take the pragmatists approach, not the idealists. You do what works! If you relent, even a small bit at the end of a long day, don't beat yourself up for it.

5. There are no perfect parents.

Perfection in parenting is impossible. Do what you can for MOST of the time and you are an excellent parent!

6. What one person starts, they finish.

It's not fair to set a punishment on a child and then ask an unwilling partner to support you in carrying it out. If Dad grounds the child, then leaves town on a business trip for two days, is it really fair to ask Mom to carry out the punishment while he is gone? If parents are divorced and living in separate houses, do not expect the other parent to carry out the punishments.

7. Agree on several core values before you have children if possible.

When you got married or became pregnant, chances are you and your partner talked about what you valued and believed in parenting. Try and come up with three core values you share and will work towards. In our family, my husband and I came up with: 1) No hitting anyone, 2) Rudeness is not acceptable between anyone regardless of age, and 3) We agreed we would raise our children rather than bring in outside care. Your family's three core parenting values might be different, but find three you both will hold up to.

8. Being supportive of your partner's ruling doesn't mean agreement.

You can state a different viewpoint, but support your partner on his choice. This is not undermining him to the children. The key here is to be SUPPORTIVE, not UNITED. Honest communication is preferable. A statement, such as, "I don't feel as strongly about the sleepover as your dad does, but his feelings are important to me, and I think you need to go and discuss this with him if you disagree with his decision."

When parenting styles are opposite

> Parents need to communicate with each other, be supportive, and decide who the issue is more important for, so they can handle it in the way they see fit.

A parent-child relationship is a linear tie. Parents get into trouble when they start to parent as a triangle. Then children see the effect they have on the marital relationship dynamics and decide who they can pressure for what they want. If each parent is more or less individual in their parenting with each child, it becomes more difficult for the child to sense wiggle room and create dissent between parents.

A parent is not responsible for the other parent's individual, unique relationship with each child. If one parent wants to be closer, he or she must do the work to bring that change about. As one mom puts it, "He gets things done his way, and I get things done my way and that's okay. But I've noticed that our relationships with the children are very different. They come to me with issues they wouldn't dare come to him about."

If a partner is more punitive in their approach and wonders why the children don't open up their feelings to them anymore, it's up to that parent to change their ways, rather than expect the other parent to become stricter. Although it's natural for partners to compensate each other methods in unspoken ways, those habits can change. Dad perceives Mom as being too lenient and naturally tends to lean towards the strict side to compensate. Or Dad has been out of town, and Mom has been more lenient on the children to compensate for lack of Dad time. These are natural dance patterns that go back and forth. If compensation swings too heavily on one side, it may be time for a private parent talk to bring out the awareness of what's happening with some solutions.

Criticizing the partner in front of the children is counterproductive to everyone. Often, modeling is the best way to teach a partner about parenting, since research shows that dads learn most of their parenting from their partners. It's okay for the children to see parents disagree, as long as one doesn't lose it and neither parent wins every disagreement. Respectful disagreement and communication to resolve an issue is wonderful for children to witness because it's their blueprint for resolving relationship issues with their future partners. There is no one right way to raise children, and just about every decision can be reconsidered. Take a time-out from your partner if things are getting too heated.

Another approach is that if you and your partner disagree, agree to try each other's way for three days. If it doesn't work out, go back to the status quo.

You can also agree to find a book or parenting course that you will both find useful. Recognize you won't agree on some of the finer points, but if you both find the major points palatable, that can be very useful for you.

As one mom from a parenting group said, "Tell him stories about the terrible things your friends' husbands do and how you are so happy he does x instead." Basic encouragement.

Tips for peaceful partner parenting

When I teach workshops with dads, they overwhelmingly say:

- Delegate the workload. Moms need to learn the mantra "I'm not the only parent here."
- Most important, Mom needs to avoid criticism of Dad's ways and methods and avoid rescues. Dad and child will find their own unique way of being together. If you disagree with Dad and the way he is doing things, model the way you want them to be done – silently. Often, Dad sees that you are having success and will be open to trying your way, if you don't point out that it's the only way to do it (aka: nag)!

When I teach workshops with moms, they overwhelmingly say:

- Dad needs to take responsibility of childcare and nurturing without being asked.
- Dad needs to know the routines and where items are without asking Mom.
- There is nothing sexier to a woman than watching her partner nurture the children.

If either parent is tempted to criticize, ask:

- Is the child in danger physically or psychologically?
- Will this cause irreparable harm?
- Do I always want to be responsible for this task?
- Is it in opposition of one of our three core values of parenting that we agreed on? If so, can I speak to him/her in private using a respectful "I-statement"?

- Is the outcome that important to me or is it more important for my partner to develop a relationship with my children?
- How can I model the change I want to see?

Father involvement is not just good for the children; it's enhancement for the couple relationship too.

When parents are divorced or separated

Even if you and your ex-partner don't get along, your children need two parents. It is even better if you are modeling respect, open communication, and problem-solving.

- Try to strive for basic agreement on three of your most important values together.
- Expect behavior changes during a divorce or adjustment time. Look for the basic signs of anger from children for each age group. (See Chapter 5) Most behavior changes include separation anxiety, regression in toilet training, fearfulness, sleep problems, and aggression; for school-aged and teenagers: rule breaking, attitude, and school problems.
- Understand that behavior changes are a means of communication from your child. They are trying to tell you their feelings about the divorce.
- Tell your child they are not responsible for the situation. Tell them often because they can forget.
- Both partners should give the children more of their time.
- Don't try to continue family traditions. It will magnify the loss. Make new ones. You now have a re-configured family.
- Keep visiting schedules flexible.
- Keep in touch with phone calls, email, and text-messaging.

When the child visits:
- Assign the child a room alone or their own personal space.
- Include the child in chores and family routines.
- Provide time alone with the child and the birth parent.
- Save the best activity for the end of the visit so it ends positively.
- Allow the child some time to settle in before a round of activities.
- Have the birth parent handle the sticky behavior issues. Be sure the discipline tools connect the relationship.

Combining two families:
- Realize that caring and love takes time to grow between stepparents and step siblings. Give it a couple of years.
- Focus on building bonds.
- Have the birth parent handle the sticky discipline issues for the first two years.

- Start the new family in a new place to avoid issues of territory.
- Let all children give input into deciding what to call the new parents.
- Refer to all children as "my son" or "my daughter" instead of "my stepson."
- Discuss adoption of children with the child and step parent.
- Children need extra security during this time of change and adjustment. Be easy on everyone. Allow them their security needs: stuffies, pacifiers, and thumb sucking.
- Include all children in household chores, rituals, and celebrations.
- Remember that hugs, listening, acknowledging feelings, and problem-solving are the best discipline tools for a newly blended family.

> At the end of the day, all you really have left is the relationship between you and your child. The laundry, dishes, and phone calls will always be there tomorrow. But will your connected feelings be?
>
> ~ Cathie Pelly, Parent Educator

2

Build the Bond:
Be the person you want them to be

> Work the relationship and the behavior will take care of itself.
> ~ Gordon Neufeld, Author

Anyone who has ever home schooled their children discovered that 24 hours a day means 24 hours. The parent and child spend a lot of time together. When I home schooled my children, their world was interlocked with mine. We couldn't spend much of that time being mad at each other. We had to learn to get along much more than the average family, who are apart for large amounts of time. It was the same with the siblings. Why spend the time fighting? Instead, we put the effort into building our relationship.

As a home-schooling mom, who also worked part time, I had to make good use of my time, which would serve to build the relationship bonds. Sometimes, that meant postponing laundry or dishes, but it was worth it. I also had to ask my husband for the same level of commitment. As a dad that was prone to traveling for work, it meant more time at home had to be focused on family and not sports or personal pursuits. Not to say that personal time isn't necessary for Mom and Dad. All the juggling of people's needs required a balanced lifestyle.

We decided to put more effort into preventing discipline problems. Good discipline is 90 percent prevention and 10 percent correction. Prevention involves building a good, solid, foundational relationship that will take minimal discipline to keep on track. It's like building a house foundation. Solid, strong walls help support the house frame.

However, no matter how good the relationship is when things are going smoothly, it's how people relate to each other in times of problems that has a direct effect on whether their bond strengthens or disintegrates. In other words, how people fight matters more. Imagine scissors cutting a piece of fabric. The fabric is your relationship with your child. The cuts are the stresses on the relationship from everyday life: peers, separations from business trips, time apart, divorce, puberty, developmental stages, death in the family, and moving. There are cuts on every side, but the little tangly threads of communication holding the fabric together is what counts. If you are still communicating through stress, that's everything.

What does a respectful relationship look like?

Healthy relationships are based on respect, trust, honesty, fairness, equal dignity, sharing feelings, taking responsibility, and good communication. Parenting is no different.

Mutual respect is:

- We listen to each other's ideas, values, and opinions.
- We are proud of each other.
- We accept each other as we are now and not how we want them to be.
- We trust each other.
- We never hurt each other on purpose.
- We don't invade each other's privacy even in the name of parenting.
- We are honest with each other.
- We understand that our feelings can change any minute.
- We forgive mistakes and learn from them rather than harbor resentments and blame.
- Our relationship is based on equality of humanness, and fairness, except for experience and knowledge.
- We both give and take equally or in the capacity of what we can (children learn as they get older).
- We make decisions that are win-win most of the time (even for toddlers).
- We both accept responsibility.
- We don't blame other people for our mistakes.
- We protect each other from harm.
- We try to think through our decisions to the best our capacity allows us.
- We overlook our many idiosyncrasies.
- We try to understand each other.
- We tell each other how we really feel.

WAYS TO BUILD A SOLID RELATIONSHIP FOUNDATION

 • Use your kindest words in the home with those you love the most.

Read together. Even when the children start reading on their own, read together out loud several times a week. Cuddle, sit together, and make it a snuggly, cozy time. If time is short, don't skip it. Continue the ritual, but just shorten the time to do it in. Many families continue this pleasant activity into the teenage years. Studies show that it helps build reading, writing, and listening skills in young children, school-age children, and beyond.

Family meal times at least once a day. It doesn't have to be dinner. In fact, dinnertime for young children is the worst time of the day. They are distracted, prone to meltdowns, tired, and don't eat well. Mom is usually pretty tired, and so is Dad. Both are not in the mood for dinner time antics. Breakfast and lunch would be a better time to meet, if possible. Meals don't have to be fancy, just the four food groups and lots of good conversation. If children are not hungry, make it routine that they come to the table to talk – they don't have to eat. Many times, my children told me they weren't hungry, but when we insisted they come to the table, they eventually did eat, and talk.

Play games together. Play board games, computer games, word and language games in the car. Children find them fun, and they pass the time while driving. They also build literacy and math skills.

Create psychological intimacy. Understand and listen more than you talk and lecture. If your child tells you a secret, keep it. Don't share it with your friends. Also, ask your child's permission to share their funny, but embarrassing stories. If they decline, respect their wishes.

Exercise together. That includes walks, classes, sports, contests, and fundraisers.

Family celebrations and rituals. Gives a child a sense of belonging, history, and predictability in the family and community. Write a birthday letter to your child every year. Talk about the highlights of the year for him, new things he did, how you feel about him and his strengths. Give it to him in a packet for his 18th birthday.

Family projects. Instead of parents doing all the work, let the children help and make it fun. Avoid criticism and focus on encouraging the effort they make rather than the end product. If your sons are helping to build the basement, make light of the fact they cut a piece of wood wrong. Comment on the precision and care they used to cut it. Gently show them how to fix the error. Comment that "mistakes are for learning!" Encouragement will make the child want to continue on projects and especially work with you.

Use driving time productively. For older children, it's a great time to talk about issues they bring up. They don't have to make eye contact and can bring up sensitive, embarrassing topics. They know there's a finite end to the conversation when you both reach your destination! Answer matter of fact, without making fun of the questions. For younger children, driving time can be used for silly games and jokes, as long as it doesn't distract you from the road. Resist the temptation to fill the time with MP3 music, portable DVDs, and book tapes. It's too precious a time. The close proximity and undistracted time together are important factors that build relationships. Sometimes driving time is the only time parents have with their children.

Share humor. Laugh together. As much as possible, find the funny in the situation. Children have an innate ability to find it for you!

Have plenty of photos of family fun times. Display them. Too often, we focus on the drudge of laundry, fighting siblings, and snarky teenagers. We and our children need to be reminded that families enjoy each other most of the time.

Have photos of Mom and Dad with the child. Display a special photo of each child only with Mom and Dad so that children know they are unique and loved for their special qualities.

Honor their unique qualities. Make daily comments about what you love in each child. Do it nonchalantly or it sounds fake. Say "I just love the way you clean up the kitchen. It really helps me." To get you thinking what unique qualities they have, or what they do, see the chart in Chapter 9 called "I like and appreciate about you."

Make the relationship a priority. Say "no" more often. Most people value family life as their first priority but then take on too many outside commitments and over schedule their children in outside activities. That leaves no time for family life. Ask yourself, when contemplating "yes," how will this affect our family and our relationship? If it has a negative effect, just say "no." When planning one-on-one time with each child, pen in a date and time in your calendar. Hold it sacred. It must be a priority on those days. When the phone rings, and you are sharing a book with a cuddled child in your lap, ask to call the person back. Children take notice of what's important to parents. Putting off a phone call for them shows, in concrete terms, you consider them important.

Many parents spend time on child related things: baking cookies for the class, volunteering to coach for the soccer team, being a Brownie leader but shouldn't consider this as one-on-one time with children. Those commitments are nice, but children don't often appreciate them as we think they might. Often, it takes time and energy away from directly interacting with our children, which they need most of all. Think twice before saying, "Yes."

Be considerate of needs, feelings, and dignity. Don't embarrass him in front of his friends and humiliate him in public. If you must speak with your child, ask to speak in private. Ask their permission to retell their cute stories. Respect their property, and ask permission to use their things. Refrain from snooping. Model and communicate that you trust them.

Look at home movies and photos together. Scrapbook and compile film snippets. Children love to see themselves and their family in great moments.

Worship together. Avoid making this an issue, though. If your child reaches the age of not wanting to attend services, keep modeling by attending yourself and let him choose. Nudge, but don't force. It's the best way to instill values.

Phone calls throughout the day to connect. Or emails. Or, join the children and learn how to text message. Just a short, "How are you doing? How is your day going?"

Take a class together. Seek out a common interest and take a class together. Many fathers and daughters take karate or wall climbing. Mothers and sons take golf lessons together, family pottery, or skiing. Many venues recognize that families wish to spend more time together, and family classes are the result. Go for a coffee and treat after.

Holiday together. Again, many cruise ships, resorts, and holiday venues recognize that time stressed families wish to recuperate lost time together. Try not to bring along your child's friend. It tends to dilute family time. Your child may grumble at first, but will interact eventually if he is not forced.

Establish family routines when your child is young. This is one of the best family bonding and discipline methods around. Some examples: family dinner is always eaten at the table, and everyone comes to the table. If every Saturday morning is family chore time from the time that children are little, it becomes ingrained. Friday nights could be pizza and family game night. Saturday night could be parent's night out alone. Set aside Sunday as family day – a day to spend together doing activities.

Be kind. Sounds simple, right? Do we really treat our family members as kind and thoughtful as we do outsiders, such as friends, neighbors, relatives, teachers, partners? Watch your tone of voice and body language. Often, we can be very polite but in a terse, icy sound. We would not use that on outsiders.

Apologize when wrong. Do it as soon as you come to terms with the fact that you may have been in error. A heartfelt, sincere apology sends the message to your children that we are all human. We make mistakes, and we can make amends.

Communicate respectfully. Use polite manners. Use "I-statements" instead of "You-statements"; listen when other family members are talking. Avoid interrupting. Interrupting is like a "verbal shove." Avoid speaking behind another's back.

Give encouragement. Everybody can use specific descriptive encouragement. "I really appreciate it when you bring your plate to the dishwasher. It makes cleaning up easier. Thank you." It tells the child what he did specifically to please you and why it matters. This builds good feelings between you both and gives him a healthy sense of self-esteem.

Expect respect and kindness from children and partner. Do not settle for less! "Nobody walks all over you unless you lie down first." (Unknown) If you expect respect, then you give your children permission to expect it also from their friends, adults, teachers, and others. You are modeling how a healthy person should be treated by others. If family members are not nice to you, walk away. Come back later and say in a calm voice, "I'm not here to be spoken to that way. You may ask me this way…" Others are more likely to hear it when things are calmer. Don't forget to use kindness and respect on them. Introduce them to others, and be polite.

Share feelings. There are basically four levels of intimacy in conversations. Each level reveals more about oneself and has a greater risk of vulnerability to the other person. Trust in the relationship must be greater for each higher level.

Level One – small talk: This is when two people don't know each other very well and discuss the weather, the mutual situation (the bus is late), or a trivial observation.

Level Two – fact disclosure: This is when two people talk about what movies are on, current hockey games, and sharing information about themselves, such as their statistics: how many children they have, what they do for an occupation, or where the playgroups are.

Level Three – viewpoints and opinions: This is an intimate sharing of one's beliefs, values, and viewpoints on different topics. This is critical for listening to without judgment from school-age children and teenagers. Accepting their differences in these areas build relationships.

Level Four – personal feelings: This is the most intimate level and the most difficult. Communicating how you feel about life's topics and your child sharing how they feel. The environment must be a safe one. You must ensure confidentiality. If you can get to this level with your child, you have a very connected relationship.

Sharing feelings, values, and beliefs, and opinions is the ultimate way to communicate trust, love, and intimacy.

Use human touch. In an increasingly litigation fearful society, appropriate human touch is becoming less fashionable. Touch is essential to nurturing. For small children, hugs, holding, lap cuddles, carrying, stroking, and kissing are as basic a need as food and water. For older children, they still crave touch. Maybe not lap holding but shoulder hugs, head pats, hand pats, sitting next to you are much desired – even in the teen years. Be aware that children may slough off touch when in the company of peers, but they still need it and welcome it at home. Let your child be the touch controller. Keep offering touch. If he is uncomfortable or doesn't want touch, respect his wishes. Find other ways, such as verbal affirmations, to show love and nurturing. We all know some children who dislike physical contact. They hate slings as babies and hate cuddling as children. A definition of appropriate human touch is touching any area of the body that is not covered by a swimsuit. Kisses are not open mouth kisses.

Play what your child wants to play. Let the child lead in play. Do what she tells you to do, rather than the other way around. This helps you become aware of your child's body language and verbal responses. Become aware of her thoughts and feelings. It helps you develop empathy to see the world from her eyes. Children love it because they get to be the "boss" and play how they want.

Respect child's property and expect respect to your property. Ask to use things, and knock on doors before entering. Don't give away anything of your child's without asking first and receiving permission. Don't snoop through their belongings or diary. Avoid grabbing toys from your child. Ask to use his things (this teaches him to ask to use your things). Don't use them if he says "no." This shows him that "no" means "no" and when you say "no" to him asking to borrow your stuff, then he will respect it more. Ask permission before allowing other children in their room or allowing them to play with their toys. Encourage all your children to treat their siblings the same. I found that the more each child asked for permission to use other siblings' belongings, the more they said "yes." It's almost as if they knew they always had the control within themselves to lend out and would not abuse the privilege. In the odd time they said "no," it was usually for a good reason. We tried to work out what the issue was so both siblings would be happy with a solution.

Family chores. What a great bonding tool! Nothing says "You are our family, and we need you" like asking children to pitch in and help with running the household smoothly. Teaching a child how to clean a birdcage or how to mop a floor provides great one-on-one time and opportunities to discuss a wide variety of things. Housework is so mundane; it's nice to have someone to work with and talk to. Children are less keen to do chores on their own though, and would prefer to work with you or a sibling.

Camp. Family camping trips are great. Young children love to camp and be outdoors. Older children don't mind if they can bring music, bikes, balls, or other pleasant diversions. Sitting around the campfire, singing, telling jokes, playing games are wonderful family memories for older and younger children, and they pick up a variety of useful skills.

Listen to music together. You don't have to talk. Just share in the moment of joint enjoyment.

Family outings. Visiting museums, other families, zoos, etc.

Bedtime rituals. Bedtime rituals are an especially intimate time. Share these duties with your partner. Since bedtime is often a time when children tend to open up and talk, both Mom and Dad should take turns listening. Lack of diversions and focused time and an opportunity to put off sleeping tends to open children up. Try to build in 20 minutes of talk time into the nightly bedtime routine. It's invaluable as a relationship builder.

Share opinions, beliefs, and values. Take time to listen to your child without comment. Invite sharing more. Even if you don't share your belief, you are building the relationship that will allow a more even back and forth sharing of views for next time. Children are far more likely to listen to you once you have demonstrated that you can listen totally without judgment to them.

Schedule one-on-one time together at least once per month. A good way to do this is to mark on the calendar, each child's birth date for each month. Sometimes, if we don't schedule time for it, it just doesn't happen. For example, every fourth day of the month, the evening is blocked off for my son. He decides what we will do that day for his special time. This is not for grocery shopping alone with him or errands or a play that I've wanted to see. This is time for me and him together (and sometimes Dad, too) to do what he wants to do. We have gone to dinner, bowling, movies, go-carting, shopping, or whatever. Sometimes, we stayed home and played games while Dad took all the other children out. Although, we try to include a child along on our errands during the weeks, this date is different because we just focus on one child.

Enter contests together. Sometimes a little friendly competition with someone outside the family strengthens the bonds inside the family. Entering a neighborhood block party Olympics as a family team can help build bonds.

Fulfill promises. When you make a promise, do your very, very best to follow through and honor your commitment. Children are watching and will do as you do, not as you say. If there is any place for consistency in parenting, it is honoring your word.

Leave caring notes to each other. In lunchboxes, under pillows, in pockets, and any unexpected place.

Give small tokens of love in the form of gifts. A small token, carefully chosen, tells a child that you were thinking of her.

Give small acts of service to each other. Make a special dessert, a cup of hot chocolate on a bad day, a paper hug.

Play sports together. Make sure both parent and child love the sport.

Build trust. Avoid lying to members of the family and checking up on your child. Mention every so often, how much you trust your child. If your relationship is good, they will value it and work to keep your trust.

Focus on and notice strengths. Every child has wonderful qualities. If it's hard for you to think of them at the time, see the chart in Chapter 9, "I like and appreciate about you…"

Give five appreciations for every complaint. This is to keep the focus on a positive climate rather than negativity. It's so easy to only see the things that bug us instead of the hundreds of things that children do right.

Give at least one appreciation every day. Everybody reacts well to being appreciated and valued. It's a basic need. We can't assume that our children feel valued. We have to say the words. They are so literal; they don't pick up nuances in body language. We need to speak up.

Maintain confidences. When your child hands you the gift of a confidence, do not spill it! Even ask the child if you have their permission to share with your partner. When the child hears you asking their permission, they can build confidence in your ability to keep it quiet.

Walk together. Going for a walk is a great way to cool down strong emotions, think together, and problem-solve. It doesn't require eye contact, so big, heavy thoughts can be addressed. It is free and healthy.

Cook and bake together. The kitchen is the heart of the family home. Many confidences are shared over communal chopping, stirring, washing, and rinsing. Don't wait for them to offer. Hand them a knife, cutting board, and some carrots then zip your lips. Give passive acknowledgements such as "uh huh," "tell me more," and "then what happened"? Don't talk too much yourself! Listen and acknowledge without judgment or offering advice, and often the conversation will flow.

Volunteer together. There are many places that allow a family to volunteer together for a good cause. Time well spent with a purposeful focus is also a great educational experience.

Family activities and hobbies together. Getting into sewing, scrapbooking, or wood-working are great ways to connect. Tackling a basement renovation or teaching a child to knit can be a great focus for conversation that slides into other topics. Be sure to praise, encourage, and acknowledge all efforts made by the children. Strongly avoid any correction or criticism. If you have to intervene for safety reasons, do it in a positive manner such as "I'm just going to roll up your sleeves here so they don't get caught in the belt sander." Instead of "You should roll up your sleeves before you start work." No person likes to be corrected. It is very discouraging. Try to word your safety rule in a positive general way. Instead of "You forgot the safety glasses again." Try "You have such gorgeous eyes; they need protection!"

Watch me! For the zillionth time during a day, your child wants you to watch them. It's important for their self-esteem and confidence and competence. This is especially important for the preschooler and school-aged years. Even if you are busy, take a deep breath and go watch. It's a short stage that will soon pass, where just a little effort from enthusiastic parents pays off huge.

A caution to family relationship builders. Limit play dates, sleepovers, and bring-ing a friend along on family outings and too many extra curricular activities. These can all contribute to a dilution of family time.

I would strongly say that even with no discipline, if most of the family relationship builders are practiced in a family, there would be almost no need for extra disci-pline. Children would turn out to be pretty decent caring, responsible people. Their needs for belonging, contribution, responsibility, communication, and autonomy have been taken care of.

DISCIPLINE MYTHS THAT INTERFERE WITH BUILDING THE BOND

Children need to be punished to behave better

Children need to be taught how to make amends, make restitution, and how to solve problems. It is better they learn these skills in the safety of the family rather than the outside world. The outside world will be more than willing to teach children about punishment.

Punishment tends to teach children not to get caught, rather than the reasons of why bad behavior is not appropriate and what to do instead. It shifts the focus to an external locus of control, meaning parents, teachers, and adults in authority, instead of the desirable internal locus of control, which is the child's conscience.

Time-outs teach children to calm down

According to Dr. Otto Weininger, author of *Time-In Parenting*, children do not have the reflective skills needed to figure out their part in the situation and what to do about it until age seven. Parents who put children in time-out expect the child to feel remorseful and think of ways to help solve the problem, when in fact, children either don't know why they are in time-out or what they did that led to a time-out. Many children feel angry and resentful in a time-out rather than remorseful or ready to problem-solve.

Many children also don't know how to calm themselves. They need to be taught the skills of how to breathe and to learn how to calm down. Many adults take courses in better anger management practices, and yet, we leave children to figure those out on their own. Learning to self-soothe and calm down is an important life long skill. Equating "calming down" with a punishment serves to diminish its necessity.

Problems not acknowledged go away

Problems tend to go underground where feelings can fester and build. They snowball into bigger ones and just breed resentment. Even if no solution is decided, at least discussion of problems helps them fade.

Children must feel bad to do better in the future

It's flawed thinking that when children do something very bad – something equally bad must happen to them to teach them a lesson. Psychology tells us that when people feel good, they do good. Children that feel bad, get revenge. Like adults, children who are acknowledged for the positive rather than constantly criticized for the negative are more likely to change their patterns and continue the positive behavior. Children have an innate urge to please adults and especially those they love. Constant criticism is not helpful for anyone. Even small amounts of criticism are discouraging. It is far better to ignore the small negative actions and acknowledge, encourage, and appreciate the good actions, however small.

Children must be taught what unacceptable actions are

They can learn by watching how the world works. It's more effective if children learn what is acceptable rather than what is unacceptable. When we point things out to people, we give them the message they are stupid and can't figure things out for themselves. Children are intrinsic learners. They will figure out what not to do if you show them what to do over and over again. All criticism is negative, regardless of how "polite" it sounds. "Would you please get off my foot?" Sounds polite and non-offensive, but it is a negative direction. "I would be most happy if you stand in your own space" tells someone what to do in a positive way. Or "My foot hurts" lets people know of your problem but leaves the dignity of deciding what to do, up to them. Most people don't like to be told what to do. But children are still learning. They still need help in how to fix the problems they have caused. They need to apologize, repair, return, fix it, replace it, compensate for it, or clean it up.

Children can be spoiled by having their needs met

Children are spoiled by NOT having their needs met or having their needs met the wrong way. Material possessions are not necessary. Love, compassion, understanding, emotional comforting, and non-sexual physical touch do not spoil a child. It makes them a better human being by showing them love and how to comfort others. These are the basic fulfillment of survival, security, and social needs and essential for human development. One mom in my class told of how her two-year-old son would cry, and all the siblings would run and comfort the child immediately. They learned how to do it by being immediately comforted when they themselves were hurt, sad, or sick.

Giving time to a child will never spoil them. Giving too many material possessions and doing things for them that they are capable of doing will spoil them.

Children can be taught independency by pushing them to be independent

The opposite is true. Children that have their dependency needs met, become more independent faster, than if they were pushed or forced to become independent before they were developmentally ready. Children that feel secure will become independent sooner. It relates back to basic attachment theory. Children need a secure base to run to for comfort and to explore from. When they are filled with security, they will cling less.

It's certainly within a parent's job to encourage a child to independence, whether it's giving up the soother, toilet training, sleeping in their own bed, going to preschool, but it's not okay to force those milestones before each child is ready. Readiness is an individual development that doesn't respect the clock or calendar. Just because the neighbors child is ready for the toilet doesn't mean that your same aged child is ready. Respect your child's uniqueness. They will master each task in their own time.

If I reward misbehavior with hugs, cuddles, soft words, and unconditional love, it will encourage the child to misbehave some more

Often, misbehavior is about strong feelings of anger, unhappiness, upset, and frustration. If we react with harshness, we are not helping our child deal with his feelings. The time to teach is not then. It's time to help him calm down. Teaching comes later and is more effective when the child and parent are connected and calm.

You are not rewarding the misbehavior. You are dealing with the emotional upset in order to set the stage for teaching. Then you can calmly speak, and the child is calm enough to hear. They will get the lesson more in connection and respect of you than in fear of your anger and punishment. Connect first, then direct.

Toddlers are too young to know how to problem-solve

Have you ever watched a toddler and a shape sorter? They have figured out a problem and are brainstorming solutions to solve it with a bit of trial and error. Perhaps they might need adult help to brainstorm solutions, but they can certainly handle the process.

Children learn self-control by being controlled

Children learn self-control by watching models of self-control. They see their parents exercise restraint in areas of drugs, eating, gambling, and spending. They learn accountability and responsibility through problem-solving and honoring their promises. They learn by watching their parents acting responsibly. But most of all, children learn self-control by figuring out where their own limits are, experiencing natural consequences of going over those limits, and receiving positive guidance, teaching, consulting, and whole lot of repetition and practice. Children also need information. When they know the reasons, they can figure out the best course of action and how to solve the problem. This develops their internal locus of control. And that internal control is what guides a person's integrity. Integrity is what you do when no one is looking.

My 12-year-old son, decided one day, when I was out doing errands, he would put himself to work. He cleaned the kitchen, baked a cake, went to the store for eggs, and sat at the table doing school work. Another time, I took the younger children to a play place for the afternoon. He didn't want to come. He stayed at home with five computers, two video game consoles, six hand-held game consoles, and a video/ DVD player. He left them all untouched! He made a choice to clean up the house, put away dishes, vacuum, and clean up scattered toys. No nagging. No parent telling him to do it. It was entirely on his own initiative. He learned self-control by watching others and seeing the importance of it first hand. He experienced the benefits of a clean house, a fresh cake, and newly acquired knowledge. Most of all, he felt a sense of accomplishment.

Children get into bad habits that can take years to correct

New habits can be acquired in about 21 days of repetition. Everybody has bad habits that require adjustment at some point in time. We all fall into them, but often, don't want to get out of them unless we are internally motivated to do so. When we are really ready to change a bad habit, we can kick it in three short weeks.

A child that gets used to sleeping with parents can get used to sleeping with siblings or alone. They can break a habit when everyone is ready. A prime example is toilet training. After using diapers for two years, would we ever get them to switch to using the toilet? Are we creating bad habits by getting them used to diapers? No. Even though we use diapers, we fully expect that someday they will use the toilet.

When the time is right to change habits, it will be done. Better early than late doesn't apply. In fact, later usually is better, because children are more developmentally ready.

Children do not have the adult rights of dignity, respect, and kindness of their feelings and body

Children have the same fundamental and civil rights as adults. In most countries' constitutions, charters of rights encompass all people, regardless of age. Besides, if we want our children to treat others with dignity, respect, and kindness, we need to treat them the same way.

Dismissing children's feelings makes them go away

Feelings dismissed by adults tend to be driven underground. Acknowledging and accepting feelings does not make the child feel them even stronger. It's the opposite. It tends to dissipate the feeling once the child feels understood and their feelings are validated. A common concern by a parent is that if they acknowledge a feeling, the child will milk it for all it's worth. If a child trips on the sidewalk, they cry. The parent comes and comforts them with a "that hurts, doesn't it?" The child then cries less if the parent just said, "Be a big boy and put a brave smile on." The parent is now making the crying harder and longer. I believe that children who are not used to an empathetic response to their feelings will cry longer and harder when they get it, just because it feels so good to have that attention and empathy. It's called an insecure attachment. If children are used to getting consistent nurturing, they will naturally get over the hurt faster because it's a response they can count on.

Children do not have an innate sense of fairness and justice

By age six, children are very familiar with rules and social conventions and have picked up norms and values within society just by watching adults and other children. Try watching a group of six-year-olds play a board game. They are very "rule" focused and have picked up fairness rules from their parents and peers. They know when they are being treated differently from the way they think they should be.

Respect must be taught

Character education states that respect must be taught. Not so. Respect must be modeled and caught. It must not be limited to certain ages, genders, classes, cultures, religions, or occupations. Children learn more from "Do as I do, rather than do as I say."

Children change their behavior if we yell, hit, nag, punish, or correct enough

Children, like adults, are more likely to change by observing a strong, influential, positive, respectful role model that they admire and respect – you, their parent. Psychological studies show that people do not like to be coerced to change their behavior, yet we do it all the time to children. If an adult doesn't like it, why would we think a child would? Why would their feelings and response to coercion be any different than an adult's? It's the most vocal, spirited, and protesting children that give us a clue that most children do not like to be corrected and coerced. Acceptance, modeling, and teaching inspires change more than constant correction or coercion.

Children who willfully disobey need strong punishment to stop it

Children don't usually wake up one day and think, "I'm going to bug the heck out of my parents today. It's going to be fun. I'm going to watch their anxiety and displeasure with glee!" Most children do not intentionally set out to bug their parents. They do try to get their own needs met, sometimes at the cost of the parent's needs. However, it's not about us. It's all about them.

When children willfully disobey, they are saying, "My needs matter more than yours right now." Usually it's a pattern of where one person's needs are met in the relationship, and they are usually not the child's. They are the parents' needs. A parent would do better to really examine what the child is communicating: are they ready for more freedom? Is what they are doing really important to them? What are my true concerns? Can we find a way to meet the child's needs and mine? Punishment rarely stops the willful disobedience, even when the parent ups the ante. Often, the child becomes more sneaky, vigilant, and resentful. If the child has experienced a long history of always having their needs ignored or quashed, they might go to great lengths to have their needs met, through willful behavior.

Children today are worse behaved than the last generation

Every generation has criticized the next for behaving worse than they did. Read a newspaper opinion piece from one hundred years ago, and many readers write about "how bad today's youth are."

THE MYTH OF THE EXPERT

In parenting, there are two experts: you and your child. If you need help and information, certainly seek it out. No professional should tell you what to do without very good reasons for doing so. Their job is to give you the most up-to-date, researched information, outline possible options, outline the risks of those options, and then leave the final decisions and risk assessment up to you. You have to do what feels right for you and your family – not for your relatives, friends, neighbors, doctor, parents, or our collective culture.

Many parenting practices recommended by the health profession are not based on evidence (studies and research) but on the professionals' cultural bias and personal experience. Feel free to question the reasoning behind the recommendations. That's your job as a parent: to discern information.

Parents and children are biologically programmed to bond together. Relationship connections have served humans well for many, many years! It has allowed us to continue the human race. We need to support, encourage, and endorse child-rearing methods that lead to strengthened bonds. We will have healthier adults and a better society in the end.

THE IMPACT OF NEEDS ON BEHAVIOR

 Misbehavior is action misunderstood.

Abraham Maslow was a psychologist that studied effective, happy, stimulated adults and found that they have several things in common. He formulated the pyramid model that all humans have needs. As we meet each level of need, we require another need at a higher level, until we reach the ultimate in human satisfaction at the top of the pyramid: self-actualization. He stated that we can't fulfill higher level needs until the lower ones have been taken care of. Maslow's model has been used for decades to explain motivation for behavior, especially in parenting, and to explain why children and parents act the way they do. His model also shows that people often have competing needs within themselves.

Maslow's hierarchy of needs is important in accepting the theory that children don't misbehave. They only act in (as we see it) inappropriate ways to get their needs met, just as we adults do sometimes.

Here are some parenting conflict examples illustrating miscommunicated needs that are often looked at as misbehavior.

Maslow's Hierarchy of Needs

Survival needs: food, water, air, touch, sleep, and stimulation

The parents need to get groceries. The child finds shopping boring and needs stimulation for her brain. She wants to touch, taste, and see all the vegetables. They have a conflict of survival needs.

The parents need sleep; baby needs to be held with touch. This is another conflict of survival needs.

The child needs to run around and be active. The parents need to eat in a restaurant. Another conflict of survival needs.

Security needs: emotional and psychological safety, attention, survival provisions, feeling safe, free of injury, illness, poverty, embarrassment, and ridicule

The parent needs the child to wear a bicycle helmet to protect his head while riding the bike. Parent needs survival provisions. The child has been teased in the past about the helmet and doesn't want to be targeted again. The child refuses to wear the helmet. The child needs a security provision, to feel safe from ridicule.

Another child needs their security blanket, pacifier, or parent on an especially insecure, clingy day. Yet the parent needs to get some work done at home to ensure a paycheck for groceries the next day. This is a conflict of security needs.

Social needs: a sense of belonging, love, friendship, nurturing, connection, relationships, acceptance, understanding, love, affection, and bonding

The parents need some couple time after putting the child to bed. The children need more social reconnecting with their parents after spending a day apart, with the parents at work and the child at daycare. The child won't stay in bed. A conflict of social needs results.

Or, the parent needs to talk to another adult at the grocery store because they ran into someone they haven't seen for awhile. Meanwhile, the child needs to feel they belong, too, and pester the parent for attention or connection.

The child is angry and needs her feelings understood (security and social); the parent is angry and needs her feelings understood (security and social).

Success needs: to feel good about one's accomplishments, to feel lovable, capable, respected and esteemed, to achieve mastery, productivity and accomplishment

The parent needs to get a work commitment done so they will be prepared for a meeting the next day. The child needs help on a homework project so they will be able to present it in class the next day. The parent needs quiet time, and the child needs help. They have conflicting success needs.

The child needs to "do it herself" when struggling with a zipper. The parent needs to get out the door on time to a meeting. Another conflict of success needs.

A point to remember about success: children need to feel significant. One way to do that is to have them contribute.

Alfred Adler, author of *The Practice and Theory of Individual Psychology*, says that children also need personal power and autonomy. We see the beginnings of this in toddlerhood, where a toddler oscillates between autonomy (power) and security (clinginess).

Self-actualization needs: to reach a person's highest potential, heightened awareness of living, personal growth and life long learning

The parent wants to take night courses to finish her degree. The child wants to take basketball lessons to enhance his game. Both need to get somewhere at night. They have a conflict of self-actualization needs.

- When we give a child lunch (survival needs), a hug (security needs), a listening ear (social needs), a chore to do (success needs), and encouragement on his art picture (self-actualization), we are meeting five levels of needs.

- When we give the parent a good night's sleep (survival needs), a job (security needs), a parent time-out (social needs), a hobby (success needs), and a chance to showcase his hobbies (self-actualization), we are meeting five levels of needs.

In all these examples, are the parents' needs more important than the child's? In some cases, the parents might say "yes." A parent's need to work may be more important than the child's need to do homework in the big picture, but on a relationship scale, the child doesn't see it that way. Their right to get their needs met is equal to the parent's right to get their needs met. And their behavior will almost always reflect that. The parent might view the behavior to get ones needs met as misbehavior, but to the child, this is not so. No one person can judge whose needs are more important. Needs can certainly be prioritized, but the optimum outcome is meeting everyone's needs at the same time. It's difficult, but almost always doable.

Most parents' and young children's conflicts revolve around the first three levels of needs: security, survival, and social. Levels three to five mostly fit parent-teen conflicts. Survival needs apply in the first year of life: sleeping and eating. The security needs are vital during toddlerhood and the preschool years. The social needs of school-aged and teenagers can also be areas of conflict for parents.

People in our culture tend to do well with security and survival needs but fall flat in the social needs category. We do not have enough models, training, or practice in respectful social relationships, as evidenced by our ever increasing divorce rate and the level of conflict in interfamilial and parenting relationships.

THE IMPACT OF FEELINGS ON BEHAVIOR

Besides needs, the other useful motivator of behavior is a person's feelings. Feelings motivate behavior. One person's actions often communicate what a person is feeling. Children are born with intense feelings: anger, boredom, frustration, joy, excitement, and their range of feelings grows. A good parent must take into account the child's feelings when they are trying to understand behavior.

Respect of a child's feelings is paramount to building a good parent-child relationship. When your child misbehaves, the first thing to ask yourself is what is the child feeling? Bored? Anxious? Sad? Jealous?

Feelings are great!

Every human being has feelings. They are as much a part of their make-up as their hair or eye color. Feelings are as real as feet. Do we need a reason to have feet? Do we question why they are there? You don't need a reason to feel angry, upset, or happy. The feelings are just there. There is nothing wrong with saying, "I'm angry" and feeling very angry. All feelings are acceptable and limitless; only behaviors are limited.

- All feelings are useful in that they tell us something. They are merely data that gives us information to act upon.

- We can't protect children from their feelings. They need to be taught how to cope, handle, and work with them. Good parenting does not mean constantly happy children. That would be unrealistic. Good parents help their children deal with their unhappy feelings, not suppress them.

- Feelings are transitory. They come and go and vary from minute to minute.

- Negative feelings in our children are hard for us to deal with. Often, we want our children to feel only happiness because then we will feel happy. When our children feel bad, we don't want to feel bad too, so we want to change them.

- Acceptance of feelings helps manage and resolve them. Acceptance doesn't mean agreement. It means you accept the person however they are at that moment.

- People are responsible for their own feelings and behaviors. "He made me angry!" doesn't really take ownership of one's own feelings. "I feel angry" is more appropriate. You can't make someone angry. You can do something, and they choose how to feel about it. How they feel about it is not in your domain of control. When our children are angry at a parenting decision we make, they are certainly entitled to feel how they want, whether happy or frustrated. We can't change how they feel.

- Children can learn calm-down tools to express and manage their feelings. (A list of calm-down tools is provided in Chapter 5.)

We need to get away from labeling feelings as positive and negative. We don't have positive or negative arms or legs, nor do we categorize other body parts that way. If feelings are as much a part of us as our feet, then we need to accept all of them, positive and negative, as vital to our emotional health. We might say we have pleasurable feelings and difficult ones.

The best way to deal with feelings is to feel them and have them acknowledged. Expressing feelings is healthy; repressing feelings is not.

Our role as parents is to help children identify what they are feeling, help them give it a name, and help them to cope with them. We also need to teach children how to recognize feelings in other people. This is called teaching children emotional intelligence. If and how feelings are expressed in the family are copied by children, so parents must be careful how they deal with their feelings. If a parent deals with sadness by eating ice-cream, a child learns that is an acceptable coping behavior.

Children that have the ability to handle their emotions, as well as deal with other's emotions with respect, have an advantage in life. Those skills are later used in the workplace and future relationships.

Of course, we need to teach children appropriate times and places to express their feelings. We need to teach them all feelings are okay to feel. There are no limits on feelings, but the resulting behaviors have limits and some behaviors are not okay. Feeling angry is okay. Hitting someone because we feel angry is not okay.

Bodies don't cover up feelings or lie about them. Look at specific body signals: red eyes, tightening, and sensations in the pit of the stomach; a hot feeling somewhere in the body, perhaps in the ears; breathing coming faster and harder; heart beating faster, voice getting louder, energy increasing, muscles tense, butterflies in stomach, accelerated blood flow. These are all body sensations that signal the brain of impending feelings.

Emotional intelligence is also about recognizing those body sensations in others. How many people can sense when someone is about to cry? They can see their eyes swell up and get red or that the person is looking very somber, possibly hunched over so no one would see their face. What is that person feeling?

Feelings come in degrees of intensity

Let's look at anger and how it can climb from mild to intense:

Annoyance – irritation – aggravation – incensed – hostility – fury – rage.

Many parents are surprised at the rage they feel – also the rage their children can feel. Parent-child relationships are so strong and intense when loving feelings are present, and yet, we are caught off guard when we feel such strong uncomfortable feelings of anger, rage, and jealousy, but they are completely normal.

More spirited children feel the strong, intense side of feelings, rather than the mild and may require more adult help in managing them, especially anger.

It's best to try and limit the amount of events that cause the uncomfortable feelings. Dealing with anger and sadness take a toll on a person's health and happiness. People who are angry all the time have higher blood pressure, higher levels of cortisol – the stress hormone in the brain, and many other side effects.

People who experience more comfortable emotions, such as joy, satisfaction, and pride, make decisions easier, have stronger immune systems, and live more energized and satisfying lives.

Expression of all feelings is good. The most respectful way to express feelings is to talk about them. Saying "I feel…" can be very therapeutic in helping people to sort out how they feel.

To a certain extent, we have choices over which events to have strong feelings about. We can make a conscious effort to let go of those things we have little control over. We can choose not to get angry at every little annoyance by increasing our patience and tolerance to things. Especially in parenting, where a lot of things can be the cause of anger.

THE IMPACT OF THOUGHTS ON BEHAVIOR

What a child thinks affects how he feels which in turn affects how he behaves.

Children are so receptive to a smile, that if a parent could make just one change in their parenting style, I would suggest smiling more often and offering hugs and affection.

~ Diana Loomans with Julia Godoy, Authors

How can two people watch the same movie and feel differently about it? The reason is because they both bring different beliefs, values, and attitudes toward the movie's interpretation. They both therefore experience different emotions about the movie. They act or behave differently afterward. For example, Gloria sees a movie (event) and because she is a happy-go-lucky type of girl, she laughs at the serious parts (beliefs), then goes home feeling satisfied at seeing an overall funny movie (feeling), and tells her friends jokes about the movie (behavior). Tom, on the other hand, sees the same movie (event). He is very serious and thoughtful (beliefs). He reflects deeply on the serious parts and then goes home feeling sad and perplexed (feeling). He surfs the internet for reviews that validate his feelings of regret at seeing the movie (behavior).

Let's look at how a person feeling angry handles the event-think-feel-behave iceberg:

One child gets a bigger cookie.

Anger starts in the mind first. It builds as we think about an event that is unfair. We may not even be aware of it building. Hey, wait a minute. Brother has a bigger cookie. Think: Mom must love him more than me. Feel: angry, but underneath, fear. Mom really does love him more than me. Behave: I am going to pinch him. Then I'll feel better about this unfairness.

How does this apply to discipline? Let's look at another example:

Event: - Child A writes a Science exam.
              - Child B writes a Science exam.

Belief: - Child A thinks they did well on the exam and that Dad will be pleased.
                  - Child B thought the exam was hard and didn't think he did very well.

Feeling: - Child A feels encouraged and wants to study the material some more.
                  - Child B feels discouraged and wants to drop all science-related studying.

Behavior: - Child A studies the science book.
                  - Child B acts up in science class and becomes a discipline problem.

What happens to this child in the belief and feeling stage definitely affects his behavior. If the parent grounds the child because he did badly on the exam, the child's belief is anger at Dad and anger at science studies. He will be feeling discouraged. If the parent tells the child how to improve his study habits for next time or how to understand science better, the child will believe he can do it and will feel encouraged to try again. The behavior of the child who is grounded will probably be more disruptive in the future. The behavior of the child who is shown how to improve will be better in that he will try again. The parent's reaction makes all the difference.

Often, children know the event and their belief but often don't understand their feelings. Get at the child's thoughts, and you may understand how he is feeling. The key is to not ask children "What are you thinking?" But "What are you saying to yourself in your head?" This starts for preschoolers around age three and a half. Children under the age of five have limited awareness of the workings of the mind and thoughts, both others and theirs.

A parent's feelings, needs, and thoughts frame their perception of a child's behavior iceberg. As adults, we can change the belief part. Much of parent education and cognitive behavior counseling does this. When parents learn that temper tantrums are a very common and a normal part of toddler behavior, they can relax and know they aren't rotten parents because their children have tantrums. They can also feel more relaxed knowing that most parents have to deal with them. Their belief changes their behaviour.

People are conditioned from infancy to think of feelings as bad. Some cultures are more closed on feeling feelings than others. It's very hard to overcome our cultural ignoring of feelings. It's so embedded in our media, communication, and body language.

Look at the following statements we say to children about feelings:

- "Don't ever let me hear you say that you <u>hate</u> your baby brother."
- "You shouldn't feel <u>discouraged</u> about what happened. It's not your fault."
- "Don't <u>worry</u>. There's nothing to be <u>afraid</u> of."
- "Swallow your <u>pride</u> and give in."
- "Don't <u>cry</u>. Everything will be okay." This is so prevalent in children's books and movies.
- "Hold your <u>temper</u>, young lady."
- "If you can't speak <u>pleasantly</u>, then don't say anything at all."
- "Don't feel <u>bad</u>. Things will be better tomorrow."
- "Suck <u>it</u> up, princess."

In those statements, we have just told a child that it's not okay to feel hatred, discouraged, worried, afraid, proud, sad, angry, resentful, unhappy, and victimized.

We could change that language to say we accept their feelings, although we don't necessarily agree with them:

- "I understand that you <u>hate</u> your baby brother?"
- "You feel <u>discouraged</u> right now?"
- "You're <u>worried</u> about that and probably a little <u>fearful</u>?"
- "You are feeling <u>proud</u>."
- "You feel <u>sad</u> right now."
- "Whoa. Looks like you are pretty <u>angry</u>."
- "Sounds like you are feeling <u>resentful</u>."
- "I hear a bit of <u>unhappiness</u> in your tone."
- "You seem to feel <u>victimized</u>."

Or, we could seek to find out more and encourage discussion.

After identifying the feeling, go back and find out the belief, value, expectation, or thought as to why they are feeling that way. For example, the child says, "I am stupid." "You feel that you are stupid?" "What do you think stupid is, and how did you come to think you are stupid?" "That's okay. Tell me more."

Notice there is no judgment or solution in the above responses to feelings. These statements just acknowledge the feeling without saying that it's right or wrong. This is called active listening or empathic listening or acknowledging feelings.

It's important to monitor our communication about feelings, and our body language.

Children's typical emotions and how parents typically react:

Emotion	Typical response	Better connection response
Worry	Don't worry.	How can you deal with the worry?
Excitement	Settle down now.	Let's go run outside and shake out our jubilation.
Anger	You shouldn't be angry.	I see you're angry, but we can't hit. Let's breathe!
Curiosity	Don't touch.	This is how to touch safely.
Sadness	Don't be sad.	It's okay to feel disappointed and sad.
Jealousy	Life isn't fair. You have to suck it up.	Sometimes, it's hard to feel generous to someone.
Frustration	Here, let me do it.	Do you want some help? It's very hard.

Children express feelings to someone who lets them. Many moms complain their children "act worse" with them instead of Dad, or they are perfect angels at school, daycare, or friends, yet they come home and unleash emotions on Mom. That is because Mom is a safe haven. She is accepting of all their feelings, and they need someone who will love and accept them regardless of the expression of emotion. The roles can also be reversed in some families, depending on which parent the child spends the most time with.

How to talk to children about feelings:
- Share with your child how you feel several times during the day and allow her to share how she feels and why.
- Make a list, pictures, or drawing of feelings and ask the child to point to her feeling. You could laminate her head picture and post it on the fridge so she can move her picture throughout the day.
- Read books and ask the child how the characters might be feeling. Express your feelings about the book and reasons.
- Watch TV and movies. Ask your child what the character is feeling and what could he do or say to solve the problem. Turn down the volume so there are only visual cues and body language that can be observed.

- Talk about feelings while doing activities together.
- Never shame a child for his feelings. Show in your conversations that feelings are valued.
- Talk about feelings after an emotional outburst, such as after calming down from a temper tantrum, screaming outburst, angry interlude, or any other emotional moment. This is a critical time for learning what the child is feeling and how to best express those feelings. Avoid discussion in the moment while tempers are still hot. Wait until after they're calmed down and everyone is ready to listen.

Children's inner feelings

Children need to develop their sixth sense: the inner voice that tells them when something is out of order, wrong, or not quite right. We call this many terms, but it's important to tell children the vocabulary for what they feel and also how to act upon it. Nagging feelings, persistent thoughts, anxiety, hunches, hesitation, suspicion, apprehension, and fear are some feelings that will keep our children safe. Ask your child to ask someone at the mall for the time. Ask them why they chose a particular person. This helps them to trust their inner feelings and assessment of people.

Never force a child to interact with someone he doesn't want to. A prime example is making little Johnny kiss Aunt Martha goodbye, even though he thinks Aunt Martha smells from too much perfume, and he finds kissing her objectionable. We need to respect a child's feelings as valid, so he will learn to respect his own feelings and trust them.

COMMUNICATION BUILDS RELATIONSHIPS

Communication is words, tone of voice, voice pitch, inflection, and body language. Most of what we say to others is shown as 55 percent body language and 35 percent voice tone. Only about 10 percent of meaning is communicated through the actual words we use.

Direct, clear communication builds healthy self-esteem and relationships. Unfortunately, children are not taught how to communicate effectively in speaking or listening. The educational process only focuses on reading and writing, which is one-way communication. Yet, most of the communication a child encounters in a day is two-way. If the schools aren't teaching it, then it's up to the parent. However, many parents don't know how to communicate effectively, either. It takes knowledge, skill practice, and a conscious effort to change the way we talk and listen to another person.

There are two important types of communication of feelings in loving relationships: I-statements and active listening.

I-statements

I-statements are the most respectful method to let someone know that their behavior is a problem. They usually begin with "I feel" or "I think" or "I believe," followed by a disclosure statement. There are four types of I-statements: positive, preventative, declarative, and confrontive.

Positive I-statements are those in which we communicate love and acceptance of the other person. "I love you." "I'm glad you are my son."

Preventative I-statements let the other person know of a warning or transition coming up in order to avoid problems. "I need the car tonight for my class."

Declarative I-statements lets the other person know of their values, beliefs, opinions, or feelings about situations. It's a disclosure statement. "No thanks. I don't like the violence in video games" is a declarative I-statement I give to my son when he asks me to play his game with him. It lets him know of my values and beliefs.

Confrontational I-statements lets the person know you have an issue with them. Direct communication solves problems and builds relationships. It is preferable than unassertive communication, such as discussing problems with others who are not directly involved. Direct communication says to the person, "I respect you and honor you enough to bring this up to you because I care about our relationship, and I know that you care too and will do your part to help solve this problem between us."

Confrontational I-statements have three parts. The three parts communicates your FEELING, (how the behavior is making you feel) and the specific BEHAVIOR/ PROBLEM, (a specific non-blameful description) and the REASON (tangible effect on you) to the child.

- "I feel demoralized, when I see the kitchen in a mess because I have to spend time cleaning it up."
- "I feel frustrated, when I hear siblings bickering, and I can't concentrate on my work."
- "I'm worried that jumping on the sofa will damage the springs, and I will have to pay for a big repair bill.
- "I feel frustrated when people scribble on the wall because I will have to spend time cleaning it off."

I-statements are great because they tend to not put people on the defensive compared to a "you" message:

- You should...
- You did this...
- You are...

Active listening

Active listening is also as critical as I-statements for building relationships. I-statements are used to communicate how you feel, and active listening or acknowledging feelings are used to communicate that you understand how the other person feels.

Active listening involves feeding back to the child both the feeling and content of their message. Observe the words and especially the non-verbal communication of the child. Look at body language, tone of voice, pitch of voice, facial expressions, posture, and gestures for clues to how the child is feeling. Try very hard to pinpoint a particular feeling and form a statement that asks the child if that's how they are feeling in that particular situation. The parent then puts his/her understanding into his/her own words and checks it out with the child. Useful when the child has a problem. Validation and acknowledgement of feelings doesn't mean agreement.

Feeling/Content:

- "Sounds like you are frustrated because _____."
- "I can see you might be feeling _____ because_____."
- "You're feeling _____ when _____."
- "It sounds as if you feel disrespected by the way I talked to you when you came home last night."
- "I understand how you may be feeling jealous...when_____."

Active listening is also called empathic listening or reflective listening. It's very different from parroting, paraphrasing, or mirroring because the active listening feedback must include a feeling word that would describe the child's feeling or emotion. Paraphrasing and parroting doesn't have a feeling word. For example:

The child says, "Michael is an idiot."
Parroting: "Michael is an idiot?" (The child would most likely respond, "Yeah, that's what I said, duh!")
Paraphrasing: "You think Michael is an idiot?" (The child would probably respond again with "Duh!")
Active listening response: "I'm hearing that you are angry with Michael for some reason?" Note the feeling word: angry.

If the feeling is a wrong guess, don't worry about it. Most children will be happy to correct you or confirm you are on the right track. The main point is you are making a genuine effort to understand how they are <u>feeling</u>, and they will pick it up. Someone trying to understand and validate how you are feeling is a wonderful relationship builder.

Many parents may protest: but how does that solve the problem? Many parents want to jump in too soon to solve the problem, and often, the child doesn't want the parent interfering. They want to solve their own problems. They just want a sounding board to vent. You could ask them if they want help to solve the problem. They will tell you. Once a problem is clarified in the child's mind, they can usually figure out their own solutions.

You are also showing the child that you accept and validate his feelings and perceptions of the situation without judgment or evaluation. It also teaches children to take responsibility for their problems. Being heard, accepted, and understood builds love relationships and healthy self-esteem.

Active listening lead-ins:
- You feel…(frustrated)
- You sound…(sad)
- You seem…(embarrassed)
- You look…(depressed)
- I hear you are saying…because you are feeling…(jealous)
- You are experiencing…(angry feelings)

For more information on I-statements and active listening, read Dr. Thomas Gordon's *Parent Effectiveness Training* or take a course which focuses on valuable practice of these skills.

Examine your filters

Often, when someone is speaking to us, our past experiences, beliefs, values, and attitudes filter the communication and alter what we hear. What we "think we hear" is not what the other person is saying. Sometimes, it helps if we go away and digest and think about what the other person said and why our instant reaction was the way it was. If your child says "I hate you" in an angry moment, what is it in your past that sets you flying off the handle at the word "hate." Note: children toss the hate word around much more casually than adults do, so it has different meaning for them.

Check what you heard

It's a good idea to rephrase or paraphrase what you think the other person has said to you, before responding. That way, you can be sure you heard them correctly.

This is different from active listening in that active listening checks on how the other person feels, not just what they said. Never assume. Always check the intent.

Avoid the shotgun approach

Discuss one or two issues at a time.

Don't interrupt

Be fully present and available to hear what the person is saying. Really digest the content of the statement. If you interrupt, you are not being fully open to what they are saying, but are proceeding forward with your own agenda. Interruption is like a verbal shove. We want to be seen as special, witty, and knowledgeable and our ego sometimes makes us interrupt. It's a difficult habit to break but a necessary one in building relationships. People (and children) who truly feel heard will value you.

Be congruent

Make sure your body language and voice tone fully match your words. Many parents say a polite "please, let's go" to their child and yank their arm impatiently and drag the child off, which is not very polite and gives the child contradictory messages.

Be clear

Never ask a question when you don't want a "yes" or "no" answer! That means don't ask, "It's time to go now, okay Sweetie?" Your child might say "no", because you asked a question. Instead, say "Sweetie, it's time to go now." End of statement.

Make sure your listener is "listening"

 "Mommy, this is important!" Scotty Arnall, age four, as he is pulling his mom's face to his.

We often waste our time, effort, and voice, speaking when the listener is not listening. They might be hearing us but are not fully present to what we are saying. Get your child's eye contact and full attention for things you really want to communicate to them. Tell them this is important and you need their attention. Otherwise, don't waste your valuable time and effort. It's the same with adults. Have you ever met an adult at a party who asks what you have been up to, and as you tell them, they turn away to say a quick hello to someone else that walks by or their eyes scan the room as they pretend to be interested in what you are saying? I often want to be blunt and say "Are you really interested in what I'm saying or did you ask just to be polite?"

Ask kindly, rather than demand

Good communicators ask for what they need or want and don't order people around, including children. People of all ages hate to be ordered and rebel in indirect or direct ways. The old saying of "It's all in the way that you ask" is never truer!

Focus on appreciation

"I appreciate…" is one of the best communication words around. People love to be acknowledged, appreciated, and feel they have contributed to someone's happiness. Children are no different. This is not a bribe. It's positive genuine communication of honest feelings.

Assess underlying needs and feelings

When in a conflict with someone, active listening and checking into the message can give you clues to what the issue is "really about." Conflicts are always about people's needs and feelings and resolution of them has to come about after they are exposed. These are communication basics for all people, from babies to elderly.

Important issues are best talked about not in anger or rushed times

You both need to discuss feelings and that can't be rushed.

PROBLEM-SOLVING BUILDS RELATIONSHIPS

All relationships have problems. If you look at the parent-child relationship in terms not of "It's you against me" but rather, "It's us against the problem" then you will be more bonded and able to work together as a team through issues.

Here are six basic steps to problem-solving:

1. What is the problem?
2. Who has the problem and what are their needs?
3. What are some options? Brainstorm.
4. Which one will work to meet everyone's needs?
5. Let's do it!
6. How was it? Did it work or do we need to adjust?

Treat all child misbehavior by looking at it in terms of a problem, and it changes your parenting to a more respectful, "let's figure this out together" type of model.

Discipline and the other parents in your child's life: friends, relatives, caregivers, and strangers.

 Children have more need of models than critics.
~ Joseph Joubert, Philosopher

We know that children are great at adapting to rules and expectations that differ from those at home. It's not confusing for them to see how different personalities, opinions, and belief systems come from other people. You only have control over the relationship between you and your child. So, if Grandma yells at your son, instead of you yelling back at Grandma (which models disrespect, retaliation, and of course, bad anger management), instead, quietly say to your child, "Grandma sometimes gets angry and raises her voice, but I believe she does not intend to hurt you. Do you feel sad because Grandma yelled at you?"

Be your child's explainer, interpreter, and buffer between him and the other people in his life. Coach him how he can deal with those people, so he can build the skills to do it on his own. You won't be there forever to protect or shield him. Teach him to do it himself. Then give him a hug and kiss. Actively listen to his feelings. State your interpretation of the situation in an I-statement. If your communication lines are open with your child, he will come to you often for guidance and advice on the other people in his lives. He will tend to avoid you if you go directly to those people and try to change the situation for him. Of course, this is age appropriate. A two-year-old would need your intervention, but a 10-year-old would not.

Other people don't intend to be rude but often have no experience with children. You will have an easier parenting life if you assume the best of people. They mean well but say things that come out offensive. Blow it off and take care of your child and you. Do something special. Brooding all day can make you very negative and unhappy.

When you absolutely need to go to bat for your child, be their advocate. You know their limits, needs, and strengths. Many unassertive women become much more assertive when they have children. It's the mother bear influence. Don't dismiss your child's needs out of deference to family members or to appease strangers. You are building a relationship with your child, not with the store clerk who yelled at your child in Shop-Mart. You don't have to cave to peer pressure or family pressure if you don't want to!

You can help your child accept the rules of other places (birthday parties, friends' houses, theatres, shopping malls, museums) by:
- Warning your child of the rules beforehand and helping him practice.
- Being aware if he is capable of following them. If you know your toddler gets frustrated at not touching things in museums or doesn't get along with particular child at a play-date, feel free to say "no" to those activities.
- If you go and your child has problems accepting the rule, you can empathize with your child while enforcing the rule. "I know that it's hard to not be able to eat in the theatre, but we have to finish our snack in the lobby. It's the theatre rules." You are still building connection with your child, but helping him to learn the ways of the world.

What you think of me is none of my business.
~ Terry Cole Whittaker, Author

If relatives are over critical of your parenting methods, remind yourself that you and your child are the experts of your relationship and what other people think is none of your business! Try and see the concern in their comments. Take the high road and reply politely that it may be off topic for discussion. Or you can say, "Thanks for the advice" and do whatever you want anyhow. Or, if it really bothers you, use an I-statement to say how you feel. If your neighbor expects your child to clean up dishes when he is over for supper, and your child doesn't want to, then your neighbor complains to you, tell your neighbor you will take care of it and then talk to your child. They don't have to know "how you took care of it." The same applies in public. Tell people you will deal with it later in private. It takes the pressure off to do an immediate reaction, like spank the child, because you think that is what the other person expects. One you may regret later. In private, you can be freer to make whatever choices come to you (including talking rather than spanking).

One day, my two-year-old son and I were at the library. I put him up on the counter so he wouldn't run out the sliding doors while I was checking out my books. Before I knew it, he pulled the red handle of the fire alarm. The alarm was blasting, while the library clerks were frantically looking around for the lost key to shut off the ear deafening noise. All the onlookers were watching what I was doing. I think they expected to see some discipline happening. I calmly said very loudly that we would deal with this later and waited until they finished my transaction, then whisked my son to his car-seat in the car. I told him that fire alarms are not for little boys to pull. He got the message. I'm sure some onlookers were expecting a punishment in proportion to the crime, but I was the true judge of what I would do, not them.

When it's your house, it's definitely out of place for anyone else to intervene. In their house, it is a different story. If you or your child are doing something to affect your host's needs then you have to accommodate them as much as you are able. It's only polite. You might want to reinforce it with your child by saying the rule is different in this house, and we need to follow the rules here.

If it's a public place and the behavior is not directly affecting the other person, you can thank the person for pointing it out and choose to do something or not. For example, if a stranger walks up to you in a playground and states it's dangerous for your child to climb on the monkey bars; you can thank them and decide what you want to do. You are modeling respectful behavior for your child, rather than flying off the handle and saying, "I'll watch my own child, thank you, you busybody!"

If you are in your house or a public place and other people keep disciplining your child in things that you don't really consider important or in ways you consider harmful to him, you could say your best I-statement: "I appreciate that you are interested in Johnny and what's best for him, but I believe it is not right to yell at children. I need you to stop." Let them know if something is bothering them, they could bring it up with you, and you will intervene with your child. If it doesn't stop, you may wish to see them without the child.

A final word on building the bond

Almost all research shows that children are more likely to comply and cooperate with those parents who they have an emotional connection with.

You and your parenting partner are modeling a bond

One thing I've noticed from teaching parenting classes is that it's very hard for one parent to treat their children with respect if their partner doesn't treat them the same way. Karen Flint, M.Ed., Registered Psychologist, provides some questions to ask yourself:

- Does he accept my right to have opinions that are different from his?
- Is he willing to listen to my concerns if I express them gently?
- Are my expectations of him reasonable and clearly stated?
- Do I have any influence with him? Is there evidence that he ever changes his behavior in response to a request of mine?
- Does he ever do things he would rather not do in order to contribute to our relationship?
- Can we sometimes reach a clear agreement about an issue that affects us both, without nasty fighting?
- Does he keep his agreements or promises at least some of the time?
- Do I believe he cares enough about saving this relationship to work hard for it?
- Does he seem to have respect for me?

If you answer "yes" to most of these questions, you are in a respectful partner relationship. Make sure you are treating him as well as you would like to be treated, and extend that to the children, too. You will have a respectful, caring, and healthy family life.

3

Discipline, Not Punishment:
Stay with your "no" and honor your words

> People remember not so much what you said, but how you
> made them feel. ~ Unknown

It was an awful day. I had to drive across the city three times to ferry my children to several activities, and we had no time for meals except for fast food in the van. It took an hour for each trip. It was hot. I was frazzled, and on the way home from my last trip, the power steering fluid leaked out of my van. My husband came home, and we took the van to the garage. There was no dinner ready, and I had to attend a meeting at 7:00 p.m. I was so tired, all I really wanted to do was to stay home and relax for the evening. Yet, I had committed myself to the meeting. My daughter asked me, "Why don't you just stay at home?" I seriously entertained the thought, but felt that all the times that I preached to her to honor her commitments, I couldn't model different standards. So in the interest of teaching my daughter (discipline) I dragged my tired body off to the meeting. Actually, it helped to lift my spirits when I got there. It was a discipline tool (modeling) that taught proper behavior and didn't hurt anyone. It made my life easier the next time I had to drag my daughter off to a commitment that she didn't want to keep. Discipline without distress.

Differences between discipline and punishment

In our classes, we say that discipline comes from the Latin word that means "to teach." Punishment means "to hurt" either by causing physical, emotional, or social pain. But in reality, both types of parent reaction "teaches" the child.

The difference is what each does to the parent-child bond while it teaches. Sometimes punishment "works" in that it gains compliance but at a grave cost to the relationship connection.

Punishment disconnects parents and child. It also produces anger, resentment, retaliation, fear, submission, or passive aggression in the child. It produces guilt, remorse, and inconsistency of action in the parent because no one likes to see their child suffer for very long.

Discipline, on the other hand, is respectful, caring, and gives attention to the relationship. Discipline does not intentionally hurt. Both sides are left feeling connected.

 It is easier to build strong children than to repair broken adults.
~ Frederick Douglass, Abolitionist

Typical uses of punishments by parents are:

Spanking, slapping, pinching, beating, kicking, and punching; anything done to the body to cause pain and uncomfortable sensations; yelling, timed time-out away from parent or caregiver; physical and emotional banishment, logical consequences, withdrawal of privileges; allowances, special stuffies, favorite toys, movies, visits with friends, TV time, and computer time, and grounding (the teenaged version of time-out).

Anything threatened by parents is probably a punishment: sarcasm, name calling, belittling, comparing, scolding, correcting, holding tightly even when he doesn't want to be held, public humiliation, and assigning extra chores.

Typical uses of bribery by parents are:

Gifts, toys, games, treats, and money; play dates and special outings; caving in to the child's wishes if they get upset enough; begging; special privileges, and generic praise.

Typical uses of discipline (not bribes or punishments) by parents are:

I-statements, active listening (acknowledging feelings), modeling, problem-solving and negotiation, childproofing and changing the environment, honoring words, staying with "no" and selective ignoring when appropriate.

PRAISE VERSUS ENCOURAGEMENT

Praise is what you say to a person at the END of the race. Encouragement is what you say to that person DURING the race.

What is wrong with praise?

Although praise can be an effective discipline technique for small children, too much is not good. It can be like junk food-addictive and not healthy. Praise is a parent's judgment of a child. We want to teach children to value themselves for what they do and feel, and not just live for other's approval. It sows the seeds of self-discipline. Praise is basically a verbal expression of someone else's approval contingent on how the child acts.

Many parents think they are encouraging children when they really are praising them. Praise can be very discouraging in the long run, especially when used excessively.

Praise is a type of bribe. Children have to earn it. They might earn it by competing and winning or by being compared to somebody else. It teaches children to please others. They also learn to want more and more of it. Because praise is contingent of the end result, every endeavor becomes a win/lose type of contest where winning is the prize. Children feel worthy only if they win and their self-esteem plummets if they don't.

Encouragement and appreciation is a gift

No one needs to earn it. It can be given to everyone based on their effort and improvement. It can be a way of noticing what is special. It can be given to a child who isn't doing well or makes mistakes. Encouragement from parents helps children feel valued just for being who they are, and it helps them to feel accepted and capable. It raises their self-esteem.

Children need to feel accepted and appreciated all the time, not just when they do things right. They need to learn to think for themselves, and win their own self-approval, not just other people's approval.

Does this mean that you will never praise your child? No. There are times when praise is helpful, such as when your child wins. "Way to go!" This is an automatic response. But when your child doesn't win, you can't give praise. Your child will think you are a fake. You can give encouragement, "You worked really hard practicing that shot." "You put a lot of time into practicing. Good for you." You will be more effective if you avoid praising your child too often. When you refrain from using praise, be sure to make up in encouragement and appreciation.

Children, especially, need extra encouragement and appreciation during stressful times and family changes and adjustments.

Praise	Encouragement
Is an expression of approval.	Is an expression to spur on: to stimulate.
Acknowledges the reaching of goals or results.	Acknowledges any bit of effort whether goal is reached or not.
Patronizing attitude.	Respectful and appreciative.
Used most often with children.	Used mostly with adults.

Encourages people to change for other's approval.

Encourages self-evaluation "What do you think?"

Long term result is people pleasing.

Long term result is to help focus own goals.

Very general, "Good boy!"

Very specific, "I appreciate the way you emptied the dishwasher. Thank you!"

Praise statements	What they mean	Encouragement statement instead
Good boy. Good girl.	If I can be good, then I can be bad, too.	I really appreciate that you made the bed. Thank you.
Jennie is my smart one.	I have to live up to that label forever or Mom will be disappointed.	Jennie worked really hard on that "A."
It's easy. Can't you do it?	I find it hard. Maybe something is wrong with me.	It's a hard task, but look, you already mastered the zipper. Keep going!
Nice picture. Excellent work. Well done. Great! Super!	Mom loves my picture, but I don't. Maybe it's really bad, and she's just saying that she likes it.	I really like the blue colors you used in your picture. Can you tell me more about it?

Some tips to encourage

Remember that encouragement of acceptable behavior is far more powerful than punishing unacceptable behavior.

Be specific:

- I see that you have picked up all your books and put them away. Thanks!
- Juice can be spilled on the rug. Please drink in the kitchen.
- I noticed that your laundry is done before the week starts. Isn't it great to start the week with clean clothes?

- I appreciate the way you mowed the lawn without me asking. It makes my life much easier!

Invite self-evaluation:

- What do you think of your picture?
- What did you learn from the spill?
- Are you happy with what you accomplished?
- What mark would you give yourself in this course?

Communicate your love:

- I really appreciate it when you play cooperatively with your brother.
- I love playing games with you.
- I love you.
- I'm glad you are my daughter.
- I value your opinion.

Focus on effort:

- You put a lot of time into writing that speech.
- You worked hard to earn that green belt.
- You picked up several items of toys. Thanks.
- You used color in a different way.

Show confidence:

- I know that you can do it.
- I'm sure that you can think of a way.
- I know that you can solve this in a way that makes sense to you.

Acknowledge the difficulty:

- That was really hard to do.
- It's a huge, difficult task.
- It's not easy to accomplish that.

OVERINDULGENCE

Many parents question themselves, why don't children need limits? Am I spoiling my child if he gets what he wants all the time? IS there a difference between wants and needs? Am I spoiling him if I do too much for him?

Overindulgent children are ones that are not embraced in love, caring, and nurturing their feelings. They are not picked up when they cry as babies and don't have anyone to acknowledge their feelings or care about what they think as children.

They are undernourished in caring, love and attention, and over-nourished in consumer goods.

What is an overindulgent/uninvolved parent?

- Lets their child wreck other people's things without speaking out, interrupting, or teaching the child how to make amends.
- Lets their child hit, push, or bite other children without intervening.
- Leaves their child unsupervised in dangerous situations: playing outside, at a beach, when the child is underaged.
- Says "yes" when their gut feeling says "no".
- Gives their child what they want, in spite of wanting to say "no," because the parent is afraid of child's reaction or feelings.

Overindulgent children have:
- Too many items bought for them.
- Too much work and chores done for them.
- No regard for other people's needs and an unhealthy sense of entitlement.

Items

Children need to know when enough is enough. They don't need every new gadget on the market for their intellectual growth or their entertainment. In fact, the smartest children tend to entertain themselves with pretty simple toys.

- Don't buy them everything. Give an allowance and let them have the power to choose and learn budgeting. Children can make choices starting at age five. Let the budget be their limit, rather than you set the limits.
- Examine your reasons. Do you feel guilty for going back to paid work? Focus on spending time with your child, rather than buying items.
- Nip peer pressure in the bud. It's okay to buy some things to help your child fit in but not everything. Giving allowance helps here too, because children make better choices if it's their money they are spending. Often the "gotta have it item" is not so important anymore.
- Modeling is also a powerful way to stop spoiling. Letting your child see you go into a shop and not buy anything lets them know that you do not need material things for the sake of having them or to feel good about yourself.
- Let them get used to the word, "enough." "We have enough candy." "We have enough money." "We had enough time at the park."

Work and chores

Working for things and allowing children to participate in the family chores and doing the many tasks they can do helps them to build their self-esteem because they know they are capable.

- Can they bike ride or find their own way around the neighborhood or do you drive them?
- Can they make their own breakfast and lunch?
- Can they do their own activity fundraising such as selling cookies and popcorn?
- Can they carry their own projects, backpacks, lunches, and equipment?
- Can they pack their own bags for camping, traveling, or outings?
- Can they plan for their own outings and trips?
- Do they do their own projects and homework?
- Can they make decisions on clothing and accompaniments?
- Can they prepare for their next day's activities on their own?
- Can they clean up after themselves at home and visiting?
- Can they care for their own clothes, health, and hygiene?
- Can they care and help with maintenance, not only in their own rooms and personal space, but also contribute to the family living space? Make the expectation that everyone helps out, with no pay, for the sake of the family. Their contribution is valued. You need them.

Other people's needs and entitlement

Consideration of other people doesn't come naturally to children. Socialization is cultural specific, and children need to know what is expected in their social group. We handicap our children when we don't teach them this. They end up making social faux pas and don't even know it, and wonder why other children reject them. Or they have a well-developed sense of entitlement that can get them into trouble with the law. Because they are not mind readers, they rely on us as guides and tutors for what they should be doing to help other people get their needs met.

- Teach responsibility. Model fulfilling commitments that you don't want to make. Advise them for doing the same. Problem-solve if they don't want to. How can they fulfill the commitment?
- Show them how to make amends when they break an item.
- Show them when they are interfering with someone else's needs.
- Be clear about having your own needs met. Use I-statements to declare what you need.

  "We need to be quiet because Granddad is sleeping."
  "I need a nap right now. Could you please keep the noise down?"
  "We need to not touch that because Aunt Grace is worried about her treasures."
  "We need to pick up that wrapper because the litter could hurt the wildlife."
  "We need to…"

- Volunteer. Give them experience and good feelings in helping others for no remuneration. It shows children how to appreciate what they have.

Part of a parent's job is to help their child handle failure, not avoid it

Children are going to make mistakes. They are going to make bad purchase decisions. They are going to fail exams. They are going to produce botched experiments, projects, and crafts. They are going to experience hurtful relationships, nasty fights, and bad marks. They are going to fail programs and awards and possibly experience a job firing.

The helpful parent does NOT rescue the child from the effects or consequences of these events. The helpful parent coaches the child from the sidelines and actively listens to the child's emotional pain, acknowledging their feelings. Then the parent offers help to solve the child's problem. If help is denied, the parent backs off. If help is sought, the parent advises but doesn't jump in and do it for the child.

DISCIPLINE IS SETTING LIMITS FOR SAFETY AND HEALTH

Discipline is about setting limits for the child when needed. All children need limits to keep them safe in body, mind, and spirit. Some limits include car seats, crossing streets, not playing with matches. These keep their bodies safe. Limits that keep their mind safe are limiting internet sites, movies, and people that may have harmful content for our child's growing mind. Limits that keep their spirit safe are limiting contact with a "friend" that damages the child's self-esteem. Or showing them how to behave with socially acceptable actions so that other children will not shun them and adults will not dismiss them.

Sometimes we have to say "no" because our children need to learn about their own limitations. They don't know that a violent movie can be emotionally damaging to them under 14 years of age. They also need to learn about curbing their own behavior to meet someone else's needs. Children are driven to fit in to their environment and their society. They want to be normal, accepted, and belong socially. Parents have to teach them how to do it because children do not naturally know.

That being said, if a parent sets no limits at all during childhood, a child will still grow up to be a functioning adult. However, they would have learned how through trial and error, by making a lot of people mad at them. It can be socially isolating. On a road without a guidebook or map, they will find their destination. But it may take longer and with a few hardships along the way, such as losing friends, losing respect of people around them, losing a job or getting into trouble at school. We don't want our children to learn social rules the hard way.

The essential component of setting limits is sometimes we have to say "no" to our child's request

True discipline is not about making a child do what he is told, making a child come when called, or making a child keep his room clean. It's about helping him to be an interdependent person in charge of his future. It's about raising him to respect other people and to be responsible and caring also to himself.

When you say a carefully thought out "no," you have to stick to it. We often issue consequences in the middle of our anger. Then we cool down. Then we don't follow through with the consequence because we are no longer mad or it was too harsh. Or we say "no" because we are hit with a barrage of requests multiple times a day, and it's sometimes easier to just say "no", so we don't have to go through the hard emotional work of thinking about each request. Sometimes we are very busy and an automatic "no" comes out to make the child get out of our hair. Then, after our child's nagging, whining, and tantrums, we change our "no" to a begrudging "yes" and feel bad about our parenting, our child, and our integrity. It's far better to say "yes" many times than to change from a "no" later.

Giving in to our child's nagging, whining, tears, and tantrums increases that behavior next time. That is not negotiation. Negotiation comes before the nagging and tears, not after it or because of it. We have to really be careful what behavior we are encouraging.

For school-age and teenagers, you could say "no, unless you have a good argument to convince me otherwise." Get them to write it on paper which develops their logic and writing skills!

Often parents say to me, "But if I say 'no', she'll get mad and throw things." Yes, she might. Your child is entirely entitled to her feelings. But she needs to learn to separate feelings from behavior. Stomping feet because she is feeling angry is okay. Throwing things because she is feeling angry is not okay.

Sometimes I ask parents to write down the reactions their children produce when they say "no."

The list includes: tantrums, hitting, and throwing, among others. These cause parents' anger level to go up. Somehow, we expect children to accept our "no" with pleasantness and politeness, which is pretty unrealistic when we can't even muster that as adults! The key is to stay calm after you say "no". You are dealing with a child's anger. You're modeling self-control and self-discipline and that will go a long way in teaching a child to handle theirs.

It's very important not to escalate anger. A parent getting mad at an angry child escalates the anger both ways. Teach with your heart, not your hurt.

One time my ten-year-old daughter was driving downtown with me and she asked for my answer on her sleepover proposal. I told her "no" and the reasons why. She became instantly angry and started kicking the garbage bag beside me in the car. I actively listened to her anger and acknowledged her feelings. No help. I was in the car under a time deadline and couldn't escape her anger. She screamed, kicked my garbage all over, and cried. I felt my anger rising. I tried to stay calm. I pulled over into a fast food place and told her I was taking a time-out and was hungry. I ordered a burger and one for her, and she followed me inside and sat down at a table and ate while she sulked. She calmed down in public. We drove the rest of the way in silence. We went into a building where I did my business, and she talked on the way home. She didn't accept my reasons, and I accepted her anger. When we reached home, we were both calm and we hugged. I politely gave her a bag, and she cleaned up the mess in the car.

If I had demanded in the heat of the moment for her to clean up the car, do you think she would have? No. It would have escalated things, and she probably would have made a bigger mess to anger me. It helped to direct her after we had both been in better moods.

Another tip is to ask your older child, school-age and up, what they would like you to do to help them calm down and get the angry feelings out. My daughter responded that she liked hugs when she was angry. She hated time-outs that her father gave her. She said that they made her feel disregarded and invalidated. It's important to ask the child in a time of relative peace how they would like you to handle their anger. Not in the heat of the moment.

When your child doesn't like your "no"

This is one of the absolute hardest parts of parenting and discipline. Dealing with the fallout from a child that wants his way. Children react differently based on personality and temperament.

 We need to help our child **deal** with her frustrations, not help her **avoid** them.

Your child will hear "no" many times in her life, not just from us, but from other people. Teaching them while they are young how to handle it is the biggest gift you can give them. Think of Veruca Salt from the book, *Charlie and the Chocolate Factory* by Ronald Dahl. Her first "no" ever, in her entire life, was from Willy Wonka. Although she felt disappointed, angry, and upset, the world didn't stop revolving, her dad didn't stop loving her, and the sun rose again the next day.

> The child who openly expresses hostility to you actually hands you
> a double bouquet. You have reared him with enough strength to stand up
> for himself, and you have made him feel safe to express himself directly.
> Working constructively with your child's anger helps him to accept all
> parts of himself without negative judgment.
> This is the basis of self respect.
> ~ Dorothy Corkille Briggs, Author

Why children need to hear "no":

- A respectful "no" is showing our children how to be assertive for your needs as a parent.
- A respectful "no" defines your limits and values. Your needs matter and are important.
- A respectful "no" models to your children how a person can set limits and not feel guilty.
- A respectful "no" is required to keep your child safe in mind, body, and spirit.
- A respectful "no" teaches your child about self-discipline.

> I wish my parents had spent a little more time correcting my behavior
> because it is important to consider that how people react to
> your behavior will affect your self-esteem.
> ~ Nicole, mom of four children

Limiting "no" to essential ones

- Use "no" as rarely as possible. Ask yourself, "Does this issue affect one of my three core values?"
- Think before you say "no". Don't make it an automatic response. That way, you are more committed to it and won't change your mind later. Try and say "yes" as often as possible. Save "no" for the really important things. Often, we ask 10 requests from our child and then say no for their one request. Realize that the more "yes" responses we give to them, translates into "yes" more often from our school-aged and teenaged children when we make requests!

Children are corrected many times in a day. That's a lot of negativity thrown at them. Eventually, the word "no" loses its impact, and children get so tired of hearing it, they learn to tune parents out. For one day, try to avoid the no word and rephrase all your correctives in positive language. Save "no" for absolute safety reasons. See what a difference it makes in the cooperation of your children!

How to stay with your "no":

- For toddlers, you have plenty of time later to teach limits and boundaries when her cognitive understanding and impulse control is more developed. Don't worry, by age 3.5, they have a much better understanding of rules and negotiation and the reasons behind everything. They also have a better understanding of consequences at age six. Again, they are too abstract at age two because you need a bit of logical thinking (logical consequences) to understand them. Logical thinking becomes evident at age six and up.

- Preschoolers can handle a bit more frustration when you say "no". They are verbal and might listen to the reasoning behind it, although they probably won't agree with it.

- School-aged can also handle "no" better. By this time, they are used to it and have coping strategies that help them deal with the frustration that results from "no."

- Starting at toddler level, explain the reason behind the "no" in very simple two word sentences. She might not understand, but it keeps you in the practice of offering explanation. Keep explaining as the child grows. This shows respect for her inquiring mind and you would give a reason if it was an adult asking why.

- Childproof everything else. If you can change the environment, it's easier than to change another person.

- Protect yourself and others and breakables in case your child throws them or hits them or you. Ignore the damage for now. (Fussing over it shows your child you care and they might use that for power struggles later.) Gently hold his hands to avoid hitting or throwing things. Soon your child will see that his actions will not change your decision, and he will drop hitting and throwing and try other ways to get you to change.

- Keep calm yourself. Remember that it's okay that your child doesn't like your decision. He is entitled to his feelings. To handle his screaming and tantrums, imagine a soundproof, plastic bubble around yourself that will keep you calm and kind and firm. Repeat a mantra to yourself, "It's okay, I'm calm."

- Don't second-guess or change your decision now. Vow to think clearer the next time round before you say "no". Honor your needs and reasons you need to say "no." You are important and valuable too!

- When your child is calmer, connect with her and then discuss acceptable ways to handle that frustration and have her help you clean up the damage.

- Together you can come up with ways to deal with the "tornado in the tummy", their furious feelings.

- Emphasize that feeling angry and frustrated and mad at Mommy is definitely okay. Throwing Mommy's statue at the wall is not okay. Does she want a hug? A stuffy? Discuss calm-down tools now. The time not to do it is in the middle of a tantrum.

Handling saying "no" in public:

Yes, it's possible to change your mind, but make it a rare incident when your children are smaller (under aged 12). By the teen years, they can see abstract thought and understand the many shades of grey under the "no." But for young children, still immersed in black and white thinking, "no" should mean "no". You must then be very careful to not toss a "no" casually about.

If you know you are going to a location or activity with lots of temptations where you anticipate a lot of "Pleease . . ." and your responding "No . . ."and your child doesn't tolerate it much, then use prevention and don't go there!

Handling frustration is a learned skill that takes many years and a gradual process. Every new step, where your child handles it better, is cause for celebration!

Don't worry what other people think. Most parents of children truly understand what you are going through. They have been there themselves. Some smile, some stare, while thinking, "Oh gosh, I remember those days and I'm sure glad it's over!" Some are silently empathizing with you and just don't know if and how to give you support.

When your child deliberately ignores your "no":
- If your child is young, move him away from the source of the problem.
- Childproof to change the environment.
- Distraction sometimes helps get their mind off their frustration.
- If your child is older, take away the source of the problem.

At the end of the day, you won't be judged by how loud your child is but by how you took charge of the situation in a respectful and teaching way.

Power struggle options:
- If it's one of your three biggest core values (permanent marker rules), such as safety, mutual respect, or property then go to the wall for it. Be strong and don't waver!
- If it's not one of your big three, you could try negotiation, collaborative problem-solving, or a compromise.(washable marker rules).
- Take a break or let it go for now. Decide to come back and do either of the above.

DISCIPLINE - Proactive	PUNISHMENT - Reactive
Focus upon the future: "Here is what to do instead."	Focus upon the past: "Stop doing that!"
Preserves mutual respect of feelings and dignity.	Ignores feelings and dignity of the child.
Raises self-esteem. Leaves child feeling good about himself.	Lowers self-esteem. Leaves child feeling bad about himself.
Teaches self-control by explaining reason behind the "no."	Teaches outside control by offering no explanation.
Parent and child feel good about each other and the relationship.	Parent and child feel disconnected from each other and the relationship.
Presents choice.	Demands compliance.
Sensible: related to misbehavior.	Arbitrary: unrelated to misbehavior.
Motivates and encourages doing better next time.	Inspires anger, resentment, rebellion, revenge, or withdrawal.
Looks for needs or feelings (NOF) that produce behavior.	Focuses on behavior only.
Child feels understood.	Child feels misunderstood.
Decreases power struggles, since the needs of parent and child are met.	Increases power struggles because only the needs of the parent are met.
Time-in: parent and child decide together on time, place, tools, and helping person.	Time-out: parent decides on time, and place, and forbids tools and helping person.
Consequences: focus upon restitution, making amends, and solving the problem meeting both child and parent's needs.	Consequences: focus on hurtin g or depriving the child to teach a lesson.

4

Punishments and Bribes Don't Work:
Look for the need or feeling (NOF)
under the behavior

Some time ago, a school-aged boy named John took his cat to the playground. He put a leash on the cat so he wouldn't get away. While John was playing, the cat got his leash hung up on the slide and was injured. The boy was very afraid to tell his parents the result. When his parents found out, they felt they needed to teach John a lesson. They took away TV for a week. John felt bad, and he did learn something. He learned that he should lie when he encounters a problem, and if he gets away with it, he won't get punished. He learned that he shouldn't leash a cat but didn't learn why.

Why parents want to punish

Punishments are used more for the person giving them than the person receiving them. They are meant to fill a need in the person who was wronged, or in the case of parents, who perceive the wrongdoing and are in charge of teaching the child that what he did was wrong.

Punishments are often about revenge and assuaging the parent's feelings of anger, frustration, and disappointment. Punishments are also about retaliation. I'll feel better if you feel bad. They are more about how we feel than how the child feels.

They can also be acidic to the relationship. Imagine your partner leaving towels on the bed. An appropriate punishment might be to take all the towels in the house and put them in a wet bathtub so none are available for use. That would surely teach your partner not to leave wet towels on the bed. That is a related, reasonable, and respectful consequence, but what would it do to your relationship? It would not help connect it in anyway. In contrast, it would disconnect it and probably cause resentment and retaliation, if not divorce!

Punishments often impede the learning process. Children become immersed in their anger, fear, and hurt and don't often get the lesson. Or the lesson they take away is that they can't communicate with their parents.

 You don't have to hurt children to teach them.

I like this analogy from Mary Sheedy Kurcinka's book, *Kids, Parents, and Power Struggles*: Think of your child as a pot of boiling water on a gas stove. His feelings are the flames driving the water to boil, and the water boiling over the pot is his behavior. Now, imagine the pot lid as the punishment. Turn up the heat (increase bad feelings) and the behavior will increase (the water will boil). Slap the lid on the pot (punish), and it will stop the behavior of water boiling over the sides – for a little while; but without the flames (feelings) being attended too, the boiling water (behavior increases) will soon pop the lid off and overflow again. Using the lid is a temporary stop-gap measure. Turning down the heat and addressing the feelings/needs will permanently stop the overflow. The lid is the punishment solution; turning down the heat is the discipline solution. Good discipline allows parents to determine the unmet needs or unacknowledged feelings and help the child find acceptable ways to meet them. Over time, the child learns how to identify and address their own needs.

Parents ask, "If I don't punish my child, will that leave her ill equipped to handle our punishing world?" It's true that we live in a punishing society. Your children will learn about punishment from all the elements in society from schools, the workforce, and other friend's parents. However, the parenting relationship is a love relationship, above all, and just like the partner love relationship, there is no room for punishment in a relationship that is expected to grow, influence, and teach. A child's first primary relationship with Mom and Dad should not be filled with fear, dread, and anger. It's one teaching-love relationship in a child's life that can be free from punishment.

I recognize that most parents feel they need to do something if a child behaves badly. That's why there are 135 tools in this book to use as "something" to do! Parents can feel that they are doing something even when a hug is all a misbehaving child needs to turn things around.

Some parents think there is a distinction between normal misbehavior of a child and misbehavior resulting from strong feelings of jealously and anger. There is no such thing as "normal misbehavior." Children don't act badly for no reason. They have very good reasons: their feelings, their needs, their motivations. As parents, we need to see the reasons and help them fix it.

THE PROBLEM WITH PUNISHMENT AND BRIBERY

The case against punishments

The many reasons that research shows that punishment is ineffective in teaching children proper behavior in the long run:

- Punishment can be inconsistent, delayed, or too mild. It is not a deterrent. Parents are not consistent, and it loses the desired effect.
- Severe punishment is abusive. Children adapt to increasingly intense punishments, which can become the point of abuse.
- Using punishments is not evidence-based. There are no studies or research that shows that punishment helps connect, preserve, enhance, or nurture love relationships.
- It creates a power struggle between parent and child. Sometimes children resent punishment so much that they will purposely repeat the misbehavior as a way of exerting their power or to get back at the parent. (The power struggle escalates.)
- Parents run out of energy to enforce. The parent must always be present to carry it out.
- A child who obeys primarily out of fear will only obey as long as she is scared. It wears off.
- Parents must stay calm when issuing, or children associate it as a way to solve anger, yet, it is very hard to stay calm.
- Punishment can foster aggression, anger, fear, humiliation, and retaliation, which interfere with the learning process.

- The child can feel so discouraged that they give up.
- Adults eventually run out of punishments. When children realize it, adults become totally disarmed, especially as children enter their teens.
- The fear and anger can interfere with the trust process in the parent-child relationship. The punished want to get away from the punisher physically and emotionally.
- Children can receive negative attention from the punisher or the sympathy attention from the onlookers, which serve to increase or justify the behavior.
- Punishment teaches that those with strength and power can control those without.
- Not all children respond to punishment, especially strong willed children. Often, the children who respond the fastest are those that "need" it the least.
- Punishment focuses on what will happen to the children, rather than how their behavior affects other people.
- Repeated exposure to punishments lessons its effects.
- Behaviors that are punished in a certain context can be desirable in another context. We want our children to be assertive with others, but not with us.
- It wrongly operates on the theory that children must be hurt when they behave inappropriately in order to grow to be responsible.
- It's temporary and transitory. Once the punishment is over, there is no further need to teach or act responsibly. The price is paid.
- It kills the very thing we are trying to teach – motivate children in positive ways.
- It tends to benefit the punisher more by providing a release of anger and frustration.
- Self-punishment is often the most severe if we encourage children to do so.
- They can be left feeling very bad about themselves, which is not good.
- It must be applied consistently or it will not work. Humans are not very good at being consistent.

Two conditions needed for punishments to work and both conditions lesson as the child ages:

- Punishments must be strong enough to be painful.
- Child must not be able to easily escape.

> We are raising a generation of adults
> averse to taking a personal time-out because
> they have experienced it as a punishment in childhood.

TYPES OF PUNISHMENT

> If the only tool you have is a hammer, then every
> problem starts to look like a nail.
> ~ Haim Ginott, Author

Time-out

Time-out is the most confusing, overused discipline method to come out of the last
two decades. Spanking has become so much out of favor that parents are reluctant to
do it for varied reasons: public support for violent solutions to problems is lessoning
and hitting a child in public is considered very risqué. However, parents still feel
the need "to do something, whatever it is" when their children misbehave. Time-
out, on the surface, looks very respectful in that the child is not being hit, is being
told to reflect, and replicates the parent authority-child submission model. However,
it still has some real concerns with the effects on the child's moral, emotional, and
physical health.

There was a magical book written on time-out in the 1990s, specifically for parents
of children with ADD (Attention Deficit Disorder). It was a behavior modification
idea that was taken to the mainstream parenting arena, and it was advertised to work
for all children's behavior everywhere and all the time – for all temperaments and
personalities. Parents loved it because it seemed respectful, was easy to do, and was
a great alternative to spanking.

It worked for curbing some children's behavior, especially children whose behavior
was already easily malleable. It worked for parents who needed to take a time-out
from their children to calm down their own anger. However, it didn't work for
many other types of children, such as spirited children, older children and children
with certain personalities. It gave children the message that when someone bugs
you enough, you need to push them away somewhere, rather than remove yourself.
It's premise is that children exist to try and bother parents, when in actuality, most
children want to please parents, but are caught up in their own emotional state in
the moment.

> The times our children need us the most, when they are dealing with
> strong feelings, is the time we want to be with them the least.
> ~ Otto Weininger, Author

Many parents insist that time-out is only used as a calm-down tool, but as we see in
the next chapter, there are many other ways to calm down.

Would you give an adult a time-out?

Imagine you just had a fight with your partner, and you've phoned your best friend. "Janice, I'm so upset! Peter was late coming home from work again, and I have just had it. I'm tired of waiting and worrying about him. We had this huge fight, and I got so mad at him, I took his dinner plate and threw it out the window! It serves him right!"

Janice says, "Judy, that was inappropriate behavior! You don't throw dinners out the window! You march to your room right now and don't come out for 46 minutes (one minute per year of age). When you've thought about what you just did, then you can call me back. Do you hear me? Now go!"

Now, did you get your strong feelings of anger, worry, and upset validated from your friend? Did your friend truly understand you? Was she supportive? Did she help you calm down? Would you phone her next time you were upset? Would you still be her friend if she reacted to you like that?

No, to all the above. Yet, how often do we react to our children's strong feelings (and inappropriate behavior) with counting one, two and then a parent forced time-out? If that's not how you want to be responded to, then it's not mutually respectful.

Here is the reaction that would have built a relationship: "That's okay, Judy. Calm down. Here, breathe with me…in…out…in…out. You sound pretty angry at Peter. It's hard to not worry when someone is late. It's okay. Do you want to tell me about it? You both will work things out. What did you think about the dinner flying out the window? Yes, you probably shouldn't have done that! What can you do next time when you are really angry? It's okay to be angry, you know. Here are some ways that I have handled it. How are you feeling now? I'm glad that you are my friend."

Let's look at the risk analysis of time-out.

Advantages of time-out

- Puts limits on behaviors.
- Invites little adult emotion, especially anger.
- Increases consistency because it's simple and straightforward.
- Helps parents to calm themselves.
- Better than spanking and hitting.
- Transferable among caregivers.
- Actual punishment is done quickly.
- Developed for children with ADD.
- Sometimes attains short-term goals of stopping misbehavior in some children.

Disadvantages of time-out

- Promises "magic" and speed, which can be an unrealistic goal in parenting.
- Fails to address long run goals of the child developing belonging and attachment with family. The child feels disconnected and banished. Not appropriate for adoptive or blended families where attachment is a critical goal in the first couple years.
- Teaches that time-out is a negative punishment rather than a positive life skill.
- Invites power struggles when the child refuses to do the time. Many children often don't go to time-out, nor do they stay there.
- The last resort is to lock the room shut and that can be perceived as abusive.
- When children pass stool, pee, or vomit because of enforced time-out, they are ignored by parents when they are trying to communicate their distress.
- It takes emotional and physical energy from a parent to fight a child to stay in time-out.
- Encourages submission to a bigger sized person. Is that what we want to teach children?
- Fails to teach problem-solving, conflict resolution, or co-operation skills, because discussion after calm-down is discouraged.
- Can incite anger, frustration, resentment, rebellion, retaliation, and getting even behaviors from the child.
- Can be addictive if the child submits. Some children go to time-out 25 times per day.
- Can increase sibling animosity when used for sibling conflicts or playmate conflicts.
- Ignores the child's needs or feelings (NOF) that led to misbehavior or fighting.
- Is a barrier to parent-child communication.
- Fails to recognize that each child is unique. Doesn't work for all children's temperaments, ages, personalities or development.
- Fails to teach internal controls and self-discipline. The child isn't taught to recognize symptoms of anger and when to take a break.
- Fails to teach thinking skills of how to fix things, how to make amends or restitution.
- Fails to teach how to calm-down when the child is in a high emotional state. Most children need a parents coaching to calm-down.
- Fails to teach children how to get what they want or need in a positive way.
- Parents must be united for the consistency to work.
- Isolates the child rather than promote connection.
- Not "mutually respectful." Adults wouldn't want it done to them especially if they were upset.
- Gives negative attention to misbehavior, which may increase misbehavior if the need is attention.
- Difficult for extraverts who need to "talk through high emotional states."

- Labels the child with unhealthy self-esteem. "The naughty child goes to the naughty step."
- Increases original and repeat behaviors because the child's underlying needs are not addressed.
- Children do not have reflective skills until age seven, to understand why they are in time-out.
- Embarrassing if done in public and the child doesn't submit to counting.
- Children in a high emotional state don't hear "counting."
- Saying to the child, "That's one, two, three!" teaches him only to stop when you get to three.
- Saying to a child, "Take five and add 15 minutes (of jail time) for the mouth", (expressed bad feelings) gives the child the message that she has no power and no way to express her feelings. It doesn't teach her how to respectfully disagree with adults, which is a long run life skill.
- Often used to help parent calm-down rather than for child's needs.
- Time-out is assumed to be effective only if time-in is really worth being removed from.
- Needs consistent follow through every time, everywhere.
- When children protest, the counting begins again. Tells children that uncomfortable feelings are not allowed to be expressed or communicated.
- Time-out models power, not peace.

Generally, parents want children to have appropriate time-out behavior such as being quiet, reflective, and still. They are supposed to behave that way for a certain amount of time. That is very hard because the time a time-out is most often prescribed is when a child is out of control emotionally. Their inability to calm down sufficiently enough to take a time-out, can ire parents. Both parties are now in a power struggle and are very angry.

We had a family friend over visiting, and their boy, about seven, got in a fight with my boy, who was nine. His mother put him in a time-out in our family room. Since I had long given up time-outs, I pulled my son away to talk to him and help him calm down. I just sat with him for a few minutes in silence. He took a few deep breaths, calmed down, and we talked. How could he resolve his angry feelings? What could he do with the tornado in his tummy? How could he solve the issue between him and the seven-year-old. We figured these issues out together but noticed the seven-year-old was still in jail time (time-out) in the family room. No one spoke to him. He was constantly pounding at the wall with his foot. Thump. Thump. Thump. He was getting angrier because he was in time-out, and my son wasn't. It wasn't until after he had gone home that I saw he had kicked several chips in the wall by his shoe thumping the paint. Clearly, he was not thinking about problem-solving. He was thinking about retaliation and revenge.

Therefore, I don't recommend using time-out for any child. It can be used as one of many methods to calm down, but to not to confuse the issue more, I will call the calming strategy of time-out, a time-in, because most often, the parent will be present, and it's not meant to punish.

Time-in instead

> There are times – many times – when a quiet, loving reconnection with a child is more effective than any consequence or punishment.
> ~ Holly Bennett and Teresa Pitman, Authors

Perhaps it's time to rethink the way a time-out is used. A time-out should be away from the aggravating situation, not the parent. Adults often take time-outs for themselves when they are angry and frustrated. They go for a walk, blow off steam at the racquetball court, or just stay in their rooms and listen to a soothing piece of music. The time-out is a useful skill to teach your children, but the way it is used is a big factor in achieving the results that you desire. If you want a great way to calm down children, focus them on their actions and restitution, and connect the parent-child relationship, try the "child directed time-in." Here are five differences between the two types:

Parent-Directed Time-Out	Child-Directed Time-In
Used as a punishment.	Used as a calm-down strategy.
Send the child away for a certain number of minutes per year of age.	Suggest the child take a time-in. Let the child decide when he's calm enough to to start problem-solving the issue. Talk softly, rub shoulders, show how to breathe.
Gives the child nothing to do and instructs the child to "think" about his actions. Often, the child is really thinking about his anger, the unfairness of the situation, and/or how to retaliate.	Gives the child calm-down tools to suit his learning style, while he sorts out his feelings: - Auditory learner: soothing music - Visual learner: paper and markers - Kinesthetic learner: Lego^{TM}, ball
Parent requires the child to be alone.	Ask the child if he wishes you or an other adult to stay and talk with him or be with him. An extraverted child may need a sounding board, whereas an introverted child may need solitude.
Parent decides the location, such as chair, bedroom, corner, or "naughty step."	Child chooses location such as bedroom, special fort, going for a walk, or even the basketball hoop.

I used to use parent directed time-outs. My son was constantly put in time-out and learned nothing. He threw blocks at the door and trashed his room while I was trying to keep the door closed and the other two children out. Neither of us were calming down. Neither of us were learning anything. Emotions were escalating. I was getting angrier, and he was too. Clearly, time-outs were not working. The books said to keep at it and show him who was boss, but he was not relenting! After weeks of that behavior, I gave it up. We never did time-outs again.

 Time-outs are for parents; time-in is for the child.

I would ask my daughter, when she was eight, what she wanted us to do when she was throwing tantrums and screaming in anger. I chose a time where we were both in a good space. We had been using time-out as a cool down strategy, whereby we would carry her to her room and shut the door. Her flailing resistance made it hard for me to keep calm. In anger, I probably carried her to her room rougher than I meant to. She would keep screaming and shouting. She told me that she wanted us to give her a hug, reassuring words, and not force her anywhere. The next time she was in a mood, I did as we had discussed. She calmed down much faster, and we were much more connected. Now, I notice that when I'm upset or one of the children are upset, she is the first person to get up and hug us!

Time-In

STAY COOL - HELP CALM - TEACH LATER

Music
Puppets
Rocking
Hugs
Touch
Distract
Drum
Play
Physical
Art
Crafts

Spanking

Twenty years ago, about 97 percent of parents spanked as a method of discipline. Today, in Canada, the number is about 63 percent, which is probably a reflection of the waning acceptance of violence in society that is believed begins in the home. Studies show you don't have to hit children to raise them properly, so the necessity of spanking is unjustified.

Parenting is hard work. There are times in every parent's career where they wish to smack the children. I've reached that point many times. In my case, the only thing that's stopped me is my commitment to a non-hitting approach and the fact that I teach discipline to parents. I really have to model it or be untrue to myself.

The Repeal 43 Committee revealed in the 1990s that approximately 90 percent of children physically killed by their parents (average of 35 per year in Canada) were attempts to discipline by use of physical punishment. The average parents accused of child abuse are not sick or deranged people. They are regular people like you and me that have allowed punishment to go too far. The controls to stop or go lighter were missing on that day. "They just lost it!" That's why even mild spanking can be dangerous. When it doesn't work, there is nowhere to go but to harder spankings, because often, spanking is a last resort tool. It's common to hit a child harder when one truly believes in the use of physical punishment, rather than when a parent doesn't believe in the use, but has occasionally felt very angry and succumbed to its use.

We know that using physical punishment doesn't doom most everyone. After all, most of us were spanked, and we turned out fairly okay. Like the fact we smoked and we are still walking around pretty healthy after we quit. But we do know that smoking is harmful for health, and we don't advocate it anymore. We also know that using physical punishment doesn't make relationships better or enhance our children's well being. There are **no** studies that show that physical punishment **lowers** the risk for negative outcomes or that it improves relationships. I liked the example that a speaker gave at a discipline conference. I could relate to her example. When I was 20 and in my partying days, I rode as a passenger in a car with a driver that was drunk. I turned out okay. Nothing happened. No accidents, no crashes, or people hurt. But I was certainly not optimizing my chances of living a healthy, injury-free life. I was engaging in risky behaviors that had the potential for damage. The analogy is the same for spanking.

If you are committed to not hitting, write a list of reasons down on paper and stick it to your fridge. Try and read it in the heat of the moment when you are angry and feeling too impulsive.

Advantages to spanking

- Fast
- Easy to do
- Relieves parent's feelings of anger and frustration.
- Gives parents a false sense of control.
- Can be done anywhere.
- Transferable to caregivers: they can use the same method.
- Young children learn to obey unquestionably for a while.

Spanking doesn't teach you anything. It doesn't solve the problem.
~ Marlin Arnall, age eleven

Disadvantages to spanking

- Parent is often left feeling guilty and remorseful when it's done in anger and then might overcompensate by spoiling or letting more behaviors slide.
- The more spankings are used, the more they have a diminishing effect on children's behavior.
- According to the Repeal 43 Committee, hitting a child can cause burst eardrums, concussions, and brain injury when the child is hit on the head. Hitting a child on the buttocks can injure the tailbone, genitals, spine, and sciatic nerve. Slapping hands can produce broken bones, blood vessels, joints, and ligaments. Psychological damage includes low self-esteem and lack of bodily respect.
- Studies show that when children's behavior is difficult, harsher punishment is not the answer although it's the parent's first choice. When parents become more punitive, children tend to become more aggressive and power struggles can escalate.

When even milder forms of physical punishment, such as light spanking, hand slapping, pinching, and pulling were used in a family to correct children, children were more likely to have:

- Higher aggression levels towards siblings, peers, pets, and anything they could lash out at.
- A higher risk of big problems such as substance abuse, criminal behavior, and sexual activity.
- A lower moral internalization whereby children learn "to not get caught" rather than do "the right thing," even when no one is looking.
- Higher levels of poor communication between parents and children, especially the sharing of feelings. Children don't open up to parents they fear some of the time.

- Even at two years of age, children learn to avoid parents rather than seek them out for comforting.
- Higher levels of child's poor mental health.
- Higher levels of aggression and antisocial behavior when the child is an adult.
- Increased risk of adult partner abuse when the child grows up and marries. Boys are more likely to be abusers, and girls are more likely to be victims. Child abuse is often repeated in the next generation.

When parents are emotionally aroused (very angry), they underestimated the force of their hits. When mild spanking occurs, severe violence is seven times as likely to follow.

> We are not saying that physical punishment is abuse. We do know, however, that the vast majority of physical abuse cases involve physical punishment within the context of discipline.
> ~ Joan Durrant, Researcher

Research from the United States indicates more reasons not to spank.

- Children who are spanked may have difficulties saying "no" to people that could put them in personally dangerous situations such as drug, criminal and sexual experimentation.
- Boys who are spanked tend to exhibit more violent and bullying behaviours and girls who are spanked tend to exhibit either extreme shyness, or underground, indirect, relationship-type bullying behaviours.
- Children who are spanked may reject their family of origin's religion, as adults, expecially if the religion advocated the use of physical punishment.
- Children who are spanked tend to grow into adults that are unhappy in their marriages. Punishing partners tend to be the immediate reaction to marital problems rather than to communicate.
- Research is consistent in that it shows that spanking increases willful disobedience behaviours in children. This is ironic in that most parents who spank generally view willful disobedience as a behaviour that definitely needs spanking or physical punishment as correction. This can erupt into a circle of increasing physical punishment and escalating power struggles.
- Children who are spanked demonstrate poorer school performance. This is not because of lower intelligence, but could be the result of lower risk taken in producing answers and solving problems. Children's ability to problem-solve depends on their creativity and tolerance for taking appropriate risks, both of which are decreased due to the chance of being wrong and being punished for it.

Logical consequences

This is another popular tool that has gained in momentum since the anti spanking campaign of the 1990s. Consequences are actions that are created or set up by parents to teach the child a real world lesson. They are often unpleasant, and although many books say they are not a form of punishment, the intent and by-product of them often does punish a child.

Advantages

- Teaches real world cause and effect.
- Can be three "R's": reasonable, related, and respectful.

Disadvantages

- Child may not cooperate and may become a power struggle.
- Hard to think up.
- Consequences are usually imposed by the parent, and they are often perceived negatively by the child, so they often don't change the way a child behaves.
- Warning consequences ahead of time; puts the child's focus on the risk of getting the consequence rather than focusing on expected behaviors. They may still choose to take the risks.
- Consequences make children feel bad, and generally, children do better when they feel better.
- Requires time, cost, and effort on the part of the parent.
- Needs consistent follow through. If a consequence is threatened, it must be carried out or it loses its threat capability. Parents find it hard to be consistent with unpleasant tasks.
- Doesn't teach child how to make amends, fix things, or solve the problem.
- Can disconnect the parent-child relationship if the child doesn't agree to the consequence.
- Children see through the contrived consequence as the parent's doing, not just the real life outcome.
- Consequences seldom address the underlying cause of the misbehavior: the need, feelings or motivation of the child.
- Children may avoid seeking parents' help in problem-solving, in order to avoid the consequence of punishment.

Yelling

Yelling is a very easy habit to get into and one that's hard to break out of. But, it can be done! If you find you yell at your children more than you play with them, it's time to look at the problem.

Advantages

- Relieves parent's feelings of anger and frustration.
- Can motivate children that are not used to it.

Disadvantages

- Produces guilt in parent.
- Loses effectiveness over time and heavy use.
- Can be very threatening to young children.
- Makes the voice hoarse.
- Disconnects the parent-child relationship.
- Encourages the children to yell back at you and at siblings and friends in order to motivate them or change their behavior.

Grounding

Grounding is the teenage version of time-out.

Advantages

- Gives parent and child time and space to connect if no hard feelings are present.

Disadvantages

- Takes time and monitoring from the parent.
- Needs consistent follow through.
- May deprive social needs of a shy or introverted child.
- Disconnects the parent-child relationship.
- Can result in power struggles
- Difficult to restrain an older child that   won't cooperate.

Withdrawal of privileges

Related to the misbehavior or not related.

Advantages

- Teaches real world cause and effect if related.
- A popular consequence

Disadvantages

- Disconnects the parent-child relationship.
- Takes time and monitoring from the parent.
- Needs consistent follow through.
- Can result in power struggles.

Lecturing

Advantages

- Gives parents the feeling that they are in control and teaching the child.

Disadvantages

- Telling children what to do takes away their initiative and inner motivation and their ability to solve the problem and feel good about it. (Asking gentle, reflective questions is better because it leaves the figuring out up to the child. It empowers them and leaves their dignity intact, while they can solve the problem themselves.)
- Children tune out if too long.
- Children miss out important points if not to their developmental level.
- Can become overused.

Threats

Advantages

- Easy to do.
- Helps parents deal with their anger.

Disadvantages

- Seldom carried through. Needs consistency to maintain effectiveness.
- Loses effectiveness over time.

Blaming and shaming

Advantages

- May help a parent with unhealthy self-esteem feel better about herself by deflecting blame to another person.

Disadvantages

- Makes child feel worthless and incapable
- When parents become impatient or have too high expectations of their children's behaviors, children can feel shame, which is hard on their self-esteem. They can also become very defiant as a result of losing the ability to make their parents proud of them. Essentially, they give up. (Patient reminders, explanations and appreciations when they are followed by children go a long way in building cooperation.)

Withholding love and affection

Advantages

- Can be a great manipulator especially for sensitive children.

Disadvantages

- Can be emotionally very damaging to all types of children.
- Can break attachment bonds or prevent them from forming.

Withholding allowances or issuing money penalties

Advantages

- Easy on the pocketbook.

Disadvantages

- Hard to keep track of penalties.
- Doesn't teach children about handling money.
- May be too far away in time to matter to them.
- Gives child the option to buy his way out of normal responsibilities and doesn't solve the parent's problems of needing help with chores.

Extra chore assignment

Advantages

- Helps get tasks done around the house.

Disadvantages

- Teaches children that doing chores are a bad thing, a punishment.
- Requires monitoring to get done properly.

Sarcasm and name-calling

Advantages

- Makes the adult feel cool, superior and powerful

Disadvantages

- Name-calling is never productive. It doesn't shame children into doing better, and usually produces anger, resentment, and emotional damage.
- Sarcasm is adult attitude. Parents model it to their children to handle anger or deal with uncooperative people. (Check your statements against this yardstick. Would you use that statement to your partner, boss, friend, or relative? If not, then don't say it to your children. It's not respectful. To get respect, you must start first by modeling it.)

Scolding and correcting

Advantages

- Easy to do.
- Sounds appropriate because the practice is as old as parenting.

Disadvantages

- Becomes habit forming
- May fix the negative but doesn't call attention to the positive
- Can be demoralizing to child.
- Hard on the child's self-esteem.
- Can produce anger and resentment.
- Doesn't teach what to do, only what not to do.

THE DIFFERENCE BETWEEN BRIBES AND POSITIVE REINFORCEMENTS

Bribes are conditional on behavior. Positive reinforcements are unconditional. Bribes are treats, toys, and consumer items that are used to be incentive for children to change their behavior. Positive reinforcements can come in many forms, such as appreciations, encouragement, recognition without forewarning, I-statements, and are used to build the relationship rather than to coax compliant behavior. If you find that you are saying, "If you do this, then I will get you this…" too much, you are probably either bribing or threatening a punishment!

Examples of bribes – usually an item to buy. Doesn't build relationships. Avoid them.

Possessions: toys, money, balloons, jump ropes, coloring books, crayons, puzzles, combs, perfumes, stuffys and games.

Consumables: fast food, junk food, candies, sweets, drinks, pop and dessert.

Examples of positive reinforcements – usually emotional relationship builders. These are desirable.

Activities: Hobbies, crafts, redecorating, preparing food, sports, gardening, barbecue, bike-riding, going to the park or playground, walking, window shopping, swimming, camping, going to the beach, watching TV, playing music, sitting, talking, bath time, and watching videos.

Social time: Verbal, specific, descriptive, encouragements, such as "I like it when we do dishes together. It makes it more fun." "Thank you." Physical encouragements, such as hugs, kisses, tickles, eye contact, shoulder pats, bouncing on the knee, laughter, rough housing and play wrestling.

Appreciation: This is verbal acknowledgement of an action the other person does or something about the other person that affects the parent personally. Appreciation always starts with "I appreciate…" It expresses only what the sender feels. It is not judgmental, as it doesn't express what the receiver is being judged by.

Encouragement: This is verbal acknowledgement of the effort that the other person is seen to be doing. It does not focus on the end result or goal of the effort, so therefore, can be given to everyone that is "trying."

Positive reinforcements are wonderful relationship builders and should be used a lot of the time. They should not be just contingent on good behavior. Inversely, they produce good behavior and they become less necessary as children begin to internalize those positives.

Children and adults have an inner need to please those they love. A common question from parents is, why should I acknowledge my child for good behavior, when that should be automatically expected? All people feel good when we do good things and when other people notice them. If it wasn't a universal feeling, there would be no volunteer work or good deeds done in the world. Remember that when a child who feels good, does good, then acknowledging and noticing his positives will help him keep doing positive actions.

Bribes and praise are very similar to punishments. Although bribes are the carrots and punishments are the sticks, they are both used to manipulate a child's behavior. Both are used to control another person.

 Positive reinforcements are more about the expression of what the sender is feeling rather than used to control the receiver.

When I ask my children to do something and they respond, "What will I get for it?" I reply with a smile, hug, and say, "My undying love and appreciation." They smile and do the task I've asked with the response, "I already have that!" It still reinforces the good feelings we have, and they are still likely to do the task, but it gives them the message that not everything in life is met with a "what's in it for me" type of response.

The case against bribes

The many reasons that research shows that bribery is ineffective in teaching children proper behavior in the long run:

- Bribes can lose their value. May be too far away in time or not big enough incentive.
- Unacceptable behavior can be rewarded, for example: class clowns get peer and teacher attention.
- Children can acquire their own prizes. To work, the prize must be desired and unobtainable by them alone.
- Prizes can be too hard to earn, such as the bell curve grading system. Young children can get discouraged.
- Acceptable behavior can go unrewarded. Parent must always be present to acknowledge it.
- Children might start to work only for the prize. Always an expectation of praise or payment. The prize may lose it's desirability over time.
- A missed or forgotten prize feels like punishment. Children who are accustomed to praise worry when they don't get it. Therefore consistency is required to maintain bribes.
- We think better of a child that acts autonomously rather than one acting only to get a prize.

- Bribes are hard to give up because they create obedience but not inner motivation, thinking skills, or initiative.
- They are quick and very easy to use, which makes them hard to give up.
- They are often wrongly used to increase self-esteem; however external motivators are seldom effective in raising self-esteem. True self-esteem comes from one's inner motivators and perceptions, not other peoples'.
- Studies have shown that the more we reward people for doing something for which they are not internally motivated, the more likely they are to lose interest in whatever they had to do to get the prize.
- Creativity declines when more emphasis is placed on the prize.
- Bribes tend to foster competition and cheating if there are limited prizes available.
- Winners begin to feel alienated by those who never get prizes.
- Some people, no matter how hard they try, never win prizes that are given based on natural ability. The end product is rewarded, not the effort. So people who try really hard and never get rewarded, feel bad.
- We all know children that behave and work hard without ever being rewarded; and children that could get a bucket of games, toys, and candy may not move an inch.
- Bribes change motivation from internal to external. The prize becomes the focus, not the enjoyment from doing the original task.
- Bribes for good behavior teach children that if they are good, they will receive an item in return. This is a bad message. Society does not give prizes for expected standards of behavior. This is real world cause and effect.
- Giving prizes for reading causes children to ask, "If this book is so good, why do they have to bribe me to read it?" We want them to think, "Reading is the basis for all other learning, so I need to learn to read." Getting homework done is a personal accomplishment, which is rewarding in itself, by feeling good. Appreciation for learning is intrinsic. You can't force it on someone.
- Many prizes are junk food or toys that are inherently bad for children. The risk is that children could become emotional eaters that use food to raise their self-esteem.
- Marks are often defended on the need for society to provide a measuring stick of achievement. But would you rather have brain surgery by the doctor who earned 95 percent or 45 percent? I would pick the 45 percent because he probably didn't pass and had to learn the same material twice and probably absorbed and internalized more than the doctor who took it only once.
- Achievement doesn't always equal effort.
- Bribes must be consistent to work, and we know that humans are rarely impeccably consistent.
- It costs the parent time and money.
- The child may feel manipulated, and the parent may feel used.

Two conditions needed for bribes to work and both conditions lesson as the child ages:

- Child must need it strongly.
- Child is incapable of meeting the need themselves.

TYPES OF BRIBERY

Play dates, extra privileges, and special outings

Advantages

- Can be powerful motivator for the right child.
- Connects the parent-child relationship.

Disadvantages

- Parents need to provide time and money.
- The child may feel manipulated.
- The parent may feel guilty if they can't provide.
- These are normal childhood learning and experiential circumstances that children should automatically get in order to develop and grow.

Cave in to the child's wishes if they get upset enough

Advantages

- Easy to do.
- Eases the embarrassment of a public tantrum.

Disadvantages

- Not providing the child with teaching and guidance doesn't help him learn his own limits.
- Tells child that you don't have any resolve and your "no" means nothing.

Begging

Advantages

- Easy to do.

Disadvantages

- Parent feels demoralized.
- Doesn't work with strong-willed children. They will do what they want regardless.
- The child sees the parent's desperation.

 Giving a child a time-out is like leaving a baby to cry it out;
both actions ignore the child's true need.

Praise

Advantages	Disadvantages
• Ingrained into our culture and perceived as normal and necessary.	• Praise is like junk food. A little bit is fine, but a steady diet makes people addictive. • Children praised too much become narcissist. Children are trained to constantly need approval by peers, family, and friends. • Praise can cause aggressiveness in children when they meet with people who don't like them. Authentic, descriptive encouragement is much better. "You got a really good mark on your science quiz and worked really hard at it!" This helps children connect outcomes to their efforts. "The kitchen is really clean and now I can make dinner." • Too evaluative and judgmental depending on someone else's approval. "Good girl" or "Good boy!"

 Correction doesn't inspire change, acceptance does.
~ Thomas Gordon, Nobel Peace Prize Nominee

Scolding and correcting: normal or nasty?

In my years as a children's organization leader, I noticed there were some special children with behavior difficulties. Most particularly, I was interested in how the adults dealt with it.

We all know those children. They may be our friend's children, our neighbor's children, or even our children. They are the challenging, "difficult to manage" children that seems to test our patience. They may be loud, inappropriate, rude, display backtalk, exclusionary, or exhibit other negative behavior. Behavior disabilities are the hardest ones to deal with in other children. We tend to hold common judgments about such children. We give the up most patience, encouragement, and support to children in wheelchairs but not to the behaviorally challenged child. We often ignore them, correct them, or subtly punish them for the way they are. Their disability is invisible, yet strikes a negative feeling in some of us.

I was a leader at a camp where there was one such girl from another group. I didn't know much about her except for her name, but I noticed for the first few hours that she would sometimes yell inappropriate, out of place questions or comments to the whole group. She definitely stood out.

The next day, during the activities, I had a closer chance to observe her. What piqued my attention this day was not the number of times that she shouted something out, but rather that each time was met with a correction, rather than an answer to her question.

When she came to my round robin activity, I decided to count how many corrections she received from the other leaders and also how many encouragements she received. In the group of four girls, she received the most corrections. I counted nine in the 30 minutes she was at our activity. How many encouragements she received? None.

A correction, even phrased in a polite "please" and "thank you" is still a negative assault on one's self worth and self-capability. "Please don't touch that." "Please be quiet." "Don't bother those girls. Thank you." "Watch out. You almost hit that thing." "You need to sit down and be quiet." "Please get off that mat." "You can't have another cookie." "Don't go out there." "Don't, don't, don't, no, no, no." These are negative corrections. It rarely inspires people to do better. If anything, it causes the person to feel even more discouraged and gives the message of hopelessness to keep trying. Most people hate being criticized. They react by feeling withdrawn or resentful. If a person feels is how they behave, then discouraged people rarely behave better.

It's so easy to correct and so hard to encourage and appreciate, because it's not our native tongue. Sometimes we were brought up with so much correction as children, that it easily slips out of our mouths as adults. We need to make encouragement our new accent. Then our children will encourage others as their native tongue.

Very often, when we criticize another person, it's not about the other person, but shows our need to criticize. Rarely do criticized people say, "Thank you so much for pointing out my mistakes and flaws. I didn't see them until you told me." Most people react by withdrawing from you or getting angry and defensive. Especially if delivered in a "you-statement." An I-statement is different. It's coming from the deliverer and is intended to be about the deliverer, not the recipient.

From the point of view of the criticizer, it doesn't make them feel good either. When you have just delivered a zinger to another person, it feels yucky. It's like shouting to the world, I need to criticize to make myself feel better and because it's familiar to me.

If someone corrected us 18 times in an hour, I think we might explode at that person. Yet, the effects on children go unseen for many days, months, and sometimes years. Their self-esteem takes a beating because they are told to "sshhhh" too much. Their questions are dismissed. They are made to feel they are always out of place. Their feelings of discouragement and anger are not acknowledged. Their confidence in their skills get a beating because they feel that they can never do anything right.

So what can adults do to change the behavior-correction-discouragement-negative behavior cycle? Stop giving negative attention to the behavior in the form of correction. Start noticing every little, teeny, tiny thing the child does right. She does a lot right, but often when we have labeled her the "difficult one", we have a hard time seeing through the negative. A practical suggestion is to fill a fanny purse belt with about 25 marbles. It will be heavy and uncomfortable to wear. Wear it for the whole day or until all the marbles are gone. Then, each time you notice something encouraging about the girl or something favorable she did, you comment on it to her and later take out one marble. Put them in a container somewhere. Each time you correct her, put a marble back into the bag. Focus on the specifics of the good deed. "I really liked the way you shared the last piece of cake. Thank you." "I really appreciated picking up that piece of garbage. Way to go!" "I really enjoyed listening to your description of dinner. Thank you." The marbles give you a visual reminder to acknowledge everything she does right and gives you great practice in picking up the small, insignificant positives in every person.

People often say, "They don't need to hear appreciations, they already know." Yet, most children and adults don't know. The most times people hear positive comments about themselves is at their funeral. Even then, they don't hear them! Yet, when people are asked if they'd like to have verbal appreciations or positive comments about them, most do. People spend their whole lives wanting to be appreciated and have others approve and like them. A simple comment goes a long way.

One day, my son had a friend over for dinner, and he did an action at the table which was not polite. My daughter piped up with "That's rude!" Then, I corrected her in front of everyone and said, "It is rude to correct people in front of others!" Then, all eyes at the table were on me. I did the exact thing I told her not to do. Children teach if we are willing to learn!

Instead of punishments and bribes, build the relationship bond

Conditions needed for a behavior change:

- The child must feel loved, honored, and respected by the parent.
- The parent must be available as a teacher, mentor, and protector of mind, body and spirit.
- Punishments must never be used.

- Positive reinforcement needs to be used liberally. Everyone wants to be recognized and appreciated by the words and actions of another human they care about.

This works on the premise that children listen and modify their behavior on the request of an adult they want to please: one whom they respect, love, and trust. It continues working, whether the child is younger or older.

BENEFITS TO CHILDREN OF USING NO PUNISHMENTS

1. Less anger, hostility, and frustration from "always losing." Anger can be turned inward or outward, but it shows in children's behavior, such as attitude, sulkiness, talking back, passive aggressiveness, working to rule, not talking, and shutting parents out.

2. Freedom from fear. Punished children can become cowed, nervous, and vigilant. They fear their parents at certain times when a punishment is expected. Often, they don't come to parents with their problems for fear of punishment and hurt. So they try to solve their problems in ways that could cause permanent damage to themselves or others.

3. Less stress, less illness. Pain, humiliation, fear, anxiety, and tension of punishment, and mixed feelings of parent love and hatred cause stress in children. Stress can weaken the immune system and cause illness. Punishments add to the stress level of children. Stress is defined as "sense of threat" to a child's well being and security.

4. More responsibility, more fate control. Freedom and responsibility gives children control over their future. Inner control promotes acceptance of responsibility. Outer control shuns responsibility. Children feel good when they can have an active part in their solutions.

5. Less deprivation and humiliation. Deprivation of needs can increase desperation of getting needs met in unacceptable ways. Attention seeking misbehavior is often the result of not getting attention. For example, a child that needs attention (which is a valid need), that keeps getting put into time-out, has their need for attention made even worse, which increases the likelihood of the misbehavior happening again.

6. Fewer self-harming behaviors. Smoking, drugs, alcohol, dangerous driving, eating disorders, and sexual activity are common reactions to fear, stress, and anger.

7. Better social skills. Children behave assertively, not aggressively when treated in a fair, democratic manner. Children who practice and experience true problem-solving relate better to adults and peers. Children who are not punished don't feel the need to punish as a way of solving disputes with other children. Children who are taught about meeting needs and expressing feelings tend to look for the same in other children. Help them meet their needs, and they tend to empathize with other children's strong feelings. Not punishing children helps group cohesiveness and lessons sibling fighting enormously. Everyone feels good when everybody wins.

8. More problem-solving competence. Children who are taught a problem-solving method rather than a punishment method tend to look at problems differently. Rather than blaming another person or figuring out a punishment, they look forward to helping the other person collectively solve a problem.

9. It's easier to parent because consistency is less important. Punishments and bribes work only on the fact that consistency is absolutely required. The biggest problem is that parents are not consistent.

WHY DO CHILDREN MISBEHAVE?

Behavior is communication. "Misbehavior" is miscoded communication. What is your child trying to tell you? Often, they don't know how to tell you in acceptable ways of what they need and default to unacceptable ways to get their needs met.

Look at this list with a friend who can provide an objective perspective, and ask yourself honestly if the point applies to your child. The discipline tool to use for the problem is listed in italics.

General needs
- Hunger or poor diet or food allergies: too much sugar, food dyes or food allergies, or caffeine? *Change environment by changing diet.*
- Tired: not enough sleep leads to tantrums and irritability. *Change environment by providing sleep.*
- Boredom: the child may need age appropriate activities to stimulate his growing brain. *Change environment.*
- Over-active: does this child have enough time, space, and opportunity to be silly, loud, active, boisterous, and noisy? Children are active and noisy by nature and need to expend energy at least every two hours. *Change environment and remove yourself.*
- Mismatched learning style: the child doesn't respond well to the way things are presented in the family. *Give information.*
- Illness or health problem: *Change environment.*
- Verge of developmental change: normal and mixed feelings accompany it. *Learn child development.*

- Needs more social activities: extraverted children need more social contact. *Change environment.*

- Needs less social activities: introverted children need less time with people and more time alone. *Change environment.*

- Hormonal changes in puberty: the child can become moody and surly. *Active listening, I-statement and problem-solve. Don't take it personally.*

- Feeling contrary: everybody feels contrary on some days – adults, children, and everyone. "It's just one of those days." *Develop "acceptance" bone.*

- Over-stimulated: the child has too much going on. *Change environment.*

- Watches too much violence: the child is exposed to too many violent programs on TV, video, and computers without adult intervention and discussion. *Change environment.*

- Overscheduled: not enough control over downtime. Young children react with fussiness, sleep problems, and appetite changes. Older children react with surliness, change in grades, or too little sleep. *Change environment.*

- Unrealistic expectations: are expectations too advanced for the child's age or developmental level? Is the child not capable of understanding yet? Remember that young children are egocentric (find it hard to appreciate other's feelings until age five), pre-logical (are unable to process thoughts logically until age seven), and aggressive (finds self-control difficult under age four). *Learn child development.*

- Rule following is widely inconsistent in the family: the child doesn't understand the rule or see that it's not followed by others. *Problem-solve.*

Attention needs

- Not enough positive attention: is there too much competition for love and attention within the family? Does the child get negative attention instead of no attention? Every human has a strong hunger for recognition, and a child will act the role that gets the most response from his family, even if the response is hurtful. Children will take 100 percent of parents' or any adult's attention if they can get it. Children, who do not get attention at home, act up in school to get teacher's attention. Attention and recognition is a basic need. "Oh, he's just doing it for attention!" negates the importance of providing this need. *Give attention.*

Power needs

- Feelings are negated: unexpressed, uncomfortable feelings such as anger, upset, scared, sad, frustrated, jealous, confused, insecure, and unhappy are not allowed to be expressed directly, so they are driven underground and expressed indirectly through sibling fights, put downs, aggression, and attitude. *Active listening and problem-solving.*

- Not staying with "no": does my child not realize when a "no" means "no"? *Model. Stay with your "no".*

- Too rigid rules: are your rules too strict that the child is rebelling? *Give choices. Change environment. Problem-solve.*

- Too many transitions: the child feels they have no control over their day. *Change environment.*

- Not enough control or choices over own life: these should grow as the child ages. By age nine, he is halfway to adulthood. Half of his life decisions should be his own. *Give choices.*

Revenge needs

- Conflicts resolved disrespectfully: do conflicts escalate because no one practices mutual respect while solving problems and conflicts? *Active listening. Problem-solve.*

- Stress: is there stress in the family system due to the arrival of a new child, illness, job loss, addiction, dissension, divorce, finances, move, holidays, and visitors? Children know when something stressful is going on, even if the adults don't talk about it or insist that it is not a big deal. Children often express the stress for the family by doing things that are hurtful or disruptive. *Active listening.*

- Insecurities: is also a form of stress. The child feels that something he values may be threatened. Could be expressed in bullying or harassment. *Active listening. Problem-solve.*

Inadequacy needs

- Labels: can affect children by the self-fulfilling prophesy. "My parents think I'm lazy, so I'm going to live up to it." *Encourage. Focus on strengths. Avoid labels.*

- Misbehavior is based on a child's interpretation of how to find belonging and significance or to fill a need or cope with a feeling. *Show and tell correct behavior. Give positive feedback. Holding, hugs, and cuddles.*

Parents need to crack the code! What is the misbehavior telling you about what your child really needs and feels? Try to avoid immediate reaction to the misbehavior and plan ahead for a positive response.

> Spankings do for a child's development what
> fist fights between spouses do for a marriage.
> ~ Jordan Riak, Activist

When parents resort to physical punishments as a last resort

When respectful methods of discipline and teaching don't give parents immediate compliance, some parents feel there are times when a spanking or some type of punishment is justified as a last resort. When it's time for the big guns – threats, or implementation of punishment, these three situations are times the parents pull them out:

1.   Repeated misbehaviors
2.   Deliberate defiance
3.   Emergency safety reasons

The first two come from an inner feeling of losing control or having your authority challenged, not being respected, listened to, or heeded. These are very rightly concerns. However, parents must remember they are still in control, even when their children don't listen.

It's not necessary to ever resort to punishments even for the big three. In fact, it can be very damaging. Here is why:

- What happens when even punishment for the big three doesn't work? Many parents are backed in a corner when that happens. They have nowhere to go except to up the ante, so the spanking might be a harder one or the punishment a more severe one. Often, parents report that even spankings don't work. Spankings tend to get harder and more frequent because of parents feeling a loss of control. When the child still behaves badly, parents throw their arms up and give up. They may retreat and let the child run wild, saying that there is no hope, and the child is out of control. The child feels they have won, but also that they have been given up on. This can be bad for their self-esteem and sense of belonging and worth.

- Punishment, even in small quantities, can be damaging to the relationship that was built on trust and predictability. A good relationship, whether parent-child or partner-partner, has zero tolerance for punishment. True love never punishes. People who truly love each other, work together to solve their problems.

- It teaches children that the ultimate control of another person is still rooted in threats and nasty things being done to them.

Sometimes parents issue a punishment for the big three and then do the teaching part. Why not skip the punishment part and go right to the teaching?

Tools for the big three

1. Repeated misbehaviors. The child is meeting a need that is more important to him than meeting your needs of cooperation. The trick here is to find out the true need underlying the behavior and address it. This can be done by:

- Acknowledging the child's feelings.
- Solving the problem.
- Ignoring the misbehavior but increasing positive reinforcement of the proper behaviour.

2. Deliberate defiance. This really gets a parent's ire and with good reason. Nobody likes to be challenged. Remember to model the behavior you want to see in your child. Being in control and authoritative doesn't mean hurting those who have little control. Deliberate defiance from a child is the result of not feeling in control or feeling they have no choices or no say in the matter.

- Walk away and stay calm.
- Avoid engaging in a power struggle. Take a parent time-out.
- Come back later when the emotional temperature of both parties is lowered and problem-solve the situation.
- Use an I-statement to say that you don't like being spoken to that way.
- Problem-solve the issue that is being defied.

3. Emergency situations. The child is running onto the road. The child is about to touch the handle of a pot of boiling water. Your first discipline tool is to supervise and protect. A spanking is not necessary to teach. You teach with your words and actions. Pulling away from danger is an action.

- Act immediately! Not to spank but to grab the child away from the danger.
- Save your sharp "no!" for such an occasion.
- Show and tell the danger after. Supervise!

Children's coping behaviors to punishments

Children tend to use flight, fight, or submit, based on their gender, age, temperament, or personality. Girls tend to submit more than boys, who tend to fight. Young children submit more than teens, who tend to fight in their rebellion or flight when they dismiss their parents psychologically. Strong willed temperament children fight more than easy-going children, who submit. Introverts submit or flight, and extraverts fight.

When punishments are used on children, they often cope in the following ways.

Fight: being negative, giving attitude, resisting commands, defying orders, giving "lip," being snarky, retaliation, deliberate disobeying, vandalizing property, wrecking things, hitting, pushing, biting, deliberately breaking rules, throwing violent temper tantrums, showing anger, bullying and trying to control siblings, friends and authority figures, competing and needing to put others down to feel good.

Flight: lying, blaming others, covering up the truth, forming alliances against the authority, not talking, ignoring, sulking, giving the silent treatment, and keeping one's distance.

Submit: withdrawing, escapist daydreaming, passive resistance, giving up, goofing off, running away from home, skipping school, feeling depressed, crying spells, being fearful, shy, timid, unassertive, scared to try new things, scared to take risks, sucking up to more powerful people to escape control, needing constant praise, assurance, feeling insecure and unsure, and second guessing oneself, overindulging in substances (food, alcohol, cigarettes, drugs, sex), getting physically sick, excessive dieting and eating disorders, being overly conformist, complying and being dutiful and docile.

Children often react to punishments and control in these ways. These are not qualities that parents want in their children. In fact, they often come to parenting classes wanting to alleviate those behaviors in their children. It's very hard for parents to focus on teaching their children long term skills rather than to control them.

Punishment and religion

Many other authors of parenting books, based on a certain philosophy of authoritarianism, some in the name of religion, espouse the importance of children submitting to an authority such as parents, God, or other adults that is certainly backed by punishment.

Their philosophy is that "punishment done by the loving hands of a concerned parent" is very different in purpose and practice than punishment that would be considered abusive. This is a point of view that helps to alleviate parent's guilt when they find their churches' beliefs and teaching are going against their parental heart felt feelings and intuition.

Guilt is arisen from actions differing from one's values. If a parent feels guilt from striking a child, it is because he was taught to love one another and be kind. Then he is told that the strike was a loving one done for the ultimate benefit of the child. That supposedly helps alleviate the guilt the parent feels in the moment.

Parents are often told that physical punishment is not abuse. It's "loving" discipline and abuse is "hostile" discipline. Some parents punish out of concern of teaching children to submit to a higher authority, rather than the by-product of ordinary parental anger. They believe that when children learn to submit to their parents, and other adults, they learn to submit to God.

There are concerns with this point of view. Not all submission is good or healthy for children or adults. Many adults do not have children's best interests in mind. Some pedophiles on the internet would love to meet submissive children because they won't resist authority. Because we are raising a technologically connected generation, we need to give children skills for assessing the intentions of adults, not just blindly submitting to whatever they want. Blind obedience should not the goal of parenting for the new millennium.

Another problem with this kind of thinking is that children do not view it the same way. Not all children submit when adults try to control them. They don't put feelings into neat little boxes. They don't think that when Mom and Dad hits them that it's an act of love that they should accept willingly. They may react with flight, fight, or submission behaviors. Often, when those children grow up, they learn that love is equated with punishment, hurt, and betrayal of trust. The family relationship in many religions is very hierarchical based, usually with the husband at the top of the power pile, wife next, and children at the bottom. We see this in studies that show that some girls, who have had strict punishing parents, often marry abusive, punishing partners. Boys that have had strict punishing parents, often become abusers in their marriages.

In parenting classes, it's very hard to teach moms (who are the ones that often go) about respect and non-punishment of children, when they are not valued, respected, and are punished as wife.

One of the arguments of authoritarian religious parenting experts is that God values discipline and orderliness. Children with strong temperaments and wills must have their wills broken down and rebuilt up in the fear of God. But what is it about God's work, the creation of the child, that needs improvement? God made children perfect, strong willed, and all. Our job as parents is to protect that spirit, not break it down and rebuild it. Are we saying that we need to modify God's work?

According to The Repeal 43 Committee in Canada, the danger with physical punishments that are meant to be loving and necessary is that parents who believe they are doing the right thing often hit harder than a parent that hits spontaneously out of anger.

Many parents quote the biblical saying, "Spare the rod and spoil the child." Taken literally, many parents believe the rod is used to beat the child. In biblical times, the rod was used by the sheep herder to guide sheep to the right way, not used to hit them with. Therefore, the statement could be taken to mean, "Teach and guide your children. Don't hit them."

Another well-known saying is "Well, I was spanked, and I was okay." In retrospect, parents are loyal to their parents' methods even though they abhorred them as children. Most people are okay in terms of outward success: education, job success, financial success, yet not okay in their interpersonal relationships. That's probably why the divorce rate is near 50 percent. Punishments and hurts are still occurring in the marital relationship because as children, we are so familiar with those tools for controlling and changing another person.

If we are truly okay in all our interpersonal relationships, there would be no need for social workers, child welfare workers, psychologists, psychiatrists, police, judges, self-help books, self-help groups, and criminal justice workers. There would be no substance abuse, crime or unwanted pregnancies. We would live in utopia.

The training ground for respectful relationships is the parent-child one. This is the model for all other love and friendship relationships. If we use the traditional model of our parents, often, it falls short in respect. We need to learn how to be kind to our loved ones, to treat them with respect, to show and tell that we value them. We need new models of parenting so our children will treat their partner in the same way.

 Yes, we were punished and turned out okay. But think of how much better we could have been?

~ Unknown

5

Good Parents Feel Angry:
Separate your anger from your discipline

> Anger is a gift that inspires us to change.
> ~ William Rivers Pitt, Author

I had a really bad day. I was under stress. I needed to get a handout ready for a class after lunch, and my printer wasn't working. I was furiously trying to get the printer working, when my two younger children started fighting. I yelled. I screamed. I threatened to put them in their rooms and take away TV for a week. After complete frustration, when my printer was already quite crippled, I went to my drawer and took a hammer to the printer. The children were in tears. I was in tears, and the printer wasn't in great shape either. I was embarrassed for demonstrating a very poor expression of anger in front of the children, and I was regretful for taking away TV for a week. I knew when I calmed down, that the TV punishment would never be enforced. The printer problem and handout problem eventually got solved, but our relationship was not yet repaired.

Most parents discipline or punish when they are angry. When children do things that make us mad, we want to relieve our hurt, often by hurting them, which may not be the best tool to teach them anything or help them solve problems. It leaves us feeling very guilty. If you are like most parents, you've probably made several parenting resolutions for the future. Yelling, spanking, and issuing empty threats are common punishment methods that parents want to reduce. If you find you are making no progress, it's easier to understand it by examining why we fall back on those methods.

Good parents sometimes feel anger toward their children. It's a basic fact of life. We need to accept that anger is normal in every love relationship, whether partner, co-worker, friend, or parent-child. How we deal with the anger can damage the relationship or make it a valuable source of teaching and strengthen the connections.

Separate your anger from your discipline (and guilt and worry)

It's far better if parents separate their anger from their discipline measures. We need to take responsibility of our actions when we are angry. Discipline means having the vision to see the long term picture and keep things in balance. A Chinese proverb teaches, "If you are patient in one moment of anger, you will escape a hundred days of sorrow." It's so much easier to watch what we say in anger than to apologize and try to make amends. Relationships are like glass, once broken, they're very hard to repair. Often, it is not the same as it was. So be very careful of what is said in anger. We do have choices and can be conscious of what we say and do.

WHY PARENTS FEEL ANGRY

The reasons parents feel angry are as numerous as there are parents. But number one on the list is "My child doesn't listen to me." Most children's hearing is fine. What they really mean is "My child won't do as I ask." This is probably the reason most parents come to discipline classes.

Other common reasons parents feel angry:

- The child doesn't get permission first in order to do something.
- The child's temperament is spirited.
- The child's developmental stage is a negative one.
- The child's personality is a difficult fit with parents.
- The misbehavior keeps repeating.
- The children are fighting, and you need them to be quiet.
- The children throw tantrums after you have said "no".
- The child hits, screams at, yells, bites, or pushes a sibling or friend.
- Your child nags you when you are talking on the phone or to a friend or busy with a task.
- Your child purposely breaks an item.
- Your child won't do as you ask in public or while visiting outside the home and you feel embarrassed that your "authority" appears weak.
- Your child talks to you with swear words, or attitude, or snarkiness.
- Your children are playing boisterously loud when you are under stress.
- Your child is demanding something right now!
- Your child is whining at you and won't stop when you say "no".
- Your child is pestering you for attention.
- Your child is too slow when you need him to hurry.
- Your child won't talk to you when you ask him a question.
- Your child doesn't share information you need.
- Your child touches something or plays with something that you've told him not to.
- Your child doesn't do his chores.

- Your child does all or some of the above when you've told him that you are having a bad day and he doesn't seem to care at all.

Anger caused by other factors:

- You have had a few drinks. Avoid alcohol. Alcohol lowers a parent's tolerance level.
- Your needs are not being met. Not enough food, sleep, understanding, personal time, or accomplishment for you to feel good.
- Stress. A stressful life, combined with the normal trials and tribulations of parenting, can lead to many angry outbursts. One of the most common ones for parents of young children is getting out the door on time. Instead of yelling "Hurry up! We are going to be late!" change your attitude to "That's okay, take the time you need." If you are late, will it really matter five years from now?
- Low tolerance level of normal childhood behaviors is due to parent personality, temperament, background beliefs, and knowledge. It is essential to read a book on child development. Knowing that children are naturally messy, noisy, self-centered, excited, or clumsy and that they are not just acting that way to get your goat on purpose can really help reframe your anger at their behavior. Especially learn about temperament and children's developmental needs and how some children and babies can't help being more needy. Also learn about developmental stages and how it's very normal that children go through "annoying" stages to develop. Look at your own family of origin and see where your blinds spots are. What triggers your anger, and what can you do about it?

What every parent needs to know about anger:

- Anger is a normal, healthy feeling.
- It's very, very difficult to listen to another person's point of view when we are angry.
- Can be neutralized by appropriate or inappropriate behaviors or expression.
- The ultimate goal of anger is to solve a problem.
- Is usually vented on those closest to us. Thus, it's a choice of if and how we vent. Familiarity with family and safety of home makes it easier to be angry there rather than with a peer group, friends, or work.
- Others can't make us angry. They do things and we react. We own our anger. Rather then say, "She made me so angry." We need to say, "I felt angry when she..." We take responsibility for our anger.
- Is often a secondary emotion caused by an unacknowledged first emotion: frustration, fear, jealousy, tiredness, hunger, embarrassment, loss, grief, and sadness.
- Anger is hard on the body. It causes stress hormones that endanger our health. Reducing the triggers help to reduce the amount of anger we have to deal with.

- Anger is usually about us feeling hurt in some way.
- Anger alerts us to change! Change can be as simple as letting go. It's not a big deal. Or perhaps it is a big deal, and you need to make major resolutions and commitment to solving the problem. If you sleep on the issue and are still angry the next day, chances are you can't let it go and need to resolve it.
- The home is a living classroom for learning how to handle anger. We, as parents have also been taught how to handle anger. When you were a child, what was your parent's way of dealing with anger? My parents yelled and swore a lot. I tend to yell a lot and my children do, too.
- Unresolved anger will resurface at a later time.
- Anger management does not mean suppressing anger. It's means neutralizing it, feeling it, and then using it productively to solve the problem.
- Anger and aggression are not the same things. Anger can be expressed assertively using I-statements rather than you-statements.
- Respectful anger does not hurt healthy relationships or people.
- Anger does not reflect badly on the character or personality of others.
- Being angry does not mean being angry forever. Feelings are fleeting.
- Feeling angry does not always happen when we think it should or when we think we have the right to be. It occurs as naturally as our feet. We don't question why our feet are part of our bodies.
- Anger seems inappropriate only when we don't understand it.
- The expression of anger shows: we care enough about the other person to tell them about it and have confidence in the relationship that one can reveal their true self.
- Anger is all about us and how we react to things. There are certain buttons that are pressed in our makeup, and we need to analyze what the problem is. When dealing with anger in children, we can't deny our angry feelings, because then our child's outbursts will trigger ours, and we will react with anger. Anger escalates other's anger. We, as the adult in the situation, need to stay calm and find healthy ways to neutralize anger.
- Punishment for expression of feelings, such as anger, can be very disastrous for children and result in the repression of feelings. Repression of feelings can have serious health risks for people: high blood pressure, stress, worry, heart attack, stroke, and many other illnesses.

FOR YOUR CHILD'S SAKE, TAKE A BREAK!
MANAGEMENT OF PARENT ANGER

A = Accept it
N = Neutralize it
G = Get away
E = Examine why
R = Resolve and problem-solve

A = Accept that you feel angry

The key is to recognize it before it escalates. Try and get it in the thinking stage before it gets to body symptoms. You could try to self-talk at this stage. Perhaps there really isn't a problem.

Know your trigger situations. High on the list are:

- Sick children or you are sick
- Trying to get something done and especially within a tight time frame
- Feeling tired, hungry, and stressed
- Messes and clutter
- Children bickering
- Trying to multitask
- Entertaining
- Constant interruptions
- Lack of control over getting a job done
- Daily irritations
- No downtime
- Messes after cleaning up
- Waiting anywhere: lineups, traffic
- Partner out of town/partner back in town
- Children not listening
- Children getting angry with you
- Trying to concentrate or focus
- Getting out of the house on time
- Not getting respect or appreciation
- Getting dinner on the table
- Power struggles
- Partners disagree
- Stores and public outings

N = Neutralize your anger in a way that doesn't hurt anybody or wreck anything

Release the energy. It is normal to occasionally become frustrated and angry at our children's behavior. However, it can be difficult to effectively discipline our children when we are furious. The impulse to give our children a big whack can seem very tempting. The key is to learn anger management techniques, which enable us to overcome our anger, which then allows us to use effective discipline later without physical punishment. In this way, not only are we disciplining our children, but we are also teaching them anger management skills at the same time.

Things to avoid:

- Yelling
- Slamming doors
- Throwing things
- Attitude or sarcasm
- Name calling
- Hitting walls
- Destroying objects
- Swearing or cursing people or places or situations
- Hitting children

Positive self-talk

We have a choice! Use self-talk to moderate those trigger thoughts that get your anger boiling. We have about 50,000 thoughts that go through our heads in one day. How many of those are negative, unproductive, and bad? How many are positive, optimistic, and cheerful thoughts?

Post this box on your fridge!

> ### Points to remind yourself in the heat of the moment
>
> 1. *It's just a stage.*
>   *All children go through stages where their behavior might be hard to deal with. It will pass very shortly. Doing nothing about it means they still will get through it and come out a decent person. They won't go down the path of a slippery slope!*
>
> 2. *It's not about you.*
>   *It's all about where they are at. Remember her age. It takes 18 years of childhood to get it right. She has genuine feelings right now and her behavior is how she copes with her feelings. It's not about trying to bug you. It's about her. She can't help how she is feeling.*
>
> 3. *Look on the brighter side.*
>   *Someday you will laugh about this or tell your friends about it, maybe even write about it!*

CALM-DOWN TOOLS

These are immediate things to do in the heat of an angry moment to help yourself feel the anger and let it go.

Auditory/verbal

- Listen to soothing music
- Listen to rock or rap music and dance and sing. Releases that anger energy.
- Sing your favorite song. It helps to focus on the words.
- Blast the radio in the car and sing
- Talk to a friend. Sharing feelings and talking to another parent or one of your friends allows you to express feelings and perhaps gain some perspective and insight into handling the situation next time. At the very least, it helps you vent feelings.
- Cry
- Record a tape expressing feelings
- Do a three minute silent scream
- Scream at the wall or in the shower
- Hiss
- Count to 10 backwards or forwards. Also try to count to 10 while taking slow, deep, deliberate breaths.
- Count to 10 while drinking a big glass of water.

Visual

- Watch an aquarium
- Read a book
- Draw pictures
- Visualize yourself in a calm place. See feelings and anger floating away from the body.
- Play video or computer games or watch a movie

Creative

- Write in a journal. Write down your angry feelings and then destroy your notes when you feel calmer. No need for careful word choice. Just write it as it feels.
- Make a poster of methods to calm down.
- Make a mad-meter out of an arrow and paper plate. Color red, yellow, and green areas. Post it on the fridge to show everyone how you feel.
- Make something
- Draw a picture
- Write poetry
- Write a letter or email but don't send

- Knit
- Make models
- Play Lego™
- Play piano or guitar

Self-nurturing

- Get a hug
- Bubble bath
- Make a calm-down place, which is a quiet corner or spot with calming devices in it to help calm-down.
- Drink from a water bottle
- Eat a snack
- Go out with other people
- Be alone (This is the traditional child time-out. Look at the many other ways you can teach your child to calm-down, other then a time-out!)

Physical

- Silent scream
- Squeeze stress or hackey sack balls or oranges
- Play with play dough
- Play Lego™ or K'NEX™ and build a masterpiece
- Clean a room, closet, or yard
- Knead bread, weed garden, or vacuum
- Dance, rollerblade, bike, throw and kick a ball, walk
- Shake off feelings
- Breathe in calmness
- Stomp, run, or jump
- Blow in an anger tube (cardboard paper towel roll)
- Hug – force a smile and a hug – it soon melts into a genuine one and you feel much better in the moment and definitely after!
- Shred paper
- Use a fuss box (a cardboard box you can go and kick the sides in)
- Make faces at the wall
- Drum
- Bath or shower
- Play the piano
- Mow the lawn
- Hit a bop bag, punch pillows, break ice-cubes. (Can be frightening to children so use carefully, or not in their presence. They will imitate you and may not be as discriminate on what they hit!)
- Make ugly faces
- Stamp feet in one place

- Hang laundry on a rack
- Wring towels
- Blow balloons or bubbles
- Do the recycling
- Clean up clutter
- Play with toys; your child might join you, and the fun dissipates the anger.

Humor

- Make a joke out of the situation
- Read a funny book
- Watch funny videos

G = Get away for a while to think

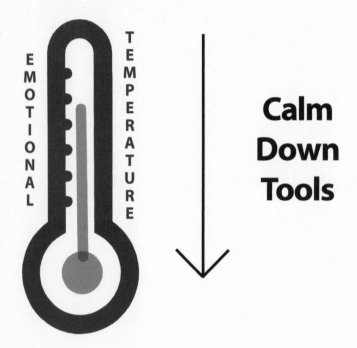

Time-out for parents

If the child is in a safe place, a time-out for parents is a wonderful way to cool off. Go to the bathroom, turn on the shower and yell, "I'm so angry!" If the children are older than 10, go for a walk. Go to a bedroom, lie on the bed, close your eyes and breathe deeply for a few minutes. Go into the shower. Time-out for you – a minute per year of age!

Avoid child time-outs when the parent is angry

When a parent is angry, children get sent to time-out. Honest parents know that the purpose is more for the parent's ability to calm down, rather than the child. This can be isolating and damaging because the child doesn't know why he is in time-out.

It helps to know where your child is cognitively at his age. Two-year-olds most often don't know why they are in time-out. They just know that Mommy is mad! Even if they know they did something to cause the time-out, they don't have the self-control developed yet to stop doing it. Dr. Otto Weininger, author of *Time-In Parenting* states that most children don't have the reflective skills that we think they do until age seven. Those reflective thoughts are the big questions of "What have I done to be here?" "What was my part in the problem?" "What can I do to make things better?" Those are all questions we would hope our timed-out children would ask, yet often, they are just thinking, "I'm so mad at her." "I'm going to get even with my sibling when I get out, and this time I won't get caught." "This is so unfair." "I hate myself and the whole world."

When a parent sends a child to time-out, she feels stretched to the limit. The parent feels upset because she is unable to control the child. She needs a break from the child and has the power to send the child away. When the child is gone, she can calm down and she feels more in control of herself, the child and the situation. It SEEMS to be working. Parents lose it because they believe they are supposed to be in control. Control is illusionary. There is no such thing as control when another human being is mixed in the equation. Children have their own control. The appearance of control is only maintained by our power as long as the children are little. It's easier to take a time-out yourself than to force another person in time-out.

Ways to take a parent time-out when the child is there

Many parents object to the parent time-out because they complain their small children just follow them screaming, whining, and complaining. How true! Children are often scared of their parents' distress and follow them for assurances that things are okay. Children need physical security and proximity at these moments. Parents often need to be alone and cool off, which can lead to a conflict of needs. There are ways to meet both parent and child's needs.

Here are some tips to be physically present but mentally time-out:

- Put a CD on the stereo and dance hard!
- Put in an MP3 player of your favorite songs to distract you.
- Have earplugs everywhere.
- Lock yourself in the bathroom. Tell the children that you love them and need to take a time-out for yourself. Turn on the fan or shower and breathe or visualize yourself in a calm place. A closet can work too.

- Breathe in, breathe out, and close your eyes.
- Distract yourself with a calm-down tool.
- Drop everything, dress your child and put him in the stroller and go for a walk outside. Exercise, fresh air, and peace and quiet!
- Put a children's video on. It either distracts you or your child, which gives both of you time to calm down.
- Get out of the car, leave the children in it, and walk around the car. Cry, deep breathe, stomp.
- Imagine a soundproof room around you to protect you from screaming children.
- Run a bath and have the children join you. Everyone's mood changes when you add water!
- What skills do you use to calm down in other situations? Try them now.

Anger in the car:

- Pull the car over and step outside.
- Breathe fresh air – know your children are watching you
- Stomp your feet outside.
- Put the car radio on and sing.
- Earplugs in the car help you to focus and get centered.
- Stop the car and go home. Leave the children at home with a babysitter or partner. Come back later to finish up the errand.

E = Examine and clarify the reasons why you feel angry

Find out what the primary feelings are. Anger is a secondary emotion caused by a primary one. Am I really angry at myself or someone else and I'm taking it out on someone close to me? Sure, I feel angry, but what's underneath that? What is the real feeling or issue here?

Most often, the primary feeling is lack of appreciation and respect. Keeping score of how you are treated compared to how someone else is treated, can also fuel anger.

Some other primary feelings in parent anger are:

- Fear – Your son gets lost in a store.
- Tiredness – You spot a mess in the kitchen left for you to clean up.
- Stress – You have a report deadline.
- Loss – Your wedding ring accidentally gets flushed down the toilet.
- Jealousy – Your husband visits his mother in law on your anniversary.
- Hurt – You go through a lot of trouble for a birthday party that your child didn't have fun at.
- Embarrassment – Dad wants the children to behave in front of his boss when he has to bring them to work.
- Disappointment – A special event was canceled.

R = Return to the person or situation and solve the problem directly

You have felt, neutralized, and expressed anger. You are calmer now. Now is the time to put anger to work to solve a problem. It helps to phrase everything using I-statements. You are in control of your feelings and are taking responsibility for them.

1. Choosing to do nothing is still a choice; perhaps this is the bait, and you are not going to bite this time. If you choose to let it go, **stop thinking about it.** Many times, we go over and over the anger situation in our heads. Thoughts tend to escalate it when we rehearse and recycle them.

2. If you choose not to let it go and you are going to take action, **choose problem-solving**. Brainstorm some options on how to handle it. Ask for a friend's help in choosing which one would be most respectful and helpful. Then choose the solution and do it.

Plan ahead for handling anger

Plan for next time. Find what works for you. Make an anger coping kit: put in a MP3 player, earplugs, a Stop! card, a new DVD you have been meaning to watch, etc. Or put a new calm-down tool in big letters on a sticky note or piece of paper on the fridge for you to grab the next time you are angry. Some parents ask their children to hold up a yellow (caution color) piece of paper to them as a signal they are getting frightened by the parent's anger. Keep trying calm-down tools until you have a few reliable ones that work for you and your child in a hurry. A planned anger response helps parents stay in control. This is also great for the children to see. They will learn a controlled reaction when handling their own anger by watching your example. If you react badly, don't worry. We are not perfect. Apologize and try again.

Breaking the yelling habit:

- Ask your children to help you regroup. They could give you a signal that reminds you that you are yelling.
- Put a mirror on the fridge so you can see what you look like when you yell.
- Leave the room, count to 10 or 1,000, and calm yourself.
- If your children are older, walk around the block.
- Try breathing out. You will have less air to yell with.
- Practice getting up and speaking to the children instead of yelling from another room.
- Get a cold with laryngitis. That will force you not to yell!

Choosing not to hit or hurt

Some parents say they "just lose it," but I truly believe they choose to act out "how" they lose it. There is immediate gratification for our physiological selves when we release angry feelings and really let someone have it. It feels better, but only in the short term. Chances are that the outburst has damaged or destroyed a part of a relationship without getting at the real problem. Often, the primary feeling is one where we feel unappreciated, overworked, over-taxed, and unvalued.

Sometimes, it can be difficult to resist spanking children. Sometimes, it seems that they are deliberately misbehaving just to annoy us. Sometimes, they act up the most when we are rushed, doing something critical, or at an occasion when we most want them to behave nicely. Often, children can feel your anxiety vibes and it makes them anxious. They react by behaving in ways we wish they wouldn't for the situation. It's a vicious cycle! We need to recognize both parent and child anxiety and take steps to reduce it. The best method is to walk away and take a brief parent time-out. You will feel so much better when you do!

As a parent, there were many times I really wanted to hit my child. Deep in my subconscious, I knew that as a parent educator, I shouldn't be doing things that I teach parents not to. How could I give workshops on handling anger when I wasn't practicing what I preach? Those thoughts were going through my head even in the midst of extreme anger. Those thoughts helped me choose not to hit. Every parent can choose thoughts and commit to not hitting their children.

I also knew that hitting is an easy way to handle frustration in the moment, and can become too common. So, I always avoided the first hit. It's almost as if one hit was too many and 20,000 would never be enough. I had to choose and promise myself never to do the first spank. I have been proud raising five children and not slapping, hitting, or spanking any of them (well, except for once). And they are a varied lot of personality and temperaments, too. Research shows that many parents raise caring children without ever hitting them. If hitting is not necessary to raise children, then why do it?

The added bonus of choosing not to hit is that I don't have to deal with guilt after. With guilt comes compensation, and that's where parents fall down in the punishment arena. They hit, feel guilty, and then over-compensate when it's probably better to use respectful teaching discipline methods in the first place. It results in more consistent parent reactions for the children.

After you are calm and in control, you are in a position to carefully consider the behavior that irritated you so much and decide upon an appropriate disciplinary response that will teach the child and be respectful.

Shaken baby syndrome

Everyone needs to know the difference between systematic "leaving baby to cry it out on a regular basis" and "I'm going nuts and am going to throttle this baby if I don't get a break RIGHT NOW!" Sometimes, babies and toddlers have days that seem to test your patience. They have crying days and you try anything and everything to stop and it doesn't stop. Don't worry about wrecking them! An isolated incident of leaving the baby to cry for 10 minutes isn't going to hurt if you are loving and attentive MOST of the time. On those bad days, you need some tender loving care right away. It's better to make a safe choice and leave the baby in the crib or a safe surface and get a grip on your emotions.

HOW TO GET MORE PATIENCE

Like in a good marriage, it really helps to ignore a lot of daily irritations. Anger is like a fish hook. We can choose to bite or swim on by. Sometimes, we just keep on swimming! Sometimes, we have to ignore the dishes in the sink, clothes on the floor, books strewn about, or we will be constantly criticizing someone for it.

Patience is a learned skill. We all have varying levels of patience, but we need to learn how to extend it for longer periods and how to loan it to our children. Part of increasing our patience is to learn child development and understand that much of what our child does is normal behavior. Learning to handle things that set us off is part of developing that patience muscle. Ask any parent home full time, and they will wonder why they have so much patience and then hand the children over to the partner who has only been home half an hour and they are losing it all ready. They don't have the same patience level because they haven't had practice developing and using it all day.

- Breathe often!
- Set aside a time limit. Say, "For the next half hour, I will be patient." Extend your time limit as you get better at it.
- See the good intent of others. They are not trying to bug you. It's not about you. It's all about them. Children are born egocentric and learn about others as they grow.
- Live in the present. Forget about the future and all that needs to be done. Relish what is happening now. When you are distressed and more patient, things get done more efficiently, even if it's later.
- Prepare for delay. Carry around a good book or something to do when waiting for others.
- Keep perspective. Has anyone died because of this roadblock? Will it really matter a year from now?
- Be grateful. When you are delayed, think of all the people you are grateful for. Carry around a notebook in your purse and write a short note to tell them what you appreciate about them. This helps put you in a way better mood.

- Have quiet time every day. Take ten minutes on the front step admiring nature, or five minutes in the shower. Even for school-aged children, remove yourself for a half hour and savor the quietness. Be sure younger children are engaged in an activity and safe. You can have a few minutes alone. Hooray for the DVD player.

- Have a time-out room for you! Make it inviting, soothing, and calming. A bedroom with crystals, a water feature, stereo with spa or massage music, candles, calming artwork, plants, books, and cozy pillows can be a welcoming, relaxing room to have a peaceful moment. If you have a TV or computer in your room, cover it with a white sheet, so it doesn't remind you of work to be done.

- Avoid multitasking. Living a more peaceful, patient life means taking one thing at a time and at a slower pace. Doing multiple things causes stress and hurriedness, which feeds itself in the frenzy.

- Accept the many areas parents must leave change up to the child. Parents can facilitate change but can't force it.

> Parents can't control their child's:
> eating, sleeping, toileting, pace
> learning, thoughts, feelings, beliefs, values, attitude
> personality, or temperament

We are taking on an adult role. Part of the adult role in parenting is leadership. Good leaders model appropriate skills. Yes, we are human, but being parents, we try to be better at patience every day that we wake up. How we deal with anger is a direct model to our children on how to deal with anger. They are watching us. Keep at it and pat yourself on the back for every minute of success!

The really, really bad days

If you are like most parents and occasionally have a really bad day, don't beat yourself with guilt. Try asking yourself, what do we all really need right now? Nourishment for the body? (Sleep, exercise, fresh air, bath.) The mind? (Read email, newspaper, book, movie.) Spirit? (Chocolate, aromatherapy, talk with a friend, a walk.) A snack, nap, drive, or a new activity helps change everyone's moods and the atmosphere of the day. Every parent has bad days. Have a Bad Day Plan ahead of time. Never mind the endless list of things that need to get done. Going to bed knowing that you held your temper and your relationships are in tact is much more satisfying than folded laundry and a clean house. Tomorrow is a new day and the chores will get done.

Apologizing for mistakes

Okay, we are human. When we slip up, like that day I took a hammer to my printer, we need to address the situation, rather than let it go. I went to the children and said, "I'm sorry for slamming the printer and I broke the house rule. Mommy made a big mistake, and I'm very sorry for doing that."

Then I said what I should have done instead. "I should have used my words instead of the hammer. Or I could have gone for a walk, taken a deep breath, or got a drink. I know that I should have taken a break. Can you think of anything else I could have done?"

Separating your anger from discipline is a learned skill. With practice, it becomes easier and easier.

Parenting blind spots

We need to be aware of our blinds spots. Little quirks we carry forward from our childhoods are sensitive areas for us. We make mountains out of molehills. As a child, I was always shifted quickly without time to gather my stuff. My parents would decide to suddenly go home in the middle of the night while camping. I would subsequently lose things and be very upset. Now, as an adult, losing things is very hard for me. When my children lose things, as all children do, I become more upset over the lost item than they do. My anger is blown out of proportion, and it helps to keep perspective if I know where that quirk is coming from. I have to make a conscious effort to not react.

DEALING WITH AN ANGRY CHILD

From happiness, sadness, and anger, children feel a whole range of emotions. Which are easy to accept? Joy, excitement, happiness? Which are harder to accept? Anger, frustration or disappointment? We feel bad for our children when other people and circumstances cause those triggers in our children. We feel even worse when we are the source. Anger directed at us is very hard for us to deal with calmly and respectfully.

We don't have many role models of adults handling children's anger. Most often, we handle it the way our parents handled it. There are not many images of angry parents in TV and other media. Often, we also feel a loss as to how to handle our children's anger toward their siblings. How do we feel when our son expresses anger to our daughter?

The one key that parents have to remember is they are not responsible for their child's anger, happiness, or other feelings. We can facilitate a happy, calm, loving environment, but the child still chooses how to feel. It's unrealistic to have happy children all the time. We can get into a trap of spoiling them to ensure they are never sad, disappointed, or hurt, and we do our child a disservice. The mad rush for the holiday "must have" toy is rooted in the desire to have non-disappointed children. Our job as parents is to help our children deal with their uncomfortable feelings, not protect them against them.

What makes our children angry?

- Unrealistic standards and expectations for them.
- Unmet needs. Even babies get angry when hungry or not changed.
- Punishment and excessive competition and comparison.
- Sibling and peer conflict.
- Feeling they have been treated unfairly.
- Feeling they have not enough control and choices over their lives.
- Goals are thwarted.
- Getting physically hurt.

Typical ways children express their anger

Babies: red face, crying and grunts of protest.

Toddlers and preschoolers: hitting, screaming, yelling, crying, tantrums, throwing things and stomping feet.

Middle childhood: teasing, bullying, sarcasm, hitting, yelling, crying, throwing, withdrawal, sulking and "attitude."

Adolescence: sulking, teasing, sarcasm, hitting, yelling, throwing, depression, withdrawal, and "attitude."

Children act out anger in direct ways such as biting, screaming, and tantrums and indirect ways such as sarcasm, attitude, and sadness. Children who feel their anger is unacceptable will act out in indirect ways. Anger that is expressed and accepted loses its destructive power, so it's always better to tackle anger directly than indirectly.

Reducing child's anger:

- Use solution-oriented, relationship-building discipline tools.
- Have realistic expectations for your child's age and stage.
- Avoid hitting (hitting teaches hitting).
- Avoid isolating your child if it compounds her anger.
- Avoid comparing your children. Celebrate each child's uniqueness.
- Avoid experiences that are too hard for your child when she is frustrated easily.
- Actively listen to your child's frustration.
- Recognize when your child is having a cranky day and avoid too many demands on her for that time. Crankiness is just like being sick. It's illness of the emotions and mind, not the body. Ease up on duties and let things slide. Tomorrow you can go back to the regular program when everyone is in a better mood.
- "Scold" the furniture or toy that was causing trouble for your child.

HELPING CHILDREN MANAGE THEIR ANGER

A = Accept it
N = Neutralize it
G = Get away
E = Examine why
R = Resolve and problem-solve

A = Accept that children feel angry

Teach them to recognize anger and develop a vocabulary for naming their feelings. You can do this by:

- Sharing your feelings.
- Encouraging your child to take ownership of feelings. "You felt mad…" Instead of "He made you mad…"
- Use angry people in stories, videos, and TV as a spring board for discussion.
- "It's okay to be angry, but you can't hit your brother." "It's normal for that girl to feel angry, but she probably shouldn't have thrown her present in the garbage. Can you think of another way she could have expressed her anger?"

N = Teach how to neutralize anger in a way that doesn't hurt anybody or wreck anything

- Make a poster of yes and no behaviors. We often tell children what they can't do, but not what they can do when they are in the heat of the moment.
- Write "yes" behaviors in green marker and "no" behaviors in red marker. Discuss this when they are NOT angry.
- Make a feelings intensity poster. Draw a big "emotion" or "anger" thermometer on a poster and laminate it. When they are angry, have them draw or color in red how much anger they feel. Have gradations from annoyed to furious.
- Role model healthy expression of anger. Hitting, yelling, and throwing teaches our children to hit, yell, and throw. Use the same list of calm-down tools for adults. They work equally well for children.

G = Teach children to get away for while to think

Teaching children to walk away from a volatile situation is probably one of the best anger tools you can teach them. Teach that the trigger is like a baited hook. They can choose to take it on and resolve it or leave it be and move on to other things. My daughter was 12 when she and her cousin were walking home from a store. They had a disagreement and both children were very angry. My daughter came home alone and I asked, "Where is your cousin?" My daughter replied, "We had a fight. I was so angry, I had to walk away." I had to explain to my daughter that her action was a good one, but in that circumstance, when her cousin was visiting from another city and didn't know where she was, it was not the best choice! We rushed into the car and found her cousin.

E = Help children examine the reasons why they feel angry

Active listening to a child's anger and really trying to understand and empathize with his feelings helps him to sort out the real underlying issues and primary feelings. Help him clarify why he is angry and what his primary feeling is. Is he jealous? Feeling victimized? Feeling tired?

Accept and validate all responses, even if the child is very angry at you. This is difficult to do but very helpful for the child. When your daughter says that she feels unloved compared to her sibling, the first words out of you are probably in defense, "But that's not true! You know I love you as much as her!" Active listening would be a response such as "You feel unloved compared to your sister? You think that I love her more?" This shows your daughter you have truly heard her feelings and not dismissed them. Then you can defend. "I really love you just as much as your sister! How can I show you that?"

Some primary feelings in child anger are:

- Fear – your child fears a loss of parent love.
- Tiredness – your daughter had too many sleepovers and is on a very short fuse.
- Stress – your children are overbooked in too many activities and not enough downtime.
- Loss – your child lost his favorite stuffie.
- Jealousy – your child thinks that you love the new baby more.
- Hurt – your child thinks you have time only for her sibling.
- Embarrassment – your daughter is yelled at in front of her friends.
- Disappointment – your daughter is not asked to the prom.

Parent words that negate angry feelings	Active listening words to use to accept them
Stop making such a fuss; it's no big deal.	I hear your anger.
Can't you be nice? Good little girls don't act that way.	You sound pretty mad at that. That's okay. Girls can feel angry just as much as boys.
It's not the end of the world.	You feel like it's the end of the world?

Parent words that negate angry feelings	Active listening words to use to accept them
You don't really hate your baby brother.	You feel jealous of your baby brother.
In this house, we never say the word, "hate."	Hate is a pretty strong word to adults. Is that the word you want to use?
Stop crying or I'll give you something to cry about.	It's okay to cry. It helps us feel better.
You're ungrateful.	You are feeling victimized or treated unfairly?
What's wrong with you?	Something's wrong? Want to talk about it?
Don't be a baby.	It's okay to feel upset.
You're not really angry; you are just tired.	You seem pretty angry and tired too.
Why do you have to be that way?	You are feeling angry?
Suck it up, Princess.	It's okay to feel angry.

R = Show children how to return to the person or situation and solve the problem directly

Help children problem-solve and generate solutions if they require assistance. Teach trading, negotiation, taking turns, brainstorming options, and choosing solutions. Walking away and letting go is also a resolution and a valid choice. Teach them to first resolve with the person they had the issue with before appealing to a higher authority.

Congratulate your child on small victories of self-control and demonstrated maturity. Learning to handle anger is a life long accomplishment. It takes years for children to practice and get it. Most children can begin to handle anger without hitting and throwing at around 10 to 12 years of age.

If we put as much time into helping our children handle their strong feelings as we do in keeping them in time-out, we would have emotionally healthy children.

Temper tantrums

Temper tantrums are typical from ages one to three and a half years or when the child is old enough to be sufficiently verbal to express his feelings. They occur when the child has a desire but can't understand their physical, mental, emotional, or social limitations. The child can't verbalize feelings of anger and frustration, tiredness, hunger, crankiness, or boredom, so they express feelings in body language by screaming, crying, kicking, or "doing the plank" (they flatten their arms over their heads and keep their bodies straight so a parent can't pick them up). Most toddlers do grow out of tantrums.

Tantrums are not misbehavior, nor are they abnormal or in need of correction. Children punished for temper tantrums learn to not express feelings. They learn how to suppress them, which is not healthy for the body or mind. Like an air mattress not being allowed to express air through the main chute, it will spring leaks in other places to compensate. Most often, children will leak feelings through their "misbehavior." **Feelings must come out somewhere, somehow** – even when parents are not comfortable with them.

There are two types of tantrums: Spill over and Power struggle

Spill over tantrums

Prevention: Food, rest, stimulation, or sleep when needed. Don't attempt shopping with a tired, cranky, and hungry child. Watch for and prevent triggers. Change the activity. As soon as you notice your child getting tired, hungry, or cranky, try a juice-box (to get their blood sugar up) and a protein snack. Try cuddling them on your lap with a good book – a great way to calm down, get some literacy skills, and enjoy some connecting quiet time together. Try and meet needs as soon as possible, as a tantrum is starting, if not before. Sometimes, boredom can't be alleviated. Parents have to get creative and invent ways for children to pass the time.

Handling: Despite your best preventive techniques, a tantrum does occur. You are not the only parent with a child that displays a tantrum in a public place. Other parent's children have done it before and will do it again. Those stares are not looks of judgment on your parenting ability. Other parents will look at you and breathe a sigh of relief that their children are normal, too. Go on about your activity as if nothing is happening. Sometimes, ignoring it helps. Hold him if out in public, or move him to a safe quiet place. Let the child feel their feelings and know that expressing them is okay. Say, "That's okay. You're angry. I'll stay with you. Calm down." In a loud voice, so onlookers know that you have everything under control, "It's okay to be angry. I know you are feeling frustrated." In a quiet time, you could ask, "Do you want me to hold you for awhile while you calm down or would you rather be alone?" Your child's reaction will give you clues as to what they want you to do. After the tantrum, carry on with your scheduled activity. Stay with child. Use soft firm voice. Encourage deep breaths.

After: Wait for the calm after the storm. Avoid talking to your child because the toddler is too upset to hear anything. Again, try and meet her needs for rest and food as soon as possible. Label your child's emotions and give her the words to use so she develops a feeling vocabulary. Say, "You were angry when you couldn't have that cookie?" The toddler usually understands the intent of the question and feels understood. It also gives them the words to match their uncomfortable feelings so they can use "their words" when they are older instead of their body language to express their feelings.

Power struggle tantrums

Prevention: Give lots of choices. Acknowledge your child's feelings of unhappiness. Pick your battles wisely.

Handling: Ignore the behavior if your child is safe. Use a soft firm voice. Do NOT give in to your child's desire. Children do not do what doesn't work. If a tantrum always gets a prize, then it's a behavior that will repeat over and over. This is the hardest part! Stay with your "no"!

After: Wait for the calm after the storm. As with spill over tantrums, acknowledge your child's feelings with an emotion word so she develops a feeling vocabulary. Carry on with your normal scheduled activity.

General tips:
- Realize it is a normal behavior. Don't be embarrassed. Every parent has been through them.
- Older children are not immune. Some children go through them into the school years. See the book *The Explosive Child*, by Ross Greene for more recommendations on school-aged tantrums.
- Make the surroundings safe.
- If your child holds their breath and you are worried about cyanosis (lack of oxygen to the brain) blow gently into the child's face or apply a small splash of water on him to bring him out.
- Avoid showing anger to your child's anger. Stay calm. Parent anger can escalate your child's intensity of their anger.
- Try to prevent tantrums as much as possible by distraction. Get down on the floor and start to play with some of their toys. They will soon join you.
- Although preschoolers are more able to use their words, they can become overwhelmed with emotions and regress back to body language tantrums.
- Avoid time-outs to deal with tantrums. Children are experimenting with their feelings. Mostly, they don't understand them and can be overcome with them. Their uncontrollable anger can be frightening for them, especially for younger

children. They need us to accept their feelings, love them with their feelings, and guide them through their outbursts with understanding, acceptance, and help. Parents can't do that if they shoo their children away during a time-out.

- Many adults still need practice in controlling and managing their emotional temper tantrums. Eighty percent of people don't lose their jobs due to technical incompetence, but rather the inability to get along with other people and manage their uncomfortable feelings.

- As a society, we have a greater acceptance of positive emotions than negative ones, yet both kind exist and are equally valid. In children, we find the positive ones don't quite bother us as much as the negative ones. At least they are easier on the ear! It's great that tantrums cease as children become more verbal and can express their feelings with words.

My son used to throw daily, almost hourly tantrums at the age of two. One day, when he was four, I was taking all five children and two friends swimming. I only had enough change in my pocket for one treat to share for all the children. I was bracing for the "after swimming-so hungry" tantrum from my son, and after I explained the situation to him, he got it! No tantrum! I could actually negotiate with him. What a difference a year or two made in his frustration tolerance!

How to move a tantruming toddler

The best way to carry a tantruming toddler is face out with one arm between the legs, grasping the other arm around the trunk and under both child's arms. You can also hold the handle of a baby carrier or shopping bags on your arm, if you find yourself in the middle of a store with a baby and a tantruming toddler. It helps to bring someone along if you know that your child is prone to tantrums in stores, just to help with packages, kicked off shoes, etc.

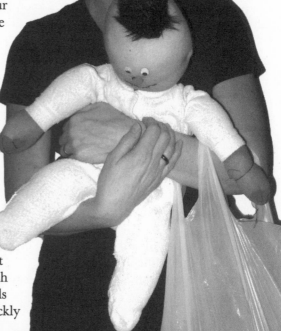

It's also helpful to schedule shopping without the child if store tantrums are a huge problem. They will grow out of it, but for now, it's the easiest thing to do. You also might wish to avoid problem areas like malls that are hard to get to a car quickly or stores that are especially difficult like candy and toy shops. Shop alone and have a partner or babysitter home with the children. This stage will only last a few months.

How to get a tantruming toddler into a car seat

Throw your packages into the driver's seat. Gently, but firmly, place child in seat. They may be doing "the plank," so it might help to tickle them to get them to bend and put the bar down to strap them in. Let them tantrum, and you could gently stroke their hair or hand while they finish. Show how to deep breathe. Softly talk. "It's okay." "Let's breathe." If the noise is too much, close the door and wait outside so they can see you and feel assured that you won't leave them. Stay calm!

Spirited children's tantrums

Spirited children don't handle frustration very well. You may experience more tantrums than normal, perhaps hourly or daily. Brandie, a mom in a parenting group, said, "I have a very spirited three-year-old who does the OPPOSITE of any requests." Three to five-year-olds are into power, and it's totally developmentally appropriate. Head off the triggers as best as you can for spill over tantrums, and never, never give in to the power struggle ones. It really increases the likelihood of them doing it again.

On the other hand, Donna, another mom, experienced the 3.5-year-old solution! It seemed that 3.5 was the magic age that spirited children changed. Temper tantrums normally dissipate after 3.5 years. They can go from daily tantrums to once a month tantrums almost overnight at that age. Children really turn a milestone when they become much more cooperative, remember things, and negotiate better. Many moms of spirited children have reported the same thing.

I have found that heading off the triggers helps for spirited children. Then if you gradually increase the triggers or expose them to frustration incidents more as they get older, they get practice at learning to handle their strong feelings better. The frequency of times they have to feel frustrated or angry naturally increases as they get older by natural consequences. Sometimes, you just can't hold a tantrum off. That broken banana just can't be fixed, and it has to be THAT banana! Tell them, "It's okay to feel that way." Help them with their strong emotions when you say no. Try to hold them (but don't force it if they refuse), speak softly with "That's okay. You can feel angry..." and try to rock them, rub their back, or rub their hand until the tantrum is over. It tells them that all their feelings are acceptable and you love them unconditionally – that the tantrum has a start and a finish. It also tells them you will not back down and say "yes" if you are engaged in a power struggle.

It's very difficult to remain calm and unfettered through it, but try! Protect yourself and anyone else. Hold their hands while speaking softly if they are prone to hit or throw during their tantrum. Save your words for after when they hear you better. Remember, this too shall pass!

HANDLING CHILDREN'S PUBLIC MISBEHAVIOR

Children's public misbehavior can be challenging for parents. I wouldn't call their actions misbehavior but rather a clash of needs. Parents need to run errands, wait in lines, and grocery shop; and children need to explore their world, declare their independence, and expend energy. Those are valid developmental tasks for children from one to four years. Unfortunately, many public places are not child friendly and do not take into account small children's needs that arise while parents must go about doing errands. For example, notice all the checkout aisles aimed to tempt young children with gum and chocolate bars? When my son was 18 months, he would unwrap a few chocolate bars and eat them while I was loading groceries onto the cashier table. I would have to pay for unwanted chocolate or deal with a screaming child while I was unloading groceries. I complained to the store manager, and he admitted the store chain puts goodies at the checkout to increase the "nag factor" of bored children.

If public venues do not take children's needs into account, then the parents must do so. Avoid them if they are trouble spots or bring your own snack. Patronize shops that do not put the treat display stand by the checkout. I was amazed to find supermarkets in England that had no candy or junk toys near the checkouts. Instead, at the front of the store, near the checkouts were mini playgrounds and play tables to amuse the children while the groceries were rung through. Apparently, an organized mother's boycott prompted retailers to make changes. That is what I call "child friendly"! Those stores met the need for children to be occupied and stimulated while mothers could watch prices being added, which is a normally boring time for children. If stores can have special services and modified checkouts for people with special mobility needs, why can't they offer modified checkouts for mothers who can't control their toddler's mobility?

Steps that parents can take to avoid public scenes are:
- Have realistic expectations. Toddlers won't sit in a restaurant chair for more than 10 minutes in spite of how much we need them too. Proper table and social manners can be taught much later when the child is older and can understand respect for other's needs. Age five is a good time to start teaching table manners. As well, parents know their child's temperament and their limits best. Some children are naturally quieter than others and can sit still for an hour in their high chair while amusing themselves; and others won't sit five minutes. It's not the child's fault for differences in their self-control. It's how they are. By age 15, most will sit still and have reasonable table manners!

- Break errands up into smaller trips. A three-to-four hour shopping trip may be too much stimulation for a toddler or preschooler to handle.

- Before going out in public, try to have a rested and fed child. Adults get cranky when we are hungry and tired. Children are no different. Shopping for groceries before afternoon naptime may be too taxing for a toddler. When the preschooler gives up naps, they still have a cranky time of day, when they used to nap. This is not a good time to shop. Bring along juice boxes and keep non-perishable snacks in the car for unexpected delays in the car or line-ups in stores.

- Distraction is a great tool for children this age. A snack works while waiting for dinner in restaurants or in stores. Bring along a special "going out" toy bag that you bring out only in public. In line-ups, children can play with a container of play-dough, a calculator, a pull toy, or a roll of tape. Older children can count things, play I-spy with you, or play rock-paper-scissors. Children's books are a great way to pass the time waiting in offices and stores. It's a great way to build literacy in everyday life and spend some one-on-one time.

- Engage your child to help. Toddlers can put apples into bags at grocery stores or carry a special brand of juice to the cart. They can even put some of your hand-picked groceries into those cute little child sized carts at the supermarket. Just watch your ankles! Offer them a choice between two acceptable products so they feel they are really helping you. My toddler learned about counting, shapes, and colors while grocery shopping because I constantly talked to him in the cart. We played lots of peek-a-boo games during waiting times.

- Take into account their high energy needs. When you are going somewherewhere children are expected to be quiet, make sure your toddler has burned off some energy beforehand. Visit a playground before the wedding or church service or a meeting. If traveling on a bus, or plane, bring a ball along to chase while in between travel times. Children need to expend energy every hour.

- Teach children how to touch objects gently. Christmas is a hard time for shopping because children watch with fascination all the sparkly, twinkling baubles they want desperately to touch. It is like showing a starving adult a pizza and saying, "Don't eat!" Exploration is a developmental task of toddlers. Children can be shown how to touch gently if they are constantly supervised. If you can't supervise, try to avoid letting them see the desired object. Run that stroller past the toy store fast before they see those enticing packages!

- Model appropriate public behavior. Usually, toddlers are too young to engage in embarrassing behavior such as swear words or out of place comments, but they do pop out, especially with preschoolers. If it does happen, selective ignoring works because toddlers do not comprehend the significance of the word yet, and may not notice the reaction it brings. Parents have to be careful of behaviors they may find funny at home but embarrassing when done in public. For example, children who pick their nose, scratch their bum, or fondle their penis as soon as they are out of diapers need to learn what constitutes public and private behavior. You could just say matter of factly, "We do that in private when we are alone in our rooms."

Handling public tantrums

My daughter was two and threw a tantrum on a plane. She wanted to get down from my lap, and the flight attendants wanted her to sit still during take-off. Take-off was delayed, and the tantrum lasted at least 30 minutes. She was screaming, crying, hitting, and flailing. I was a captive show with 238 other people watching my parenting skills!

Despite the best of intentions of avoiding public scenes or trying to prevent them, a tantrum may occur. Sometimes, a parent has to run an errand at the wrong time or forgot to pack a toy or snack, and the child emotionally explodes. What can a parent do? Take a deep breath and remain calm. You are the adult. So you are expected to be calm, even when the embarrassment and subsequent anger is rising up in your throat. Our job as parents is to teach self-control. The best way is to model it. Calmly pick him or her up, and take her out to the car, restroom, or a quiet place to wait out the tantrum.

How do you cope with people's stares? Ignoring helps. We feel that other people are judging us. Some might be, but others may be silently empathizing and remembering their own days of dealing with toddlers. Often, they really do understand but don't know what to say or do to help you. Have confidence in your parenting. Say in a really loud voice, "It's okay, Natasha. I'm here," while you wait until the tantrum is over. Or, "It's okay, we are going to leave now." People know that you are calm and in control, or at least look that way! Take a deep breath. Avoid threatening your child and raising your voice. Avoid threatening to leave the child. You never would anyways, and it destroys trust and attachment between parent and child. Anger tends to escalate anger. One of you has to remain calm, and it isn't likely to be your toddler.

If people make a rude comment, you can politely say, "I am taking care of the situation" and carry on doing what you plan to do. You know your child best and can advocate for them. Many well meaning friends, family, and strangers, especially those that say, "all that child needs is a good spanking," may not know the needs and developmental capabilities of young children, or they forget what it is like to have to constantly meet those needs.

When we see other parents coping with a toddler tantrum, it may be nice to offer them some words of encouragement. A simple "It's hard when toddlers have tantrums.

You deserve a nice cup of tea!" or "It's tough parenting. Is there anything I can help with?" Often moms need a hand to carry the baby, push a stroller, or handle packages while they carry their screaming child to the car. A smile can even go a long way to alleviate a parent's embarrassment and often helps both the parent and the child. When my daughter was having the airplane tantrum, the flight attendant patted my shoulder and said, "You're doing fine." I felt instantly better and less anxious. My daughter probably picked up on my feelings and felt better, too.

Dealing with an angry older child (not temper tantrums):
- Actively listen and hold the angry child if they consent. Rub their back. Put their hand in both of yours and gently rub.
- Teach self-calming tools in a calmer time and remind them in the turmoil time.
- Be a "feeling releaser" listener rather than a "fact finder" listener, especially when dealing with fighting children who are very angry at each other.
- Acknowledge your child's anger and assure them you are available to help.
- STAY CALM even if the anger is directed to you. Deep breathe. Visualize calm.
- Fake it until you make it! You can choose to stay calm.
- Later, after the emotional temperature has gone down, help the child
  see the problem and generate some options for a solution.

Children learn how to deal with anger by how anger is managed by the parents in the home. What are they learning from us in how we deal with anger?

ABOUT APOLOGIES

When the child needs to apologize to someone else: nudge, don't force!

This is one sticky area in discipline. My son Scotty was three and a half. We were at the local science center. He was playing with the sticks and threw one at his brother. The stick went flying and almost hit another mom that was sitting down. Fortunately, it hit the wall. I grabbed Scotty and insisted he apologize. Of course, he wouldn't. By this time, he's feeling like he's on stage and embarrassed and shy. I temporarily let it go. We went to a new activity, and he calms down. So do I. We talk about our feelings and reconnect. I then suggest it would be the right thing to do to go back to apologize. I didn't force it. I forgot about it and went back to talking to my friend. I noticed five minutes later, Scotty went up to the mom and said he was sorry – on his own terms, in his own time, and in his own words and way.

Apologies must come from the heart. They almost never come when forced or in the emotional heat of the moment. They can be taught by modeling, not forcing the words. Parents never apologize in the heat of the moment. Why do we make children? Because it's more about our social embarrassment and need for social bandages than about how the child is feeling at the moment.

When one child hits another, the time to ask for an apology is not while he is still mad! As the parent who witnesses this, shower the victim with attention and mend his wounds. Say, "Sorry for the wound," so you are modeling an apology to the hitter. You are expressing sorrow for the victim. It doesn't excuse what the hitter did. It shows empathy from the observer parent. When the two children have cooled, you could model an apology or ask that one be given. Nudge, teach, offer advice, but don't force!

It can be difficult to handle the parents of the other child who may expect an apology from your child. It's best to be direct and say to the other parent, "Jared is too upset right now to apologize, but we will still deal with this." Or, "We will make this a teaching moment." It lets the other parent know that you are conscious of the social rules, and you are teaching your child about amends. It doesn't say you will force an apology, and it still respects your child's need to apologize in his own time and method. You could also apologize yourself to the parents for your child's behavior. It shows them that you know the social rules, and you care about their feelings and it's great modeling.

When the child needs to apologize to you

Tell the child you need to hear an apology to get past your hurt. This puts the focus of change on you and your needs rather than something he must do. Again, nudged apologies come faster than forced ones.

When you need to apologize to the child

Do it when it needs to be done! Be sincere. It doesn't undermine your parental authority or respect. If anything, children have more respect because it takes a big leap to admit wrong and make restitution for it. It helps to calm a child's anger and resentment if they have been treated unfairly. It's great modeling for the children in teaching how to do it sincerely and with respect.

COUNTERACTING PARENT STRESS

 It takes a village – to cherish a parent, to nurture a child.

Moms are so down on each other and themselves, with little in the way of public recognition but lots in the way of judgment. We need to spread a sign of support, a show of appreciation, not judgement when we see a mom dealing with a toddler tantrum at the playground, a mom with a mouthy teenager in the mall, or a mom with a sulky school-aged child in the school. Mothering can be hard, unsupported, and unappreciated work. Yet, society needs parents to nurture our next generation of citizens. What job could be more valued? Send three emails to parents you know every day to tell them they are appreciated.

Ways to counteract parent tiredness

Parent tiredness is a key factor in parent anger. When we are tired, everything seems so much worse, from the state of the house, to our child's behavior. Try to get more sleep.

Here are some tips:

- Sleep when you can. Forget about "everything that needs to be done." It doesn't look so daunting when you are rested, and things will actually get done much faster.
- Have your partner take the children out so you can nap.
- If you can't sleep, at least try to have some downtime – some quiet to rest and relax.
- Join a babysitting co-op and trade off childcare duties with another mom so you can sleep or get stuff done.
- Accept offers of help and take people up on it. People love to feel needed!
- Demand time for what energizes you: talking on the phone, reading email, reading the newspaper, having a cup of tea or watching a favorite show.
- Use music to relax or energize you. Even the best tunes can spice up a dreary task.
- Know that tiredness doesn't last forever. Your children will get older and need less supervision, and you can nap more often. Parents report that once their youngest child is about five, they can get much more sleep.
- While children are young, put on a video and do the one-eyed snooze. This is lying on the sofa, dozing, but still being half awake for keeping an eye on little ones. Get them to sit beside you so you know where they are. Play the "Sleeping Beauty" game.
- Keep cold. Drink cold water, and put on a cold fan to keep awake. Soak your feet in a bucket of cold water. It keeps you awake.
- Chew peppermint or cinnamon chewing gum.
- Look at the humor in the situation. Look at humor in life. It can give you energy.
- Find time to exercise or go for a walk. Fresh air helps to keep awake. Sitting down in a stale-air room will keep you tired.
- Go to a play place with the children and a friend. Stimulating conversation and coffee can help keep you awake. Bonus: if you tire the children out enough, you can have a nap when they nap afterwards.
- Drinks lots of water. Leave it out on the counter or you won't get around to doing it. A lot of tiredness can be related to dehydration.

- If you are driving home and the children fall asleep, park the car in the driveway with the parking brake on and engine off, and don't disturb them to get them out because they could wake up. Instead, go in the house and grab a pillow. Come back into the car, and snooze in the back seat while they are napping in their car seats. When they wake up, you wake up, and bring everyone in the house.

Start a babysitting co-op

Are you alone in the city with no family or relatives to baby-sit? Do you need occasional babysitting to get your hair cut, visit the dentist, have a nap, nurse a cold, or enjoy an evening out with your partner? Perhaps a babysitting co-op is the answer.

To find a babysitting co-op in your area, check the community centers, mom's time-out groups, or churches to see if one already exists. If not, check with other moms at the playground while you are supervising your children. Many co-ops exist by word of mouth only.

If your community doesn't have one, it's easy to start. All you need is another mom and some agreed upon rules, tokens, and structure. Here are some considerations:

Numbers: Aim for about 10 – 12 families. Not too big that you don't know everyone and not too small so that you run out of phone numbers before you find a commitment to baby-sit your children whenever you need it.

Tokens: Use wood disks, poker chips, or painted coins. Many co-ops start with 30 hours allocated to everyone to begin, and everyone leaving has to hand in 30 hours. Tokens are made in different colors to represent one hour and 1/2 hour tokens. In my co-op, we pay one token per hour for the first child and a quarter token for each additional child in the family, per each additional hour. That way, larger families are not penalized too much. Some co-ops charge a half token for second and subsequent children.

Rules: Keep the rules to a minimum, and make sure that all charter members agree to them. Some general considerations are that the mother is the one babysitting, unless otherwise agreed to. During the day, the children to be babysat are transported to the babysitters'. In the evening, the babysitter comes to the children's house to sit and puts the children to bed in their own domain. Meals, transportation, and outings are negotiated between the two parties. A discipline policy should definitely be discussed at the charter member meeting. Communication is important so misunderstandings are avoided.

Structure: Some co-ops have a secretary that one would phone and request a sit. The secretary would then phone the lowest token holder first to fill the sit and go down the list if needed. The secretary position is rotated monthly. Other co-ops have each person do their own phoning for sits, which has the advantage that the person can choose who their child likes to play with the most. Generally, the person with the lowest number of tokens should be phoned first. Regardless of structure, members should meet monthly on a rotational basis, at each others' house, to discuss token counts, arrange future sits, and problem-solve any issues that come up. Moms really look forward to the monthly meeting as it's a social visit and support group also!

The advantages of babysitting co-ops are many. To children, they are like a play date with their friends. Often, babysitting other children helps keep yours occupied, and the babysitter can get more done too! It's inexpensive, and parents have the security of knowing that an adult is in charge rather than a teen. Many moms like to baby-sit at another's house in the evening, as they are free to do some quiet work, read, or hobbies once the children are in bed – things they wouldn't otherwise get done in their own home. Perhaps the most compelling advantage is that the social and support network of similar aged children and parents is wonderful to have in this day of isolated nuclear families.

Time for yourself

One of the toughest things a parent or anyone in a close relationship faces is giving herself permission to take a time-out for herself – personal satisfaction time. Don't feel guilty; it's a necessity. Schedule regular time so everyone in the family gets used to it, and it becomes non-negotiable. Mom could take a few hours on Saturday and Dad on Sunday to do whatever they wish to do. If a parent is single or the other partner travels a bit, try swapping childcare with another parent or set up a babysitting co-op. Or try to schedule in personal time through the week while the children are occupied in the house. What could you do in five minutes, 20 minutes, or two hours? Make a list:

- **Five minutes:** check email, have a cup of tea, go outside for breaths of fresh air, try to go to the bathroom alone or open mail.
- **Twenty minutes:** read a magazine article, watch a bit of TV, have a quick bath or shower, talk to a friend on the phone or read the newspaper.
- **Two hours:** go out if you have childcare, nap, or watch a movie at home. Don't clean, organize, or do chores! This is time to nurture you, not the house!

Sometimes children need about 10 or 20 minutes of focused time and then they are filled up on attention and will leave you alone for some time to yourself. They will engage in a solitary playing activity. However, if you force them to leave you alone when they are lacking attention, they probably won't leave you alone because they are still low on attention needs. Giving attention is the best way to solve this, rather than punishments or harsh words.

Examine your "to do" list with a critical eye and choose only those items that absolutely have to get done that day to meet your families needs. Trim everything off the list. They will get done eventually. If you are a type "A" driven person, move the items off the list today to another day in the day timer so you can feel that they will get done sometime.

Put Dad to work. Outings Dad could take children to: grocery shopping, pet stores, hardware stores (children love the escalators and ceiling fans), errands, playgrounds, parks, picnics, bike riding or sports events. My children's favorite was just riding the city train, with no particular destination in mind.

Try to aim for a regular night sleep every night. Half of all discipline problems could be solved if only parents get a good night's sleep. Meet your needs for meals and water. Many moms don't drink enough water and feel tired and dehydrated. When you feel better, minor irritations of parenting, such as a toddler's tantrum, affect you less when you are in a better space.

Time for couples

Set aside one night a week to be together – at the very least, one night a month. Pick your anniversary date and book a sitter in advance for those dates. Often, with a sitter coming, it's less easy to bow out if one person is tired or busy. Go out, or plan a romantic evening in. Every time my husband and I went out, we came back feeling connected and happier for getting together.

It's also important to set aside 15 minutes a day for couple time. Grab a cup of tea or glass of wine and head to a quiet place, such as the sofa, the deck, the front porch, the bedroom, even the bathroom if you have to. We used to take the children to the park and talked together while sitting on the park bench. Try to talk about feelings, opinions, and values rather than just the details of life running smoothly. Instead of, "Will you pick up the dry-cleaning tomorrow?" try, "How did you feel when you were rushed at work today? That must have been hard for you?"

Try to keep one room in the house that is a retreat space– one room with no toys or clothes lying around. Perhaps it could be a hobby room, office, guest room, workshop, or sewing room.

Begin couple time when children are toddlers. By the time they are school-aged, they will get used to waiting for Mom and Dad's attention for a short period of time. Of course, toddlers and preschoolers are a bit young to understand how to wait, but definitely by school-age, children can estimate what 15 minutes is and give you both some space.

When Dad comes home from work, his spending time with the children helps in filling up their attention needs – so they will give you some time later.

Find time to connect throughout the day. Kiss and hug at every goodbye. Touch and cuddle whenever you can. Phone each other at work. Write notes on the babies diaper to give to the other person when he changes the baby next. Leave notes on pillows and in lunches. Spontaneous, appreciative notes keeps the love flowing! The greatest gift you can give your children is a loving Dad or Mom in a secure couple relationship.

Time with each child

Do it often enough so each child will feel special. Let them lead the activity. Have no other siblings along. In our house, we used the birthday date to allocate special time. My son was born on September 4, so every fourth of the month is his "special date" with Mom or Dad or both to pick an activity he wanted to do. We booked off all the dates a year ahead, so we knew not to plan any other activity that evening.

DE-CLUTTER YOUR LIFE

Too much stuff, obligations, and people can make our lives stressful and leave us with a short fuse of anger. We need to occasionally do some pruning.

Your stuff

Material stuff is nine times less important to happiness than personal resources, such as family relationships, friendships, contributing to others' lives, and celebrating life events. Most storage is procrastination of decision-making. Where do I put this stuff? What do I do with it? Or, if you have an idea of what to do with it, you have no time to put it in action and keep putting it off. How many broken items are stored with the best intentions of fixing them?

Often, we search for new and bigger houses or renovate for more storage space when we should be going through our stuff and pruning it. Keep what we need for our life today. Most people store too much stuff. Only 20 percent of the house should be allocated to storage, including bookcases, dressers, closets, cupboards, shelf, and storage containers.

An organized house reduces your stress level. No, you don't have to get rid of everything, as my husband often fears! Just keep what you love and use. There are many great books in the library to help you streamline your house.

Your relationships

When people look at de-cluttering, they tend to focus on objects. They also need to focus on the cluttering people in their lives. By de-cluttering people, I mean we need to examine all the relationships in our lives and prioritize and redirect our energies to those relationships that give us pleasure. Now, I'm not saying you have to dump your partner because he annoys you from time to time. I'm saying we need to look at the equity in the relationships. All give and all take is not healthy for you or the other person. It's not fair to you when you give 95 percent and receive five percent back. We have to re-evaluate those ties we are maintaining only out of a sense of obligation and duty. And yet, they take up so much time and energy that we could use to make our lives less stressful.

For example, when Aunt Martha calls (and we all have someone like Aunt Martha in our lives) and complains for two hours daily about her aches and pains, all the bad things that have happened to her, everything that's gone wrong in her life, and she spends five minutes listening to how you are, it's not fair. You can feel the life energy being sucked right out of you. You hang up feeling like a limp balloon. Then you take your annoyance out on your toddler by getting angry because he just spilled his juice. Put a boundary there. Give Aunt Martha five minutes of your most focused, empathetic listening, and then say, "Sorry, I have to go now."

Moods are contagious. Associate with positive people and you will have a more positive outlook on life. When we surround ourselves with people who nurture us, they feed our ability to nurture others. Drop the "should's" and "ought to's." Focus on the people in your life that really matter to you, who are kind to you, who give you nurturing, support, and affirmations. Who do you want to make more time in your life for?

Your obligations

De-cluttering obligations requires prioritizing and redirecting your energies to those things you really want to do with your life.

You should love your work 80 percent of the time. If not, redirect your energies to what you really want to be doing. If you had five years left to live, would you be doing what you are doing today? A friend once told me that you should find out what you love to do and then find someone to pay you to do it. If you can, turn a hobby into a business.

Drop the should's and ought to's and cut down on your commitments. When we rush from activity to activity, we become stressed and lose our patience. Who do we take it out on? Often our children. It hit me one day, while serving a fast food lunch to four children in the back of the van. I was trying to navigate the fastest road in our city with the fries flying in the back seat. You could have heard me yelling all the way across the city, when the ketchup dripped all over the upholstery. Too much to do and no time to do it. Rush, rush, rush!

Slow down. Life becomes so much easier on a "child's pace". Instead of saying, "Hurry up, we're late," say "That's okay, take the time you need." Seriously look at what needs to be cut down or out in order to slow your adult pace.

Learn to say "no." When you do add a new activity, drop one you are no longer interested in as much, so you keep a flow through calendar rather than just adding and adding. Keep in mind to add driving and preparation time to activities. A one-hour meeting can really take three hours out of our day when those factors are considered. We need reflection and downtime as much as we need activity to keep balance in our lives. What do you want to make more time for?

Does baking homemade cookies for your child's class, offering to coordinate the yuletide pageant, or sitting on a school committee really benefit your child directly in terms of one-on-one, direct attention time? No. These types of commitments eat into the time with your child. You must step back and really examine the reasons you are doing this. Is it for your needs or your children's? It is adding stress to the family or reducing it? Is this the time in your life that is appropriate for this type of commitment or would another stage of life be better? Some things might have to go on the back burner. There are good causes, but maybe it's time for someone else to step up and volunteer. Think about your children, you and your partner. Is this best for all of you right now?

Do some serious life de-cluttering and you will reap the benefits. You will have more time, patience and energy for the people you love, the things you love to do, and more space to do it in. Feel the exhilaration, the sense of freedom, the enjoyment of a lighter load! It's worth it.

CLEAN OR PLAY?

There I am sitting on the floor of my four-year-old and five-year-old son's bedroom, and I am happily, contently, and blissfully absorbed playing parking lot with rows of Lego™ and little metal cars. Then I spot it. Dirt! I see a ledge that I have never seen before at this angle. How often do you see your house at a small child's point of view? It was disgusting! A ledge full of five years worth of dust, grime, and grease that has never seen a dust cloth. I abruptly changed from my blissful state into a panic, consumed with guilt, because I really should not be playing with toys when dirt is silently breeding in little nooks and ledges. It was almost enough to ruin a perfectly wonderful day of enjoying my children. I can just hear the tape of society's expectations playing in my head: a good mother has a spotless house. A good mother has everything in place and has perfectly clean children. She herself must look exquisite. Dinners must also be cooked nutritiously and homemade. STOP! It is time to replay the messages in my head. Besides, I love playing Lego™, the children love playing with me, and my partner loves us all in a happy mood, so if I have to endure a dusty ledge in my face while doing it, then so be it! Over the years, I have collected poems and quotes for my fridge that helped to alleviate the dirty house guilt. Here are some:

- "Our home is clean enough to be healthy and dirty enough to be happy."
- "If you want to see my house, please make an appointment; if you want to see me, please come on in!"
- "No one says on their deathbed, 'I wish I had a cleaner house'."
- Sign on the front lawn, "I'm not growing grass, I'm growing children."

The housework will always be there. The children grow up so fast.

Helping children play independently

"Moooooooooom, I'm borrrrrrred!" Is this the dreaded statement coming from your children on school holidays? Previously, you might have rushed to the phone to arrange a play date, or changed your plans for the day to include your children, or make a whole pile of suggestions of what to do, only to be met with cries of "That's stupid!" Some parents even go to great lengths to sign their children up for back to back day camps in order to escape the inevitable boredom cries that occur over the summer. Boredom is great! Embrace it! Instead of avoiding boredom, help your child deal with it.

Helping your child deal with boredom means releasing parental responsibility from it. Children need to learn to play independently and require practice in initiating activities themselves. They also need this skill when they have a group of friends over and whine, "There's nothing to do!"

First, parents need to get over the idea that they are responsible for filling their children's time. Nobody can make another person feel bored. Boredom is a state that the child owns, and thus, they are the best person to alleviate it. Children today are surrounded by so many toys, games, and play equipment, they can easily get visual stimulation overload. Too many play choices mean that they choose nothing. Mention the word, "chores" and children can easily become "unbored" if they really want to. A parent's job is to provide a stimulating play environment and then leave it up to the child to decide if and how to engage in it. A parent's job is not to be the entertainer of children. That's the child's job.

Some things parents can do to facilitate children's independent play:

1. Give them the gift of uninterrupted time.
2. Pack away the TV and unplug the computer, or at least, cover them up with a sheet for part of the day.
3. Pack away 90 percent of the toys, games, and puzzles they own.

4. Continue to rotate the remaining 10 percent of toys that are left out, preferably on a weekly basis, so that each time something is brought out, it appears new and exciting to the child. Be sure there is no more than 10 percent of toys out at all times.

5. Leave a lot of unstructured play materials around. (See Chapter 9)

6. Pull books from the bookshelves and leave them lying around on the floor and tables. Children tend to not pull individual books from shelves themselves, but will pick one up if the book catches their eye.

7. Put on a video and start watching it. Quietly leave when the children join you and are engaged.

8. Pull out a board game, set it up, and leave it out in the open.

9. Pull some ingredients out of the cupboard and allow the children to make "potions," or leave out a simple recipe and the ingredients.

10. Pull out art supplies and leave them on the table.

11. Pull out the sewing machine, or hammers, nails, and wood pieces.

12. Leave out a bucket of costumes or interesting dress up pieces from the thrift store.

13. Pack away half the gifts received from birthday parties. Bring them out one at a time a few weeks later.

14. The best play ideas are 20 percent toy, 80 percent kid power.

For some activities, the parent should be present and accessible for help from time to time, such as cooking, sewing, and woodworking. Help the children, but don't do it for them. Be a resource person for the play, not a director. Don't forget to play with your child. Parenting brings back play and fun for both parent and child.

6

Your Child Is Unique:
All the factors that affect discipline

 Instead of preparing the path for the child, prepare the child for the path. ~ Unknown

In our family of five children, we have three spirited ones, one slow-to-warm-up child, and one very easy-going child. In terms of personality differences, we have two extraverts and three introverts. We have one child whose love language is gifts, one is touch, one is acts of service, and two whose language is words. We have two visual learners, one auditory learner, and two kinesthetic learners. We have a child who is spatially intelligent, one who is logically intelligent, one who is intelligent in interpersonal relations, and another who is linguistically intelligent. The other child has intrapersonal intelligence. How can I possibly use the same discipline tool for each child when they are all so very different? Add to the mix of different ages, stages, and birth order, and wow! Discipline needs to be unique for each child, capitalizing on their strengths and helping to teach them in a way that it's easiest for them to learn.

DEVELOPMENTAL <u>MILESTONES</u> (THE AGE OF AGES AND STAGES)

Developmental milestones are those <u>physical, emotional, and cognitive milestones</u> that children go through, such as age of walking, talking, and sitting up, or using fine motor skills. Most children develop the new skill and add it to their accumulated body of knowledge. For more information on developmental milestones, see books by The Gesell Institute of Child Development.

DEVELOPMENTAL <u>STAGES</u> (THE STAGE OF AGES AND STAGES)

Developmental stages are <u>behavior stages</u> that encompass emotional, social, and cognitive milestones. According to Jean Illsley Clarke, author of *Self Esteem: A Family Affair*, these stages are recycled and revisited often throughout child and adulthood.

The developmental stages are:

Babies: "Being stage" zero to six months
Babies and toddlers: "Doing stage" six months to 18 months
Toddlers: "Thinking stage" 18 months to three years
Preschoolers: "Power and fantasy stage" three to five years
School-aged: "Structure and skill development stage" six to 12 years
Teenagers: "Identity, separation, sexuality stage" 13 to 19 years
Adulthood: "Recycling stages" 19 years onward

As your children reach a new stage, they can regress backward to a previous stage for a few days or weeks, until they move forward again. This is normal. A responsible teen decides to ride down the railing of a steep stairwell, just like a preteen would. He'd be regressing back to a previous stage – trying out "skill development" again. An adult starting a new job, learning new job skills, recycles back to the "structure and skill development" stage of school children. It's okay to make mistakes. A divorced adult meets a new love interest; they both go back to the babyhood "being" stage of wanting to be nurtured and loved unconditionally for just existing.

Children's developmental stage can often be viewed as misbehavior if parents don't understand what they are, how children exhibit them, and move through them. Most children go through stages and come out of them through no interventions from parents. Because milestones and stages are very important for understanding behavior, they are listed under each age group in Part Two. For more information on developmental stages, see books by Jean Illsley Clarke.

TEMPERAMENT

We used to think babies were born as blank slates and could be molded, changed, and taught, depending on the parenting style. Now we know that children definitely come out of the womb with their own personalities and temperament. Temperament is the "how much" of personality. It's the intensity.

Dr. Stella Chess and Dr. Alexander Thomas did wonderful ground-breaking work on temperament traits. They categorized three types of temperament and focused on eight areas that children differ in temperament.

Three types of temperament:

- Easy going or low keyed – 40 percent of children
- Slow to warm – 15 percent of children
- Spirited or high need – 10-15 percent of children

An easygoing child may have a mild temper tantrum and is easily distracted when they don't get a candy bar at the store. A high needs child will have a violent, screaming, thrashing tantrum that won't settle for an hour if they don't get the candy bar. Most high-need, "strong willed" children can be very challenging for their parents. They don't need more discipline, they need greater understanding.

These are on a continuum. A low persistence child will be easygoing, but a very persistent child will be on the spirited side of temperament.

It's important to remember that temperament is no indication of parenting style. A high need baby will grow into a high need child and no difference in parenting will change that.

Eight Areas of Temperament	Easy Going Child	High Need Child
Persistence	Loses interest.	Pushes to continue.
Sensitivity	Not bothered.	Bothered by noise, crowds, stimulation, light, smell, texture, taste and sensory cues.
Adaptability	Not bothered.	Bothered by surprises, transition and change.
Intensity	Mild reactions in temper tantrums, nightmares, protests.	Intense reactions.
Regularity	Predictable eating, sleeping and toileting patterns.	Unpredictable and irregular.
Activity level	Stays put with a low level.	Unusually active for age.
First reaction	Jumps in to new activities. Embraces new ideas, places and people.	Cautious.
Mood	Even-keeled and steady.	Unpredictable and changes rapidly.

So, easy going children are easily distractible (great for toddlers), not bothered by noise and light, so they sleep anywhere and eat anything. Easily adaptable, they travel well and are easily moved between caregivers. They have mild tantrums and usually recover from hurts very fast. They are easily put on a schedule and have regular eating, sleep periods, and potty times. They sit still for long periods in baby carriers and do not get bored easily. They participate easily in new activities and wake up happy and gurgling.

Discipline is generally easy for these children in that they respond most times and get over unhappiness fairly quickly. Because they adapt well to the adult world of schedules and conventions, they are easy to mold into a family life.

Slow to warm children are somewhere in the middle. They are stronger in some areas of temperament and less so in others.

Spirited, strong willed, or high need children do not easily fit in the adult world and may be perceived as needing more discipline, but this is not true. What they need is more adaptation in the adult world to meet their unique needs.

High need children are not easily distractible, so it's hard to use distraction as a discipline tool. They are bothered by noisy crowds and stimulating environments, often becoming over-stimulated and stressed, and need to shake off the anxiety with a temper tantrum or two. They are slow to adapt to new situations and don't transition very well. They have intense reactions to injustices, with massive tantrums that may include vomiting and head banging. They are very irregular and difficult to schedule. They have a high level of activity and never sit still. They are constantly on the go and into things. They won't stay in strollers, car-seats, or carriers. As babies, they want to be held most of the time or changed from carrier to carrier often. They often approach activities carefully. Their mood is very irregular, changing from minute to minute. They will be cranky one minute and happier the next. As babies, they cry a lot even when all the reasons have been checked by the parent. High need babies and children need extra effort in empathic parenting. Let's look closer at the high need spirited child, because, often they present extra problems in discipline.

The spirited child (high need) characteristics
Babies:
- Want to be held all the time
- Don't schedule well for eating, sleeping, and toileting
- Cry for no "apparent" reason
- React strongly against sleep training
- Won't stay for long in carriers, strollers and restraints

Toddlers and preschoolers:
- Smart – won't play with toys, mostly real items
- Frustration tolerance slower to develop

- Every day is unpredictable
- Mood swings in minutes
- Wakes up generally unhappy and crying
- Early night terrors and awakenings
- Severe separation anxiety
- Goes through most daily requirements: dressing, diaper changing, meals, bath, or tooth-brushing with negativity
- Clings in new situations and with strange people
- Wants to do everything themselves
- Not easily distractible
- Violent, intense tantrums
- Very active for the age
- Picky eater
- They are THE BOSS and things have to be done their way, in their time.
- Still requires a lot of attention and physical contact

School-aged:
- Very structured and needs routines
- Better tempered if gets adequate sleep and food
- Very determined in needs and wants
- May dislike clothing blends
- Requires a lot of physical contact
- May still have temper tantrums if goals thwarted
- May still have periods of separation anxiety and clingyness
- Need a lot of control over their lives
- Usually very intelligent

Teenagers:
- Not easily swayed by peers
- Requires a lot of physical contact with loved ones
- Moodiness is intense
- Determined and self-directed
- Handles responsibility well and has perfected coping skills
- Is suited for leadership and initiative roles

Discipline for spirited children

Do you have a child that when you send to time-out, you have to close the door and hold the knob? Even then, he's throwing books, blocks, and Lego™ at the door in anger? Do you have a child that sneaks out the bedroom window when he is grounded for the week? Do you have a child that when you spank her, she says, "that didn't hurt one bit!" and you know that if you spanked her harder, you are so angry, you may never stop?

You probably are raising a spirited child. They have many wonderful qualities and a keen sense of self-determination and autonomy. Yet, they are also very clingy in the early years. They do best with a very patient, non-controlling type of parent who will give them their direction and help them to make choices safely.

Spirited children are not the ones you want to engage in a power struggle. Avoiding power struggles with them doesn't mean that you let them "win." It means that you are not even going to pick up the battle armor. You are taking a more quiet, guiding approach by being their mentor, coach, and protector, rather then their director, controller, or dictator. You understand their unique needs and are providing for them.

For spirited children, keep your "must uphold" rules to three. In our house, matters of 1) safety, 2) hitting and 3) mutual respect are absolute issues that I will notice and deal with, no matter how tired, sick, or worn down I feel, no matter how tired, angry, and frustrated my child is. That doesn't mean I will take action right away. It means the action will be dealt with at some point, except in the matters of safety, which requires immediate reaction. Of course, if a child insists on running out in the street, I will immediately grab them out of harms' way. But the teaching will come later. I will let everyone calm down for a while and then deal with it.

Ask yourself: is this an issue I'm willing to battle for? Don't worry about spoiling your child by backing down too much. Backing down on non-essential issues shows you are not willing to engage in power struggles. I have personally found that my three spirited children, around the age of 3.5 years, became more receptive to the word "no," as they were able to handle frustration in increasing amounts. Up until then, I used the "change the environment" discipline tool to avoid areas of frustration for them. Being so self-directed, they couldn't understand their physical and emotional limitations and if it was easier to avoid many direct confrontations in their day, then that's what we did. By about age four, they could handle more talking, negotiating, and the reasons behind their limitations, so it was much easier to teach and guide.

Spirited children also need their physical needs met regularly in order to stabilize their moods. Carry a juice box or a cracker package wherever you go so they have an instant low blood sugar remedy. It can avoid a meltdown. Regular meals, naps and nighttime sleeps are important. As soon as they awake, a quick drink of juice helps temper their moods.

Allow spirited children their full range of emotions. Give them plenty of choices and decision-making powers. Give them a longer rope than you might for other children. They have an inborn need to have greater control over their lives.

Don't worry about treating them differently than the rest of your children. They are unique and you have to treat all your children uniquely. Some have greater needs in certain areas than others. Your children will notice that each child's needs are met – not equally, but as they need it, and they will feel comforted and secure by that knowledge. For more information on temperament, see books by Mary Sheedy Kurcinka and Dr. William Sears.

MATURATION THEORY

Arnold Gesell, Frances Ilg, and their colleagues at Yale University School of Medicine have been leaders in the research of child development. Many other researchers have followed and enhanced their original theories of child development. One theory is the Maturation theory. It's basically when a child is ready to do something, he will do it, and no amount of practice, nudging, or discipline will speed things up. Some children just naturally take longer to develop. As parents, we can nudge, but the child's natural development will decide exactly when and what he can do.

Implications for discipline

Every child is different and will mature and develop on their own schedule. Their time of readiness has nothing to do with intelligence, parenting style, or discipline techniques. It's just the way they are.

Although all children develop in the same sequence all across cultures, development is very much an individual matter. All children eventually pull themselves to stand and then walk and then learn to talk. But the ages of when children do those things are individual and unique.

BIRTH ORDER

The place the child draws in the family has an effect on the child's perception of himself and who he is. We, parents and society, often label children. They feel they have to live up to that label in order to belong as part of the unit we call family. Children have an inborn need to belong. If they perceive they only belong in a certain way, that's the way they act. Society and parents often have particular scripts for children to behave based on their birth order.

First-born children

Traits: perfectionists, reliable, conscientious, critical, serious and self-reliant.

Discipline tips: Give privileges with age. Encourage participation and fun in family activities, and encourage cooperation in activities with younger siblings. Stop their "mothering" or "fathering" tendencies by not putting them in charge of siblings a lot of the time. Encourage fun and free spontaneity. Reinforce that mistakes are for learning and it's okay to make them.

Middle-born children

Traits: mediators, sociable, independent, lots of friends, outside interests and a free spirit.

Discipline tips: Encourage help with household chores. Ask for their advice and opinions. Encourage individuality of their likes and dislikes. Emphasize their uniqueness. Avoid comparison. Put them in the number one position some days so that they get the first serving, the first name signed on the Christmas card. Encourage their private space. Get them some new things, too, instead of hand-me-downs. Encourage caretaking of younger siblings.

Youngest children

Traits: manipulative, charming, messy, blames others, precocious and rebellious.

Discipline tips: Give chores and responsibilities. Encourage age appropriate responsible behavior. Encourage independence and capability by letting them do things themselves. Let them express opinions. Give them some new items and special things, too. Although it gets harder, don't do any less than you did for the first or middle child. Help them join teams, volunteer in their school, enroll them in lessons, or assemble their baby book.

Only children

Traits: self-centered, mature, popular, questions many things, reliable, perfectionist and adult-oriented.

Discipline tips: Give lots of opportunity to develop friendships – churches, interests, play-schools, play-dates and group activities. Encourage sharing and problem-solving in conflicts. Let them find things to do when they are bored. Don't take them everywhere with you. Avoid discussing adult problems with them. They are children even though they may act mature. Keep experiences age appropriate. For more information about birth order, see Kevin Leman's *The Birth Order Book*.

Parenting perspective: beware the toddler-new baby syndrome

Many parents have their second child when their first is a toddler. Often, with the newborn, the older child looks so much bigger and well...older. Beware! Often, that perspective demands more grown-up behavior and bigger expectations than is appropriate for the toddler age. You have a new helpless baby and not much more brain power in your toddler than a baby that also has intense curiosity and outstanding mobility. Your toddler still is not capable to refrain from running onto the road, darting out to cars, spilling juice, having potty accidents, and many other babyish things. Your toddler can't understand your new demands. Have patience, perspective, and perseverance. He will become more responsible starting with preschooler age, but not much before.

When my first-born was four and I had a three-year-old and a one-year-old, I thought he was so grown up. I had much higher expectations of behavior than was appropriate. I thought he should know better because he was older. When my youngest was four, he was so babyish, and we forgave him for so much more. Each child in the birth order really does have a different parent!

LEARNING STYLES

Every child takes in information and processes it in different ways. There are three basic learning styles that people have:

Auditory learner: About 15 to 20 percent of the population predominantly learns this way. They need to <u>hear</u> instruction. They love to chatter and socialize and often talk to themselves when working on a quiet task. They are easily distracted by noise, but definitely prefer music to art. Children prefer phonics instruction for learning to read.

Visual learner: About 60 to 65 percent of the population learns this way. They need to <u>see</u> instruction. They do better with the "look-say" approach to learning to read. They have creative imaginations and daydream, and draw detailed, colorful pictures. They remember faces more than names and often see details rather than the whole picture.

Kinesthetic learner: About 10 to 15 percent of the population learns this way. They need to <u>do</u> the instruction, step-by-step, to learn it by methods of building models, producing something, taking things apart or by using the body in some way. They fidget and touch things constantly, which gives adults the impression, that they are "not listening." In reality they are. They are good at body movements, such as dance and sports. They love to touch and be touched and have difficulty with handwriting, verbal, and written instructions. My son used to jump on the sofa and wander around the living room when I was trying to read a bedtime story to my four children. I would yell at my son to sit and listen, but to no avail. Eventually, I banished him to bed. Once, while in bed, he recited the whole story word for word. I was amazed that he was listening very carefully while he was jumping all around the room. He needed to move his body to learn and take in information. When I learned about learning styles and multiple intelligences, I felt guilty for not allowing him to learn the way he does!

Implications for discipline

When you consider that discipline is all about teaching, you realize the importance of getting the message across to a child who may learn in a different way than the teacher. We may be auditory learners and love hearing instruction and wonder why that child is not "hearing" us! Most parents love to teach in the style they learn, which might not be the best for their child. We have to discover how our children learn and try to teach in that style.

Take your child's learning style into account when trying to get him to do something. Don't yell from the sofa! Most people are not auditory. You have to get up off the sofa, make eye contact with the child, and tell or show him what to do. A lot of effort, but will count as exercise and keep you slim!

Post pictures of tasks that need to be done in a day to remind a visual learner of what he needs to do. Have children do chores so they learn how to do them. That is great for kinesthetic learners.

Have tolerance for children that do not sit well in "circle time" in programs and preschools. They are often kinesthetic learners and are not trying to misbehave or be rude. When adults knit (kinesthetic learner) or doodle (visual learner) in my classes, I no longer feel that they are not listening. They need to do it in order to process the information. That's okay.

Schools are great at providing educational experiences for all learning styles from Kindergarten to grade four, but the higher grades have more demanding curriculums that make presenting in all learning styles more challenging. Parents need to advocate for their child in the school. If the curriculum is predominantly presented in one style, their child may be missing out of the knowledge or may be labeled a behavior problem.

How to know what the learning style is for you and your child

One way is to have them make popcorn. If you sit in another room and tell him the instructions, is it easier for him? Can you give him the box and have him read the words or if you draw pictures and help him see the instructions, is it easier for him? If you are in the kitchen and show him each step while he does it, is it easier for him?

When you relax and listen to music, do you prefer to:
1. Hum along? (Auditory)
2. Daydream? (Visual)
3. Dance or tap your feet? (Kinesthetic)

When you learn a new computer skill, do you prefer to:

1. Listen to tech support talk you through it on the phone? (Auditory)
2. Read a book with diagrams? (Visual)
3. Have a mentor sitting beside you and showing you what to do? (Kinesthetic)

If you had to sign up for one of three, which would you choose:

1. Music class? (Auditory)
2. Art class? (Visual)
3. Exercise class? (Kinesthetic)

If you attended a gathering, which would you remember the next day:

1. Peoples names, but not faces? (Auditory)
2. Peoples' faces, but not names? (Visual)
3. Who said and who did what? (Kinesthetic)

When standing in a crowded bus, which would you do:

1. Listen to your MP3 player? (Auditory)
2. Look at the advertising posters? (Visual)
3. Fidget or tap your feet? (Kinesthetic)

Generally, a child presents a preferred learning style at about age four. There are many tests on the internet to help you find your child's preferred style. Test yours, too, so you will know what your bias is. There is plenty of information on learning styles on the internet, and in education resource stores.

MULTIPLE INTELLIGENCES

In 1983, a Harvard psychologist, Howard Gardner, wrote a book called *Frames of Mind*. It took the education world by storm. It proposed that every person had eight different intelligences and were stronger or more able in some than others. It challenged the traditional emphasis in schools on only three intelligences (linguistic, visual-spatial, logical intelligence) measured by the standard Binet IQ tests. Gardner proposed that people are intelligent in many ways that our society and educational system doesn't recognize or value. He also proposed that parents need to recognize how their children are intelligent; because discipline is so rooted in teaching and education, it has widespread implications for how we teach children according to their intelligence.

> Every child is gifted.
> ~ Thomas Armstrong, Author

Multiple intelligences differ from learning styles in that people have only one learning style, whereby everyone has all eight intelligences but are strongest in one or two. Learning styles are strongly linked to the intelligences. People who are linguistically intelligent are usually auditory learners. Spatial intelligent people are generally visual learners and bodily-kinesthetic intelligent people are most often kinesthetic learners.

Eight ways of being smart

1. Linguistic intelligence: word smart – the ability to use words effectively.
2. Logical/mathematical intelligence: number and logic smart – involves the capacity to work well with numbers and/or to be adept at logic and reasoning.
3. Spatial intelligence: picture smart – involves the ability to visualize pictures in one's head or to create them in some two or three dimensional form.
4. Bodily/kinesthetic intelligence: body smart – the intelligence of the whole body (athlete, dancer, mime) as well as with the hands (machinist, jeweler, surgeon).
5. Musical intelligence: music smart – involves the capacity to carry a tune, remember musical melodies, have a good sense of rhythm or simply enjoy music.
6. Interpersonal intelligence: people smart – involves the ability to understand and work with people.
7. Intrapersonal intelligence: self smart – the intelligence of understanding oneself or knowing who they are.
8. Naturalist intelligence: nature smart – involves the ability to identify the natural forms around us (plants, birds, rocks) and includes sensitivity to other natural occurrences such as cloud formations, weather prediction, and geologic activity.
9. Spiritual intelligence: sixth sense smart – Gardner hasn't officially examined this as intelligence yet because he is researching whether it fits the prescribed criteria for intelligence.

Implications for discipline

Logical intelligence: Use reasoning, negotiating and consequences that focus on logistics of solving the problem.

Intrapersonal intelligence: Use goal setting, asking reflective questions and one-to-one chats as well as contracts.

Nature intelligence: Go for a walk in natural areas and talk.

Bodily/kinesthetic intelligence: Role play problems and act out solutions.

Spatial intelligence: Use charts. Read a book or watch a video about children's behavior and how the problem was solved. Draw pictures and diagrams.

Interpersonal intelligence: Use family conferences and collaborative problem-solving. Have your child teach a younger child about the behavior.

Musical intelligence: Sing the rules! Use music as a calm-down tool.

Linguistic intelligence: Talk out problems and solutions. Tell your child stories from your childhood. Read stories and book-tapes about how to deal with the problem.

For more information on multiple intelligences, *In Their Own Way*, and *7 Kinds of Smarts*, by Thomas Armstrong and *Frames of Mind*, by Howard Gardner are great books.

GENDER DIFFERENCES

There has been a lot of research lately on gender differences and how the female and male brain is wired. Some skills and abilities are predominantly female wired and others are male. As much as we tried to herald a gender-neutral parenting environment, children still behave in different, gender related ways. Ask any parent who has hosted a birthday party for 10 girls and a separate party for 10 boys. You will be guaranteed there were definite differences observed!

There are structural and functional differences in boys and girls brains caused by sex hormones. Generally, right brained people tend to be more creative, artistic, spatial, musical, and flexible. They have better long term memory and look at things in the big picture. They rely heavier on feelings.

Left brained people tend to be more logical and mathematical. They have more developed speech, short-term memory, are detail oriented, and excel in sequencing and problem-solving.

One study from the University of Minnesota showed that boys have more testosterone, which organizes their brain and nervous system in a way that they will be more physically active. This does not operate in a vacuum though. Socialization, environment, temperament, and personality all play a part in gender differences. Parents can consciously choose to make the socialization of their children gender neutral, yet, there are subtle influences that children notice and parents may not. For example, we raised our children with dolls, tea-sets, cars, and video games. Both our girl and boys had access and free invitation to choose to play with whatever they wished. They did up to about age four, when their friends started imparting comments that influenced their choices. The children would notice when we went to a fast food restaurant and the clerk would ask, "Do you want a boy toy or girl toy?" Inevitably, the boy toy would be some kind of car and the girl toy would be a doll, usually pink colored!

In consideration of discipline, here is a summary of what recent research has proposed about gender differences.

In their play styles, boys tend to like more space to play, and power in play (rockets, engines revving and boosting), competition (racing cars), and physical movement. Girls tend to like more social interaction (associative play), role playing (dolls), and co-operation in their play.

In the areas of multiple intelligences, females tend to be more linguistic intelligent: better at fine motor activity and social play. They are also more intrapersonal and interpersonal intelligent. Males tend to be more spatial and visual intelligent: better at hitting targets and playing computer games, as well as logical/mathematically intelligent. Males can better rotate an object in their mind. In bodily/kinesthetic intelligences, females have an upper edge in fine motor and boys in gross motor.

Boys have a larger amygdala, which is the internal part of the brain responsible for emotional arousal, physical activity, aggression, and competitiveness. They have a smaller corpus callosum that connects the two sides of the brain. Girls are more likely to use both sides of the brain on tasks, where as boys tend to use one side or the other. Could explain their inability to multitask! Boys' brains tend to mature more slowly, which may explain more high-risk behavior in the later teen and early adult years.

There are profound differences in the way both genders learn. More males are enrolled in special education classes than females, possibly due to the theory that males are more physically disruptive during classes because they need to move their bodies while taking in information. Boys learn best by moving around and manipulating objects. Educators may think that boys are misbehaving, when they really just learn differently. Boys are 10 times more likely to be diagnosed with Attention Deficit Disorder and boys are also more likely to drop out of school.

Boys tend to score lower on standard tests in Language Arts. Boys typically prefer non-fiction reading material, such as manuals, reference books, and comics, and rarely see male reading models throughout their school years. Girls prefer fiction, and most often, the themes offered through the curriculum are "chick lit" rather than the action orientated themes that boys prefer. Boys learn better through computer technology. Online courses may help to rescue boys from dropping out.

Girls are often left out of the high tech sector in education: computers and engineering. In an age of increasing majority of female enrollment in university education, only 28 percent of computer science degrees and 18 percent engineering degrees are earned by women. Most computer games that involve problem-solving under pressure are marketed to boys. This is a serious problem if high tech jobs will be the fastest growing occupations, as predicted. Girls tend to suffer from lower self-esteem in the junior high years of age 12 to 14 and tend to do more poorly in science and math during those years. A possibility would be to incorporate math, science, and technology into language arts, history, and music classes, which is where girls excel and vice versa for boys.

Implications for discipline

Some discipline tools might work better for boys and girls, based on their differences. What this means in discipline is that girls can verbalize how they are feeling better because the emotional center is in the amygdala, and the language, reflection, and reasoning is in the center of the cerebral cortex. Boys' emotions center only in the amygdala, which may make it hard for them to discuss or express feelings, although socialization does play a part too. For little boys, it's easier to hit than to "use their words," but it's a skill they can practice. If boys prefer competition, games like "whoever cleans up their room first gets to forego emptying the dishwasher for two days" may work better. Boys prefer action, so it might help to spice up chores a bit with some physical action. Girls would prefer collaborative approaches, such as "let's all pitch in to clean your room, and then we will all pitch in to clean your sister's room and it will all be done faster." Girls would prefer talking or telling stories to get the point across. Boys may "listen" better if directions are presented in body language, whereas girls may hear the verbal command better.

If anything, an understanding of gender differences may help create new ideas of how to motivate your son or daughter in homework, chores, and responsibilities. A good resource for gender differences is *Boys and Girls Learn Differently! A Guide for Teachers and Parents*, by Michael Gurian, Patricia Henley, and Terry Trueman Jossey-Bass.

PERSONALITY TRAITS

The personality traits we dislike in childhood are often the ones we value in adult-hood. Boisterous, noisy, and active children often grow up into extraverted and fun adults. Argumentative children grow into adults who can healthily assert their needs and excel in debating. Stubbornness as a child can grow into determinedness as an adult. Annoying, tedious, questioning and curiosity as a child can grow into life long learning and curiosity as an adult. We need to look at the positive side of the trait that we are stressing over in our child!

There are many types of personality assessments available on the internet and delivered through instructors. One of the most famous is the Myers-Briggs Type Indicator®.

Myers-Briggs® personality preferences

Myers and Briggs were famous for producing 16 types of personality preference. It helped people understand why conflicts developed between different kinds of people and what to do about them. It can be valuable in parenting to find out why certain behaviors in our children seem to strike a nerve in us as parents. Most often, it's a personality difference or personality collision, rather than a behavior problem perceived by the parent. It's important to remember that personality preference tools are a help in understanding people, and should not be used to label people or excuse behavior. Also keep in mind that people are not black and white. We have many shades of gray.

Some of Myers-Briggs® personality preferences are:

Introversion (I) and extraversion (E): How does one prefer to get their energy?

After a stimulating day, do you or your child need quiet, alone time or need to go out and visit people to recharge their batteries? Do you like to direct your energy to deal with people and their situations in the "outer world"? Or do you prefer to direct your energy to deal with ideas and information in the "inner world"? In our world, introverted people are often viewed as social lesser beings because they are not always the life of the party. However, introverts have many positives, too. Introverted children often outpace their extraverted peers in sensitivity, creativity, reflectiveness, and independence. As an introverted mom of five children, I sometimes feel overwhelmed by the noise and business of the household. Married to another introvert, and knowing that some of our children are extraverts that demand high energy activities and conversation from us, we know enough to spell each other off for a much needed quiet break to recharge our individual batteries. My daughter is also introverted and too many back-to-back social activities leave her pretty grumpy.

Feeling (F) or thinking (T): How does one prefer to make decisions?

How do you prefer to make decisions: from the heart or head? Do you use values, personal beliefs, and gut feelings? If so, then you are using the feeling approach. Or do you prefer to use a more logical reasoning, analytic analysis, deductive reasoning, and statistics? Then you use the thinking approach.

Sensing (S) or intuitive (N): How does one prefer to process their information?

Do you prefer to deal with facts, statistics, logical, objective arguments based on what you know? Or do you prefer to deal with ideas and new possibilities? Do you like the big picture given to you all at once, such as the entire course outline, or small pieces first leading in to the big picture? Perhaps being given just one chapter at a time helps your process.

Perceiving (P) or judging (J): How does one prefer to organize their life?

How do you organize your life? Are you neat, planned, stable, organized, and time conscious? Do you try to follow directions to a "T"? Or are you a go-with-the-flow type of personality, exploring new spontaneous opportunites and maintaining flexibility as the possibilities arise?

When you put these four preferences together, you get a personality profile that helps determine who you are and why you do things. There are 16 possible combinations that make up personalities. It's the same with your children.

Implications for discipline

When I have to work with a perceiving person, as I'm a judging person, I can run into trouble. I like to stick to the agenda with a class, keep to time commitments, and get very frustrated when the co-presenter doesn't. She's not misbehaving! She has very different personality characteristics, and they don't coincide with mine. It's the same with parenting and marriage. Understanding personality differences can be beneficial in understanding the dynamics you have with each child and also your partner.

Some parents need to control

Recognize your need for control as a personality characteristic. Judging parents can be very controlling and find it difficult to deal with the flexibility and spontaneity necessary in parenting. Children throw you curveballs everyday, and it can be incredibly frustrating to deal with if you don't recognize it's an irritation and work for changes. I am a judging person. (This is not to be confused with judgmental, which means an entirely different thing.) It is very hard for me to not be controlling in my parenting.

Controlling parents often make for more power struggles and behavior problems in children that are anxious for autonomy, choice, and decision-making. A controlling parent and a spirited child can be one of the most challenging combinations of personality and temperament! Try to channel your need for control in other areas of your life, other than parenting. Control can be very destructive to any love relationship and needs a healthy balance with the other person's need and ability to control.

Introversion and extraversion

Recognize your child's need to be quiet or boisterous. Some children have more social needs than others. Provide outlets for them. Don't force children to participate in circle time or preschool or sports teams, if they are homebodies and prefer solitude. Solitude is not the same as being a loner. Introverted children need their own space to retreat to.

An extraverted child's constant questions and talking is not to get you worn down. It's their extraversion nature, and they can't help it. They are extremely social people and love the phone, play dates, MSN™, and computer. Build in some quiet time for you each hour or day if you are an introverted parent with an extraverted child. Extraverted children tend to hate time-out. They often need to talk out their problems and feelings with another person, preferably a parent.

Feeling or thinking

Feeling children have more empathy for others and you can relate a moral story easier for them. They like harmony and enjoy pleasing people. They are good at seeing the effects of choices on other people's feelings. Thinking children need to have the logic spelled out for them. They tend to be firm and tough-minded. They respond more to people's ideas than feelings and need to be treated fairly. They may hurt people's feelings without knowing it.

Sensing or intuitive

Sensing children need the details first. They notice cracks in the wall and crumbs on the floor. They are realistic and practical and have a lot of common sense. They like to be given lots of examples when listening or reading. They prefer to solve concrete, practical problems rather than abstract ones. Teach them desired behavior in little steps.

Intuitive children tend to look at the big picture first. They find too many details boring and unnecessary and don't need them when receiving instructions. They also don't bother with details when they are speaking or writing. They prefer abstract problems and get impatient with practical ones. Teach them behavior by generalizing.

Perceiving or judging

Perceiving children need fewer schedules and more downtime. They don't need to be told "now" but "in the time period of lunch to dinner." They should be allowed a room or space to keep as cluttered and messy as they wish. They adapt well to changes and are extremely flexible. They may have trouble making decisions and have difficulty finishing projects. They may postpone unpleasant jobs and may get more done under a deadline pressure.

Judging children need to be structured and have schedules. Having an easygoing perceiving, "go with the flow" parent can be a challenge because they are a highly structured personality, and if the parent doesn't provide it, they may need it from somewhere: school, Scout groups, team sports, and clubs. Otherwise, they misbehave because of anxiety resulting from too much "go with the flow". They like to get things done and may make decisions too quickly. They like to use agendas, lists, goal-setting, and schedules.

For more information on how personality fits with parenting, a good book is *Nurture By Nature*, by Paul Tieger and Barbara Barron-Tieger.

LOVE LANGUAGES

Developed by Dr. Gary Chapman and Ross Campbell, MD, love languages are the most effective ways (for that particular person) that people use to say "I love and care about you," other than the standard, "Use your words," which not everyone does.

For example, my 15-year-old son loves having me make him a cup of tea. I sometimes get exasperated because I figured he was old enough to make it himself, and it would save me time not having to wait on him. But I realized his love language was acts of service. When I made him and brought him a cup of tea, he felt loved by me. Then, armed with this knowledge, I decided to do it willingly. Another child loves to give me gifts he made or bought. Another child loves to stroke my cheek, sit in my lap whenever I'm sitting down, or rub against me when we are both standing.

There are five love languages. Each is unique. Punishing a child by using one of their love languages can be particularly stinging to that person. If I wanted to really hurt my son, to punish him for a misbehavior, I would snap at him, "Make your own cup of tea."

The love languages are:

- Gifts
- Acts of service
- Words of affirmations
- Quality time together
- Physical touch

Cathie Pelly, parent educator, says to observe how your child expresses love to you. If he brings you little trinkets (gifts) or perhaps loves to rub against you when standing (physical touch) you know what his language is. Listen to what your child requests the most often (acts of service, hugs). Notice what your child most frequently complains about such as not enough time together (time). Give your child a choice between two options, such as "Would you like a treat (gift) or to go to the park with me (quality time together)?"

Implications for discipline

We often, without knowing, use love language tools for punishment, and it can be very damaging for the child whose preference is that love language. Here are some ways we punish:

Gifts: We take away or give away valued possessions of the child. If they don't clean up their toys or clothes, we use a logical consequence and throw out or give away their valued stuffed animals (they had received as a gift from you). This could be particularly damaging to a child whose love language is gifts.

Acts of service: Ignoring a child or making them do extra chores as punishment. Withholding affection would also be damaging because it makes them feel unloved.

Words of affirmation: Swearing, scolding, or correcting a child could be particularly damaging.

Quality time together: Time-outs or taking away a special event that involves the parent can be hurtful.

Physical touch: Ignoring by shunning or any type of physical punishment, such as spanking, slapping, pushing, or hitting, hurts a child whose language is physical.

We must be very careful to not punish or even discipline (teach) using a love language preference. It can really hurt that child more than we know.

SENSITIVE CHILDREN

Parenting clingy, sensitive children is a challenge. You want to nudge but not force. Find balance between pushing and protecting. Sometimes a bad experience can set them back. They are more affected by sensory input of all kinds, such as new people and surroundings. Their brains process more sensory information, and they notice more about their environment. As children get older, parents can talk to them about ways or strategies to help them cope in unpleasant situations. Start with something your child wants to do and go over ways to do it. Don't expect him to tough it out and endure. That can cause a setback. Encourage all the little positive strides he makes. Fears, scary movies, and strange people can affect sensitive children. Strange surroundings, being away from parents and home, sleepovers, and overnight camp can also stress a sensitive child. Don't force those events, even if his age mates are doing them. Your child is unique and requires unique parenting.

BRAIN DEVELOPMENT MILESTONES

It's very important to know where your child is at cognitively, so to understand why they think and act the way they do! The following is information based on Jean Piaget's Theory of Cognitive Development, as well as many modern books on child development. The research on children's brain development and mental health is growing exponentially and medical journals are a great source for up to date information.

Zero-two years – sensori motor stage – thinking is in the here and now

No real teaching can be processed yet. Your child's job is to explore and express emotion. This is the stage for parents to just keep abreast of damage control. Your child still pretty well has a baby brain but has an athlete's body.

One year

- Just beginning to realize she is a separate person from caregiver or Mom.

Two years

- Out of sight, out of mind; can't hold a memory. When Mom is gone, she's gone. Separation anxiety peaks.

- Doesn't understand time-out or what she did wrong and can't connect the action to the consequence.

- Can only sit still for a few minutes.

- It's the beginning of empathy and recognizing crying in others. Wants to help stop it because she may feel uncomfortable with another person's distress.

- Impulse control is very bad; knows "no," as Mommy is mad about something but not that she was not supposed to do something. Can better process, "Do this," instead of "Don't touch." Not doing something is an abstract concept that two-year-olds can't understand yet.

Three-five years - preoperational stage – thinking is based on perception, not logic

It helps to ask questions to check out the perception that your child is basing their thinking on. Preschoolers are still very egocentric, where the world revolves around them and not many others. Has better self-control of emotions, and tantrums will lesson as they can talk about their feelings better. Can simply negotiate in terms of what is in it for them because of ego-centricity.

Three years

- Can verbalize her feelings a bit.

- Can start simple problem-solving with two options.

- Begins to understand ownership and hence, sharing.

- Is radically honest in what she feels and will say direct things to people, regardless of the social acceptance. ("I hate this present." "Your house smells.")

Four years

- Temper tantrums lesson considerably as frustration tolerance increases.

- Separation anxiety eases; has enough memory power to understand that her parent usually comes back.

- Begins to understand different rules for different people and different parenting styles.

- Can delay gratification and wait for five minutes without distraction.

- Most adults can remember early memories from this age on.

Five years

- Understands "no" means "don't do."

- Can only sit still for about 10 – 15 minutes.

- Complies with simple requests 40 percent of the time.

- Develops more self-control.

- Can handle frustration and anger better, but still hits occasionally.

Six-12 years – concrete operational stage – can reason, but thinking is still limited to what familiar places, people, and events they know in their immediate life

Six years

- Can't multitask yet; too many instructions gets child confused.

- Can do simple chores at a time, such as emptying the dishwasher or putting all the blocks in a room in a basket.

- Beginning to learn how to sort.

- Understands apologies and sorry.

- Can begin to carry a small coin purse with allowance, but still needs reminding to not lose it. Parent actually has to constantly watch to make sure it's not lost.

- Can begin logical thinking of consequences and recognize how she plays a part in them.

- Cause and effect is now understood more logically.

- Begins to know what is dangerous but doesn't often know why.

- Loves the concepts of rules and the making, breaking, and enforcing them.

- Has a hard time with losing in sports and board games; may cheat to avoid losing; has a hard time dealing with sportsmanship behavior, such as congratulating the winner.

- Is honest to her feelings, so has a hard time reconciling social behavior, such as pretending to be happy for the winner while feeling bad for losing.

Seven years

- Can begin to empathize with other people's needs and feelings and can more easily self-sacrifice to meet other's needs.

- Has been considered the age of reason, by law; can begin to understand logical concepts based on familiar, tangible concepts in their world.

- Can start reflection skills on own behavior.

- Can sit still for a half hour to 45 minutes.

- Can begin to plan what is needed to do to participate in her activity (get equipment, uniforms, snacks) for sports, music, dance, art, scouts, and other activities.

- Begins to understand difference between reality and fantasy.

- Begins to comprehend and judge time.

- Begins to understand what is dangerous and why, but will forget when occupied with other thoughts; she knows it's dangerous to run into the road, but forgets when caught up in the excitement of a game.

Eight years

- Begins to remember where she hid or put special things and how to retrieve them. Before this age, parents have to remember where the child put things.

- Begins to wait with more patience in situations: waiting for the museum to open, waiting in restaurants, waiting for parents to finish phone calls.

Nine years

- Can cross the street alone because has ability to judge distance and timing of cars.
- Can understand two or three directions at once.
- Can get ready for activities and sports on own initiative.

10 years

- Can problem-solve enough to stay home alone and deal with little problems that come up.

11 years

- Stops hitting another person when angry.
- Can understand social implications of lying and swearing.

12 years

- Does chores without nagging and reminding; can begin to accept responsibility for a pet and the care of pet.
- Appreciates other's views and feelings and needs; can begin to see more gray areas than black and white points of views.

13-19 years - formal operational stage – children get their abstract thinking skills

They can separate and formulate opinion. They can talk, problem-solve, negotiate, argue, discuss, reflect, explain, and debate. They can understand gray areas but are still formulating their opinions and beliefs. They are finding out who they are as people and where they fit in their families, and communities.

- 12 years – is the age where the law in Canada provides that children are responsible for their crimes. They have enough understanding of actions and consequences to be prosecuted for crimes but are still young enough to escape adult prison and be treatable and rehabilitated.
- Can learn to do most adult tasks with direction and teaching and practice.
- Can understand child development, empathy, and problem-solving enough to baby-sit other children.
- Can be expected to attend services, meetings, dinner parties, and adult conversations.
- Can understand abstract concepts such as death, divorce, politics, and religion.
- Can sit still and listen for more then an hour.
- Can fully take on total responsibility for homework and education.
- Can begin to take on responsibilities of a paid job.
- Can fully take on assigned chores and should not need reminding to do them.
- Can handle money concepts, such as stocks, insurance, mutual funds, savings, credit cards, debit cards, and other abstract forms of money management.
- Can begin to evaluate risks for behaviors.

20-25 years – continual development stage – moving forward into adulthood, but still occasionally regressing!

Recent research indicates that the frontal lobes of the brain are still developing (the last part of the brain to develop), which is the part that controls the logical thinking, planning, and understanding consequences. This may explain why young adults still do some crazy things!

Implications for discipline

It's very important to know what is going on in a child's head. We want to know what they are capable of understanding for their age. Most misbehavior can be divided into two categories:

- Children don't understand their behavior, and they don't know better.
- Children do understand the outcome of their behavior and choose to do it anyway.

Often parents need to learn the differences before they decide to intervene when they think the child knows better, but doesn't.

Both categories depend on the child's cognitive ability. Both require different discipline approaches. The first should be heavy on the teaching side so children learn. The second should be heavy on the active listening and problem-solving side to find out why the behavior is continuing.

Almost all children from all cultures have the following normal characteristics:

- They start out ego-centric and self-focused and become more aware of others as they grow. When children begin their logical thinking around age seven, they can understand other people's feelings.
- They can put themselves in danger, as their curiosity grows faster than their body or brain development.
- They are learning all the time and are exceptionally curious.
- They are naturally messy and don't know how to clean up.
- They are naturally noisy, boisterous, and excitable.
- They are naturally shy in groups.
- They all want to feel big, proud, and important.
- They have their own dream world.
- They are naturally very active until about age 12 and need bursts of physical stimulation between quiet times.
- They operate on their own pace, not in the hurry up world of their parents. They are not time focused.
- They control how much they eat, sleep, learn, and toilet. Parents can't control these functions no matter how hard they try!
- They don't know how loud they are.

- They have conflicts with things, people, and situations, just like any other person on the earth.
- They naturally want to please those people they love.
- They are spontaneous and do things without thinking.
- They are completely honest.

Implications for discipline

Children are unique and need to be accepted for their unique characteristics. Some characteristics, such as developmental stages and milestones, birth order, and maturity levels will change with time, growth, and patience! Other characteristics, such as temperament, personality traits, love languages, sensitivity, learning styles, multiple intelligences, and gender traits will not change as the child grows and parents need to accept and love the child unconditionally.

> All of these characteristics are natural and children learn how to adapt to a more adult life as they grow. It takes at least 18 years to practice and perfect it. That's why we call it childhood.

Part Two:

Tools From the Trenches

THE ALL TIME BEST DISCIPLINE TOOL EVER: A HUG

When there are power struggles, conflict, and angry outbursts in the home, a great way to break the cycle and send positive energy and vibes is to simply give someone a hug. It might be rejected, but chances are it won't. If it is rejected, just remember how much you love the other person, and imagine yourself hugging them. The other person (whether it be a toddler or teenager) will probably welcome the connection. You are the adult. You can make the first move. Give your child a hug today.

Discipline tools

All of the tools in the next five sections are accumulative. Starting with tools for babies, all of them can be used for the older age groups, as well. There are new tools for each age group that work particularly well for that age. Some tools are in every section because they are universal relationship tools, such as problem-solving, change environment, parent time-out, I-statements, and modeling, but they are used in different ways for that particular age group.

NOTE: The success of the tools is directly proportional to the strength of the bond you have with your child. If you have sworn off punishments, the bond will be great, and these tools should have maximum success. If you are interspersing punishment with the tools, you may have limited or no success. If these tools don't work in changing your child's behavior and increasing your mutually respectful parenting relationship, then give up punishments, work on building the relationship bond in the areas described in Chapter 2, and then try the tools again in a few months.

Another very important point to keep in mind is that if you are unsure if your child's behavior or developmental stage is normal, ask someone who has experience with a lot of children: a mom of several older children, a child care worker, or paediatrician. They will be able to tell you if your child has a mental, emotional, or behavioral disorder that is out of the normal range.

7

Discipline Tools for Baby 0 - 1 Years:
Attachment

 Babies' needs haven't changed much over the past thousands of years, but cultural practices of meeting those needs change every generation.

When I mention discipline for babies, I think parents imagine a baby isolated in a time-out room or a baby being spanked. That is not what I intend! When I ask parents when they start to discipline children, I get all kinds of replies ranging from conception to two years of age. Some parents think discipline begins more into the toddler years, when their babies are crawling, walking, and getting into things. One mom suggested that discipline began the day her breastfeeding five-month-old bit her nipple.

A 1994 Statistics Canada survey showed that 19 percent of U.S. mothers spanked their children under one year of age. Many babies in the second half of the first year are beginning to crawl, toddle, and walk, and with their newfound mobility, they are reaching out and touching things and exploring objects that are not appropriate. That's when parents begin to wonder how to say "no" and teach their baby not to touch. Often, mild hand slapping begins and some parents choose to spank.

Another discipline method that parents use is shaking the baby. Parents are told very often to not spank or hit the baby. But out of frustration with the baby "not listening," the parents shake the baby. With the prevalence of Shaken Baby Syndrome evident in newborns to children four years of age, we really must look at the roots of the syndrome, which is most often, discipline. Parents must know that a baby can't understand the word "no."

We discuss discipline tools with a baby for two reasons. First, the baby year is a time for bonding, attachment and relationship connection; a solid concrete foundation that effective discipline is built upon. Also, the literal interpretation of the word "disciple" means to teach. We "teach" babies from the moment they are born, by our responsiveness and nurturing, that they are loved and cared for.

YOUR BABY'S DEVELOPMENTAL STAGE

From the ages of birth to one year, your baby is in the "being" stage of development. His job or tasks that he must accomplish this year is to develop trust, be loved, be recognized by his caregivers, and form attachments with the major caring person in his life. He needs to learn to trust his parents and caregivers to meet his needs and learn that the world is a safe, predictable, and good place to be.

Typical baby behaviors

- Cries and fusses to make needs known and communicate feelings.
- May cry incessantly at times where the cause can't be uncovered.
- Cuddles and sleeps.
- Makes a lot of sounds, such as gurgling, screeching, and babbling.
- Looks at and responds to faces, eyes, colors, and moving objects.
- Imitates those around him.
- Explores his surroundings with all of his five senses (see, hear, touch, taste, smell) as he gets more mobile; puts many objects in his mouth to taste them.

DEVELOPMENTAL MILESTONES

These are approximate milestones – children can have great variation in the time-table that they do things.

Physical milestones

- Two months – begins to smile.
- Four months – hand to mouth transferring of objects begins.
- Five months – teething begins.
- Three to four months – settles into a predictable pattern of eating, sleeping, toileting, playing, and fussy times. Crying is drastically reduced.
- Six months – can sit up with adult support.
- Eight months – can begin crawling.
- 10 months – can pull himself up to tables and explore.
- 12 months – can walk and begin to explore at a higher level. Can reach and touch everything!

Psychosocial milestones

- Eight months – beginning of stranger anxiety. Does not like to be held by strangers.
- 10 months – beginning of separation anxiety. Does not want to leave main caregiver.

Cognitive milestones

- Around a year old, realizes that Mom is a separate person from him.
- Develops "object permanence," where they realize things can exist, even if they are hidden.

PARENTS MATTER

Unhelpful parenting behaviors

- Leaving the baby to cry for more than 90 seconds, day or night.
- Not picking up and cuddling the baby when upset, hurt, or sick.
- Not providing sleep, food, holding, cuddling, or stimulation when needed.
- Not actively looking for the baby's facial or body language cues for her wants and needs.
- Not providing protection from unsafe environments.
- Limiting the baby's exploration by keeping her contained in containers (car seats, swings, playpens) too long.

Helpful parenting behaviors

- Holding, singing, speaking, and reading to the baby.
- Nurture the child through touch, words, actions, and feelings.
- Provide consistent love, safety, protection, and nurturing care.
- Provide food, warmth, sleep, stimulation, touch, comfort, and security as the baby communicates the need, rather than on a calendar, clock, or other schedule conducive to the parents' needs rather than the baby's needs.
- Provide parent self care.
- Get in the habit of reading and learning about child development.

DISCIPLINE TOOLS FOR BABIES

Parent time-out
Fulfill needs
Learn child development
Substitution
Supervision
Prevention
Redirection
Change environment
Distraction
I-statements
Active listening
Spend time together
Parental problem-solving
Holding, hugs, and cuddles

Parent time-out

Maintenance time-out: This is essential. Because parents are loving and give much of their time and energy to children, as they should, often, they need a time-out. They need time away from home and responsibilities to do hobbies, self care, socializing, and to be good to themselves so they can come back home and be good parents. Some parents need time in the home and would prefer everyone else, such as partner and children, to go out. Children's bedtime and naptime provide a built in time-out for parents, but it is not the time to get things done. It's your time: to refresh and rejuvenate yourself. You will be a much better parent.

Anger time-out: Parents need to take time to calm down before they can think clearly.

Fulfill needs

One of the most important baby discipline tools. Give babies what they need. Babies are purely motivated by simple basic needs: hunger, tiredness, loneliness, attention, boredom, touch. These are basic needs that can easily be provided by a caring, tuned in parent. Don't forget the baby's emotional needs. The field of infant mental health (birth to age three) is a growing specialty, which recognizes the importance of early experiences in shaping a child's relationship with their family and the larger world. Problems that show up in elementary school or even earlier in daycare often have roots in the child's experiences as a baby.

Learn child development

This is the second best baby discipline tool. Knowing the cognitive development of babies helps to assure parents that babies and toddlers can't manipulate them. Manipulation is a higher order thinking skill that babies simply do not have yet. It's an old folklore that is still passed along to parents today, in spite of what we know about brain research. It also helps parents to understand their child's separation anxiety at bedtime and before parent outings.

Substitution

Your baby is playing with a sharp paring knife she found in the dishwasher. Holding out a shiny big spoon to catch her attention and then gently taking away the paring knife while she is focused on the spoon is the way to use substitution. Essentially, it's taking away her focus on one thing and enticing it with another. It's very easy to use on babies and toddlers because their attention span is so limited.

Supervision

Children up to the age of 10 need constant supervision by an engaged, aware, and responsible adult, 24 hours a day, every day of the year. Supervision should never take the place of discipline. Even when children "know better," they make mistakes, and for safety reasons, should be watched.

Prevention

Knowing what are problem areas and eliminating them is a great tool. If you know (from previous experience) that your child will draw on walls with markers, then put the markers up high on a shelf until you have time to supervise their use. If you know your child is curious about everything, make sure she doesn't see things, so you don't have to say "no" and endure a tantrum. If you know your child wants to touch everything at the mall, go shopping without her.

Prevention also includes having a plan ahead of time about what you are going to do when a behavior happens. If the baby goes through an inconsolable time crying during supper when you are trying to get dinner on the table, sometimes it helps to have a plan. How will you deal with that in the future? Can you freeze ready-made casseroles ahead of time? Can you hire a mother's helper for those two difficult hours? Can you order in dinner through the week? Having a plan helps you to feel in control.

Redirection

Redirection is a wonderful tool for babies and toddlers. If your child is crawling to the shiny stack of CD cases, pick her up and point her in the direction of the plastic bowl cupboard and get her interested in an item or two. Again, her limited memory and attention helps to make this tool effective.

Change environment

Childproof! It's easier to change the environment or situation, than another person. Make your home safe, stimulating, and easy to access for your child. There are resources at your local health unit on how to make your home safe for your child's age. As an exercise in my parenting class, I hand out a plate of cookies to parents and then take it back when they reach for one. It demonstrates the concept that it's very frustrating to not have something that is enticing and dangling in front of them. It would have been better to not have offered the cookies in the first place. (After I made my point, I do offer the cookies!)

If you had an elderly mother come to live with you, wouldn't you modify your home to accommodate her needs? Do your children have a right to have their needs met in their home? Is it their home too? We put a lot of effort into decorating a nursery but fail to take into account a baby's or toddler's needs. Objects that are accessible need to be appropriate for her. Inappropriate items should be out of sight. This is better than slapping hands for touching breakables. Move the breakables up high or out of sight and out of reach for a few years.

Distraction

Distraction, like substitution or redirection, works on the limited memory of your child. It's moving her attention from one thing to another, more appropriate focus. Your child is squirming while diaper changing. You can't clean her properly, and she is focused on the change and how much she doesn't like it. You keep a basket of seldom seen toys right by the change table to distract her and keep her hands busy. Or change her standing up, behind her, while she can look at herself in a mirror. Or change her while she is watching a baby video.

I-statements

We do these all the time for babies. We don't necessarily say the "I" part, but they are mostly positive I-statements. Positive I–statements are the only ones babies need. Say positive statements many times a day, so you are in the habit of focusing on the positive aspects of child behavior. You'll be well in practice for the toddler years.

- "I love you!"
- "I'm so glad you are my baby."
- "I can help you feel better."
- "I can get you what you need."
- "I think you are the cutest most wonderful baby."
- "I love your sweet little smile!"

Active listening

This conveys acceptance and total understanding of where that person is right in the moment. It doesn't mean agreement. It lets the baby know you are validating her feelings. (The feeling word is underlined.)

"Oh, you little sweetie, you are <u>upset</u> because your diaper is wet? Here, I'll change you!"

"Sounds like my little baby is <u>hungry</u>? We will feed you right now."

"Did that sound scare you? It's okay to feel <u>scared</u>. Mommy will give you a hug."

Spend time together

<u>Stranger anxiety:</u> Around eight to 15 months, stranger anxiety will set in. Your child will look at other faces anxiously and look for your face, which is familiar and comforting to him. Avoid passing him around at this stage if he looks uncomfortable or starts crying.

<u>Separation anxiety:</u> This begins around 10 months and could last until three or four years of age. It's a resurgence of clinging, as your child becomes aware that

you can leave him and feels anxious when you do. He does not know when or if you will ever be back because his brain can't think that abstractly yet. If you must leave him, say a firm goodbye and leave him in the arms of someone loving. They can console him when you are gone. Meet his dependency needs, and he will feel secure letting you go. Try to minimize separations at this stage. Children, who have been separated from parents for too long, become extra clingy and need extra security before they let go again. Parents away on vacation, business trips, or out for the day sometimes experience this renewed clinginess. It's the same with older children who have been away at camp or holidays and away from their parents. They will become extra clingy for a while. Some children are more intense about letting go. Some are more okay with it. Accept where your child is at and adjust your separations accordingly.

Parental problem-solving

Have you ever watched a one-year-old with a shape sorter? They are problem-solving. They take what they know and apply different possible outcomes to see if it still works. Tap in to their creativity and brainpower to help them explore possibilities. You will guide them in their problem-solving by coming up with most of the ideas first, but they will soon catch on. As you do most of the problem-solving, talk out loud to get them in the practice of talking out loud. "Hmmm…let's see how we can solve this problem. Should we put the square block in or the round block?" Of course, they won't quite understand you yet, but you are getting into the habit of verbal problem-solving. You need this skill for toddlerhood and older children. They learn the method of problem-solving by watching and listening to you do it. Children are great mimics!

Holding, hugs, and cuddles

Every human being needs touch and cuddling, no matter what age. It's a basic need. If nothing else, it helps your baby. When they cry, try picking them up as soon as they start. Babies who are responded to in the first 90 seconds show better security and fewer anxieties than babies and toddlers that are not responded to or ignored or scolded for crying. Babies that are not ignored cry less in the long run. Even easy-going temperament babies need a lot of hugs and cuddling. When your children are grown, you aren't going to say, "I wish I had a cleaner floor." You will probably say, "I wish I held my baby more when she was little."

SPECIAL BABY BEHAVIOR CONCERNS
SLEEP ISSUES

Sleep is the holy grail of new parents. It's the number one parenting problem in almost every baby class that I've taught. Parents have a hard time to adjusting to the reduced sleep that parenting brings. There are tricks to try to get baby to sleep, but much is based on temperament, personality, birth order, and all the child's unique characteristics that parents can't change. Much of the sleeplessness of parenting has to be dealt with in terms of parental acceptance. Your child is unique and won't sleep like any other baby.

It helps to think of your child as a special flower in your garden. You have been given a special seed and your job as parent is to find out how much water, sun, food, and care it needs.

Temperament and sleep

High need children often do not schedule very well. They do not adapt well to sleep training or separation from parents during the day or night. Consider your child's personality and temperament before deciding on a sleep training program. Regardless of the program, be sure the baby is not left to cry it out. That is damaging to the baby's emotional and psychological development.

Cognitive ability: are they scared or stubborn?

One-year-olds still have limited memory and almost no cognitive reasoning skills. Therefore, they have no means to "manipulate" parents. When you are out of sight, you are pretty well out of memory. They have no concept if, or when, you are coming back. So when you leave them to cry at night, they may be left feeling abandoned, distressed, and insecure. Often, the child with a limited memory "gives up" hope that comfort is coming and resorts to self coping techniques to offset the loss of the parent at night. To a parent, it looks like the ignoring is "working." A baby is left wondering what happened to Mom, who usually comes quickly during the daytime distress, but not during the nighttime distress. They don't understand the difference. They may stop crying to cope with the isolation but are left feeling devastated.

Behavior versus feelings

Many parents think that "crying it out" "works" in that the child stops crying and goes to sleep. However, we have to question the term "works." The plan works in that it enables parents to not have to get up at night, and they can get some sleep. It can be successful for some children in shaping their behavior, but at a cost to their emotional wellbeing. When parents say "it works," they are not taking into account the residual emotional damage to their infants' task of developing trust.

We also know that sleep problems are never done once. Often sleep training has to be repeated over and over due to typical upsets in sleep patterns: travel, teething, separation anxiety, guests, over-stimulation, hunger, thirst, ear infections, night terrors, and nightmares, illness, vaccinations, developmental milestones, and family changes/stress.

Attachment theory

The first three years of a child's life are critical years for developing attachment and trust with the parent. If a child is not responded to most of the time with comfort and nurturing when they are sick, upset, or hurt, they can develop attachment problems. This inconsistency can affect how secure and anxious the child is during waking hours. They can become clingy and dependent. It's what experts call an insecure attachment, whereby the child receives nurturing at some time and not others.

Brain research

Recent advances in MRIs (magnetic resonance imaging) done on small children's brains show the stress hormone, cortisol, impedes brain cell connections. New research is also testing saliva for cortisol as an indicator of a baby's stress levels. Therefore, it's imperative for parents not to leave the child in distress for extended periods of time. New research shows that early distress experiences by a pre-verbal child is retained and stored in the amygdala centre of the brain, which controls emotions and may contribute to later emotional problems, such as anxiousness, low self-esteem, and insecurity. It's a myth that we aren't affected by experiences we had as a tiny baby, just because we didn't have language to tell anyone about it yet and that we can't remember what happened before we could talk.

Babies don't develop object permanence until they are at least 10 months old. That means when parents are out of sight, babies don't know they are still around, even in another room. Sleeping next to a baby ensures their security in knowing that the parents are near because baby can see, touch and smell them.

Reframe the situation

A poll by the U.S. National Sleep Foundation found that 69 percent of parents reported frequent sleep problems. If 69 percent of parents are experiencing their children's sleep problems, it seems that frequent waking is developmentally normal and not a "problem" at all. Perhaps it's just an occupational hazard of having small children!

A certain number of children are born bad sleepers. The parents read every book and try every trick, but the child still won't fall asleep, stay asleep, or wakes up too early. If there was an easy answer, there would not be a need for more sleep books!

The situation can change in a few weeks or months. Your child's developmental stage will be different and things will get better on their own. If you are currently meeting your child's needs for emotional closeness and security, it will enable him to become secure, happy, and independent as he grows older.

All children have insecure periods in their lives where they need more closeness and comfort. It's not an either/or meeting of needs. How can you meet your sleep needs and his need for comfort and closeness? Do whatever works for both of you so that everyone is sleeping and no one is crying.

Most children that have slipped into the habit of being parented back to sleep can develop self induced sleep habits by the time of their second year molars, around 2.5 years. This could be longer for high need children.

Reconsider co-sleeping. Cultures where children and parents sleep together have almost no sleep problems in children. In North America, routine co-sleeping was common until the invention of central heating in the 18th century. Since then, many children do not respond well to nighttime separation.

Babies have not changed in their needs over the last 10,000 years of evolution. Humans are the only mammals that put their children to bed separate from them. You would never see a lion mother put her cub to sleep in a bush 10 feet away from her. Sleep practices are very much influenced by culture.

In my classes, many parents discuss the prevalence of even school-aged children cuddling up in the family bed for nurturing, security, and non-sexual touch and comfort, in a lifestyle of hurried contact and two parent working families. This was taboo even 10 years ago.

Monika, a mom on an email list, says, "In our family, co-sleeping has created children who LOVE bedtime. We never have a fight when it's time to hit the sack. I recall my entire childhood being a bedtime war zone. After a long hard day of parenting, the LAST thing I want to do is end the day with a screaming fight."

So don't abandon your crying baby at night to teach her to sleep. Rather, focus on teaching new sleep associations: sleep with Dad, white noise, music, special sleep blankets, sing, put on a movie, or use an aquarium for white noise. Before you put the baby down, make sure she is drowsy and awake so she is aware of the sleep association. Often, they are in a light sleep for the first 20 minutes and then wake up, need their sleep association, and drift back into deep sleep for a few hours. How do you tell if your baby is in a deep sleep? Raise her arm and see if it falls lightly or plunks.

THE SAFER FAMILY BED

Your baby has been crying for hours in the middle of the night. Nothing will calm her. Finally, she settles in your arms but awakens and screams the minute you set her in her crib. Out of exhaustion, you take her into bed with you and both you and baby snuggle in for a cozy sleep.

Except for North America and Europe, most people in countries around the world sleep with their children. The trend is also increasing in Canada, although many parents don't like to admit to the practice. They worry about safety concerns, and advice from friends and relatives that once their baby is in bed with them, they'll never get her out. But no studies have shown this to be so.

There are many ways to have a safer family bed. Some parents try the sidecar approach. They put the crib next to the bed. The lowered crib side is moved right next to the bed. Some parents just get rid of the box spring and put a king size mattress down on the floor so there is no danger of falling. Just as adults are aware of the edges of their beds and seldom fall off, mothers and babies become astutely aware of each other as they sleep, so rolling over on baby is not common if certain precautions are taken. The risk of suffocation and falling can be reduced by the following tips:

- Never put a baby to sleep on a waterbed.
- Never sleep with a baby while under the influence of drugs and alcohol (even over the counter drugs) or if a partner is under the influence of the same.
- Never leave a baby unattended on an adult bed.
- Keep pillows, comforters, and sheets away from a baby. Dress the baby in a warm sleeper and Mom in a warm cotton turtleneck, so the upper body doesn't get cold.
- Always put a baby on her back to sleep.
- Avoid siblings in the same bed. If siblings do share a bed, Mom should sleep between the siblings and the baby.
- Make sure there is no gap between the bed and wall, or the bed and headboard.

There are many advantages of sleeping with baby:

- Mom can breastfeed without Mom and baby fully waking up. More sleep for Mom means a happier Mom.
- Sleep sharing facilitates increased connection with a baby when Mom returns to work.
- The baby has increased touching and tactile stimulation.
- Increased father-baby connection if the father is in agreement with sleep sharing.
- Increased awareness of close proximity between Mom and baby may synchronize their breathing patterns and prevent SIDS (Sudden Infant Death Syndrome).
- Babies experiences less stress of crying and separation anxiety, which is good for healthy brain development.

Since the infant's developmental task during the first year of life is the development of trust, the family bed is ideal because it helps Mom immediately meet the infant's needs for food, security, warmth, and closeness.

For parents who are worried that their children may never leave their bed, rest assured! Children's habits can be broken in about three days, so when the family bed is no longer working for the family, new sleep arrangements can be accustomed to in a very short time. There is no research that family beds are damaging to children emotionally or cognitively.

Research shows that 43 percent of babies who were sleeping through the night began waking up again later. All babies wake two to seven times a night. Some put themselves back to sleep and others need parents' help. It helps to be boring in the middle of the night. Avoid playtime but comfort baby back to sleep.

Sleep begets sleep. An overtired, over-stimulated child becomes cranky and harder to put down to sleep. A well-rested child actually sleeps better.

"I do not think adding abandonment to the already complicated task of falling asleep is the answer. Teaching them new associations is the answer. This is why the bedtime ritual is so important. For some reason, it is hard for children to 'let go' to fall asleep. They need certain things to be done to feel comfortable. I like to think of it as a mini death: a letting go. And we should teach them that they are fine to let go (of consciousness) because we are there for them. Of course, I will also say that complete fulfillment of her needs should never compromise your ability to parent. Sleep is the key, and if you find you are getting angry, then it is a wake up call to change something," says Shay, mom of a toddler.

Soothing a crying baby

It's 8:00 pm and your baby won't stop crying. You've checked for signs of illness, and she seems healthy. She's just not happy, and you are desperate to sooth her. What can you do?

Infants cry because it's the only way they can communicate their needs. Between the ages of birth to three or four months, the average infant normally cries one to three hours a day, most often at suppertime and early evening. It's often thought that they need to discharge the energy from the day.

About 20 percent of babies are born with a fussy, spirited, high need temperament. They are not trained to be fussy, and their temperament is not a reflection of your parenting skills. They are just fussy babies that need extra care and attention all day long (and probably night too).

Another 10 to 20 percent of babies are afflicted with colic. Colic is different from temperamental fussiness and is a regular pattern of crying that lasts for four hours at a time, between two weeks and four months of age. It occurs most days. The reason is still not clear but recent research points to an immature nervous system rather than gassiness, as previously thought.

Some strategies to soothe a crying baby:

- Check for illness. As you get to know your baby, you will have intimate knowledge when things are not normal for her. Trust your "gut feeling" if you think she is sick or something is seriously wrong. Call your local health nurse or medical advice line or take her to the hospital emergency.
- Offer food next. Even if you've heard that babies should eat every 1.5 to 2.5 hours, perhaps she is going through a growth spurt and needs to "cluster" feed for several days. You can't overfeed a baby. She will turn her head away from breast or bottle and not suck if it's not food she is looking for.
- Check her diaper. A heavily wet or poopy diaper won't bother some babies but will irritate others.
- Check for gas. Try carrying the baby with your forearm around her tummy and gently rub her back. Or lie her down on your forearm with your inside elbow supporting her head and your hand supporting her pelvis. Gently rub her back with your other hand.
- Check for prickly tags on clothing or hairs and threads wrapped around toes or fingers or neck. The baby may be in pain from some kind of irritant.
- Check if the baby is too hot/too cold. Babies should wear the same amount of clothing layers that you do.
- Check if the baby needs more sleep. Some babies wake up and seem fussy. Try not to disturb them and encourage them to go back to sleep by patting their tummy and saying "shhhhhh".
- Motion really calms fussy babies. Walk, dance, and rock. Go for a walk in the car or stroller.
- White noise from a fan, vacuum, hair blower, running water, or dishwasher can help too. Buy a white noise machine that will play white noise or nature sounds or make your own recording.
- Carry your baby in a sling, wrap, or similar carrier. Studies done in cultures, where babies are constantly carried, show that babies cry very little. Warmth, touch, and motion work magic for babies because they simulate life in the womb.
- Wrap your baby in a blanket heated from the dryer. Then rock her.
- Music or humming may help calm the baby.
- Loosen clothing or swaddle the baby. Flinging arms and legs can upset some babies. Others like loose clothing that allows movement of arms and legs.
- Babies that are over-stimulated from too many activities can be soothed by a dark, quiet room with gentle rocking, a swaddled body and perhaps a soother if they take one.

- Burp baby. Maybe it's gas.
- Change the position she's in.

Inconsolable crying

If your baby's doctor diagnoses colic or you have a fussy baby, get support systems in place for you and partner. If you start feeling helpless, frustrated, and angry because your baby is still screaming, hand her over to a partner, friend, or relative that can give you a break. Make a list of her likes and dislikes to post on the fridge for the caregiver. If no one is around, make a safe choice and put the baby down in the crib, while you take some deep breaths and calm down. It's okay to take a breather, even if the baby is screaming. Everyone has different tolerance levels to an infant's crying, and it can affect a parent very deeply.

> There will be times when you have tried everything you can think of and no matter what you do to comfort your baby, he still can't stop crying.

It's not something they can control. The parent's reaction and tolerance level to crying determines whether or not they can hug and cuddle the crying baby but still remain calm to the noise. It's hard on parents because they want to help and stop the crying. Inconsolable crying is normal from three weeks to three months at certain periods of the day. Usually, the "arsenic" hour from 4:00 to 8:00 pm is the worst. It's the time that Mom is most stressed and tired from the day and trying to get dinner on the table and welcoming home family members. Trying to comfort the baby may help the parent by giving them the feeling that they are doing something, but if parents are intolerable to the crying, then putting baby in a safe place is the better thing to do.

For your baby's sake, take a break!

Be conscious of your partner's tolerance levels, too. Spell each other off from holding the baby to take a break.

Shaking a baby can cause blindness and damage the retina as well as cause brain damage. It only takes a few shakes and a few seconds to damage a child for life, or kill him. Be sure that anyone you leave baby with can tolerate crying or put the baby down also. It's okay to know your limitations for tolerating crying. Attachment parents have a hard time listening to it because they are so in tune with the baby's feelings and needs. It's okay to let it go and put the baby down for a few minutes to deal with your anger and frustration and helplessness. Walk away and regain control. There is a big difference between systematic letting baby cry it out and leaving baby for 10 minutes to get a grip on your own feelings.

Even though it doesn't seem like it at the time, this crying stage passes very quickly. From four to five months of age, the baby's crying time decreases immensely.

NURTURING CHILDREN'S SECURITY NEEDS

> **♛.** Babies, toddlers, and children whose dependency needs
> are met promptly and empathetically become much more
> secure and independent sooner than children whose dependency
> needs have been dismissed or ignored.

The dictionary definition of security is: untroubled by danger and apprehension; confident, safe against attack or threat of attack. According to Maslow's Hierarchy of Needs, security is a very important need in the baby, toddler, and preschooler stage. A secure child becomes an independent child that has a healthy self-esteem and confidence in their world, community and family.

Allowing the child to fulfill his developmental stages and needs within safety limits and with the unconditional love of his parents will help build a child's security.

Parent actions that build children's security

Sleep: Allow the child to sleep when needed. Avoid sleep training by abandonment methods such as crying it out. Leaving a baby to cry it out in distress, whether it is daytime or nighttime, does not help him form trust or security, nor is it respectful to the child.

Crying: Responding to baby within 90 seconds drastically reduces their crying time. Picking up a baby in distress does not spoil a baby. It's giving them what they need.

Separation: Avoid separation if your child has a difficult time separating from you, especially prevalent during the ages of one to four.

Bottles, soothers, and loveys: These items are a great comfort for children. Avoid taking them away because "they don't look good," or "I feel judged for having an older child still with a soother." These are reasons that meet the parent's needs but not the child's. Bottles and soothers don't become a danger to teeth or mouth structure until a child is five. So unless there is a good medical reason, allow the child his comfort item.

Playing/socializing with others: Respect a child's need to be with you. Perhaps he is introverted and needs to assess the social situation before jumping in. Many young children have a hard time being in another room when parents are visiting others. Allow children to play at your feet if it makes them feel more secure.

Allow your child to decide when they would like to participate in day camps, preschools, sleepovers, sleep-away camps, overnight visits to grandparents, un-parented birthday parties, and yes, even school. Many children are not ready to be separated for most of the day from parents at age of four or five. **There is nothing wrong with them!** They are following thousands of years of children who have been with their parents until adolescence. It's our culture and biases that insists that children be "independent" at such a young age.

Fears: Avoid making fun of or dismissing fears. They are real. Children need your acknowledgement of their fear, but also your calm assurance that certain things will not harm them.

Closeness and touching: Children have a strong need for these. Give freely. Hold them when they need it, carry them when they need it, let them lean up against you, and hug them when they need it.

Feelings: Allow children safe expression of their full range of normal emotions.

Routines and predictability: Adults love to know what is going to happen next, and children thrive on it too.

Unconditional love: Children are secure if they know they are always loved, no matter what.

Parent actions that reduce children's security

Broken attachments or inconsistent attachments: Being nurturing one day and cold the next; leads to the child not knowing what to expect.

Inconsistency and broken promises: The rare time is okay. Routine broken promises are not okay. The child learns not to trust.

Threat of abandonment: "Come now, or I will leave you here." This common threat breaks trust and causes insecurity. It's better to say, "I'll never leave you here alone. But we have to go now." Pick the child up and go!

Conditional love: "Good boy. I love you." Tells the child that only good boys are lovable. Your child needs to feel lovable even when he is grumpy.

Too much separation: Babies that are left alone while sick, hurt, or upset will have to cope with their strong emotions by themselves. They may feel abandoned and unable to form close relationships later on.

HOW A BABY AFFECTS THE MARRIAGE

Many people advise a couple to get away from the baby and work on the couple relationship. They say they need time to themselves. However, it's very hard to separate relationships into neat little corners: Mom and baby into one corner, and Mom and Dad into the other corner. Parents can stay connected and not have to feel they have to get away from the baby in order to do so. The baby is an inseparable link to the two parents. If the parents can only connect when the baby is away, the relationship might be in trouble. It's important for couples to stay connected in many ways. Communication is the most important. It can get couples through too little time together, too little sleep, no sex, too much work, isolation, and opposing parenting styles.

Here are some tips

Sleep deprivation: Help each other by tag team sleeping. Trade nap times for getting up with the baby time. Alternate who gets to sleep in on weekends. Have your partner take the baby out, so you can nap.

No sex: Schedule sex. It doesn't sound romantic, but it works for several practical reasons. When it's on the calendar, it's a given and moms have time to rev up and look forward to it. Dad could help by taking over childcare duties, so Mom can do some pampering and get in the mood. Dad knows that once a week is a regular time, and he doesn't have to guess…is this the night? Mom knows that sometimes they can cuddle without expectation. Since it's not "Tuesday," they can just cuddle without feeling guilt.

No time together: Have a date night. Plan a romantic dinner and put the baby to bed early. Do it regularly, at least once a week. Again, scheduling will keep the commitment. It's hard to say, "I'm too tired" if there is a babysitter showing up at your door at 7:00 pm.

Overwork: It helps to have a frank discussion on division of duties. Dads compare what they do, to their dad's contributions, and find they certainly do more now. But Moms compare what they do to Dads, and Dad may fall short. The perception of contribution can lead to disharmony and resentment.

Isolation: Mom, get out with your peers at least once a day. If you can't get out, get on the phone, email, instant message, or text message.

Opposing parenting styles: Agree on a few core "permanent marker" parenting values. Then let each other parent as they want with their own "washable marker" guidelines for the rest of the issues. Model what you want to see. Discuss compromise. Decide who the issue is more important for or who has researched the issue more.

Advice from new Moms for new Moms:

- Ask for help.
- You are the best thing for your baby.
- Trust your instincts.
- Decide what's right for you.
- Be flexible in getting things done.
- Don't stress about the worry, guilt and fear that comes with first baby.
- Mistakes are okay. They help the learning curve.
- Have food ready and frozen.
- Bank sleep before the baby comes.
- Don't try and be Super Mom. You are GOOD ENOUGH!

 Build your parent-child relationship first;
and your child's résumé later.

8

Discipline Tools for Toddlers 1 - 2 Years:
Action

 In times of stress, we parent how we were parented.
We can consciously change the pattern.
~ Patricia Morgan, Author

Most parents believe that REAL discipline starts at the toddler stage, when they are up and getting into things. Parents believe if they don't nip many behaviors in the bud at this stage, the behaviors will grow and become monstrous later on and their children will be destined to become criminals because they were too lenient when they were toddlers. NOT TRUE!

The toddler stage is not a stage for real reasoning yet. They are just beginning to learn they can't have their way all the time. Hence, the temper tantrums. The toddler's physical development allows for lots of freedom and access to danger, yet his brain development has no self-control, internal restraints, logical reasoning, or negotiation. This is critical. The most parents can do at this stage is keep the toddler safe by childproofing, supervision, and teach by redirection and substitution. The good news is the toddler is still small enough to pick up and move around, away from danger and non-parent approved situations. Real teaching and discipline can come later in the preschool years, when brain development is much more advanced.

YOUR TODDLER'S DEVELOPMENTAL STAGE

Your toddler is in the "doing" developmental stage. She is quite mobile and curious and that will propel her to explore everything! This is very normal and necessary for her developing brain. She is experientially learning through her senses what her brain will be processing abstractly years later.

Typical toddler behaviors
- Explores, explores, and more exploring with all her senses! Mouth, ears, eyes, touch, feel, nose. She is curious!

- Tests reality by pushing boundaries. Starting to learn to think and follow simple instructions the odd time. Follows simple two-word commands and sometimes resists.
- Feels all feelings. She can learn she has strong feelings but doesn't know what to do with them yet.
- Expresses negativity. Learns to say "no" and learns the power of the "no" word.
- Alternates between clingy behavior and independent behavior. She wants to explore on her own but be able to retrieve her caregiver at will.
- Uses body language to express negative feelings: hitting, biting, pushing, etc.
- Wants to do everything themselves. "I do it!"
- Dawdles because is so easily distracted.

ONE-YEAR-OLD DEVELOPMENTAL MILESTONES

Physical milestones

- Clumsy with a spoon. Eats with hands. Explores textures. Can hold cup but drops.
- Most front and side teeth in.
- Drops morning nap. Sleeps around two hours in afternoon and 11 hours at night.
- Can undress socks, hats, and shoes.
- Stands without help, walks, can run and climb but may fall.
- May crawl or walk up stairs with help.
- Builds with two or three blocks or objects.
- Pincer grasp develops.
- Weight gain begins to slow down. Quantity of food intake drastically reduced.

Psychosocial milestones

- Continues to form a bond and trust with caring adults.
- Most play is solitary and parallel with other children, but may want caregiver close by.
- Feels surprise, distress, disgust, pleasure, anger, sadness, fear, and joy.
- Enjoys rhythm and likes to dance to music.
- Repeats an activity, based on other's reaction or to attract attention.
- Kisses or hugs a familiar person.
- Shows fears: animals, thunder, vacuums, theatres.
- Around 18 months begins to understand "no" is a sharp powerful word, but doesn't get that it means "not do" something.

Cognitive milestones

- Sensori-motor cognitive stage (age zero to two) – thinking is here and now.
- Intensely curious.
- May understand common words when accompanied by gestures: bye, Mama, ball.
- Can begin to understand sign language. Uses words or gestures to express wants.

- Understands simple questions: "Where is your shoe?"
- Says simple words. (two to 50-word vocabulary)
- May smile or laugh at self in mirror. Recognizes self.
- May sit and look at pictures in a book for a very short time.
- Imitates housework and other adult activities: driving, talking on phone.
- Offers another child or adult an item but usually wants it back.
- Short attention span of one minute. Is easily distracted.

TWO-YEAR-OLD DEVELOPMENTAL MILESTONES

Physical milestones

- Becomes stiff or floppy when protesting. Does "the plank" (stiffens torso) during tantrums.
- Spills a lot. Can hold bottle and cup. Proficient with spoon.
- Molars appearing.
- Sleeps around 1.5 hours in afternoon and 11 hours at night.
- Can undress shirts and pants.
- Jumps with both feet.
- Climbs on or off an adult chair.
- Points to most common objects when named.
- Likes to help with housework.
- Can turn door knobs and twist open lids.
- Can walk down stairs holding a railing.

Psychosocial milestones

- Begins to express and handle feelings through tantrums and body language because "words" are not there yet.
- Plays parallel with other children.
- Definite food preferences.
- Additional emotions are empathy, frustration, and pride.
- Begins to trade toys and take turns but may not want to!
- Protective of own toys, and caregiver, especially at home.
- Shows aggressive tendencies: slapping, biting, pushing, hitting.

Cognitive milestones

- Begins to think and solve simple problems, such as big puzzles and shape sorters.
- Begins to learn to follow simple directions.
- Says some two-word sentences: "More milk." "All gone." "Me go."
- Says "What's that?" a lot.
- Understands simple directions: "Go get your coat."
- Understands more words than they can speak.

- Earliest memory begins. Selective: remember things of importance or out of the ordinary to them.
- Identifies three to five body parts on self.
- Beginning to play imaginatively: feeds a doll.
- Short attention span: several minutes.
- Imitates environmental sounds when playing: train "choo-choo".
- Calls self by name.
- Mixes up him, her, them, me, you.
- Can make simple choices between two options.
- Enjoys repetition: nursery rhymes, action songs.

PARENTS MATTER

Unhelpful parenting behaviors

- Saying "no" a lot – some parents say it up to 35 times a day. Using negative language instead of positive language "Don't touch," "Don't," "No, no, no."
- Leaving out treasures to tempt toddlers so they learn the word "no." Unfair to expect that at this cognitive age.
- Dismissing or making fun of toddler's strong feelings.
- Punishing or scolding temper tantrums. Telling a child not to feel angry is like telling a child not to sleep!
- Punishing or scolding toilet accidents.
- Telling people that their child is in the "terrible twos."
- Expecting sharing or cooperative play with the other children.
- Blaming, shaming, and criticizing child or making fun of lack of competence.
- Taking away security items and self soothing comforts before child is ready such as bottles, breastfeeding, soothers, stuffies, diapers, special blankets.
- Forcing child to say "Sorry."
- Getting angry at child for typical toddler behaviors: not sleeping, not eating, toilet accidents, dawdling, temper tantrums, touching forbidden items, hitting, and not "listening."

Helpful parenting behaviors

- Childproof the environment and make it safe to explore.
- Recognize parents have no control over eating, sleeping, toileting, and learning. The parent can facilitate those processes, but not force them.
- Allow the child to develop security on his own timetable and not on the experts' or other people's timetable. Allow soothers, bottles, loveys, and other security items.
- Teach ways to accept and express all feelings, whether positive or negative. Teach alternatives to hitting, by modeling proper behavior.

- Give simple, clear instructions and reasons for directions.
- Nurture child through touch, words, actions, and provide love, safety, and protection, food, warmth, sleep, stimulation, and security.
- All baby helpful parenting behaviors.
- Plan dawdling time into the day.
- Read, sing, and speak to him.
- Let child do it and acknowledge the difficulty when they are having troubles.

DISCIPLINE TOOLS FOR TODDLERS

This is the time for damage control, not moral teaching!

Give information
Stay with your "no"
Change environment
Plan ahead
Routines
Hold, carry, restrain, and remove
(child from the environment)
Give encouragement
Selective ignoring
Make request a game
Fulfill needs
Pretend that you need help
Active listening
Teach personal boundaries
Time-in
Help the child complete the task
Parental problem-solving
Give attention and spend time together
Say "no" another way
Allow ownership of feelings (uncomfortable and comfortable) and appropriate expression.
Use positive commands rather than negative
Allow child own space and share-free possessions
I-statements
Supervision
Parent time-out
Natural consequences
Model
Stimulation
Redirection
Distraction
Substitution
Holding, hugs, and cuddles

Give information

Toddlers are beginning to understand cause and effect, but very simply. Explaining information is more to get you in the habit for the preschooler years, than it is for toddlers to retain anything significant.

Sometimes, toddlers benefit from one word, "Hot!" "Yucky," "Dangerous," as you move the child or move the object. It helps their language development and gives them information. Signing with a toddler can also help foster communication.

Stay with your "no"

It's important to mean what you say and say what you mean at this early stage. When you have thought about the request or situation and very firmly decided that a "no" would be most appropriate, you need to stay with it and not change your mind. Make sure you have really thought about it before you issued the "no" so that you are not wishy-washy in your own mind. If you are clear, firm, and adamant in your mind, you will convey that to your child and stay with your no, in the face of tantrums, whining, screaming, and protests.

Change environment

> When I'm big, I can touch stuff in stores!
> ~ Scotty Arnall, age four

One the of two best toddler discipline tools. Toddlers are very mobile with little brain reasoning. Make it easy for you and her and avoid temptations. You have plenty of time to teach in the preschooler years. Change the house and yard to suit her abilities. Put the things you don't want her to touch or get into, up high or out of sight. Put locks on the doors and cabinets. Block off areas that are out of bounds, such as stereo systems and DVD players. Use door locks or gates. Anchor bookcases and TVs to the wall to protect the climbers. See your local health unit for information on making the car, house, and yard safe for your toddler and preschooler.

Duct tape works wonders when traveling. It is great for closing drawers, keeping toilet lids down, blocking off outlets, and many other uses.

Plan ahead

- Anticipate problems and plan ahead – e.g. carry a stroller if you know they won't walk.
- Avoid play places if you know they get frustrated and hit other children.
- Avoid taking them shopping if you know that can't understand why they can't eat everything in the checkout aisle.
- Provide toys while changing diapers.

- Diaper change standing up in front of the mirror or DVD movie.
- Clip nails or hair while the child plays in bath or is sleeping.
- Consider sleeping in clean next-day sweatpants or clothing so getting in and out of pajamas is not another thing to fight about in the morning.

Routines

Toddlers love routines. They need them in order to provide security and predictability in their lives. In fact, adults love routines. When I do a class, people sit at the same place week after week. They drive the same route to work and do things in the same order. It gives structure, security, and order to our lives. Toddlers can't tell time but can tell that, after a bath, comes teeth cleaning. After teeth cleaning comes story time. After story time is bed. The more routine an event is in a child's life, the more they won't question it when it's introduced later. Routines can be built around mornings, hygiene, clean up, leaving the house, eating, naptimes, and bedtime.

When time is pressed, such as when the family gets home late from a concert, don't skip a part of the bedtime routine. Shorten it. So keep story time, but make sure it's a really short one.

Many of these routines won't be embedded until the preschooler age around 3.5 years but they can start practicing them now. Don't expect compliance to adult requests anymore than 10 percent around age two and perhaps 40 percent around age 3.5 years.

Here are some examples of routines even an 18-month-old can do. They may not understand it, but if you keep saying it and backing with action, the rules will become routine to them.

- Candy after meals only.
- Teeth brushed first thing in morning and at bed.
- Breakfast comes after morning hygiene is done.
- Bath and hair wash once a week.
- Chores done every week or daily.
- No swearing or bathroom talk in public.
- No masturbating in public.
- Always say "please" and "thank you."
- No shoes in the house.
- Put back what you use.
- Clean up if you spill.
- Adults need a path to walk in your room.
- Towels need to be hung after showers.
- Clothes go in the basket.
- Swimming stuff in the laundry.
- Everyone carries stuff in from the car including garbage.
- Everyone carries their plate from table to dishwasher.

- Everyone carries their own backpack.
- No talking and eating in theatres.
- No toys left for days in kitchen and main living areas if not in use.
- No taking things without asking.
- No shutting off someone else's game or movie without asking first if they are done.
- No hitting to solve problems.
- No splashing water on the floor in the bathroom.
- Put computer disks, marker caps, videos back in cases.
- Clean up one game before another is brought out to play with.
- No put downs or name calling to solve problems.
- Dishes should be brought back to kitchen.
- Garbage goes in garbage.
- Lights and toilets needs to be turned off.
- Coats get hung on hook or thrown in basket.
- Socks come off into basket.
- It's bedtime after a snack, bath, teeth brushing, and book.

Hold, carry, restrain, and remove (child from the environment)

Toddlers are still small enough that you can hold and carry them to cross roads and parking lots and restrain them from danger. If they are about to run into the road, a spanking will not help them understand the danger. Restraining them and moving them back to a locked yard will keep them safe until they are old enough to know better. Redirection at some times may require physically picking them up and putting them down again in front of something more interesting. That's okay and necessary. Restraint is not the same as hitting and can be an effective discipline tool to protect them and keep them out of danger.

If your child won't hold your hand when crossing traffic, pick him up and carry him, even while he's kicking and screaming. Don't say anything. Restrain and carry on with going in the car and going home. When he calms down, acknowledge his feelings.

If they don't want to leave a play place, scoop them up and go to the car. Strap them in the car seat and go back in the place for their shoes and food. NO lectures or talking! Just action! Actively listen to their disappointment when you are in the car.

Carrying toddlers helps keep them focused. For instance, if you have to run a quick errand to the mall and you know they get distracted by the candy machine if they walk, then pick them up to carry them.

 Treat a child as though he is already the person
he's capable of becoming.

~ Haim Ginott, Author

Give encouragement

Avoid praise. Give encouragement. Praise focuses on the person and encouragement focuses on effort. Everyone deserves encouragement for the effort they have put into a task, whereby praise is only acceptable when the job is done well.

"You put a lot of care into pouring the juice." (even if she spills)
"Thank you for helping sort socks." (even if they aren't quite matched)
"I appreciate it when you carry your plate to the kitchen." (even if it lands in the garbage!)

Encouragement helps a person keep doing what you appreciate. Next time they will improve on their own, because everyone notices their own mistakes. Most people (and children) don't need them pointed out, and appreciate it when you don't!

Selective ignoring

Selective ignoring is a behavior modification tool that works really well in that it doesn't give negative attention to encourage the child to repeat the negative behaviors. Parental intervention and attention often feeds the situation, especially if the child is not getting a lot of positive attention from the parents. Be sure to recognize the child's need for attention and increase positive attention by focusing on him when he does something well. Selective ignoring (also called extinction) is paying no attention in words or actions to the child's negative behavior.

This works well for bathroom talk, swearing, lying, mild sibling fighting, and other habits that may be annoying, or embarrassing in public or at home. Tantrums can be selectively ignored, also minor squirmishes with siblings. Bringing attention to those instances sometimes makes those events worse. Ignoring may lesson the event's occurrence.

Selective ignoring goes against the parent's grain of wanting to do something because it makes them feel in control. Being in control makes parents feel they can make their life and their children's life smoother. But life isn't smooth. Sometimes things just go away or get better when we let it go.

It's easier to tell a parent to "just ignore it" than to give them something concrete to do. Here's how to "selectively ignore." Walk away, ignore, and focus on something TO DO. Have a cup of tea, phone a friend, go for a walk. Or, pretend you are in a soundproof bubble and hum to yourself. Focus on a mantra, such as "this will pass too!" or "I'm a good Mom." MP3 players also really help to tune out.

Make request a game

All children love games! Adults do too. Anything you can make a game out of, from eating vegetables, to brushing teeth, to doing chores will be fun. Sure, children will eventually learn that not everything is fun and games, but that day will come soon enough. Your desire to get the job done means that using any means possible to do it is allowed, especially through those developmental tricky times.

My husband developed a game during tooth brushing. After our children opened their mouths, he would brush, all the while saying what he saw in their mouths. "I see that you ate a giraffe today, and a police car, and a waterwheel, and a huge freezer of ice-cream and a…" The children looked forward to what he would invent and loved having their teeth brushed.

My son was three and wouldn't get into his car seat. We played the "like this?" game. He would make a pose and ask me, "like this?" and I would say "no." I would only say "yes" if he was sitting down in his car seat, and I could strap him in. He would go through four or five poses and then sit down to get the desired "yes," complete with clapping and extreme happiness from Mom. Caution: once you play a game to get a task done, you will have to keep up the racket for a few months! They will hold you to it.

Fulfill needs

Give food, sleep, drink, water, stimulation, activity, attention, touch or quiet.

Toddlers and preschoolers need food every two hours. Their tummies are about the size of a ping-pong ball. Three snacks and three meals per day are necessary to keep up energy levels. Let them eat for 20 minutes, then remove them from the table to clean up.

As toddlers move from one nap to no nap at all or from two naps to one, they are tired and cranky earlier in the day. That is usually around 4:00 pm. Add water! Give a bath. Allow them to play in the sink or spend time in the outdoor pool, supervised, of course. Water helps get through the cranky, sleepy times.

Shopping can be a hard activity with a toddler. It can turn into a clash of needs. Parents need to run errands, wait in lines, and grocery shop. Toddlers need to explore the world, declare their independence, and expend energy. Since public venues don't take children's needs into account, parents have to do it. That often means planning ahead to meet needs. Before going out in public, try to have a rested and fed toddler and bring toys to keep her busy.

Have realistic expectations. Parents know their own child's temperament the best. Some children are naturally quieter. Some are more active. But not many toddlers will sit still in a restaurant chair for more than 15 minutes – no matter how much we want them to.

Plan short outings. A four-hour shopping trip is too much for a child to handle. Bring along special toys that are for outings only. You should also be willing to build something fun into the trip – a quick peek at the fish tank in the mall.

Be cautious about encouraging behavior at home that you might find embarrassing in public. It might make everyone laugh when he burps loudly or sticks out his tongue to people at home, but it will make you cringe when he does it in public. Toddlers aren't capable of being tactful.

Pretend that you need help

Tap into your toddler's ability to empathize and "help" you. They love to feel needed and useful. Give them age-appropriate jobs and express sincere appreciation. When your toddler won't hold your hand crossing the street, pretend that you need help crossing, and say "Will you take my hand to help guide me?"

Active listening

When our children are babies, we are awesome active listeners. They can't talk, so we guess how they are feeling from their body gestures, facial expressions, and voice tone. They don't need to "tell" us how they are feeling. We can guess pretty accurately. When we can't, we keep on trying until we know the feeling and can solve the problem. However, when our children grow into toddlers, we tend to lose the ability to detect feelings because our toddlers show more uncomfortable feelings than comfortable ones.

We are pretty uncomfortable handling their uncomfortable feelings. Often, those feelings of boredom, frustration, anger, and jealousy are hard for parents to take, especially when delivered in the form of a tantrum or if the parent is the target! Sometimes parents worry that acknowledging feelings might make them worse or make them occur more often, when the opposite is true. Acknowledging feelings and validating them makes the toddler more emotionally healthy and will lesson and help him resolve those feelings.

Teach personal boundaries

Toddlers require their personal space, just as adults do. For adults, it's about 18 inches around us. Toddlers may require more, perhaps up to about three feet around them. They may push, bite, or hit if someone inhibits their space. Teach them to put up their hand to signal to others that they need space. You could also step in and speak for them. Say to the other child, "Alex doesn't have the words right now, but she would like you to stay back. How does that sound?" or "Kim isn't finished playing with the doll. When she is done, you can have it." Or provide space by sitting just inside their boundary zone and blocking others from entering. As a parent, you are teaching the child to use their words, which is much more helpful than to hit, bite, or push. However, it may not work in high stress situations. Relax. They will get there!

Time-in

Time-in is about dealing with an emotionally upset child by staying there with her and helping her deal with her strong emotions using calm-down tools. After everyone is calmed down, it's also a time that involves problem-solving and conflict resolution between a child and a situation or another person.

It's time consuming but so important. If childhood is not the time to teach socially acceptable behaviors and how to work through problems with people by using our words, then when is the best time? Certainly not when the child is 20 or 30. Yes, it takes time. But it's a much better use of time than keeping a child restrained in time-out or another punishment.

One example of time-in occurred when my son, Marlin, eight, hit his friend Jared with a stick. I comforted Jared in Marlin's presence, and asked Marlin to run and get a bandage and cloth. When he brought it back, I bandaged Jared up and gave Jared hugs and full attention. In a few minutes, Marlin was calmer (he hit his friend because of his anger and strong emotions) and was able to listen to what I had to say. I asked Jared to tell Marlin our rule about hitting. I asked Marlin to come and apologize when he was ready. Then Jared and I went to do something else. Later, Marlin must have thought about the bad thing he did and gave Jared his stuffy as an apology offering. Then the two went off to play again.

I could have sent Marlin to time-out, but he would not have learned anything. I could have made him apologize, but it wouldn't really be from him. Time-in took about 30 minutes, and it was time well spent in teaching restitution.

Help the child complete the task

Toddlers need lots of help and often enjoy parent company when doing things. They love to vacuum, sweep, and dust alongside a parent, often not with toys, but with real tools. Parents need to take time for training a child. Around preschool and school-age, parents and children can work side by side. Around teenagehood, parents can step back and let the children do it by themselves.

Parental problem-solving

Can toddlers solve problems? Yes! But at this age, we have to guide them through it. My son was two when we came home from shopping one day. He spotted his ride-on toy in the front yard and wanted to go ride it on the sidewalk. I had two needs: to get the groceries in the fridge and freezer as it was a hot day and to make sure he was safe and supervised in the street. First, I defined the problem. I said, "Oh dear, we have a problem. I need to get these into the house, and you have to be watched out here. What can we do?" My son was barely talking by then, and didn't say anything. I then outlined the possible solutions. "I could get your brother out here to watch you, or I could stay here and let you ride for five minutes? Which one should we pick?" He chose the second option, so we agreed on a solution. He would ride for five minutes and we would then go into the house. That was basic problem-solving. I did most of it, but the important thing was I used the language for how to do it, so he was familiar with it and catches on to the process. Children need to be familiar with "problems," "solutions," "needs," "agreements," and "is it working?" Many times now, my children come up to me and say, "We have a problem" rather than, "Shelly's bugging me" or "Johnny spilt his juice." Even the three-year-old says, "Mommeee…problem here!"

 Dealing with problems is a life-skill, not just a discipline issue.

Give attention and spend time together

Attention seeking behaviors have likely brought your negative or positive attention in the past. Give unlimited amounts of positive attention and ignore the negative attention seeking behaviors.

Say "no" another way

A response of "no!" from our child can be amusing or perhaps it can be irritating, but in general, it doesn't change much of what we do because we have the resources and the authority to keep doing what we want. But for the child, a succession of "no's" coming from the parent can be much more frustrating. I encourage you to soften this response to your child, with positive alternatives:

- Indefinite delay "Yes, but later."
- Specific delay or when/then "When we get to Grandma's, then we can have ice-cream."
- "Yes," with qualifier. "Yes, after dinner." "Yes, you may eat your Easter chocolate after breakfast." "Yes, you may ride your bike after your homework is done." "Sure, let's play after the dishes are done." "Yes, if you brought your allowance with you?"
- "Let me think about it." Instead of an automatic "no", you always have the right for time to think about your decision. We often make better parenting decisions, ones we don't regret later, when we've allowed ourselves time to think about what we are really being asked and what response we want to give.
- "When…, then…" This technique is especially good for transition times. "<u>When</u> we get in the car, <u>then</u> we can watch the hot air balloons on the way home." "<u>When</u> we get to Grandma's, <u>then</u> we can have the ice-cream we

brought." This works great to establish a routine and help toddlers discover the order of events in their world. One event follows another.

- Give information instead of a "no". "I think that running is not allowed in this store. We need to walk." "If you keep diving into the pool, instead of jumping, the lifeguards may ask us to leave, because it's not safe." Don't worry about giving too much information. Your child will take in what they understand.

Allow ownership of feelings (uncomfortable and comfortable) and appropriate expression of them.

"It's okay to be angry, but let's hug this stuffy rather than hit your friend." Children that are talked to and listened to frequently have better social skills and communication skills as they grow from toddlers to preschoolers.

Use positive commands rather than negative

Positive commands create positive attitudes. Using positives also helps promote feelings of being valued, supported, respected, motivated, and very capable.

"Let's jump from the sofa to the floor." (instead of "stop jumping on the sofa")
"Walk." (instead of "don't run")
"Sand stays on the ground." (instead of "don't throw sand")
"Let's eat at the table." (instead of "don't eat in the living room")

One of the best signs I ever saw was "Children left unattended by an adult will be fed coffee, chocolate, candy and be allowed to play with sticks, and given a puppy to take home." It was a humorous, positive way to say "Don't dare leave your children unattended."

Allow your child his own space and share-free possessions

There are many items in our house we don't want to share. I wouldn't share my video camera with anyone, even my best friend. Your children have special possessions they don't want to share, either. It helps to have a playroom or corner of the kitchen that young children can play with communal toys. Items not sharable are stored in your child's bedroom. At an early age, children must be taught to not explore people's bedrooms, which are personal space. You must allow your children a room or corner of their room or even a shelf, if space is limited, to call their own. Toddlers play best if there are enough of one type of toy to go around.

I-statements

Use as few words as possible! I-statements are those sentences that begin with "I." The more you express your feelings by saying them, the more your children will catch on to the language. My two-year-old son was extremely mad one day. He stomped upstairs and said, "I'm so swustrated!" What a great way to express unhappiness!

Supervision

It's a must for small children. Good discipline is 90 percent prevention and 10 percent correction. Supervision is part of prevention. Never, ever, leave a young child alone.

Parent time-out

You just walked into a room totally turned upside down and can't deal with it. Walk away and get relaxed. Make sure your toddler is safe and occupied. Breathe!

Natural consequences

Natural consequences are when the parent doesn't interfere with the outcome of the child's action. What happens because of the child's action just happens. If a child won't wear mittens outside and won't listen to your voice of reason, then let them out without mittens to experience the natural consequence themselves. Their hands will get cold. Carry mittens in a bag, in case they really get cold, to keep them safe.

 Children learn better by discovery than by being told.

Model

Have you ever watched an 18-month-old "talk" on a cell phone? He can really imitate an adult. It's often scary how young children are when they pick up on adult behaviors. Your children are watching you. Is what you are doing what you want to teach?

Stimulation

An active, busy, engaged child is a happy child. Make sure your house is child-friendly. Toddlers need any kind of toddler toy, anything chewable, wearable, touchable, hearable, seeable, and doable. They love ride-on toys and board books. Put out of reach anything not appropriate to touch, smell, hear, and taste.

Redirection

With their very short memory span, redirection is one of the best discipline techniques for toddlers. Change the situation by gently steering or moving the toddler to another activity. This stops his undesirable behavior. This can be used for all kinds of misbehavior, whether the child is throwing food at the walls or fighting with another child over a toy.

If you notice your child is about to hit a sibling, grab their hand and say, "Come help Mommy unload the dishwasher." You don't even need to mention the previous object or situation. Just refocus the child's energy to something else.

Distraction

When your toddler won't leave a toy behind when leaving a friend's house, play place, or a store, entice their focus away. Distract with a treat, a display, or something else. In a store, let them carry the item while you shop, then put the desired toy on the checkout counter as you are leaving, telling the clerk that you don't want the item. You have to be sure your child doesn't damage it or you will have to pay for it! Acknowledge your child's feelings of sadness if he notices the toy is left behind. Chances are he won't notice. If he starts screaming, quickly scoop him up and leave the store. You don't have to punish him. You are exercising discipline by leaving.

You can also encourage your child to say "Bye-bye" and "See you later" to the toy. Tell the child that the toy must stay with its own family or it will be missed. Sometimes, they can understand that.

Substitution

Trade focus for another focus. It's the same as distraction but usually with an object. The child wants juice, but you can offer chocolate milk or whatever is more acceptable to you. Sometimes, you have to sell it to the child, though!

Holding, hugs, and cuddles

Absolutely essential at any age! Toddlers crave physical contact. The more they get it, the more their touch needs are met.

SPECIAL TODDLER BEHAVIOR CONCERNS
THE "NO" WORD

Why toddlers say "no":

- They need to assert independence and they need to achieve a measure of control over their lives.
- They need to begin separating when secure and cling when insecure.
- They need to explore and discover.
- They need to express their strong emotions.

When a toddler says "no!" they mean:

- I want to do it myself.
- I don't want you, but I want you. I am overwhelmed by conflicting feelings.
- I don't know what I'm feeling, but I'm feeling it right now!

- I can't share because I don't understand the concept of ownership yet.
- I want to have some control over what happens to me.

A toddler's favorite word is "no." It is a strong, powerful, in-control word. It sounds decisive, meaningful, and packs a punch. No wonder two-year-olds overuse it. It makes them feel powerful! Not surprising, when they can only see past kneecaps and still require so much help to get through their daily routine. They like it so much, they use it even when they mean "yes"… "Do you want some ice-cream?" "No!"

Toddlers and all children control four areas of their lives: eating, sleeping, toileting, and learning. Learning to let go of control is very difficult for parents who are used to making all the choices and decisions for another person for a whole year. Thus, everything can be a power struggle, if you let it. Offer choice in those areas as much as possible. Two choices are good for a toddler. Make sure both choices are acceptable to you. This gives the toddler a feeling of independence and control over her life. Decide what is important and what huge issues you will control.

Helpful parenting strategies to get through the "no!" stage:

- Offer many choices between two or three acceptable options.
- Offer many chances for toddler to try mastering a task. Give them time to try.
- Respect your toddler's desire for separation or clinginess. If your toddler is clingy, she is filling up on security. Let her. She'll become much more independent if you allow her to be clingy, than if you push her away.
- Childproof your surroundings for safe exploration and discovery.
- Reduce your use of the word, "No." Use "later," "after," "when/then," "yes, after," "not now, but you can have…" "Let me think about it." "Maybe…"
- Accept and acknowledge all feelings. Only behaviors have limits.
- Don't expect a child under three to share their possessions.

TOILET LEARNING

No amount of punishment or bribes will speed along toilet training. This is one area that falls under the maturation theory. All children's bowels and urinary plumbing mature at different rates. Some can hold their pee and poo longer than other children in order to reach the toilet in time. Sometime between the age of 18 months and 4.5 years, your child will be ready to use the toilet. The process goes much faster the older the child is. Some parents have found that providing incentives like candies and new underpants helpful in motivating, but only if the child is developmentally ready. Punishment can cause serious psychological damage, as well as delay progress.

A child is ready if:

- They can stay dry for several hours between diaper changes.
- They have the cognitive ability to know when they are about to pee and poo before it happens, and can hold both so they have time to get to a toilet.
- They can pull down their own clothing, wipe with toilet paper, and reach the taps to wash their hands.
- They are in a fairly cooperative stage and somewhat interested in the process.

Try to avoid potty training if:

- You have a new baby in the house and are dealing with jealousy from the toilet trainee. About half of all two to three-year-olds will regress during this time.
- Your toddler is going through a particularly negative stage.
- Your family is experiencing a major life change such as a move, divorce,or travel.

Regression and accidents are normal. Two steps ahead and one step back. Clean up the accidents matter-of-factly and keep encouraging progress.

HANDLING EMOTIONS

Toddlers have a growing array of emotions that can erupt out of nowhere. They do not inhibit their feelings. They are totally in the moment and are raw and intense. Most of the time, they don't know what they are feeling or how to handle it. That's why time-outs are not good calming tools for toddlers and preschoolers. They need adult help in managing their emotions. Sometimes they have a mixed bag of emotions and fall apart or zone out in an almost catatonic state during temper tantrums. They don't hear you or respond to active listening. Wait it out. They will eventually calm down.

Toddlers are not very verbal. Unlike adults who have learned to express their feelings in words, toddlers do not have the vocabulary to describe how they are feeling or have the reasoning skills to understand why they feel like they do. They use the only "words" they are familiar with: screams, howls, lying on the floor holding their breath, sobs, whines, yells, and cries. They are not misbehaving. They are expressing feelings. They are communicating. They are trying to manage the tornado inside them the best way they know how. The feelings are the same as adults. The expression is different. Adults can talk about their feelings. Toddlers can only show them.

Toddlers are driven by curiosity and energy. They are exuberant, happy, and love life. They embrace their world and seek to explore it as much as possible. They inhale every flower and savor every lollipop. They laugh whole heartedly from the depths of their bellies at the things adults have forgotten to laugh at. They never stop moving, afraid they might miss something interesting. They love to run, jump, and climb. They can scribble, paint, feed themselves, help with clean up, and push buttons on machines. They take immense pleasure in gazing at the moon. They point out every fire hydrant, ladybug, and plane. They love balloons and sleep so soundly with their little bums in the air. They freely give everyone big, sticky wet hugs and kisses that don't quite pucker yet. They pad around the house in those soft fuzzy blanket sleepers with the padded feet that go pitter-patter, and they look like angels when asleep. When the messes are all cleaned up, and the tantrums over, your toddler is still your cozy, warm, and cuddly baby.

TODDLER SLEEP PROBLEMS

When children are toddlers, there is very little risk of suffocation, so sleeping with parents is easier. Here are some possible toddler sleep arrangements:

- Toddler sleeps in own bed – parent soothes and gradually leaves in baby steps.
- Toddler sleeps with parents in their bed.
- Toddler sleeps with siblings in their bed.
- Toddler sleeps on living room sofa, while parents are still up, and then parents move him when they go to bed.
- Toddler sleeps on the floor on a mattress or airbed next to the parent's bed.
- Toddler starts the night in his own bed and may climb into parents bed when needs to, probably in the middle of the night.
- Toddlers starts in parent's bed and get moved to own bed when asleep.
- Parents take turns sleeping with toddler in own bed.
- Parents alternate sleeping with toddler in the guest room every third night so one parent gets a solid night of REM sleep.

 Whatever works so no one is crying and everyone is sleeping safely is the right option for your family.

Sleep is important. Seventy percent of growth hormone is secreted during sleep. But it's still one of those things that is totally under the control of the child. Parents can facilitate it but can't force it.

Some toddlers still sleep with and nurse with Mom during the night. By about age 3.5 years, most toddlers are okay with sleeping in their own bed, and their night nursing has become negotiable. They are able to talk with Mom about when and where to nurse. Many Moms want to night wean their toddlers by two years or sooner. Often, holding, cuddles, and a sippy cup of water is enough to help toddlers stop night nursing and go back to sleep. Other Moms have said, "Num nums have gone to sleep and will wake in the morning to feed you!" Some Moms found it helpful to leave their toddler with Daddy at night to sleep and cuddle with and not feed for a few nights.

If parents understand the reasons why toddlers and preschoolers don't want to go to bed, they can address those needs. Separation anxiety is a huge issue. Sleeping with a child for a few years doesn't mean they will never sleep in their own beds any more then using diapers for a few years will prevent a child forever from using the toilet. Most children sleep alone, in their own beds, in their own rooms, by age 12. By then, they will insist on it!

Wherever a toddler sleeps, be sure to have a bedtime routine: a snack, bath, then pajamas, teeth brushing, and finally a story. Kiss goodnight, and have a brief talk. Children tend to open up just before bed. That's why it's great for Dad and Mom to alternate putting children to bed. It's a time for intimate conversations that really builds relationships. It may help to stay with your child while they "let go" and drift off.

Leave them in their own room with a white noise machine, fan, or to watch a movie from bed. If they get up, attend to their needs. Usually, it's not a drink of water or scary monsters under the bed. It's their need for more parent cuddle time and attention. Bring them downstairs to cuddle and lay on the couch while you watch your adult show or carry on with your adult activities. Keep the focus off them and onto what you want to do. It's your time. They will fall asleep but secure in the fact that their parents are there.

WHY TODDLERS DON'T UNDERSTAND RULES

Toddlers DON'T understand rules! Even the word "no" is very abstract to them, in that you are telling them NOT to do something, when the idea pops into their mind to do it. If I said to you, "Don't think of the color white," what is the first thing you see in your head? Something white!

They also have very poor impulse control; so naturally, they want to do the very thing you don't want them to do. And since their desire to do it is stronger than their desire to obey you, it looks to you that they are not listening or deliberately disobeying you when they are just doing their job of exploring. Preschoolers are much more able to appreciate rules than toddlers.

They don't have abstract thinking skills.
Rules are abstract. A don't rule is a double abstract. It may draw more attention to what you don't want.

They are in the here and now.
The rule he knew yesterday has been displaced in his head.

They can't multitask.
They can't hold too many thoughts in their heads at once.

Their brains drive them to explore.
Everything in their being says "touch, taste, eat, look, hear!"

They have almost no impulse control.
Their brains don't allow them to restrain themselves yet.

They don't understand cause and effect.
They can't relate what they did to cause Mom's anger. Especially true during a time delay of more than a few minutes.

SEPARATION ANXIETY

As a baby grows into toddlerhood, they begin the cognitive awareness of existing separate from their mother. At times, they welcome this separateness. At other times, the concept scares them, and they feel insecure. It is a push/pull type of emotion. They want to be independent to establish an identity as a unique person with unique tastes, desires, and wants. Yet, they are scared of change and of possibly being too separated from mother. Separation anxiety starts in babyhood, peaks in the toddler years, and decreases in the preschool years.

From a toddler's point of view, physical proximity equates with security and confidence. The further a toddler is separate from his mother, the more likely he will lose her (in the toddlers mind). Hence, the push/pull of competing desires: closeness/independence, security/growth, explore/attach. Children will go through this push/pull emotion in many of their growing phases even to the teen years. It's just the loudest protestation at toddlerhood. So if your child is screaming, crying, and protesting when you leave, congratulations! You have built a healthy secure attachment with your child!

To minimize separation anxiety, decrease the number of times you have to leave your child. She needs more security of you around. Give it to her. Around three or four, she will naturally be able to understand that you are coming back and will protest less when you leave for work or activities.

Tips for when you must leave:

- Acknowledge feelings: "You are sad that Mommy is leaving?"
- Leave a special item (that smells of you) for her to take care of while you are away.
- Have a leaving routine that you follow all the time. A special hug, wave.
- Don't sneak out! Say goodbye, kiss, and leave her in the arms of the caregiver. If you don't say goodbye and sneak out, your child will feel insecure and cling every time you leave the room.
- See if caregiver can come to your house.
- Try to leave the same time, place and with the same caregiver each day to establish a routine.
- Choose childcare arrangements thatoffer the most consistency of caregiver so they can develop an attachment to them. (Don't worry, you will never be replaced!)

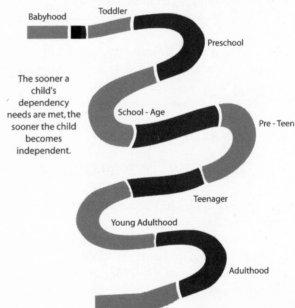

Dependence and Independence

Babyhood
Toddler
Preschool
The sooner a child's dependency needs are met, the sooner the child becomes independent.
School - Age
Pre - Teen
Teenager
Young Adulthood
Adulthood

When we moved to a new house, my daughter was nine. She felt insecure and lonely and spent the first month camped in our bedroom on an air mattress at night. She felt more secure that way, and we let her. After a month, her needs were met and she happily moved into her own newly decorated room. It would have been a longer, worse time if we had denied her finding security and pushed her out of our room.

Children go through insecure times at various stages:

- New sibling arrival
- Change in childcare arrangements
- Starting preschool or kindergarten
- Friend moves away
- Divorce or separation
- Death in the family
- Major world events, such as 9/11
- Moving to a new neighborhood
- Entering junior or high school
- Meeting a new love interest
- Starting a new job
- Moving out

PICKY EATING PROBLEMS

Babies eat more food relative to weight in the first year, compared to any other year of their life. By age one, food consumption drastically reduces. If you can get one good meal into a toddler in a day, you are doing very well!

It helps to think about the division of responsibilities between parent and child. The feeding relationship helps to lesson the need to bargain, bribe, and punish a child to get them to eat. It allows for healthier eating habits and social eating relationships. According to an informal poll of my parenting groups, about 25 to 30 percent of parents feel their toddlers are picky eaters. Toddlers are definitely more interested in exploring than eating, so more food may be on them, the tray and the floor than in their tummies! That's okay. It's just a stage.

The feeding relationship

The parent's job

What: The parent controls what food is bought, stored, cooked, and served. Parents control the money and shopping at this age and make most decisions of what to buy.

When: The parent decides when snack and meal times will be. Toddler's tummies are about the size of a ping pong ball, and they need food and drink every two hours. Three meals: breakfast, lunch, and dinner, and three snacks: mid-morning, mid-afternoon, and bedtime per day is recommended. The parent keeps the food on the table for 20 minutes and then puts the food away until the next scheduled meal or snack.

Where: The parent decides where eating and drinking will take place. Eating at the table should be encouraged to minimize the risk of choking while running, walking, or climbing. It's also a good habit to get into, as non-aware eating can lead to weight issues. When children eat while watching movies, playing video games, or computers, they are not consciously enjoying the food or even paying attention to what they are eating. Although, I have noticed you can easily slip a plate of raw vegetables and dip under their noses while they are playing video games and the whole plate is gone in minutes. I don't even think they notice what they just ate!

The child's job

If: The child decides if he will eat, according to his internal hunger cues rather than the clock or schedule. A meal is only a small part of the day's food intake – only 1/6. If your child chooses not to eat, don't worry. He will make up for it at some time later in the day, next day, or in a few days.

How much: The child decides what quantity will satisfy his hunger. This also helps him decide his internal cues.

More eating tips:

- Food jags are normal, where the child eats nothing but peanut butter and jam sandwiches for three weeks or a longer period of time. That's okay. As long as it's a healthy food, don't worry about their nutritional intake. Most parents who worried about nutrition, found that their toddlers did eat a variety of foods when they kept a log of their food intake over a week or two week period.

- It takes 15 tries to accept a new food. Have a one bite routine – try one bite (the no-thank-you bite) and see if your child likes it. If they don't, let them spit it out. Don't turn the one bite routine into a power struggle. Young children have very sensitive taste buds and they definitely will change overtime.

- Toddlers like to feel like they are getting something special. Presentation is everything. Vegetables and fruits arranged in a face will appeal to them when a regular tossed salad is ignored.

- Toddlers usually don't eat much at dinner. They are tired and cranky at the end of the day. Track their lunch and breakfast intake.

- Toddlers usually prefer finger type foods.

- Cut a bathmat in half and use it on the highchair seat so they don't slide out.

- To save time, don't use dishes. Put the food right on the tray. Then the plate won't be thrown.

- Give baby a spoon for each hand and then you can feed him with a separate spoon. It keeps his hands busy. Give a butter spreader to help preschoolers cut food.

- Let a toddler practice drinking from a sippy cup in the bathtub.

- Fill toddler glasses only one third full, and make sure all dishes are plastic.

- Cool hot food by dumping in an ice cube.

- Be aware of microwaving mugs with the attached plastic straws on the outside. The liquid in the straw heats first and can cause burns because the toddler drinks it first.

- For fun, serve food on doll or play dishes.

- Think variety: fill an ice cream cone with egg salad, tuna salad, pudding, or yogurt for easy eating.

- Use the football hold to help get the toddler to the sink and use your other hand to splash water on his chin and guide his arms under the sink to wash. Store clean shirts in the kitchen to save running to the bedroom after meal times. Wash food encrusted shirts within a day or two or the food will become moldy.

- Clean highchairs and strollers in the shower. Run water and let the encrusted food soften. Works as well outside in the summer with the hose.

- Dumping, mushing, and throwing food are exploratory behaviors. A little food exploration is part of development. When the food deliberately hits the walls, or the food exploration is testing your patience on a stressful day, it's a signal that mealtime is over. Remove your child from the eating place.

- If the toddler doesn't sit still at mealtime, schedule a burn up activity right before mealtime, and they will have used up some energy. Before a restaurant visit, go to a playground. In fact, this works well for any event that requires a certain amount of sit still time: weddings, church, movies, concerts. Be thankful for 10 – 15 minutes, as this is all you might get!

- Let them feed themselves with non-messy foods like peas and bread pieces while you can still feed the messy stuff with the spoon.

- Try serving finger foods with dip or sauce. All children love sauces to swirl.

- Serve mini portions of old favorites: pancakes, muffins, meatballs.

- Let them pour their own juice using the dishwasher door as a counter surface. Then you can just close the door after they spill and the mess goes into the dishwasher.

- Serve a tray of carrot sticks, broccoli florets, red pepper, and salad dressing as you are getting dinner ready. Guaranteed it will be gone!

- You can pretend to sprinkle sugar over the cereal and nobody will notice the difference. Just wave your spoon over and your toddler will think you put sugar and salt on their food.

- Young children tend to like their food separated. Avoid casseroles if possible.

- Serve dessert along with the meal. Don't elevate the status of dessert as more desirable by declaring it the prize for eating the lesser valued dinner items.

- Purée vegetables to hide in soups and sauces.

- Make sure dessert is healthy. Fruit, yogurt, ice-cream and oatmeal cookies are all very healthy choices and part of a balanced diet.

- Avoid classifying food into "good" and "bad" categories. Use "more nutritious" and "less nutritious" so you get your child into the habit of making better food choice decisions.

- Avoid punishing or rewarding a child with food items.

- Treats are occasional foods. They wouldn't be called treats if they were served every day. Designate a treat day.

- Avoid bargaining using food. Parents who say, "Eat four more bites of your hamburger and then you can have your toy," are setting themselves up for power struggles. Children learn very quickly that parents want them to eat, and by refusing, they can get attention and control. Give children attention for positive behavior and control in the form of choices. Don't make eating a power struggle.

- Preserve the social function of food. A comforting, social, happy atmosphere at meal and snack time and a wide variety of healthy foods is all that's needed for childhood nutrition.

TODDLER AGGRESSION IS NORMAL

Richard Tremblay, wo holds the Canadian Research chair in child development at the University of Montreal, says in his study of 2,000 babies, more than 90 percent of the mothers of 17-month-olds reported their toddlers were physically aggressive towards others. Children with siblings demonstrated this behavior earlier. The Globe and Mail stated that toddlerhood was one of the most aggressive stages in human development and 95 percent of children grow out of it. They become less aggressive as they learn to delay gratification, use their words, and problem-solve social issues.

Some toddlers are more aggressive than others, but this is not just a factor of parent modeling. Tremblay indicates other factors as indicated below.

- **Temperament:** Spirited children put more energy into getting what they want and could be more aggressive.
- **Frustration:** Tiredness, hunger, and anger stimulates aggression.
- **Parent punishment**: If a toddler is spanked, they are more likely to hit others.
- **Parent style**: Ignoring a baby's cry and becoming angry with baby is linked to aggression.
- **Sibling conflict management**: Conflict is normal and can be reduced by certain parenting strategies.

Suggestions for handling aggression

You are having a pleasant coffee and a chat with your best friends, when suddenly your toddler whacks your friend's toddler with a toy truck. There is wailing from the startled child and a stunned, embarrassed silence from the parents. All eyes are on you as to what you are going to do. What can you do that is respectful, immediate, and teaches your child proper behavior?

First, recognize that whining, hitting, pushing, and biting are pretty normal behaviors of children aged one to four. They are trying to get their needs met, whether for attention, personal boundary space, or that super interesting toy they've been eyeing. The problem is their verbal skills are still very limited and they resort to body language to say a) how they feel, and b) what they need/want. Our role as parents is to discourage their unsociable methods and encourage the polite methods to get what they want. That means, we have to "give them the words" to use, back it by taking action, and repeat it often!

Whining:

- Ignore until they stop.
- Tell them to say it again using their "normal" voice.
- Model the "normal voice."
- Give the desired item instantly when the normal voice is used.
- When in a peaceful moment, ask for "inside, outside, whining, church, and normal" voices so they can tell the difference in voice tone, pitch, and variety.
- Pat your head and pretend you can't hear the "reception" when the tone is whiny. Pretend that interference clears when the request is less whiny.

Hitting, pushing, biting

Of course, your first order of business is to apply first aid and comfort to the injured child. Then you need to address the attacker. Not all these suggestions will work all the time, but you need a lot of tools in your toolbox. Try some individually or a combination:

- Find the attacker's need. Do they want the toy, more personal space, attention, a reaction, revenge or choices? Ask them. Tell them how to ask for what they want. Use simple words.
- Make eye contact.
- Say "Ouch! Hitting/biting/pushing hurts!" or "I don't like that!"
- Don't expect sharing until age three.
- Restrain your child in your lap or carry him away to another space to calm down with you.
- Rocking your child or rubbing their backs and using a soft, repetitive voice helps your child to calm down also.

- Show disapproval in body/facial language and your voice tone.
- Save your loud and sharp "no!" for times like hitting and for safety or emergency situations.
- Have a lot of similar toys and space to redirect your child to.
- Actively listen: "You're <u>frustrated</u> that he grabbed the toy? You want your toy back?" "We can't hit, but we can ask to have the toy back."
- Teach your child to put up his hand to ward off space invaders.
- Teach I-statements: "I don't like that." "I want the toy." "I'm not done."
- Allow your child his own time to give up a toy. Gently remind him that someone is waiting, but don't force him to give it up. Let him choose when.
- Instead of always saying, "Hurry-up," you could try, "Take the time you need." Meeting your child's needs encourages him to think about other's needs.
- Supervise.
- Say "Ouch, that hurt Mommy!" when they bite or hit and put them down and walk away.
- Teach your child to walk away from annoying situations.
- Say "No! We don't bite. Biting hurts."
- Dramatize your pain and sorrow, so the child knows that you are truly disappointed.
- Give your child something else to bite. "People are not for biting. Here, bite this."
- Remove your child from the situation, but don't banish your child to a room alone. Sit with your child to help her calm down.
- Teach "breathing," "the silent scream," and "stamping feet" when your child is angry.
- Teach "trading" and "taking turns."
- Stay calm yourself.
- Don't grab toys from your child. Model the behavior you want. Ask for the toy and wait for consent. Always ask to use things that belong to your child.
- You could apologize for your child to the victim, to model what you want to see him do in the future.
- Tell the other child that your child needs space but doesn't have the words to say so yet, so could he please give him some room.
- Shower the victim with attention. Have the victim repeat the rule of "no hitting—hitting hurts" to the attacker. Remove the victim and take them with you to do something else. Be sure to increase the attention to the attacker in peaceful times. Show them positive ways to get attention.
- Increase one-on-one time with the attacker.
- If hitting between two children repeats, find something else for one child to do and separate them.
- Acknowledge the feelings of each sibling or child and repeat it for the other child to hear, so they can start to learn empathy and conflicting points of view.

- If hitting repeats, children may be hungry, bored or tired. Fix the underlying reason.
- Model politeness. Use "please, thank you, no thanks" with your children.

Discouraging aggression:
- Tell your children it's unacceptable.
- Limit media exposure.
- Model gentleness. Don't throw, hit, or bite back.
- Step in when play conflicts escalate. Don't ignore. Children need to learn how to deal with it at a toddler, preschooler and early school-age levels.
- Teach problem-solving and calm-down tools.
- Provide healthy outlets for rambunctiousness.
- Acknowledge when children are cooperative with each other.

Some toddlers learn these skills faster and easier than others. Be patient. They need a lot of repetition and practice. After all, that's what childhood is for!

Power Struggles

It takes 2 to tangle!

If there is only one in the boxing ring, there is no power struggle!

9

Discipline Tools for Preschoolers
3 - 5 Years: Action and talk

 It's not me against you. It's us working together against the problem.

Preschoolers are a fun bunch! They are easier to talk to, share play with, and are really growing into little people with opinions and quirks. They are starting to follow instructions about half the time. This is the age where real discipline starts. Their brains are learning so much during this time and their social world is expanding to include preschool, teachers, play dates, friends, friends' parents, and neighbors. They are starting to appreciate differences in the rules, customs, food, and the way things are done. They like simple jokes and unusual twists and they provide a lot of fun and play in parenting.

YOUR PRESCHOOLER'S DEVELOPMENTAL STAGE

Preschoolers are in the "thinking" stage of development. Their minds are expanding and growing and they have a bit more restraint in their bodies, but still not a whole lot of self-control. One mom was describing how she was rushing out the door while saying "Hurry up, we are late again!" and her four-year-old son replied, "What does 'late' mean, Mommy?" It shows how even at four, a child is unable to know abstract concepts such as time.

Typical preschooler behaviors

- Learns the difference between reality and fantasy.
- Tests reality and fantasy through experimentation and experiences natural consequences of their behavior.
- Becomes aware of power – who has it, how it's used, and how to get it. Starts learning about power by watching and engaging in power struggles with peers, siblings, and parents.

- Begins to learn socially acceptable behavior by watching models. Learning basic information about the world, himself, his body, his role, and how things work. Learning who he is and how he is in relation to other people in his world.
- Beginning to learn about rules. Young children under five follow rules less than half the time. It's normal and developmentally appropriate.
- Engages in fantasy play with imaginary companions. Tries on different identity roles by imaginary play with other children, dress up clothes, etc.
- May lie as a result of wishful thinking and fantasy, not malice.

THREE-YEAR-OLD DEVELOPMENTAL MILESTONES

Physical milestones

- Improved appetite. Uses fork. Learning to pour. Can use cup handle.
- May drop afternoon nap or nap for one hour and sleep 11 hours at night.
- Very active: climbs, runs, darts about.
- Can remove all clothing and pull on simple clothes.
- Builds tower of eight cubes.
- Imitates speech of others.
- Can peddle a tricycle.

Psychosocial milestones

- Plays co-operatively with other children. Begins to share a toy when asked.
- Begins to express feelings with words.
- Egocentric in thought and action but empathy beginning to develop.
- Anxious to please and conform.
- Accepts self as an individual.

Cognitive milestones

- Preoperational cognitive stage (ages two to seven) – thinking is based on perception, not logic.
- Can only think of one variable at a time.
- Animalistic thinking: belief in inanimate objects having life. "Stuffies" are real.
- Begins to learn how power affects relationships and begins to learn socially acceptable behavior.
- Mythical and magical explanations readily accepted for natural phenomena.
- Combines words in two-to-three word sentences such as "me do it."
- Vocabulary growth is rapid: understands 300 – 1,000 words.
- Longer attention span of about 15 minutes.
- Begins to follow simple directions: "Put the toy in the box".

- Remembers and tells about things that happened two to three days ago, but may not be accurate or in the right order.

FOUR AND FIVE-YEAR-OLD DEVELOPMENTAL MILESTONES

Physical milestones

- Proficient at pouring and eating with spoon, fork, and cup.
- Has no naps but sleeps 12 hours at night.
- Cuts with small scissors and starts to hold paper and crayons appropriately.
- Very active. Begins to skip and hop. Can whirl around and turn somersaults. Can throw overhand.
- Can ride scooter or a two wheeled bike with training wheels.

Psychosocial milestones

- May have imaginary companions and engages in imaginary and fantasy play with other children.
- Hates to lose games.
- Begins sex role identification.
- Additional emotions are social related: guilt, insecurity, envy, confidence, humility.
- Enjoys interacting with adults through reading.
- Developing a bit of self-control and delayed gratification for five to ten minutes.
- Begins to obey and respect simple rules.
- Likes to be independent, often refusing help.
- Begins to show sympathy and guilt.
- More fears with increased awareness of dangers.
- Few inhibitions, especially socially, where they are very honest and blunt.
- Some tension outlets occur – nail-biting, nose-picking.
- Enjoys silly and non-sense poems, rhymes, and jokes.

Cognitive milestones

- Still in preoperational stage.
- Begins to learn consequences of one's behavior. Cause and effect are still difficult concepts to master. Just starting to connect personal actions with other people's responses.
- Asks many, many questions about everything: how, why, when, what, and where?
- Begins to distinguish between edible and non-edible substances.
- May understand the word: "Soon," and "Wait a little while."
- Can follow two related directions: "Close the book and give it to me."

- Understands questions about a story: "Where did the bunny go?"
- Sentences are three and four words long.
- Gives directions as "Fix this for me."
- Memory is rote. Must start from beginning to remember items in their order: numbers, song verses.
- Often confuses sequence of events.
- Has no concept of time as we define it but in sequence of events: count days in "sleeps."
- Completes four to five-piece puzzle.
- Longer attention span: about 20 minutes.
- Organizes toys by color and size.
- Relates from an experience from two to three days past.
- Does not recognize limits. Just beginning to learn them.
- Inventive with words – makes up words to suit situation as "gadzillions".
- Learning self-control but takes much practice.

PARENTS MATTER

Unhelpful parenting behaviors

- Teasing or taunting child about their abilities or aspects of their developmental tasks.
- Discouraging the child from talking or asking questions.
- Laughing and discounting child's fantasies and play.
- Discounting fears, anger, and uncomfortable feelings.
- Expecting more reason, understanding and logic at this stage. Not within the child's capacity yet.

Helpful parenting behaviors

- Respond to questions with honest, thoughtful, answers.
- Teach, model, and encourage appropriate behavior.
- Talk about boundaries and help solve problems.
- Have predictable routines and rituals.
- Accept imaginary companions.
- Don't accept lying. Help the child identify differences between fantasy and reality without punishing.
- Listen to child's recount of dreams, thoughts, and questions.
- Nurture child through touch, words, actions, and feelings.
- All accumulated helpful parenting behaviors for babies and toddlers.
- Provide parent self care.

DISCIPLINE TOOLS FOR PRESCHOOLERS

Stay with your "no"
Honor promises
Give a choice in time or place
Give warnings of transitions
I-statements
Get eye contact
Give choices between three things
Use the when/then rule
Show and tell correct behavior – role play
Clarify expectations
Use a timer, clock, or calendar to set time limits
Reflective questions
Stimulation
Tell a story with an appropriate moral
Make the opposite request
Change environment
Be polite, kind, and firm
Pick your battles
Parent time-out
Give positive feedback
Parent guided problem-solving
Model
Active listen
Connect, then direct
Time-in
Natural consequences
Show how to use their words
Give information
Give attention and spend time together
Supervision
Holding, hugs, and cuddles

Stay with your "no"

This is the most important discipline tool for this age. Preschoolers can better understand "no" and if you honor your words. Follow through whenever you say something, and it should lesson nagging and whining later on. You need to be credible. Mean what you say and say what you really mean, even if your child is protesting violently. Be sure that you have thought it out and you really mean "no."

Honor promises

If you agree to provide something or go somewhere, do your best to follow through. Children notice when you follow-through or are wishy-washy. They count on your word. If you really can't take them to the park after work, don't promise it in order to get out the door.

Give a choice in time or place (if no choice in action)

If there is a job that needs to be done and your child doesn't have much choice about it, you can still build in some choices about time or location. "Would you like to have a bath or go swimming?" Make sure both choices are acceptable to you. Choices, such as, "Do you want to stay here or go home with Mommy?" are not acceptable if you want your child to go home with you right now. Don't give them a choice that you can't honor. A better choice would be "We have to go now. Would you like to walk or have Mommy carry you?" Other choices are "Would you like to clean up the toys now or in 10 minutes?"

Give warnings of transitions

Most young children have a hard time with transitions. It helps to warn them of the next impending activity. "In five minutes we are leaving to go home." Young children can't tell when five minutes are up, so you can also rephrase it in terms of how many more times the activity will take place. "Three more slides and we will go." "Finish your house and then we will clean up the blocks and go home." Then go!

If your child has a hard time with transitions, sell it to your child. Talk about the next activity. "I'm craving a drink. Want to go to the car and get a juice box?" or "I think the birds (your pets) are getting lonely at our place." (Or you can use a favorite stuffed animal name.) "We should go home and visit them."

Try to plan unstructured time in your day where you don't have to rush off some-where and the child could possibly determine leaving time. He feels like he has some control over some things.

For children that struggle with time concepts, show them another way. Five fingers, then four fingers, then three fingers, and so on. One mom shows her child by decreasing the space between her hands. Every five minute warning, the space decreases six inches until there is no space left and it's time to go. You could adjust the space/time left to fit your needs.

Sometimes I will say, "We have to go now. Take your last slide" and my son would say, "No, I want three more last slides." Then we negotiate. It's very important to leave on the "last" that you agreed on, otherwise, the child will not believe you when you say "this is the last time." Just pick them up and go to the car. You may have to carry them flailing and screaming, but you have honored your promises.

Avoid saying, "We are leaving in five minutes, okay?" if you really plan to leave in five minutes. Never ask a question that you might get a "no" answer to! It's better to say, "We are leaving in five minutes." Period.

I-statements

One day, my son was really angry when I put him in the car seat. He was screaming "Stupid Mommy!" I frowned and said, "I don't like that!" and turned around and continued to drive. I gave him my best "I-statement" for the situation, and I really meant it with my body language. Again, at this age, use as few words as possible.

Get eye contact

Parenting is an active sport. Go to your child, and engage eye contact with them, so you know they are listening and hearing you.

Give choices between three things

Toddlers can handle two things. Preschoolers can handle three. Choices allow them power and independence within the safety of your guidance. Choices actually raises the chemical in the brain called serotonin, which is the "feel good" chemical.

Some parents ask what to do when their child won't make a choice. If you've given them the opportunity, and they refuse, then you certainly can make the choice yourself.

Use the when/then rule

This is also called "Grandma's rule" and is used as a positive reinforcement tool. It's a promise of something pleasant in order to entice a child to do something they may not wish to do at that moment. Basically, you say, "When_____ then _____ will happen." It's not a bribe, but a reminder of the natural order of things. It's very helpful for moving preschoolers and toddlers through daily duties.

"When you get your coat on, then we will go to the park."
"When you finish your milk, then we will have dessert."
"When you get into pajamas, then we will read books."

Show and tell correct behavior; role play

The acorn really doesn't fall far from the tree. In order to raise a responsible citizen, the parent must show she is one. Preschoolers are great imitators. Let's take birthday parties for an example. Children need some advance social role play preparation. Teach them the words to "Happy Birthday." Role play how to give a gift and how to let the birthday child open their own gift, and blow out the candles. Prep them that they might not get a treat bag. Also tell them which areas are off bounds in people's houses and that they need to ask to use anything. Your preschooler will not remember all this, of course, but it's the beginning of social learning.

Clarify expectations

 Children are likely to live up to what you believe in them.
~ Lady Bird Johnson, First Lady

Tell your children exactly what specific descriptive behavior you expect. You may need to use pictures to show what you mean or show them actual items. For example, "We are going into the bank. You may look out the window at the trains. You may not run, scream, or swing on the dividers." Give them a reminder if you see them doing it while in the bank. If they don't comply, then finish up quickly and leave. Change the environment and do the banking next on your own time.

Share expectations before any big event. Give specifics. Say, "We are going to Grandma's and you can't run around the house playing chase, jump on the sofa, or scream." "We are going to a quiet meeting and you must sit and play with your crayons and paper." Be aware of time expectations for small children. A quiet meeting lasting longer than 20 minutes may stretch your child's capabilities. Don't forget a last minute refresher just before entry. If they can't comply, take them home, stay calm, and make arrangements next time for childcare.

Use a timer, clock, or calendar to set time limits

This helps in that the child will sometimes respond better to a neutral force imposing limits instead of Mom or Dad. When the timer or clock goes off, it's time to end an activity. It is also helpful if another adult sets a limit, too. A preschooler will listen to a bus driver asking him to keep his feet off the seat better than if it's another endless request from Mom.

Reflective questions

Instead of telling what will happen, ask what they think might happen if they do something. It's really interesting to get inside a child's head and see how they are thinking. Be genuinely interested. Avoid being sarcastic. A simple, "If everyone took a candy bar without paying the store, what would happen to the store? Would they make any money to feed their families? How would they feed their families then?" This is a great technique for preschoolers who are trying to figure out the "why" questions. It also encourages moral thinking and helps with oral expression skills. Say, "If you jump on my kitchen bench, it will break. Where will we sit for supper then?"

Stimulation

In these years, children love to play with everything. Their creativity and imagination soar. They love to play different games, scenarios, and plays. Favorite toys are people, cars, markers, puzzles, simple building materials, bikes, balls, playdough, painting, crafts, sandbox, water play, and sports equipment. Even though your child is at an age where you don't need to cart a diaper bag, you might want to still bring a bag or backpack of interesting toys, paper, and markers, wet and dry snacks, spare shirt, and wipes with you on every outing. Preschoolers still have limited attention span for boring activities.

HOW TO HANDLE WAITING TIMES

Bring a roll of masking tape in your purse. Keep a supply of little toys from fast food restaurants (ones you don't mind losing) or pick up stickers from the dollar store, small kaleidoscopes, flashlights, magnifying glasses, or toy cars. Something new is always more appealing. Tiny picture books you can read or they can look at pictures; a pen and small notebook they can scribble in. Snacks are also great. If they take long to eat, or unwrap, even better! If you have brought nothing, teach them "rock, paper, scissors" or "I spy" or even make up a story.

Tell a story with an appropriate moral

Use a similar situation the child was involved in. Ask reflective questions on how the character in the story might feel and what would help? This is much more effective in lecturing as the child almost always gets the point but doesn't feel accused or defensive.

Preschoolers are notorious for telling stories, especially tall tales. You can handle it by laughing and saying, "What a great 'story' – let's write it down." You validate their creativity and let them know that it is fiction, which helps them save face. At this age, their lying isn't malicious. It's an extension of their fantasy world. Still, you want to help them know the difference between reality and fantasy.

Make the opposite request

After repeatedly asking my four-year-old son to get his shoes off the seat of the bus, he insisted on doing what he was doing. Then I asked him to keep his shoes ON the edge of the seat, and he immediately took them off! I believe my parents called this technique, "reverse psychology"!

Change environment

Don't think manipulating the environment is just for babies and toddlers! It's an effective tool for even preschoolers and school-aged children. It works on the premise that it's easier to change the environment than another person!

This is the age that preschoolers can really do a lot for themselves. Putting plastic bowls, cups, and cereal in a lower cupboard means they can get their own breakfast in the morning. It helps you and them. Try to look at your house and see what daily routines can be made easier by changing the setup. Pack away (for awhile) those items that cause a lot of discipline problems.

The ages from three to seven are really bad for helping a child to learn how to lose graciously. Children can take losing very hard. I packed away the board games (and banned competitive games) during those ages because the children would get such hard feelings. It's a stage they all went through. They lose quite graciously, now, but I sure had to do some childproofing then.

> The number one discipline complaint is that children "don't listen."
> What parents really mean is that the children don't
> do what the parents ask.

In class, I ask parents to list on a board all the actions they want their children to do during the day, beginning when they get up and when they go to bed. The list might look something like this:

Wake-up, brush teeth, get dressed, brush hair, get out breakfast items, eat breakfast, put away dishes, gather papers, gather items needed for the day (sports equipment, signed letters), jackets, outerwear, shoes on, get into car, get out of car, go to daycare, or preschool. Assume they stay for lunch. After daycare or school, put jacket on at daycare or preschool, put on outerwear, put on shoes, gather papers, artwork, and take home items, get in car, stop at store on way home, get back to car, go into the house, hang up jacket, put art away, put shoes away, get snack out, eat, clean up snack, play, pick up toys, help set table, eat supper, help clean up, play, get a book for bed, have a bedtime snack, brush teeth, take clothes off, put clothes in laundry, get into bath, dry, clean up water, get into pajamas, get into bed, and go to sleep.

> Parents discover that most of their day with their child (and most of their
> conversation) is 90 percent directives – everyday.
> It's no wonder the children stop listening.

The above list has at least 50 items for a preschooler to do on time every day. That's not even counting the directives they have to follow at preschool or daycare. That's a lot of things to prod another person to do. The list is even longer for school-aged children when you add homework and after school activities to the list.

Any tricks parents can use for moving the preschooler through are helpful:

- Routines where one action follows another help to cut down interruptions.
- Changing the environment so that items the child needs and actions they must do are very easy to reach and do.
- Visual reminders, such as pictures posted at stations and checklists, help the child remember without parent nagging.
- When/then incentives.
- Connect with eye contact and a kind word, then direct.

Recent studies from the University of Minnesota show that children don't develop the ability to multitask until age 16 or so. That's one reason why when children say, "I'll do it later" and they forget because they can't hold too many instructions in their minds while they are on task doing other things like homework, playing computer. We moms are experts at keeping details of a running to do lists in our head, but children lack those brain pathways.

Be polite, kind, and firm

Politeness and kindness can be combined with discipline. Use your sincere please, and thank you!

Pick your battles

The children ask for 10 things in a row and we say 10 "no's", then expect them to comply with all of our requests. No wonder we get a "no" back. If some things are not a big deal and saying "yes" would count toward brownie points, do it! It's just relationship common sense that people we do nice things for, tend to want to give back.

Parent time-out

Still necessary.

Give positive feedback

We all love to be appreciated. We all love to have someone grateful for what we do. We all love to be noticed and have our work noticed. We love to have our work displayed (trophies, blogs, photos), and we all love to be acknowledged publicly. Positive emotional feedback is what we crave and so do our children. Our human need for attention and recognition are sometimes sabotaged by parents, who think that good behavior and good acts should happen without being noticed. Some parents worry that positive feedback would undermine parent authority. Quite the opposite. It helps children respect parents, feel good about themselves and seek improvement.

Parent-guided problem-solving

Children love to brainstorm. Have them first come up with several ideas that you will write down. They love to see their ideas on paper. It validates them and makes them feel important. If they can't move forward, you could make a suggestion, "How about...?" Preschoolers are very adept at this, and it's a great time to start learning the problem-solving process. For more on the problem solving process, see Chapter 10.

Model

Ever notice how many couples drive together, and the woman is in the passenger seat and the man is driving? What books say this is the rule? Even two-year-olds pick that up. They not only look to you, but also to the people driving outside the windows, movies, TV, billboard ads to understand why parents sit as they do in cars.

Watch especially how you treat other people, from your partner all the way to the grocery clerk who gave you wrong change. Your children are picking up tone of voice, words, actions, and reactions, and they will copy them.

Modeling is an extension of social learning theory. All people imitate people those who they admire and respect, not people they hate and fear. All children are great imitators. Modeling is such a powerful force, that it's included as a tool in all age categories. In fact, if all parents did was model correct behavior and didn't correct their child on any negative behavior, children would be keen to learn how to behave properly in society, based on how the adults act. Many cultures do this, and it works in their child rearing.

> Modeling the behavior you want your children to emulate is the single most powerful thing you can do to teach them anything.
> ~ Carol McD Wallace, Author

Active listening

Preschoolers are learning language fast and picking up the "feeling" words vocabulary. My son, at three, hated the dentist. He wouldn't cooperate in getting dressed to go there. I actively listened to him by saying, "You seem <u>afraid</u> to go to the dentist? Are you <u>worried</u> that he might hurt you?" He responded with tears and nods. I hugged him and let him cry. After a few minutes, he said, "Let's go." With absolute surprise, I realized the power of active listening. He wanted his feelings heard and validated before he was ready to move on and face the action. If I would have responded with "C'mon, you are a big brave boy, and you can handle it." We would never have got out the door!

Connect, then direct

Pretty well every parenting strategy works better if there is a strong emotional connection between parent and child. Look at the situation from their point of view, empathize, and then offer a direction. "This TV show looks like fun, but I really need you to put your shoes on now." Remember that their attention span is very focused, so you may have to put their shoes on while they are watching! Remember, talk, and then back it up with action!

Time-in

It's the next best preschooler discipline tool, and it's not even about discipline. It's about spending quality time together building the relationship. "Watch me...keep watching. Will you watch me?" is a statement from preschoolers begging for time and attention. Time-in is not just about helping calm your child or solve problems. It can very a positive way to build the relationship when things are going well! Preschoolers love to have parents see their latest accomplishments. Take a few minutes and really watch. Smile and say a few kind words of appreciation

Time-in also involves going to your child, holding her and hugging her whenever she is distressed, upset, hurt, or sick. It's nurturing words, attention, and physical touch.

Natural consequences

One day my son was with me in the store. He really wanted a truck, and I said "no" to buying him one. He started to fuss, scream, and carry on. He looked at me and kicked me. If I was a spoiling parent, I wouldn't be able to stand his unpleasant feelings, and I would be feeling pretty bad too. To alleviate both our unpleasant feelings, I would give in and buy him the truck. The next time he wanted something in a store, he would do the same thing because it obviously worked.

I'm not a punishment parent, but I'm not permissive one either. When my son kicked me, I used a natural consequence. If my friend or partner kicked me, I would have looked at them with hurt, said loudly, "I don't deserve that." And left them. I would not call them for a good long while, until they contacted me to apologize. My son needed to learn that also. I looked at him in the store, held his hands, and said, "I don't like being kicked. That hurts!" in a very loud, angry voice. I then left my shopping and drove him home in silence. I had to go back later and finish shopping. Once home, we never spoke for awhile. And here is the natural consequences part: I didn't want to interact with him until he apologized very sincerely. I needed time to feel better.

We parents do so much for our children. When people treat us badly, by kicking us, or hitting us, we can choose not to do any favors for those people. It's not meant to punish them. It's honoring our feelings of anger, hurt, and sadness when our children treat us like doormats.

When we withdraw our offer to do nice things for children, we show the real world workings. People just don't do you favors when you treat them badly. It's a lesson that preschoolers can learn. And sincere apologies make all the difference. It may not come with words from a preschooler, but in actions, such as him giving you a hug or giving you a teddy bear. If your child apologizes, be sure to not hold grudges. Forgive, hug and forget.

Modeling natural consequences is another way to teach. We need to show the children how to make restitution by following through, ourselves. Our daughter heard that I left a case of pop in my husband's car. At –24 degrees in the winter, the case burst. My husband didn't yell and scream at me, but he had an expectation that I would clean it up. I apologized to him and negotiated a date that I would clean it. And I did. The children saw that I got a bucket of water and soap and a scraper. They were keen to know how I did it and also wanted to eat the frozen sweet!

Natural consequence checklist
- If you break it, fix it.
- If you use it, put it back.
- If you lose it, replace it.
- If you need it, ask for it.
- If you damage it, repair it.
- If you drop it, pick it up.
- If you make a mess, clean it up.
- If you promise it, follow through.
- If you hurt it, make amends.

Show how to use their words

Often, we say "Use your words," but preschoolers that are very emotional have a hard time knowing what words to say. It's easy for a preschooler to be overwhelmed when they are tired, hungry, or stressed. That contributes to being unable to ask for things in words. Say, "Here is how to ask...'Mommy, I want to play outside, please.' Can you say that?"

Give information

Even with preschoolers, we have to say the same things 20 times a week. Use the same phrases over and over again when reciting rules: "Touch the cat gently. Dishes go in dishwasher. Use your indoor voice. Treats after meals." It means explaining the same thing a hundred times until they get it! And they will eventually get it. You will know because they say the same things to "the children" when they are playing house and they are the mommies!

Give attention – spend time together

Children at the toddler and preschooler age are notorious for demanding attention. This is the age of "Mommy, watch me." "Mommy, can you read me a book? Mommy, can you play with me?" Do it often and as long as they need you to. It's an important developmental need. Often, it takes less time to sit down and focus attention on a child and fill up their needs, than to constantly demand they "find something to do and leave you be," or discipline them when they don't leave you be. Be proactive and give lots of attention. It's much more positive and quicker in the long run. Especially, if you have a day where you need to get a lot done.

Supervision

Supervision is still a must for preschoolers 24 hours a day. When preschoolers misbehave, it's usually from the lack of parent supervision. Preschoolers still have a lack of self-control and need to be watched.

Holding, hugs, and cuddles

Sometimes hugs, cuddles, and kind words of appreciation are hard to give to a child that has been testing the limits and pushing your buttons all day. But the old saying, "love them the most when they deserve it the least" really rings true. Sometimes, the child that deserves appreciations the least really needs it the most. A kind word, some positive attention, reinforcement of love and appreciation, a special hug and cuddle can really change the day's mood. It can be hard for adults to switch gears and be appreciative with a kind comment, hug, or thank you, but it can really turn things around. Much more effective then a time-out or spanking.

Many parents ask, "What if my child has just hit another child and I reward him with some cozy, huggy time-in? Won't that increase the behavior?" Yes, if he is attention deprived, and that's the only time he gets attention – when he is misbehaving. No, if he gets attention in other positive ways, and you never, never forget to add the teaching and talking at the end of the hug. Sometimes, children need a hug first to calm down and be assured of love. It's a way to connect with them. Then, when they are tuned in to listening to you, the teaching part begins. It's very important to add the teaching part after the hug so the message sinks in and stays with them.

SPECIAL PRESCHOOLER BEHAVIOR CONCERNS
PRESCHOOLERS AND SELF-CONTROL

During the 1960s, psychologist Walter Mischel conducted the famous "marshmallow test" with four-year-olds in the preschool at Stanford University to assess each preschooler's ability to delay gratification. Each four-year-old was given one marshmallow. They were told they could eat it immediately or, if they waited until the researcher returned in 20 minutes, they could have two marshmallows. Some children in the group just couldn't wait. They gobbled down the marshmallow immediately. The rest struggled hard to resist eating it. They covered their eyes, talked to themselves, sang, played games, and even tried to go to sleep. The preschoolers who were able to wait were rewarded with two marshmallows when the researcher returned. Twelve to 14 years later, these same children were re-evaluated as teenagers. The preschoolers who were able to delay gratification had the same abilities later in life.

Learning self-control takes a lot of practice and maturity. When we tell preschoolers not to touch things in stores at Christmas, they are still learning self-control and may not listen. That's normal and okay. They will learn eventually. By school-age, delayed gratification and self-control is much more developed in children so expectations can be higher. Until then, it's not fair to punish preschoolers for diminished self-control. We can tell them not to touch, but taking action and removing them works much better.

Many parents of school-aged children admit, in hindsight, that their expectation of behavior in the preschool years was a bit high for the capabilities of their children. Parents often breathe a sigh of relief from attending parenting classes, knowing they are not the only ones experiencing challenges, but also that their children are very normal in their development and behavior.

POWER STRUGGLES

Three-year-olds are big at testing the rules stage, and it's perfectly normal. Preschoolers are learning about power and how they can wield it. In fact, I would worry if most children didn't go through this stage. It's a stretching of their brains and finding out what happens "if I do this or that." Or "How is my power different when I'm with Mom or Dad? Or my brothers? Or my teachers? Or in church or on a Tuesday?" It's a learning process, where preschoolers find out the positive ways to use their power, such as empathy, friendship, and cooperation, and the negative ways to use their power, such as bullying, refusing to eat, and going to bed.

HOW TO NURTURE YOUR CHILD'S CREATIVITY

A preschoolers' world revolves around fantasy and imaginative play. There is much you can do to nurture their creativity. A creative child has an immense gift to brainstorm solutions to any problem and this skill will get them far in life.

Beyond academics: What do parents teach?
Leadership: Give the child leadership roles when school-age.

Self-esteem, self-worth, and self-confidence: Accept them for who they are and be secure in the knowledge they will take healthy risks. Let "You can do it!" be your mantra.

Oral expression: Let them tell you their stories, fantasies, fears, explanations, and ideas.

Listening skills: Listen to them and show them the importance of hearing others.

Initiative: Avoid squelching their ideas even if they seem far-fetched. Encourage negotiation and problem-solving. If they wish to set up a lemonade stand in the middle of winter, help them. Let them discover their own mistakes.

Creativity: Supply them with what they need, add encouragement, and let them go at their projects. Encourage them to think outside the box.

Curiosity: Encourage questions. What if? How? What do you think would happen? Answer their questions with another question to help them discover the answer.

Community involvement: Volunteer as a family. Time well spent.

Interpersonal and intrapersonal skills: Actively listen and use I-statements. Help them develop a feeling word vocabulary and how to use to. Help them discover and feel their feelings and recognize them in others.

Motivation: Avoid bribes and punishments. Emphasize good feelings from accomplishment. "Doesn't it feel good to have a clean room?" Is better than offering a cookie.

Cooperation: Show the benefits of cooperating. "See how much we get done when we work together?"

Persistence: Model the benefits of persistence in your own life.

Positive optimistic attitude: Fake it until you make it. Laugh and the world will laugh with you.

STAGES OF PLAY AND HOW FRIENDSHIP EVOLVES

- Babies: solitary play – watch others but not much interactive play.
- Toddlers: parallel play – watch others and grab toys to see reaction. Gives toys back to see reaction.
- Preschoolers: associative play – beginning to play together but still in own world of fantasy. Some bits of "you be the mommy, and I'll be the kid" type of imaginative play. Friendships largely based on who is close by and able to come over.
- School-age: cooperative play and interest play – much more fantasy, imaginative play, with or without props. Friendships are based on similar interests. When girls and boys are with same sex groups, they will forego what they want to play individually and go with the group to fit in.

- Teenagers: interest and value based friendships. Developing deep, meaningful, reciprocal friendships that adults have.
- Adults: interests and similar lifestyle friendships.

TIMELESS TOYS FOR ALL AGE GROUPS

Unstructured play materials: Unstructured toys are ones that focus on process and experience and not the end result or goal. There is no right or wrong way to play with them. Children of all ages can use them to different abilities. A box of blocks can be used by an 18-month-old to stack or a 10-year-old to build elaborate structures and tunnels for a train set. Children can also project their own meaning on the play. It helps them express their feelings, fears, and whatever is going on in their life at that moment and can be very therapeutic. Materials can be combined in many different ways. They stretch a child's imagination by drawing on his creative abilities to play with them in many ways. He gets to make all the decisions of how the play goes and that can build self-esteem. Unstructured toys tend to be the best value toys because they span the ages and are usually kid driven, not battery driven!

Examples: blocks, markers and paper (not coloring books), paints and paper, goop, play dough and clay, people and cars and houses, dolls and clothes, glue, paper, scissors, and bits, cardboard boxes, pots, pans, spoons and plastic containers, ride on toys, bikes, play kitchen, food and dishes, cash register, balls, pails, sand, water and containers, Lego™, K'NEX™, and other building materials, dress up clothes, sidewalk chalk, box of odds and ends craft materials, tape and boxes, stuffed animals, puppets, and plastic animals.

Structured play materials: Toys can only be played with in a certain way. Often, they come with instructions or batteries. Children lose interest after they mastered it or become frustrated with it because it's too difficult for their development.

Examples: puzzles, craft kits, shape sorters, board games, computer games, coloring books, play dough kits, building kits, paint by number kits, remote control cars.

School-aged children still carry on imaginative play through playing house, theatre, puppets, pirates, aliens, action figures, and construction materials. However, computer games hold enormous appeal because of the ability to go places never seen before and try on different identities in a safe way. Creativity, imagination, and problem-solving still occur but through a different medium.

Opportunities for free play tend to diminish the older a child gets and it's even worse through the teen years, due to the increasing reliance on structured activities and lack of downtime thanks to a more rigorous academic program. We need to preserve unstructured time for older children so they can freely play, enjoy being creative, and de-stress their lives.

The best summer was when we dug up the roots to two huge spruce trees we had cut down in the backyard. Our whole backyard was one giant mud puddle. Pails, shovels, toy cars, people, and a garden hose provided 20 neighborhood children with days and weeks of building fun. Their parents weren't too impressed when I sent them home to use their own bathroom, but the children had a blast! Mud, dirt, water, sand, props, and imagination. What more could they ask for?

Toddler, preschooler, and school-aged play ideas that encourage creativity, imagination, initiative, and problem-solving:

- A big rubber bin filled with puffed wheat, rice, lentils, trucks and cars, measuring spoons and cups make a great indoor sandbox.
- Crayon rubbings with white paper over coins, is fun to do.
- Darken the room and make shadow puppets.
- Buy an old turntable at a garage sale. Put paper on the spindle and give markers and crayons for children to draw on while it is spinning.
- Throw an old mattress on the basement floor and let the children jump. Old couch cushions work great for forts and old sheets for roofs, walls, and drapings. Tables and chairs would also hold sheets for fort play.
- Save junk mail, envelopes and stickers and let the children play post office.
- Allow the children to use your video camera to make Lego™ movies after you've given a care lesson and are supervising.
- Encourage combining toys. If your son carts the play dough out to the sand box to make breaded patties, let him! Most people keep play dough and sand separate, but your child doesn't have to.
- Get a basic car track that you put together in a line. Then use pillows to make hills and valleys. See how far the cars will go.
- Play doesn't have to be goal orientated or productive. It's okay to daydream and listen to music or stare out the window and watch clouds.
- Fill the baby bathtub or bowls with soapy water and let them play.
- Use a small stool as a play table in the bathtub and give them cups to pour from and in.
- Get a small trampoline to jump on. Or designate certain sofa cushions for jumping on and fort building.
- Use rubber jumping balls (with handles) in the house to work off excess energy during cold winter months. It won't damage wall corners and helps develop your child's balance.
- Blow bubbles from bubble solution on the kitchen floor. Use the excess soap to mop the floor after.
- Use a shaker filled with cornstarch that they can sprinkle outdoors.
- Let child help with garden chores, such as weeding and digging.
- Fill empty plastic soap containers with colored water to squirt pavement or snow.
- Put a plastic swimming pool under a slide.

- Paint the house with water filled pails and paintbrushes.
- Let children wash the car, bikes, or bike trailer.
- Give a toddler a clean dustpan for a snow shovel. (Put rubber gloves over a child's gloves so they won't get wet when they play outside with wet snow days.)
- Get big boxes from appliance shops for forts.
- Use old receiving blankets for capes and doll blankets.
- Have a bedroom dresser with drawers for storage of art materials: old bits of wrapping paper, string, tubes, egg cartons, paints, brushes, magazines, paper scraps. Or have an easy to reach craft box of odds and ends: ribbons, cards, paper, markers, scissors, glue or glue sticks, glitter, paint, rulers so the children can help themselves and create a craft that is unstructured and entirely of their own imagination.
- Drape old sheets over the bunk-bed top for a puppet or stuffie theatre.
- Spread sofa cushions over the floor for islands.
- Use nail polish to fix holes in inflatable toys.
- Any small gadget or appliance that is broken is wonderful to take apart and unscrew with parent supervision. Check out second hand shops and garage sales for free stuff.
- For easy clean up of puzzles, put a colored dot on the back of each puzzle piece. Easy to separate and put back.
- Use a portable carpenter's tray to carry markers, scissors, and rulers. Makes for easy cleanup and moving around the house.
- Have a dedicated craft table if you have room. Sometimes building projects take more than a few days and will be out of the way.
- Paint with toy car tires or anything with texture. Roll a marble in paint.
- Melt broken crayons into foil lined muffin cups for mosaic crayons.
- Pre-hammer some nails into wood scraps and let preschoolers hammer the rest in. They love real tools.
- Have a decoy drawer of real, unused, broken items that are old cell phones and keyboards.
- Draw on an old shower curtain a number of roads, buildings and city features so they can customize a car play mat.
- In a bathtub with no water, put your child in naked or with just underpants and add a bowl of chocolate pudding. Allow finger painting on the walls. Just hose down the walls and your child with a little soap afterwards.
- For children past the tasting stage, put small amounts of shaving cream in a muffin tin and tint with food color. Allow finger painting on the tub walls.
- Spread the sheets out on the floor and have a picnic in the house.
- Let the children ride bikes on the concrete basement floor.

STRATEGIES TO PREPARE YOUR CHILD
FOR THE NEW BABY'S ARRIVAL

You've brought your lovely new baby daughter home from the hospital, and you eagerly show her to your three-year-old son, who pats the baby lovingly. Five minutes pass, and your son says, "Mommy, give the baby back to the hospital and come play with me!"

Whether the new baby is your second or fifth child, the whole family will have to go through an adjustment phase.

"Sibling rivalry is the natural, normal competition between brothers and sisters vying for their parents love and affection. It exists in every family to some degree," said Dr. Spock, the eldest of six children. The following information may help your family experience a smoother transition.

Before the new baby arrives:
- Encourage your child to share your pregnancy with you by talking to the baby, visiting the doctor, and feeling the baby move. Take your child to the ultrasound visit.
- Read books or watch videos with your child, about pregnancy, giving birth, and having a new baby in the family.
- Arrange a caregiver and explain to your child who will care for them while you are giving birth.
- Make or buy a "welcome" present for your child to give to the new baby.
- Visit a friend with a new baby. If possible, watch breastfeeding.
- Avoid fostering unrealistic expectations about a new playmate.
- Put a picture of yourself in the child's room.
- Speak of the baby as "ours."
- Involve your child in choices, such as baby clothes, decorating.
- Show pictures and video of the child as a baby.
- The change in routine should be done well before the baby arrives: bedtime, clothes, toys, and Dad takes over some duties.

During the hospital stay or birth:
- Have a gift from the new baby to your child.
- Let the first visit at the hospital be "family" only.
- Have a camera ready for the child to take pictures.
- Have a framed picture of your child on the bedside table.
- Greet your child without the baby in your arms.
- Bonding tip: put your child's finger in the baby's palm. The new baby's reflex grasp will hold on.

- Remember your child is anxious to see you, not the baby.
- Let your child hold the baby. Supervise!
- Let your child announce the news to family and visitors.

At home after the birth:

- Discourage visitors for the first few days, if possible.
- Let your child come with Daddy to pick up Mom and baby at the hospital.
- Allow your child to take part in the baby's care, according to their capabilities, and desire.
- Have a supply of wrapped gifts to give to your child when friends bring baby gifts.
- Talk about your child's accomplishments to visiting relatives.
- Don't force positive interaction. Your child may feel indifferent or negative towards baby.
- Older children can assist in making birth announcements or fill them out.
- Encourage your children to phone relatives and share the news first.
- Mom and Dad should spend time alone with each sibling, especially Mom. It's tempting to spend all the time holding the baby, but make the effort to put the baby down or hand off to the other parent and spend time with the older child.
- Learn ways to include the older child when caring and attending to the baby. Put a stool next to change table so the older sibling can see.
- Avoid sending the older child away to relatives and friends. They need to feel included and valued, not shoved off.
- Don't leave baby alone with the older child. Avoid leaving baby carriers on couches, tables.
- The more positive interaction the two siblings have, the sooner a bond will develop and grow. Ask yourself how you can foster attachment and bonding between the siblings when they are fighting and you need to step in and discipline.
- Give extra hugs, cuddles, smiles, patience, and understanding.
- Give your older child new privileges: later bed, pouring juice, things they like to do, help Mom with cooking.
- If you are stressed, get support rather than take it out on the children.
- Don't expect "older child" behavior from your child, such as waiting, crossing roads, etc., if they aren't ready.
- Avoid getting a new pet.
- "Tell" the baby the rules about hitting. It takes the attention off the child. "We don't hit. Right, baby?"
- Keep on going to the older child's activities as much as possible.
- Have a special basket of books, games, or toys to play with your child while nursing the baby.

- Don't blame lack of time on the baby. Use any other reason.
- Emphasize positives such as "Baby can't have juice; only big children get juice!" Point out that the older child can go to park, stay up later.
- Do your fussing, cooing, and awing over the new baby in private. Even if it's your fourth or fifth child, you will still do it!
- Interpret the baby's signals for your older child. "Look Johnny, baby is smiling at you! I bet he can't wait until you can play blocks with him."
- If the baby stops crying when the older child walks in the room, point out that the baby must have been very happy to see him.
- Emphasize the positives of the new family size: look, we fill the van now. Look, we have more people at our table. Look, everyone gets more Christmas and birthday presents!

Encourage communication:

- Ask your child what they like/don't like about the new baby. Accept all responses. Don't answer with, "Yes, but..."
- Acknowledge the challenges, "Mommy sure spends a lot of time feeding the baby, eh?"
- Be patient and reassure your child you will always love her, if she shows signs of jealousy, regression, or aggression.
- Acknowledge your child's feelings. You don't have to agree with him in order to accept and validate them. To help him express them, ask "How do you feel about the baby?" Have him draw a picture or give him a doll or puppet and ask him to show you how he feels. Your child will have mixed feelings, such as excitement, envy, anger, hope, indifference, or loss, especially of the "old" family and routines. Show him that all feelings are acceptable, although there are limits on behaviors. The more your child can express his feelings directly to you, the less chance he will act out in negative behavior to you or the baby.

Possible behaviors when the babymoon is over

It will depend on your older child's age, verbal ability, temperament, personality, birth order, and anger management practices in the family.

Regression: Most young children regress with the following behaviors. Allowing them a demonstration of these behaviors will satisfy their curiosity and help them become independent much faster, than if you deny them the babyish behavior.

- Potty training/night dryness – accept that it will happen.
- Breast/bottle feeding – indulge bottles. Go with your comfort level about breastfeeding. Many mothers nurse toddlers and preschoolers, so it's not an abnormal action. Many toddlers who have stopped nursing will try the breast out of curiosity, but not resume breastfeeding.
- Baby talk – indulge.

- Acting silly – indulge.
- Thumb-sucking – indulge.
- Trying out baby's gear – indulge.

Aggression:
- Hitting you or baby – don't let them. Hold hands, say "no", and redirect.
- Temper tantrums – ignore and acknowledge feelings after.
- Biting – say "no", and give something safe to bite.
- Mauling – ignore if the baby is safe. Give attention later.

Clinginess: Indulge, and fulfill needs. Meeting their need for security builds independence.

Whining/attitude: Ignore, but meet needs when asked for respectfully.

Deliberate misbehavior: Ignore, keep everyone safe, encourage and notice good behavior, and childproof.

Meal/sleep disturbances: Minimize nighttime separations with parents. Secure children move into their own rooms faster than children forced to sleep alone.

Negative suggestions: Be positive. Say, "No, we can't give the baby to another family, but I can understand sometimes it's hard to listen to a new baby cry."

You look at your first child and wonder if you will love another child as much. But you soon discover that love spreads like candlelight. As you light another candle from the first, the new flame doesn't take any fire away from the original candle. Your child will eventually discover it, too.

SIBLING RIVALRY REMEDIES

"Your children fight?" people ask incredulously, when I am presenting a parenting workshop. My answer is, "Of course! Every person in a love relationship fights." I prefer to say that every relationship has conflict. It's normal and inevitable to disagree. However, the determining factor in the quality of the relationship is how the fights get resolved.

 Fights are about feelings.

Conflict happens between partners, parents, relatives, friends, neighbors, co-workers, group members, governments, countries, and everyone else. Why would the sibling relationship be any different? You know it's going to happen. But like many things in parenting, it's better to know what you are dealing with and have some planned strategies.

Reasons Children Fight

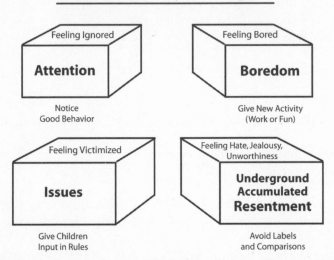

First, know there are four basic types of sibling conflicts. Each conflict type is driven by an underlying feeling. Most all relationship fights are generally about feelings and not so much about the presenting issues. So the best way to deal with sibling fights is to deal head on with the feelings rather than the issue. Here are the reasons children fight and what the child's underlying feelings are:

Boredom The underlying feeling is – you guessed it! Boredom! What better way for your child to have some fun than to bug someone he knows is going to give him a great reaction?

- **Unhelpful parent strategy:** Ignoring the fight; punishing the child.
- **Helpful parent strategy:** Give your child a new, interesting activity that is work, fun, or something to do with you or someone else. Grab a book and the victim and start reading. Everyone calms down, gets some literacy skills, and the other child may come and join you. Casually separating the children also helps, but don't make it an enforced time-out.

Parental attention Your child is feeling left out, unloved, ignored, or un-noticed. Your child is silently screaming: "Notice me, whether negatively or positively, just notice me!"

- **Unhelpful parent strategy:** Giving negative attention in the form of a punishment, time-out, or time spent playing judge and jury, is unhelpful.

- **Helpful parent strategy:** Avoid punishments. Ignore the fighting, but give more individual time and attention later when the fighting has subsided. Get up and retreat to the bathroom, closet, garden, or basement. Often, the fighting subsides when there is no audience.

This is your wake up call. The children need more individual attention. Avoid giving attention immediately at the time of the fight. You don't want to encourage the negative way of asking for the need to be met, but you do recognize the need and should attend to it later. When one sibling is constantly fighting with another, I make a concerted effort to give that child more attention, hugs, and cuddles, and kind words. I find that they then respond better to the other siblings. Schedule a date night or time alone with just that child.

Acknowledge pleasant sibling interactions when they occur. Many parents tell me they are "afraid" to notice and acknowledge kindness among siblings, because then the magic will stop and they will start fighting. But children really need to know that loving relationships is desirable.

Try to not think of the group of children as bundles. Schedule rituals unique to each one. My daughter and I do Girl Guide activities together, separate from the boys. One son loves to read, so I read his series of books so we can find times to talk about them together. Just with him and not the other siblings. One child loves movies, so just the two of us go together. When your child asks you to "watch me," make a concerted effort to watch, as long as he needs you to. Fill that attention need.

<u>Issues</u> Your child is feeling victimized, angry, frustration, or injustice over a reason.

- **Unhelpful parent strategy:** Playing judge by directing who the perpetrator and victim was and how restitution should be made. Taking away fought over toys or privileges. Punishing both children regardless of the issue.
- **Helpful parent strategy:** Avoid punishments. Avoid sending them to separate rooms, and avoid taking the toy away. You want them to learn how to solve the problem, not avoid it. Your role is to facilitate the problem solving process.

<u>Accumulated underground resentments</u> This type of fighting usually occurs when the other three types of fights (boredom, attention, and issues) are resolved by unhelpful parenting strategies. When the parent steps in and tries to solve the children's problems or punishes sibling fighting, the child will harbor resentment toward the parent and the other sibling. The resentments are acted out when children relentlessly pick on their siblings and constantly look for ways to bug them discretely. This underground revenge drives the parent bananas. There is no real issue presenting itself. If the parent's approach is to help the children solve his sibling problems respectfully, this type of fighting rarely surfaces in siblings.

Your child may be feeling accumulated hatred and resentments toward their sibling and may also be feeling jealous, unworthy, unloved, victimized, unvalued, or discarded.

- **Unhelpful parenting strategies:** Group punishments, taking away toys or privileges, comparisons, and labeling; being a judge who decides the outcome rather then the children doing it.
- **Helpful parent strategies:** Notice generous, loving, caring, behavior and point it out to the children in specific language. Avoid labels and comparisons. Love each child uniquely. Encourage accomplishments and efforts of each child. Avoid punishments of any kind to anybody. Accept and acknowledge all feelings of each child, even if you don't agree with them. Give a lot of individual attention and time to each child. Teach children conflict resolution and problem solving and mentor them through it.

How you deal with sibling rivalry determines how the children treat each other. If you punish them, they will punish each other. If your approach is to work on "solving the problem in a mutually respectful way," they will also take the same approach. It's "us against the problem," not "sibling against sibling."

RESOLVING ISSUES WITHOUT RESENTMENTS

Problem-solving so everyone wins

 My feelings are broken! ~ Scotty Arnall, age three

First, you need to help them calm-down. Your role is not to judge or to find out what happened and pass resolutions. Your role is to facilitate the problem-solving process and help the children find their own resolutions.

Accept and acknowledge each child's feelings and point of view and try to help them express it to the other child. They could tell or draw a picture. Youngest child goes first. Help them brainstorm and come to a solution that both children will agree to. Let the children be assertive, and don't force one to give in if they don't want to.

Some other ways to decide things: (You must be sure both parties agree to the process and its results. These are methods where there is a clear winner and a loser. If they don't agree, find another way that both will win.)

- One child divides and the other chooses first.

- Pick a number between one and 10. The child closest to the number you have written down wins.
- Flip a coin.
- Voting with a majority wins.
- Have a special kid day where they get all the privileges: first pick of desserts, favorite seat, choose the TV shows. Keep track and remember to alternate days.
- Make one into two. For example, when two children are fighting in the kitchen, divide the ingredients into half so each get their own bowl.
- Entice one child to another activity.
- Find the humor.
- Take turns.
- Arrange a time schedule. (My children learned how to count and tell time this way!)

Children, ages five to eight tend to be sore losers in games. I packed away all competitive board games during that time because none of the children could handle losing. Age nine is much better at handling the frustration and able to try cooperative games.

Some Moms have tried sending each child to a different corner of the room or ends of the sofa. They must stay put until they give each other permission to leave or get up or work something out. Each has the power and control of themselves and the other person.

Sometimes it's helpful to temporarily turn off the computer or TV or whatever they are fighting over until they have all agreed to a plan. Then it can go back on again.

Try distracting one child with, "Johnny, I need your help here" if you see that he is getting into a tousle with the other child.

It's okay to intervene in sibling fights. Facilitate conflict resolution for toddlers, preschoolers, and school-aged children if there is a real issue presenting itself or boredom. If attention is the problem, then ignore it unless there is a chance of someone getting hurt. By the teen years, the huge amount of time you spent teaching conflict resolution should have paid off. They will know how to resolve things in an adult, respectful way. However, before you jump in, you might want to ask, "Is this something you both can resolve yourself, or do you want me to help you?"

Celebrate your children's fights! What a great opportunity to teach relationship skills and conflict resolution skills that they are bound to need later in life.

Sibling Conflict: Facilitate, Not Judge

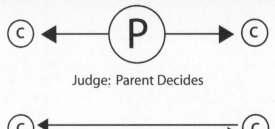

Judge: Parent Decides

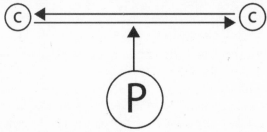

Facilitator: Parents Help Problem-Solving Process

When children cry "It's not fair," they really mean they have it hard and no one else does. Or they don't like what's happening or they are doing too much for not enough back. Children don't need an explanation or defensive argument. "Everyone is working as hard as you, dear."

What they do need is their feelings acknowledged. "You feel overworked in comparison to the rest of the family?" "Yes!" (You don't have to agree with her. You are validating her feelings.) Then go into problem-solving. "What do you think would equalize the workload better?" Maybe she does have a genuine unequal workload? Truly listen to why she thinks something is unfair and what could be done to resolve it for her.

You do not have to maintain equality at all times. Just commit yourself to giving only what each child needs. One child is bound to get more because they need more, but the important point is that each child feels secure knowing that when he needs something, it will be given to him. In *Between Parent and Child*, author Dr. Haim Ginott states, "We do not love all our children the same way, and there is no need to pretend that we do. We love each child uniquely, and we do not have to labor so hard to cover it up. The more vigilant we are to prevent apparent discrimination, the more alert each child becomes in detecting instances of seeming inequality. Unwillingly, we find ourselves defensive against the child's universal battle cry, 'no fair!'"

> Fair is not equal. Fair is resources given
> to each child according to need.
> ~ Adele Faber and Elaine Mazlish, Authors

Children need to learn this. They are not equal in terms of abilities, personality, age, or needs. What one child needs, the other doesn't. Or maybe they do at a different point in time. It's not so much that a child needs to have every whim met, but they need to be secure in the knowledge that when they have a need, it will be met in the family. Everyone looks out for and takes care of everyone else.

When looking at fairness issues, find out what your child needs and meet those needs.

Tips for smoother sibling relations:

- Allow them the choice to not share. Encourage sharing, but don't force it.

- Insist on a family rule where "everyone" asks permission to use another person's items. This includes parents too!

- If you want your child to share an entertainment item, such as a board game or TV, then give it to everyone as a family gift. One year, Santa brought one son a handheld game and my other son a video game console. Each would not share with the other siblings. We had more battles in the house over ownership and rights. I learned to ask Santa for family gifts next time!

- Insist on no put-downs, rudeness, aggression, or name-calling in the house, by anybody. If it happens, use your best I-statement: "I don't like name-calling. I want you to use an I-statement to say if you don't like something." Model how to say it. (One time my child responded, "Okay, instead of saying, 'You suck!' I'm going to say, 'I feel that you suck!'") Sigh! They will get it eventually!

- Some parents feel so angry when their children fight that they resort to hitting, yelling, and shoving. Model calm-down tools so the children can see what to do.

- Model how to treat other people with concern, assertiveness, and respect. Your children are watching how you treat your adult siblings, your partner, and the store clerk.

- Never label your children. "Here is my son, Johnny, the math whiz." The downside is that Johnny now feels he has to live up to the label, and no other child can be a math whiz in our family because Johnny now has the role. Better to say, "Johnny earned a 90 percent on his midterm math exam."

- Never, ever, compare your children – to each other and to others outside the family. Appreciate their uniqueness and acknowledge their special qualities to each of them. Each child has them.

- Examine your past. We tend to play out and project our sibling roles onto our children's. My friend fought with her sister and became estranged as adults. She expects the same of her own two daughters, even though they have the potential to be close. Are you repeating unhealthy relationship patterns and unknowingly allowing your children to treat each other the same way?

- Babies show empathy in their first year of life. Encourage empathy and good works by acknowledging when they do occur between siblings. Shower them with your appreciations.

Model respectful conflict resolution with your partner

Yes, it's okay to "fight" in front of the children – respectfully. When they are adults, children may have very poor relationship conflict skills if they don't remember how their parents fought. They have had no model. Watch very carefully how you resolve conflicts with your partner. Even young children are very aware of how respectful you are in disagreeing with your partner. Do you yell at each other? Hit or push? Name call? Swear? Throw things? Slam doors? Expect the same behavior from your children when they fight.

Do you use the calm-down tools to help when you are steaming mad? Do you truly listen to each other without interrupting? Do you paraphrase or actively listen to what you heard from your partner to be sure you heard the message? Do you avoid blaming and work on win-win solutions? Are you willing to let go of "positions" and give according to what you both need? Do you get to an agreement? Do you kiss and make up? Do you do this in front of the children? If so, congratulations! Children need to learn it.

Sharing

Look around your kitchen and master bedroom. How many items are you willing to loan out to your friends with small children, who might break, destroy, or lose your items? I'll bet there are not many things you would willingly share with the knowledge that you probably won't get it back in one piece. Why do we expect the same level (or more) of sharing from our children?

A child is not cognitively ready to share until age three, although many parents expect it from one-year-olds and on. Children need to understand what ownership and loaning means. They are pretty abstract concepts to someone who believes that possession rules! How many times has your child handed you an item of theirs at the park or party and said, "Here, Mommy, protect this for me." To them, holding on to an item means that you keep it.

Some tips to encourage sharing:

- Pack away special non-sharing items before a play date.

- Have similar or same items for toddlers to play with.

- Get in the habit of asking permission for the playmate or sibling to use the owner's item. Make asking permission to use something a requirement for everyone in the family, including parents. Children will model that and start asking permission as young as 2.5, but they won't handle a refusal as elegantly.

- Allowing her the power to say "yes" or "no", often results in cooperation and a yes. If the answer is "no", that must be respected. But you can point out that you want to make the guest happy and have fun, so what could be substituted?

- Model sharing yourself. "I would like to share a cookie with you. Here, have some of mine."

- When you notice sharing, make a big deal out of it.

- Avoid making a child feel bad when he doesn't want to share. It's his way of being assertive. If he truly owns the item, then he owns the right to say "no" just as adults do.

- Allow the child time when he wants to share. Say, "When you are finished with the fountain, Scotty may have it." This lets the child know that someone is waiting, but gives him control over when to hand it over and lessons the anxiety of having to give it up immediately.

- Ask first. Just because a child doesn't play with their toys anymore, doesn't mean they don't value them. (Remember, a gift may be your child's love language.) Ask their permission before you give them away to a sibling or the Goodwill.

Ideas to keep children from fighting while traveling in the city or on holidays

Stimulation ideas:

- Lego™ rolled up in a fitted sheet is a super toy. Easy to carry and clean up.
- Use travel-sized games or put essential parts of games in Ziploc™ bags (leave the bulky boxes and cases at home).
- Keep library books in the car for everyday car travel. You always know where they are!
- Keep water, juice boxes, and non-perishable snacks in the car. Children are more apt to fight when hungry, thirsty, and tired.
- Keep catalogues in the car so children can "shop."
- Book tapes, paper and markers, magnetic games and sticker books, are fun.
- Put a firm briefcase or backpack beside the toddler chair to keep toys in. You may have to sit in the back to offer toys and retrieve them.
- Drive through the night or leave very early (3:00 am) the next morning. Be sure someone at the other end can care for the well rested, active children while you sleep.
- Word puzzles, books, journals, sketch and writing pad are fun.
- Keep a map that they can mark up with tallies for distance and scale.

- A CD player or MP3 player or handheld games are compact fun.
- Put dice in a clear plastic toothpick container to shake in there so they don't get lost.
- A portable DVD player (great while visiting relatives with non-childproofed houses) can be a life-saver.

Practical ideas:

- If the fighting gets really bad, pull over and refuse to go until things have settled down. Children hate waiting.
- Leave the DVD cases at home and find soft padded cases to put all DVDs into, preferably with envelopes separating them.
- Inflatable balls are great. Stop occasionally and use them during pee breaks.
- Pack a pillowcase with the extra coats and fleeces that are too hot to wear in the car but needed outside, so children can nap on them.
- Plan a treat at the end of travel such as swimming pool time.
- Don't forget earplugs for Mom and Dad. Sometimes, with the best reparation, you just have to listen to it!

MANNERS

Manners need to be taught at preschool level, reminded at school-aged, and modeled in the teen years (although you should be practicing manners from the time your child is a baby!). Manners is our ability to show others consideration and to make them feel comfortable in our homes, and the situation. These involve teaching children how to: hold doors for others, offer space to others who need a seat, parking space, or cart more than we do. Offering what one is eating or doing. Not impeding someone's desire to get somewhere or do something. Saying hello and goodbye to visitors at the door. Not watching TV or playing games while friends are over. Waiting to be offered things rather then helping oneself. Using the more formal last names unless invited not to. Cleaning up after oneself at the fast food restaurant, at a friend's computer, in a friend's parents carpool, etc. Asking permission to use anything that's someone else's. Especially important is manners surrounding technology. Teach children about email, cell phone, and text messaging etiquette. Remember that, just like a newcomer to our country, your child doesn't know manners naturally. It's a process of learning.

CHORES OR ALLOWANCE OR BOTH?

The Meriam Webster Dictionary definition for chores is "a difficult or disagreeable task."

Is it no wonder that children and parents hate doing them? First, I think we need to name it something more pleasant. "Duties" gives the task an air of importance, responsibility, and belonging.

The question most parents ask is should they pay allowance for their child doing chores?

The answer is **no**. Chores and allowance should both be given to children and not contingent on each other because they have separate purposes. The purposes are learning. They are not to control children, which is the true purpose of tying allowances to chores. If children don't receive money, how else can we get them to do chores? If you pay money to do chores, you are really giving them the option to buy their way out of doing them. My son once said, "No, I don't feel like washing the car today. You can keep my allowance. I don't need to go anywhere this week." That doesn't reach the purpose of chores, nor does it ease Mom and Dad's workload!

Paying for chores teaches children that:
- all good deeds are financially rewarded.
- they can buy their way out of doing chores by not accepting the reward.
- the bigger the deed, the more they should be paid.

Children need chores:
- to help Mom and Dad's workload.
- to learn new life skills.
- to learn how to be responsible and capable and build self-esteem.
- given because they belong in the family.

Children need allowance:
- to learn how to handle money.
- to give power, choice, and autonomy in choosing purchases.
- to learn how to save, spend, and generate more money.
- to cut down on nagging for items in stores. "Did you bring your money? Do you have enough to buy it yet?"
- given because they belong in the family.

How much allowance?

The standard rule of thumb is, beginning at age five, when they can understand exchange, give them one dollar for every year of age per week. Be careful, they still are young enough to lose their wallets or purses. Many parents gasp at that amount, so I ask them to add up how much frivolous money they spend on their child in a week. One Mom's list was a movie rental $5, ice-cream treat $2, slush drink $2, and dollar store toy $2.

The same Mom with a 10-year-old would have given him $10 for that week allowance. He probably would have spent the same amount on the same things. The amounts that parents or children spend are pretty much the same, but who decides and who controls is different. It's now in the hands of the child. Sure, he will make mistakes. He will spend all his allowance on a used video game and have none left for movie popcorn when he goes with his buddies. That's how he learns to budget and make better choices.

Debbie, a Mom in my class said, "I found that when I limit it to a couple dollars here and there, they only buy junk food or dollar store trinkets. It was only birthdays and Christmas that they could obtain bigger toys and coveted items. So we upped the amount plus the number of things they would have to cover, such as movie tickets, hockey game treats, new toys they want and video rentals. Now, we see less junk food and dollar store items and more substantial items they have saved for."

So, the child has run out of allowance and needs extra money for a special event coming up. Do you pay for "extra" chores over and above their regular duties? My question is: does someone pay you for extra chores around the house? When it needs painting? When the car needs an oil change? When you have to work overtime and you are paid salary? No.

"The simple economics of work-for-pay isn't something I feel is necessary to give my children practice at 10 years before the fact. I expect it to be a pretty simple matter for them to master once they're ready for the workforce. On the other hand, community values and family obligations (that they aren't paid for doing) strike me as a much harder lesson to teach, so I intend to use chores to help me familiarize my children with these ideas." says Miranda, MD and home-schooling mom of four children.

How much chores?

Age three is a good age to start chores. They love to help at that age. They can empty wastebaskets, bring in groceries, push a vacuum around, and mop a floor. The objective is to get them in the habit of doing it regularly, not to get your house cleaned!

Our children have to do chores that occur every week and every day. Sometimes, there are extra chores, such as cleaning up an overflowing toilet that they just need to learn how to do – a useful life skill that will never be covered in school!

Children should be given jobs to do that go beyond just keeping their own territory clean. In our house, children's rooms are their own territory and they have full discretion on decorating and cleaning standards, except for food, which is not allowed in their rooms, due to the possibility of rats and bugs. However, they need to help out with family and household duties, such as dishwasher emptying, garbage take out, meal clean up, vacuuming common areas, cleaning bathrooms, and toy clean up.

Even if you have hired a housecleaner, your children can participate in other jobs, such as repair work, laundry, recycling, yard work, and meal preparation. Or, if you have housecleaning every other week, get the children involved in the in-between weeks, just so they are in the chore loop.

What if they refuse to do them?

Hand over more control. One of the greatest outcomes of studies on motivation is that the more choice and control one has, the more they are motivated to take action. If the goal is being dictated by someone else in control, then people tend to subtly sabotage it. Therefore, choice of chores and control over when, where, and how to do them may be what children need to motivate them. My teenagers often clean their own room – perhaps about once a year. They decide enough is enough and go at it. They see, however, that I clean my room about once a week, (okay, I'll be honest here and say it's more like once a month!) so they know that other people have different standards. My daughter hates doing chores but loves babysitting, so she can contribute by looking after the younger ones while everyone else is doing chores. You could write down all the chores that need to be done that week on a whiteboard and have children "sign up" for what they want to do. Those who sign up first get the preferred ones. Have them mark down the day and time that they will be done.

Emphasize the contribution to the family. Children need to do service work. It helps them feel good about themselves, their capabilities, and accomplishments. Everybody needs to feel needed. We had laminated chore cards with duties on them such as "water plants," "mow lawn" and a wall hanging that had pockets for each member of the family. Even the parents have pockets so the children realize that parents work around the house, too (for free).

Make it together time. Work alongside and you will find that they are more cooperative. You both will have fun, listen to music (be sure to provide background tunes), and have some interesting conversations. My son, 13, often comes grocery shopping with me and helps load and unload groceries. We have some wonderful talks.

Emphasize the new skills learned. Teaching how to do chores takes time. But it's time well invested. Encourage the value of the skill learned, and they will want to learn more.

Appreciate effort. No matter what the end product looks like, profusely express gratitude and acknowledgement. When my son was 11, he used to bring me breakfast in bed. Sure, the tea was cold and the eggs runny, but the gesture warmed my heart!

Make it fun! We tend to forget about making dreary, repetitive chores fun. The more people involved the merrier. Play some energetic music out loud. Tell jokes. Let children stop and play while cleaning the bathroom sink. Limit weekly chores to two hours on a Saturday or Sunday, where everyone gets down and dirty. After two hours, and everyone's done, bring out a treat. This also emphasizes belonging: We work together and then play together.

> All the great things are done for their own sake.
> ~ Robert Frost, Poet

What chores when?

I picked up a video at the store the other day called "Toddlers Who Work." I was curious and watched it with my youngest son, who was three. He loved watching the video! It had no talking, just music, and toddlers helping their parents making beds, emptying dishwashers, cleaning the car. It was amazing. It got me thinking about cultures that have no toys. Those children are beside the parents all day. Why try to keep the children entertained with toys, when they are perfectly capable of working alongside you? Children have been working alongside their parents for thousands of years. Somehow, we've stopped that. I know they don't do a great job and sometimes the mess is more than worth the effort, but it sure pays off later. The benefits are that the children get into a routine. They are taught how to do things. They feel like they belong and are part of the family and can be counted on. They build a healthy sense of self-esteem by feeling capable, and they are a big help getting things done. Everyone wins.

At 18 months:	put things away.
At age three:	put things away, empty wastebaskets, be a "gopher" (which means the parent hands the gopher an item that needs to be put away somewhere else, they run and do it, then come back for more), empty dishwasher with your help, hand things to you, sort laundry, set table, and pick up socks.
At age four:	sort videos and put away, help with recycling, and vacuum floors.
At age five:	water plants, empty dishwasher, and take out garbage.
At age six:	put pillows in pillowcases, and mop floors.

At age seven: answer phone and take messages.

At age eight: use microwave and toaster, strip and change sheets.

At age nine: vacuum sofas, put away their laundry, prepare their own breakfast, pack their own lunch, and prepare a dinner for the family using the microwave or oven.

At age 12:   all aspects of dinner, including stove use, clean-up, wipe counters, put food away, wash pots, load and unload dish-washer.

At age 13 and older: pay bills, do own laundry, handle a clothing and necessity budget, and shop. Shovel walk, mow grass, sort video games, put away, and gather up library books. Make own phone calls, appointments, and play dates. Ask for help from salespeople, purchase own clothes, gifts, use an ATM machine, and take the bus. Ask for directions when lost, handle difficult people, and read bank statements. Clean bath-rooms, and do minor repair work.

Remember the toddler shout, "I do it!" They want to do things for themselves without your help. When we take over for our children all the things they should do for themselves and the family, we rob them of the confidence, sense of belonging, and accomplishment of a job well done.

BUILDING A HEALTHY SELF-ESTEEM

A healthy self-esteem is not measured in quantity of high or low. **It's basically about a child feeling that they have as much <u>value</u> as everyone else in the world.** Here are some ways to build your child's healthy self-esteem:

- Love and accept them for who they are.
- Spend time alone with each child.
- Avoid labels and criticism.
- Give positive affirmations every day: "I love you."
- Give duties and responsibilities and acknowledge effort, not just the finished product.
- Teach that mistakes are for learning and growing and are okay!
- Let them make age-appropriate decisions.
- Be involved, watch, attend, and cheer loudly!
- Celebrate successes with them and others.
- Watch them when they want you to.

- Introduce them and include them in your adult social conversations.
- Seek out their opinion and listen with full attention, even if you disagree.
- Watch your language. Instead of: "You will spill it." "I'm too busy." "Sometimes I wish I never had children." "Why can't you be like your brother?" Try: "You can be careful." "Sure, I have a minute." "I love being a parent." "I'm glad you are you."
- Play with them and take them places.
- Be proud. Display their talent. Place netting over a wall and attach artwork, crafts and writing with clothespins. Laminate art for placemats or use a clear plastic tablecloth for displaying artwork underneath the table.
- Hang and display art everywhere – shows you value the child's efforts.
- Give time and attention, not material things. Children know what you consider important.

I LIKE AND APPRECIATE ABOUT YOU...

Skills, talents, abilities, aptitudes, and intelligences to appreciate and acknowledge in children:

Spatial/visual intelligence

Drawing and painting	Photography	Recall for details
Active imagination	Map skills	Candle making
Directionality	Creative	Cartoon drawing
Ceramics	Cake decorating	
Cutting and pasting	Movie making	

Logic intelligence

Computer savvy	Organized	Problem-solver
Abstract thinking	Math and numbers	Thinking games
Decipher codes	Common sense	Science
Quick thinker	Good memory	Researcher
Video game player	Reading directions	

Bodily/kinesthetic intelligence

Role playing	Acting	Creative movement
Dancing	Magic tricks	Mime
Puppetry	Card tricks	Puts things together
Taking things apart	A specific sport	Running
Athletic	Strength	Graceful
Endurance	Balance	Dexterity
Coordinated	Nice handwriting	Puzzles
Carpentry	Model building	Jumping

Fast runner
Knitting
Macramé
Doll making
Quilting
Embroidery

Catches and throws
Crocheting
Fabric arts
Weaving
Needlepoint
Sculpting

Tree and rope climbs
Origami
Calligraphy
Sewing
Printmaking
Pottery

Musical intelligence

Play an instrument
Rhythm
Reads music

Choir
Remembers tunes
Responds to music

Singing
Songwriting

Intrapersonal intelligence

Takes initiative
Patient
Courageous
Adaptable
Humorous
Noncompetitive
Self-confident
Thoughtful
Responsible
Generous
Neat and tidy
Insightful
Happy
Dependable
Good problem-solver
Truth teller
Disciplined
Religious studies

Follows through
Reliable
Caring
Brave
Giving
Forgiving
Flexible
Easy going
Outgoing
Confident
Determined
Gentle
Open
Proud
Optimistic
Serious
Affectionate
Recognizes and
manages own feelings

Trustworthy
Sensitive
Hard working
Curious
Appreciative
Negotiator
Calm head in
emergencies
Spirited
Reflective
Interdependent
Truthful and honest
Mature
Prompt
Motivated
Loyal
Sense of humor
Concentrates

Interpersonal intelligence

Friendly
Good host
Leader
Good loser
Good-natured
Fair
Cooperative
Peacemaker

Remembers names
Good guest
Follower
Tells jokes
Good sportsman
Takes turns
Shares appropriately
Fun

Supports others
Good phone skills
Good winner
Helpful
Polite
Team player
Empathetic
Encouraging

Includes others

Honest

Recognizes others feelings

Volunteer with others

Solves group problems

Humorous

Speaker

Childcare

Good storyteller

Good listener

Memory

Play production and direction

Linguistic intelligence

Reads for enjoyment

Remembers facts

Debates respectfully

Spells

Vast vocabulary

Creative writing

Joke teller

Handwriting

Confident speaker

Poetry

Storyteller

Second language

Physical appearance

Neat

Special feature

Clean

Takes care of clothing

Healthy posture

Nature intelligence

Nature observer

Recycling

Collecting rocks

Explorer

Curious

Hikes and camps

Astronomy

Farming

Environmentalist

Mountain and rock climbing

Backpacking

Gardening

Wildlife protector

Cares for animals

Science collection

Life skills

Cleaning up

Vacuuming

Taking out garbage

Home maintenance

Gift giving

Dishes

Wiping

Laundry

Money management

Polishing

Remembers chores

Organization

Cooking and baking

We wish our child to have every skill, talent, or quality on this list. Obviously, that won't happen! No one can possibly possess all of these. However, each person in this world has some qualities. Acknowledge them and appreciate them often.

10

Discipline Tools for School-aged Children 6 - 12 Years: Talk and action

Quit harassing over daily irritants, comment and praise the positives a lot, and save your ire for the really big stuff. ~ Rona Maynard, Author

There is a reason that children don't start their formal education until age six. Their brains are not mature enough to handle formal learning. So why do we expect children zero to five to instantly learn and behave from discipline, when we know they can't remember four times five yet?

If the preschool years are the time to start learning social rules, the school-aged years are prime years for teaching right from wrong and how to fit into their families, communities, and the world. They are not into the hormonally charged emotional years of teenagerdom and have enough brain capacity to understand basic logic and reasoning behind the rules. They are young enough to not pay dearly for mistakes, yet old enough to solve problems. They have quite a bit of self-control and moral thinking. They still see parents as the center of their universe and still want to please them. **These are the best years to teach and guide.**

YOUR SCHOOL-AGED CHILD'S DEVELOPMENTAL STAGE

School-age refers to children aged six to 12. Preteen also refers to children aged nine to 12. In this section, I have included preteens in the larger category of school-aged, yet made distinctions where necessary. This is the stage of learning about structure and organizational skills. Children are in the prime years of developing life, academic, and hobby skills. Sports, activities, and friends take up a larger portion of their time.

Typical school-aged behaviors
- Develop skills through activities, sports, chores, and education.

- Experiments with structure, learns time management, scheduling, and deadlines.
- Learns about consequences of their actions.
- Needs to experiment with and explore social rules and roles. They learn to argue, question, and honor rules. They also learn to test and negotiate rules. What are they for? How are they made? What happens when rules are broken? How different are other families' rules?
- Make lots of mistakes and learn how to solve problems.
- Needs to try out her own values and ways of doing things to get her needs met.
- Needs to disagree with others and find out they are still friends.
- Needs to learn to separate reality from fantasy.

DEVELOPMENTAL MILESTONES

Physical milestones

- Growth spurts and extreme differences are evident in children of the same ages.
- Preteen girls tend to be more advanced than boys.
- Bone growth is faster than muscle development.
- Sexual characteristics are developing.
- Fluctuations in basal metabolism causes restlessness.
- Preteens may tire easily.
- Ravenous appetite, picky eaters or peculiar tastes are present.
- Belt of fat develops around waist.
- Visual acuity develops around age nine (ability to judge time and distance of moving cars).

Psychosocial milestones

- Have better developed impulse control and delayed gratification. Can now wait for longer periods of time.
- Even-keeled from ages six to nine; from 10 to 12, emotions may be erratic.
- Greater anxiety, and self-consciousness about physical and sexual changes.
- Sensitive to criticism and correction.
- Strong need to belong to family and peer group.
- May exaggerate and over-dramatize problems.
- Increasingly able to identify and label own feelings and feelings in others.
- Still have fears: dogs, sharks, heights, losing parents, the dark.
- Can begin to use "self talk" to calm down.
- Easily upset by things not fair or right.
- Disregards personal hygiene from ages six to 12.
- May still be quite open and affectionate in private.

Cognitive milestones

- Concrete operational thinking using reasoning rather than perception to justify their judgments. Can think logically and expand knowledge, but thinking is still limited to concrete, tangible objects, and familiar events.
- Intensely curious and growing in mental ability.
- Is really moving out of the "it's all about me" stage into thinking of others feelings and viewpoints.
- Asks a lot of questions, gathers information, and practices skills.
- Belongs to same sex groups, clubs, and friends.
- Compares, disagrees with, sets, breaks, and experiences consequences of rules.
- Moral development not quite there. Still black and white thinking. Increasing sense of right and wrong and societal rules.
- The average Kindergarten age child has the attention span of 20 minutes maximum.
- A 12-year-old has the attention span of one and half hours.
- Age 11 or 12: may be argumentative as they develop critical thinking skills to debate gray area type of issues that have no one right answer.
- Eager to solve real life problems.
- Age six to 10: still need reminding, supervision and teaching to do chores.
- Age 11 on: can do chores without reminding or supervision.
- Knows the difference between real and imaginary things.
- Loves bathroom talk.

PARENTS MATTER

Unhelpful parenting behaviors

- Avoiding non-sexual touch like hugs, holding, and cuddles.
- Emotional distancing.
- Refusing to help build skills.
- Downplaying the importance of learning and making mistakes.
- Parentifying your child. Making him responsible for fulfilling your needs.

Helpful parenting behaviors

- Treat your child with mutual respect. Don't do anything to him that you wouldn't want done to yourself!
- Encourage daily physical activity and allow the space in your yard or house to be boisterous.
- Mistakes are for learning! Acknowledge difficulty in tasks and encourage how to solve the mistake.
- Avoid intense competition or pressure with sports, music, or activities.
- Provide health and nutrition education with choices.
- Provide sexual health education.

- Don't over-react to fads in clothing and mannerisms.
- Invite input into rules and problem-solving parent-child issues.
- Walk away from "attitude" and power struggles.
- Encourage healthy, respectful disagreement and listen with empathy.
- Encourage them to develop their intuition and gut feelings about people and situations.
- Assist them in finding solutions to their own problems instead of staying in distress.
- Encourage explorations of their ideas and values and how to express themselves.
- Provide daily unstructured down-time.
- Encourage their friends at your home and let them choose their own friends.
- Protect family time and family activities from interruption by friends.
- Respect their privacy and possessions.
- Have one-on-one regular time together without siblings.
- Use appropriate touch of hugs, holding, and cuddles.
- All helpful parenting behaviors from previous age groups.

DISCIPLINE TOOLS FOR SCHOOL-AGED CHILDREN

Stay with your "no"
Ignore provocations
Plan ahead
Natural consequences
Reflective questions
Active listening
Problem-solve
Stimulation
Family conferences
I-statements
Connect, then direct
Spend time together
Change environment
Model
Give gentle reminders in preferred
learning style
Re-evaluate limits
Use humor
Walk away from power struggles
Teach calm-down tools
Clarify expectations
Skills chart
Walk away from "attitude"

> Schedule daily downtime
> Give input into rule setting
> Show the child benefit of behavior change
> Reward truth and honesty
> Have a favorite kid day and alternate days
> Have a "yes means no" day and vice versa
> Contracts
> Parent time-out
> Holding, hugs, and cuddles

Stay with your "no"

Your "no's" should be getting further and farther between. Your child is halfway to adulthood and needs to be making choices and decisions on their own behalf. Yes, they'll make mistakes. But mistakes are great learning tools and at this age, they are not too costly yet!

Ignore provocations

Refusing to participate in the power struggle doesn't mean that you lose. It means you are the adult and can think and remain calm enough to take a break from the emotional situation. You can always come back later and address things. Responding to provocations will encourage them because the perpetrator is getting what he wants – a reaction. Ignore it, but also keep in mind that someone is sending a powerful message of unhappiness that you will need to address at some point soon.

Plan ahead

If you know your child is going to have a problem, see if you can plan ahead and minimize it. For example, if one sister is invited to a sleepover and one isn't, make plans for a special night for the left behind child, so that she can feel better about it.

If you know your son is having a friend over that tends to get rambunctious and trip and step over fragile toys when they get into a chase game in the house, remind everyone of the no-chase rule before they come in, and put away the breakables before hand. Just in case!

Natural consequences

Some of our child's best teachers are those things that happen outside our control. People and situations intervene to teach our child lessons. I brought my children and their two cousins to an amusement park one day. My eight-year-old son spit from the Ferris wheel chair onto my 12-year-old niece, who was right underneath and who was very angry. I was watching from another chair. When we all got off, my niece told the Ferris wheel operator about it. The operator came over to me and asked if it was okay if my son cleaned up the cars. I said, "of course." I could have said "no" and be on our way, but why miss a valuable opportunity? The operator handed my son a spray bottle and paper towels and he spent 10 minutes cleaning up the cars. He learned that it was not appropriate behavior and learned what it took to solve the problem. Perfect discipline.

Reflective questions

What if? "What did you learn today from dropping the milk jug on the driveway?" "What happens to the sidewalk if everyone dropped one gum wrapper on it everyday?" What and how questions open up the conversation better than "why," which can seem accusing. These only work if you are willing to listen to the response and if you are sincerely accepting of your child's perception of the world. Avoid all sarcasm. You are not trying to teach. You are trying to get your child thinking through their understanding of the world.

Active listening

 The most important thing in communication is to hear what isn't being said. ~ Peter F. Drucker, Professor

Active listening is one of the most important discipline tools for this age. It helps to build the relationship for the teen years coming up. If you have been using it in parenting up to now, it should come easily and natural for you. A mom in one of my classes had two boys in grade one and two. She picked both boys up from school for lunch, and they were hitting each other in the car on the way home. She got home and told each to go to a different corner of the house. She realized they were stressed and angry over different things. She acknowledged their feelings and actively listened. "John, you seem very mad at your brother." "Andrew, you are pretty angry, too." "Let's try to calm down and then we'll talk." She listened, talked, and discovered they weren't really mad at each other. The brothers were handy targets to take their school related stresses out on. They each calmed down after she listened to them individually. They felt better that someone cared to talk about their day. Unfortunately, there was no time to make or eat lunch, so they went back to school with an apple, chunk of cheese, and a lighter heart.

Problem-solve

This is another great discipline tool to use in parenting school-aged and teenagers. The true essence of discipline at this stage is learning how to solve the problems they have caused themselves and other people. Problem-solving involves a lot of active listening from parents to find out what the real issue is, I-statements to communicate feelings and brainstorming for solutions. Solutions may come in the form of:

- Apologizing
- Repair
- Return
- Replacing
- Compensating
- Cleaning up

Overindulgent parents don't teach problem-solving. They ignore problems and hope they go away. Responsible, caring parents teach this essential skill to their children and practice it in their own lives.

Stimulation

Bored children become discipline problems. The parent's role is to be sure to have age appropriate stimulating activities on hand if the child chooses to occupy himself. The parent's job is not to entertain the child but have entertainment available.

Children this age are into skill development. Their toys encompass sandboxes, trampolines, bikes, scooters, every kind of sports equipment, chapter books and series books, collections of toys, and other trinkets. They are into workshops, crafts kits, like beading and candle making, electronics, playgrounds, computer games, art supplies, puzzles, models, building forts out of any material, board games with definite rules, imaginative role playing games with props, and activity kits, such as wood burning, rock tumbling, chemistry sets, sewing supplies, and also building sets. Remote control cars are popular, too.

Family conferences

Family conferences are a great way to deal with issues and problems of living together for school-aged children that are able to sit and talk for longer periods of time. These can start as early as five years of age and older. They are basically a meeting of the family members to discuss upcoming plans and/or problems experienced previously. Plans include what to do for the weekend or holidays or what is priority for the week. Who is home and who does what? It can also be used to solve problems that affect every member of the family, such as computer time. If the problem is just between two people, such as Mom and daughter, then a family conference is not the time to problem-solve. Other members will get bored, distracted, or over-involved if the issue doesn't affect them.

Family conference guidelines

- Any person can call a meeting but it must be a mutually agreed upon time. Items agreed upon at the meeting should be continued until discussion at the next meeting.
- Make sure everyone knows the permanent marker rules are not open for discussion. This is a great time to discuss all those washable marker and pencil rules.
- Some families find that Sunday nights, after dinner, are a great time for a meeting. Dessert is served, and everyone is in a good mood.
- Be sure to write down everyone's suggestions when brainstorming. No matter how silly they are, they deserve to be treated with respect, written down, and sincerely considered.
- It can be a positive time, too: time to plan vacations, weekend activities, show and tell, and plan a special event.
- Family members can take turns chairing the meeting and being the recorder of issues resolved and actions taken. Young children should be given markers and paper to record at their level. Keep a permanent record of resolutions, persons involved, and date.
- School-aged and older teens may be wary of the process if it's new to them. Talk about the process and how it works. Guarantee everyone will have their needs met. Don't force them to participate, but if you truly want them to buy into the process, you need to consider and value their input.
- Agree on basic ground rules: no name calling, no put-downs of others or their ideas, no blaming, no interrupting. Everyone must share airtime.
- Keep it short. Meetings that slog on are a drag for everyone. One hour or a half hour is long enough.
- Have an agenda. Post the agenda on the fridge at the end of every meeting for the next meeting. If a child starts balking about bedtimes in the middle of the week, and the family meeting is on Sunday nights, then ask him to write "bedtime" on the fridge agenda so the problem is discussed and resolved at the next meeting. This helps to cut down problem-solving in the middle of the problem, when everyone is trying to rush out the door, get dinner on the table, or dressed in the morning. Problem-solving works better if all members involved can concentrate, relax, brainstorm, and think in peace.
- Start introducing meetings to the family on positive issues so they learn the process.
- Start with appreciations and end with appreciations.
- Make decisions with consensus, not voting. If a solution that everyone agrees to can't be reached, come back again and try next meeting.
- End the meeting on a fun note: watch a movie with popcorn, go out for ice-cream, or do some other fun thing.

I – statements

Body language can be an effective I-statement. When your child calls you a name – simply turning around, walking out of the room and ignoring her is an honest, effective reaction to her behavior. "I don't like that!" Of course, you do need to work on the relationship if she is calling you names. Be sure you don't react by name calling back. When the parent-child relationship is good, there is no name calling present on either side. A hug is also an I-statement. "I love you!"

Connect, then direct

> Resistance is the child's way of cooperating by showing the adult what doesn't work.
> ~ Edmund Sprunger, Violin Teacher

All people, including children, are more likely to cooperate when you invite, not order! My son, 12, was blowing the horn loudly at a hockey game. I noticed there were several older people in the audience turning around to see who was blowing the horn inappropriately. He was having fun and didn't see what was going on. I said to him that I saw there were older people in the audience that looked bugged by the loud noise. Perhaps we should keep the horn blowing to only when goals were scored. I didn't command him to do it. I only offered my wisdom, experience, and knowledge for him to make a decision, based on the information I gave him. He decided to do it or not. He chose to accept my knowledge and complied to not blow his horn. The strength of our relationship allowed him to trust my advice and take it.

If children are used to being commanded to do something, they will often rebel. If the suggestion is made, along with an assurance from the parent that the child is capable of making the right choice, then the chance of them making the right choice will be higher, especially if the child is used to having suggestions made, not ordered or commanded. Try saying, "The decision is up to you, but I think it might be in your best interests to finish that book report this weekend, instead of next weekend when so much is going on." Children will comply much more than with, "You have to finish that book report this weekend or no TV next week!"

Spend time together

> Remember that children need to be supervised at least until age 10.

Often, the time that school-aged children and teenagers want to talk is later at night, preferably before bed. Take advantage of that time to find out what is really oing on in their lives. I know parents get tired at that time, but the energy spent on children in such a positive way pays handsomely more than the energy spend on discipline problems during the day if we don't take the time to listen.

Walk or drive instead of using the carpool. Some of my best conversations with the children are when we are driving or walking. One night, I was walking home in the moonlight from a neighbor's barbecue with my 14, 13, 11, and seven-year-old. It was dark, and we stopped in the playground across the street. We had a fun, fantastic time that built memories. We laughed and talked about recent events, memories, and jokes. It was a moment out of the ordinary. Those are often the best parenting times.

Change environment

Yes, you still childproof for school-aged children! Add, delete, and change the environment if there is a problem. For example, when my husband worked in Peru for two years, I had to drag all four children to various activities that only involved one of the children. So, three children were bored. Being bored, they fought. The fighting behavior was bad, but I decided to change it, knowing that the underlying feeling was boredom. I bought the three children used hand-held game consoles to keep them busy while waiting for the child in the activity. It worked! No more fighting.

Model

 Modeling is discipline taught 24 hours a day, 365 days of the year.

The second most important tool for this age. Model the behavior you want. If you want your child to read, read yourself. If you want your child to be honest, don't lie about his age to get an admission discount. If you want your child to go to church, go to church yourself.

A great example was when my husband and I would go to a party. We would be marginal to drive home sober. We left the car behind on purpose to show the children that it's okay and normal to leave the car and get a taxi or bus home. Inconvenient? Yes. Made an impression? Yes! Teaching discipline is not easy. It requires inconvenience, but modeling is the best way to teach.

It's easy to model when the task is easy and fits into our schedule. But you have to remind yourself who is watching you. If I break a commitment to do an errand with a friend, and my children notice, but I rant on and on about responsibility and commitment, then they can see right through the hypocrisy. Integrity is doing the right thing even when it's hard and inconvenient.

Give gentle reminders in preferred learning style

Try to use less than 12 words. Talk, and then follow up in action. You've asked your child to politely empty the dishwasher twice. Now, you go up to him, acknowledge his fun at playing computer, wait until he can pause, and say, "Please pause, and let's go." Then you help him get up, walk with him to the dishwasher, crack a joke, and hopefully he empties it. He will get the message that you follow through talk with actions. That is more effective than yelling and threatening. Or, write a comic bubble with the word "dishwasher" on a piece of paper and go up to him and put the bubble next to your lips. He will notice!

Or, write a letter from the dishwasher, saying how full it feels, and how much it would love to be purged. Sign it, love, "Dan, the Dishwasher."

Re-evaluate limits

Perhaps now the child has outgrown the limits and feels the need to expand his independence and world; that he has the maturity, knowledge, and gumption to try. The parent needs to let go and let him try his wings. Attitude remarks and cries of "no fair" often are indicators that the child is ready for more independence. Seriously look at his maturity and capability before saying "yes" or "no". Children's capability levels are often way more ahead of their parent's security levels! Give him a chance to grow!

Many preteens start to separate from siblings and the family and want more privacy and their own time. Children, who previously loved to share rooms, may need more space. When your child wants a new limit, have her write an argument to convince you of her new request. It builds her writing skills, teaches negotiation and gives you time to think through new boundaries.

 The greatest gifts that you can give your children
are the roots of responsibility and the wings
of independence.   ~ Denis Waitley, Speaker

Use humor

Humor is such a powerful learning tool and often overlooked. It has to be truly fun humor and not sarcasm that can be hurtful.

Walk away from power struggles

Pause for a minute. Get cool and control your own emotions. Then, look at the situation. What are the real underlying feelings and needs? Come back and listen to your child's point of view, and listen to how you really feel. What is the real problem?

Controlling, power oriented parents could often get involved in a struggle with controlling, power oriented children. The problem is that parents are teaching children that to get your way, you must control others to win. Those who struggle the hardest and the longest win. You just have to be the biggest and strongest. This gives children the wrong message.

But if a parent backs down and never get their needs met, that teaches the child they don't need to respect their parent's needs. In power struggles, nobody wins, except the person who walks away in the heat of the moment. They win for everyone, by taking time to calm down and chill out. Then, more cool heads can get together and think of win-win solutions to the problem.

Teach "calm-down" tools (instead of time-out)

Time-out is a valuable skill for children to learn. But they don't learn it by being forced into one by a parent. They learn it by watching a parent use it for herself. Parents can model time-out and many other calm-down tools discussed in Chapter 5.

Clarify expectations

Once you say a statement to your child, such as, "You promised to mow the lawn by 4:00 pm because we are having company for a barbecue.", ask your child to repeat what you have just said, so he understands the directions and you know that he does too.

Skills chart

It's not for stars and stickers but as a great visual way to check off what the child has learned, knows, and needs to do. This is great for visual learners and spatially intelligent children. It also helps to build self-esteem.

Walk away from "attitude"

School-aged children learn social aggressiveness from their peers, parents, and siblings. This is the age they learn that hitting, pushing, and physical aggression is not appropriate and they have enough self impulse control to refrain from doing these things.

Unfortunately, aggression takes the form of something quieter and less detectable. They use social aggression. This is verbal abuse, ignoring, or exclusion of activities to peers and siblings, and "attitude" and backtalk to parents. These strategies are still as hurtful as fists to others but much less detectable.

Parents must be careful to not use attitude themselves and also not allow siblings to talk to each other disrespectfully in the family. Allowing the child choices and appropriate control over his life will go a long way to enhancing his sense of control over himself, enough so he doesn't feel he has to control other people through social aggression. Recent studies show that social aggression is learned behavior. It's not innate; so it can also be unlearned.

Attitude is sarcastic anger. Your child has a pressing need, but has to find a way to express it appropriately and assertively. Try to meet the needs as soon as he expresses it in a more respectful way.

It's important not to take personally, the "I hate you," and "You are so mean!" messages. They are merely volatile and emotionally wild statements of emotional people that usually have no more deep meaning than when a toddler says "I hate you." Parents think "hate" is a strong word, but children toss it around like a ball. It's the same with door slamming.

Children should be able to express their feelings, but rudeness is not acceptable. Expressing feelings and wishes respectfully is assertive behavior and what we wish to encourage in our children. If possible, grant their wishes when they ask respectfully. Teach them to start with, "I feel…"

Schedule daily downtime

Should you let children opt out of organized activities? If you have chosen the activity and two sessions didn't go well, you gave it a try, and let it go. Let the children drop it. If they begged you for the activity and now want to drop out, make the point of persistence and keep at it. If they are waiting by the door with uniform and supplies then you keep going. Avoid signing school-aged children up for activities that they are lukewarm about. You can't force a child to like an activity that you think might be good for them. The power struggles will stamp out any enjoyment and learning in the long run. This includes sports, music lessons, art, and any other activity. Children who are enrolled in nothing other than school have just as equal chance of success in life as an overscheduled child. Perhaps more, in that they have had much more downtime to reflect, dream, process information, and relax.

Give input into rule setting

Those that make the rules, generally follow the rules!

Show the child benefit of behavior change

Show movies with a message. Tell stories of friends children. Tell your own stories from your childhood. Read stories of fairy tales and books. Sometimes, children need to see benefits before they change.

Reward truth and honesty

Don't punish! Acknowledge difficulty of being honest and thank them. Give them your help. If your child returns a lost wallet and the receiver doesn't say thanks, make a special outing for your child to celebrate "the right thing to do." Encourage the good feelings you both have.

Have a favorite kid day and alternate days

This helps in sibling fights. When the children are squabbling over car seating, computer time, and who gets the first piece of dessert, you can designate the favorite kid day. The favorite kid that day gets all the first choices. This only works if you give each child a day. All the children in the family must agree to it. My friend was describing this to me and related the horrified looks from strangers who thought that she was being discriminatory in her parenting!

Have a "yes means no" day and vice versa

This is a fun way to handle rules. When a child asks for permission, you say "no," which means "yes" and vice versa. Be sure everyone understands this is a game.

Contracts

For preteens, contracts are great. They are written agreements of what both the child and parent agree to. You both need to add, subtract, change, and agree to the conditions and sign it. Display it somewhere for all to see. They are often the written resolution of a problem-solving session.

Parent time-out

Get out yourself and have some fun!

Holding, hugs, and cuddles

When children grow to preteen age, parents tend to stop hugging, cuddling, and touching their children. Moms tend to stop with boys, and dads with both genders. Yet, children who are entering puberty and are insecure about their changing bodies still need to feel they are lovable and huggable.

Teenage girls, who are sexually active, often miss the body contact, hugs, and cuddles from their dads and seek it out in sexual activity with boys their age.

It's important for both moms and dads to continue to touch their children in non-sexual ways. Hugs and cuddles while watching movies, sitting close together, pats on the shoulder, head, and arms, kisses on the cheek, getting tucked in, hugged, and kissed at bedtime can continue until the child or teenager says "no". If you are not sure how your preteen/teen feels about it, ask them.

SPECIAL SCHOOL-AGED BEHAVIOR CONCERNS
PROBLEM-SOLVING

Next to hugs and modeling, the third best all time discipline tool for school-aged and teenagers is problem-solving. Children learn problem-solving by doing it. Family conferences are a good way to learn problem-solving, but are best when the issue affects everyone in the family. Most problems are between two people and can be resolved by the two people. For ages two and up, problem-solving is a mutually respectful way to fully meet parent's and child's needs at the same time. It's not a compromise. The aim is for an honest full win-win solution for everyone. For children not used to the process, you need to set the stage a bit:

- Explain the six-step process.
- Assure they will get their needs met, guaranteed.
- Break the ice with friendliness and an appreciation.
- Tell your child that you wish to solve discipline issues in a different way and would they be willing to try this with you? Gain their trust.
- Be honest, direct, and specific.
- Express thanks for input and co-operation.
- Stick to one issue at a time.
- Select an appropriate place and time for discussion. As children get familiar with the process, you can do stand up problem-solving on the spot.
- As children can see they get their needs met too, they will be more committed and willing to participate in the process.

Six steps to problem-solving

1. What is the problem? Gather information and figure out what the problem is. Turn off all distractions, such as TV and games.

2. Who is involved, and what are their needs? Look at the underlying needs rather than positions. Actively listen to find out what your child's needs are and what your needs are. Needs differ from positions. Positions are already formulated solutions that don't address underlying needs. Positions are like the table-top and needs are the legs. The "needs" hold up the "positions."

3. Brainstorm. What are our options? Both you and child brainstorm ideas together. The child goes first. Accept all ideas no matter how outrageous. Write all ideas down on paper so the child can see you writing and knows you are taking them seriously. Aim for at least ten ideas for children older than five. Younger children, aim for two to five ideas. You'll find that the first few ideas might be positions/solutions. Do not evaluate any ideas at this point.

4. Evaluate. Which one will work for everyone's needs? After everyone's brains are empty of ideas, evaluate them, and consider the consequences. Choose the outcome that best provides a win-win solution for you and the child.

5. Do it! Implement the idea. Record it in the family conference minutes, in a contract, or on just a piece of paper as a reminder. Get everyone to sign it.

6. Did it work? Does it need tweaking? Do you both need to problem-solve it again because it's not working for someone?

Here are some examples:

Trampoline

1. Problem:	How many children should go on the trampoline at once?
2. Needs:	Heidi wants to play multiple child games on the trampoline. Mom wants to limit people on the trampoline because she is worried about safety. Marlin wants to have only one child at a time because he likes it to himself.
3. Brainstorm:	**A.** Only three children at a time.
	B. Only four children at a time if everyone stays in their space.

        C. Only one child at a time.

        D. Only four children, unless boys are on, and then it's one at a time.

        E. Only one child at a time if Johnny is visiting.

        F. Only four children, unless neighbors are over, then it's one at a time because they are not used to the space and feel of it.

4. Evaluate: **A, B, D, E** doesn't meet Marlin's needs, so we cross it off; **C** doesn't meet Heidi's needs, so we cross it off; we agreed that **F.** will work for Mom and Heidi and Marlin, if he gets some time to go on just by himself.

5. Do it: We wrote down the rule "four family members can be on the trampoline at one time, as long as they stay in their spaces, and Marlin gets some time to be on by himself."

6. Did it work? Yes, four people seemed to keep everyone safe and still have the fun of games.

Lunch

1. Problem: We needed food for lunch and had to use up two hours before our next appointment.

2. Needs: Mom was out with four children and didn't want to go back home for lunch before the appointment or she would have difficulty getting the children back out of the house again. She wanted to have lunch and use up time. She suggested going to a fast food play area but only one child wanted to. Marlin wanted to go to Taco Time™, and Heidi wanted to go Burger King™. Travis wanted to go to Dairy Queen™, and Chris wanted McDonalds™. The children argued.

3. Brainstorm: **A.** All go home and stay home.

        B. All go to McDonalds™ and play in the play place.

        C. Drive around and forget lunch.

        D. Go to Safeway™, get fixings, and have a picnic.

        E. Drive to each favorite fast food place and get the desired lunches.

4. Evaluate: **A** didn't work for Mom, **B** didn't work for Chris, **C** didn't work for anyone – we were all hungry, **D** didn't work for anyone – they wanted fast food favorites (although it would have been a compromise; it was not a 100 percent meeting of needs). **E** worked for everyone. Mom had to spend time to feed everyone, and everybody got to eat their favorite lunch.

5. Do it:	We drove to each drive-through restaurant and ordered one lunch. It was funny to see the look on the cashier's face, as she handed one lunch out to a car-full of children.
6. Did it work?	Yes, everyone got their way, and everyone was happy.

Computer time

1. Problem:	Everyone wants time on the computer and feels the other siblings gets it more.
2. Needs:	Heidi wants to have it first. Travis wants at least three hours, and Chris wants a turn, too, but has to leave for an appointment.
3. Brainstorm:	**A.** Give each child tickets for an hour of computer time each. As they take time, they hand in tickets. **B.** The person on first gets one hour, the second person gets two hours, and the third person gets three hours for waiting the longest. **C.** The child who has to leave first gets the first time on the computer. **D.** We shut off the computer for the day and nobody gets it (Dad's idea). **E.** We draw up names, times, and sign-up slots for the next day. Appointments are scheduled in, and children sign up for their slots around their times away from home.
4. Evaluate:	**A** met everyone needs, **B** the person who had to go out didn't get their time. **C** everyone agreed. **D** nobody agreed except for Dad. **E** everyone agreed.
5. Do it:	The deal was that computer time was scheduled around appointments and with a sign-up sheet. Everyone could schedule their time to fit around their schedule.
6. Did it work?	It worked well, until nieces and nephews came for summer holidays and nobody had appointments. Then we had to revisit the problem-solving process again.

Is the process time consuming? Yes, at first, but the more the children get used to the process, and the more often it's done, the faster it becomes. You don't even have to write down suggestions anymore because the children will remember them. Can every issue be problem-solved? Most can. There are some days when I thought, would it be easier to just be a dictator and tell them what they are going to do! It was tempting! But then I realize how much time is spent on enforcing discipline on children that don't have buy-in to the solutions. They learn a critical life skill in the process: how to work out problems with other people. Teaching children problem-solving is a much more effective use of discipline time than punishing sibling fighting, power struggles, and rebellious behavior.

Other methods to solve conflicts

- Meet in the middle: This isn't a true 100 percent win-win solution. It's more like 50 percent/50 percent, but it is a compromise.

- The agreement volley: Ask one child for a solution. Ask if the other child agrees. When the other child says "no", then ask them to come up with a win-win idea. When they have one, ask the first child if they agree. When they say "no" (a big surprise if they say "yes"!), then ask for an alternate idea. Keep going until they agree on something. This could take a long time, but the children will catch on that the sooner they agree on something, the sooner they can get with the plan. (It helps if you put distracting items on hold, such as the TV, video game console, or the computer that they are fighting over. Both parties want to get on with the action and will work to a solution faster!)

- Hold court: Teach the children how to appoint each other as the judge, lawyers for opposing sides, and the jury. Teach them the "court" process, where the lawyers speak for the clients and restate their opinions without the emotion involved. The judge keeps the order and the jury decides the outcome. My children start this out very serious and end up laughing.

- Duct tape the children to each other until they settle it (by Marlin, 11). See, I wrote down all suggestions, no matter how silly!

When your child doesn't keep to agreements

It builds your child's self-esteem by helping him to feel good about himself when he honors commitments to others. It builds self-discipline too. Sometimes you need to help your child keep to their agreements. You could say, "How can I make this easier? What can I do to help you keep your agreement?"

For example, my daughter, 11, agreed to go to karate three times a week to finish her next belt, and then she had the option to quit. She wanted to take karate for two years but its appeal was wearing thin. We sat down and together, decided which three nights she would go, based on her choice of what were fun classes. However, on the night she agreed to go, she didn't want to. I asked what would help her keep her agreement. She said it would help if I stayed and watched. I decided I could do that. And I did. She went and kept to her agreement and even had fun.

Alternately, you might have to problem-solve the issue again. If one person doesn't keep their agreement, it often means the problem was never solved to a truly win-win situation. The person wasn't really having their needs met. It may be time to go back to the drawing board and brainstorm some new solutions.

Problem-solving sibling issues

Brainstorming ideas and coming up with solutions that meet both children's needs are essential for sibling harmony. Here is how parents teach the process:

- You facilitate the problem-solving process; they watch.
- You and they do the problem-solving process together.
- They do the problem-solving process; you watch and guide.
- They problem-solve, and you hide!

Benefits of problem solving:

- Uses the wisdom and experience of the child, as well as of the parent.
- Only the process needs consistency, not the outcomes. Outcomes are flexible enough to meet everyone's needs.
- When everyone participates in making rules, the rules are more likely to be respected.
- Parent's and child's needs are deemed equally important, and both are met.
- Everyone feels listened to, loved, and respected.
- Children and adults get practice in problem-solving, brainstorming, and creative thinking skills. These skills are essential for success in today's world.
- The method strengthens relationships by facilitating growth, good feelings, and intimacy.
- The method allows parents and child to deal with conflict rather than avoid it.
- Doesn't require the use of power, bribes, or punishment.
- Not a compromise, which is still half-win, half lose. Both parent and child would have to give something up to get needs half met. Problem-solving allows both parent and child to have needs fully met by focusing on needs and not positions.
- The child learns self-discipline and responsibility.
- Problem-solving enables children to work out their conflicts respectfully with siblings and friends.

> Children, like adults, flourish best when given support and encouragement for what it is they're doing right, rather than a lot of criticism for what they are doing wrong.
> ~ Thomas Gordon, Author

NAGGING

Ask any adult who is trying to quit smoking, lose weight, stop drinking, stop speeding, or exercise more, whether bribes and punishments issued from another person helped them achieve their goals. Did nagging, lecturing, threatening, or forcing them to change, help motivate them? Why would preteen and teenage children feel any different?

Nagging is giving people information that they already know.

~ Patricia Morgan, Author

SCHOOL PROBLEMS

Warning signs that your school situation isn't working:
- Unhealthy self-esteem
- Deterioration of social behaviors
- Disruptive attention seeking behaviors increase
- Reluctance to go to school
- Physical symptoms such as stomach cramps, nausea, and dizziness

Why children resist school and homework:

"It's too hard." They may not be developmentally ready for the concepts.

"It's too boring." They may already know the material.

"It's not fun." Their learning profile does not fit the material delivery.

"I'm fiercely autonomous and resist anything my parents and teachers promote."
Due to my temperament, personality type, and developmental stage.

"I'm a curious independent thinker and want my questions answered, rather than having to answer somebody else's questions." I don't see the point in doing busy work when my time is better served somewhere else.

"I'm being bullied and I'm scared." A very common reason.

Suggestions for getting more co-operation and fewer power struggles:
- Give choices in subject matter, time, or place of study. Would the child like to do Math or English first? When is their best, most alert time of day? Would they like to study in their rooms or on the couch?
- Supplement the material in a fun way and gear it to the child's learning style. Is he an auditory, visual, or kinesthetic learner? Use a math music audiotape, math videos, or chocolate chips for math concepts. Great games for Math and Language Arts are Scrabble™, Battleship™, card games, Monopoly™, Fraction Pizza™, and many others.
- Contact the teacher. See if your child can follow their interests as much as possible, if not in format, then in content. The child has to write an essay, so he could write about his passion.
- Avoid power struggles. Put your relationship building first. Try and approach homework another way. Listen to why your child doesn't want to do the work and brainstorm ideas together on how to get the work done.

- For those hesitant writers, try being the scribe, while the child dictates ideas. Or try letting them write on the computer, which is easier on little hands. Or let the child dictate into a tape recorder and then copy down what he has spoken.
- For those hesitant readers, try picking up an enticing children's book and reading out loud. Your child might come join you if it's not forced. Model reading yourself. Cuddle on the couch with a child and make reading a fun, cozy, exciting time. Use vocal variety and stop when the child is no longer interested.
- Keep a routine going when you figure out the best time of day for homework. After school, after supper, or before bed. This has to work for you and your child. Some parents like to get homework out of the way and done by supper, but perhaps the child needs a break from academics and needs to let off steam in the back yard first. Be kind but firm in sticking to a routine that works.
- Have a written contract each week, month, or year that is signed and agreed to by the parent and child, about what work must be completed for that time period.
- Realize that most children and adults will learn what they need to know, when they really need to know it, and will not be hindered by lack of previous learning.
- Never punish for not doing the work. You want to create a climate for life-long learning and enjoyment of the pursuit of knowledge. Your job is to facilitate homework and learning. You can't force a child to learn, and you can't stop a child from learning.
- Talk to the teacher and problem-solve issues that come up. Be sure that your child is present and fully participating in the problem-solving process. You have done your homework by active listening to your child and found out the underlying issues and feelings. You may need to help your child find their voice and talk to the teacher or send an email.
- By the age of 13, homework becomes the child's total responsibility. Until then, you need to help your child learn time and task management skills.

Much of what children learn is invisible to us. Their amount of interest in a topic is directly related to how much knowledge is absorbed and retained. When they are left to their own devices, children learn new information and skills when they have a need to accomplish a particular task or goal. So, instead of trying to fill your child with information, be a facilitator of learning; leave interesting things lying around, such as science kits, games, books, and videos. Pique their natural curiosity. Introduce topics and subjects, but let it go if you observe your child's disinterest.

If you want your child to develop essential skills of initiative, co-operation, and a passion for learning, you can't do it by shoving worksheets at them. Encourage their interests, questions, and help them look for answers. Spend homework time helping them to learn what they really want to know. And don't forget to have fun because the learning doesn't stop when the school bell rings.

 You can't teach somebody anything, if they don't want to learn it.

CONSEQUENCES: DISCIPLINE OR PUNISHMENT?

Consequences are the natural outcome from our behaviors. Every action has a consequence. For our children, consequences are a powerful learning tool that tells them if a decision was a responsible one or a careless one. Experiencing the consequence from their action helps them to modify their future behavior to enjoy better outcomes. But learning goes beyond just experiencing consequences. It involves learning how to solve problems.

<u>Natural consequences</u> are those outcomes that happen without the intervention of parents. Outcomes are determined by events, people, or just by circumstances. Parents do not interfere with the natural learning that will occur.

Sometimes, letting children experience the natural consequence of their action is too dangerous, such as letting a two-year-old run out into the traffic in the street. Parents must interfere. In this case, supervision is a better discipline tool. <u>Logical consequences</u> are set up and enforced by the parent. They may or not be related to the behavior.

People working in the juvenile court system often say that children end up there for two reasons: They have a very unhealthy sense of self-esteem, and they have not had to face the consequences of their decisions and actions. They have been rescued from any unpleasant effects.

How to make consequences non-punitive

There are several guidelines when using consequences as a respectful and effective discipline tool. Most consequences are thinly disguised punishments that are made palatable to parents under a new name. I don't recommend them because children can see through them as a punishment and lose respect for the parent. Here are some guidelines for making them non-punitive if you must use them.

Consequences must be related to the behavior. A messy room might mean that the floor is too cluttered for Mom to put away the child's laundry, so the child must do it himself. An unrelated consequence would be the video console is confiscated for a week until the room is cleaned up.

Consequences must be reasonable. Expecting a two-year-old to earn money to replace a broken vase from their carelessness is unreasonable. It would be reasonable to have the child "help" with the clean up by picking up the large non-sharp pieces and putting them in a box for the garbage.

The parent must feel comfortable with the consequence. Telling a child that the play date will end if the child hits the other child one more time may not be enforceable if Mom is enjoying chatting with the other mom on the play date and unwilling to cut the time short.

Consequences must be respectful. Would you treat your partner, friend, or neighbor with the same consequence? If you loaned your saw to a neighbor and they left it out in the rain then returned it to you rusted, it would be very reasonable to expect they clean it up or replace it before its return. That would solve your problem of having a rusty tool. The same action would be a reasonable, respectful expectation from your child. You must show him how to meet it.

Consequences must not be used as a punishment. How to tell?
- If you threaten a certain outcome to get compliance, then it is being used as a punishment, which could invite a power struggle.
- If you come up with the problem-solving solution and insist on it rather than get input from your child on how to solve the problem, it's probably a punitive consequence.
- If your child thinks it's a punishment, rather than a way to make amends or solve the problem, then it probably is a punishment! Ask your child for their opinion. Is the solution meant to hurt them or does it solve a problem?

The best consequences focus on teaching restitution, making amends, and solving problems. Consequences must be solution orientated. If a child spills a drink because she was careless pouring, she wipes up the mess. No further punishment or consequence is needed. A child who hits another child needs to be separated, calmed down, and told the rule. The restitution part might be to offer the other child a toy, hug, or an apology. No further consequence is needed.

Here is another way to look at it. Your son rides his bike without a helmet – again. You've nagged, begged, pleaded, and informed him of the dangers of riding without. Next, you've issued consequences! You've taken the bike away and put it in the garage for a day, then a week, and then a whole month. You've done everything the parenting books say for a consequence to work. It's reasonable. Anyone can live a day without a bike. It's respectful. You're not hitting or calling him names. And it's related. No helmet, no bike. Simple to understand. But the problem is he is still riding a bike without a helmet! The situation could turn into a huge power struggle every time you take the bike away.

Clearly, the consequence has not worked. Why not?

Consequences won't work, because it's punitive and also because the underlying need/feeling (NOF) of the child is not addressed. A child who consistently refuses to wear a bike helmet, even after having the bike locked away several times (and this is a common logical punitive consequence that parents take), may have a good reason for not wearing it. Perhaps he is being teased because it looks babyish. Maybe it's prickly or doesn't fit right. Active listening and mutual parent-child problem-solving are better tools used to uncover and address the underlying need.

Make sure the consequences are solution focused rather than pain focused. A common concern is, "Won't my child ever learn the consequences of his actions if I don't set up logical consequences? The more unpleasant the better?" Of course, he will. The rest of the world will be happy to teach your child the consequences of his actions. Sometimes, it will be painful and inconvenient for him, but only you, the parent, can provide the safe haven of your loving relationship to teach him how to solve problems, make restitution, and amends. That's the harder job. The outside world is too busy to teach him those. You can! And the bonus is you'll enjoy less power struggles and more connection in your relationship.

When used properly, non-punitive consequences teach children appropriate behavior in a positive way and should be in every parent's discipline toolbox.

The rule	Reason	Consequence as punishment	Consequence as solution
food must be eaten sitting down	safety reasons	food is removed	problem-solve why the child is running and eating at the same time

The rule	Reason	Consequence as punishment	Consequence as solution
don't throw water over the bathtub	it floods the basement through the air intake	get out of tub	help clean up, give info, and distract with another activity
no jumping on beds	springs get wrecked	remove from room	get something else to jump on; substitute
no throwing toys	hurts people or things	take toys away	find something else to do; redirect

messy rooms must be cleaned up of toys	respect for others' safety	toys go in a bag to be taken away	clean up mess together; show and tell correct behavior
children must stay close in public	can get lost	child has to stay home	buy a child leash; plan ahead

> The only way we can fully protect someone against his own mistakes and the uncertainties of the world is to make him a slave. He is then defenseless before OUR whims and weaknesses. most people would prefer to take their chances with the world. They have the right to that choice.
> ~ John Holt, Author

SWEARING

Swearing has worldwide appeal. Every language has its profanity swear words. The key to parenting a child who swears is not in controlling or eliminating all swear words, but in teaching when, who, and where it might be okay to do it and not to do it. Ninety-five percent of adults swear. Why wouldn't children?

In the times you are connecting with your child, gently teach your children why it's important to not swear at certain times. Provide some examples and let them decide:

Is swearing appropriate at:

- The playground with little children around versus a private party with peers?
- Dinner with Grandma or picnic with buddies?
- Everyday conversation with friends or when you slam a finger with a hammer?

GROUNDING

Grounding is the teenagers "time-out." The same concerns with time-out apply to grounding except that grounding a teenager can be very hard to enforce. Don't use it. It's a punishment. Problem-solve the situation instead.

SLEEPOVERS (WAKE-OVERS!) AND PLAY DATES

It's perfectly acceptable to expect that your child's friends will follow the family rules at your house, even if they have different rules at home. Areas to consider are:

cleaning up messes, behavior and conduct rules, cooperating with siblings and others in the home, and respecting family values around computer games, movies, and phone use.

Some tips

- Stimulation: It helps to have a structured activity for school-aged children for at least part of the time.
- Change environment: Put a video on and lights off to settle children down for bed.
- Plan ahead: Ask guests to bring their own pillows, towels, and sleep bags to cut down on your laundry.
- Natural consequences: Be sure to get parent's contact info in case you need to send an uncooperative child home.
- Clarify expectations: The first time a child visits, go over family rules with your child present. It can be done in a fun and friendly way.
- Change environment: Pack away any toys that are not sharable or are breakable. Be prepared to hear whispers and giggles after lights out. It's normal and fun!

PEER PRESSURE

> Peers were never meant to be nurturing; they compete for nurturing.
> Parents have an innate capacity for nurturing.
> ~ Gordon Neufeld, Psychologist

My eight-year-old son excitedly told me about a birthday party trip to a popular play place. He casually mentioned he had a fun and bumpy ride in the back of the parent's van. Upon further inquiries, I discovered that several boys rode in the back of the van with no seat belts. For eight years, I taught my son not to get in a car that didn't have a seat belt for him. I taught him to say "no" to any adult that would urge him otherwise. It still didn't work. He, along with two other boys, succumbed to peer pressure and didn't question the decision making of the adult in authority.

Peer pressure is influence from people of the same age, group, or affiliation to behave in the same way, regardless of individual attitudes, feelings, or beliefs. It can be positive and healthy, or negative and destructive. And it's with us all our lives, even as adults. Humans have a basic need to belong, in our family, peers, and our social groups. However, peer pressure is most powerful during the school-aged and teen years, when your child is venturing forth and discovering his self-identity outside the safe confines of the immediate family. Our children's overriding desire for acceptance is normal and a healthy developmental stage. Our goal as parents is to help our children cope with negative peer pressure while growing to healthy interdependence.

Children are exposed to many influences: video and computer games, advertising, other people's values and opinions, news reports, etc. Some of these are good influences and some are not-so-good, depending on how these influences fit with our family norms. Our children are going to encounter values, attitudes, and beliefs that are different from our family's values throughout their lives. So what can parents do? Parents can subtly influence the choice of peers but cannot control the choice completely. There is much parents can do to influence peer relations if they know three main points of why peer pressure flourishes.

Peer pressure has more influence when:

1. The need for acceptance in a peer group will become much greater if the child's needs are not met by family. These needs are: acceptance of themselves, unconditional love, understanding, fun, the need for control and autonomy, the need of skill mastery and self-confidence.
2. The more the child needs approval, the greater the possibility he will override his beliefs and attitudes with the prevailing behavior of the peer group.
3. Children often find their unrealized personality characteristics in friends. For example, a shy child will gravitate toward a more outgoing child.

Let us look at the positives of peer pressure. Peers provide encouragement and challenge to engage in positive activities. A good example is the popularity of Harry Potter™ books. Many parents are overjoyed to find their children reading what their peers are reading. Peers can provide positive pressure to join a soccer team, stop bad habits, work on community projects, eat healthier, or even set up a business. Peers also ease some of the stress in the major transitions in life by providing a same aged confidence. Peers listen, understand, and provide a sounding board. Children need to go out in the world and test the values learned at home. The peer group is the next logical step in the world, as well as peer's parents, other adults in the workplace, and volunteer settings.

Peers teach compromise, negotiation skills, and fair play. We can teach our children all we want about losing graciously in a soccer game, but a friend will teach our child actual consequences if they display obnoxious behavior. They might not speak to them for a while. Another positive is that children gain experience in reading the social norms of groups, which is excellent practice for being a discerning adult.

The three warning signs of negative peer pressure are:

1. Your child is heavily dependent on approval by others, including you. He may consult friends on small decisions and worries obsessively about what peers will think of what he bought, said, or did.
2. Your child won't take responsibility for his actions when in trouble and blames his peers instead.
3. Your child is secretive about friendships and won't bring friends home.

What can parents do?

1. **Look at your child's unmet needs.** Look beyond his behavior. Does he need more attention, self-confidence, encouragement, and understanding? You can give it!

2. **Build a connection with your child.** Spend time with him. Give him unconditional love. He won't want to do things to hurt his relationship with you.

3. **Give respect.** Respect his space and belongings. Avoid criticism. Treat your child with politeness and kindness and he will come to expect it from his peers, too.

4. **Build your child's healthy self-esteem.** Help him develop his talents and abilities to give him confidence. Every child excels at something. Encourage him, rather then praise him, to avoid over reliance on approval from others. Focus on the effort, not the results of his activities.

5. **Don't overly value your child's outer looks.** Carol, a mom of five in my class says, "Does your child have a smart brain (and every child does excel at something) and a kind heart?" Emphasize those qualities that are under their control.

6. **Choose your battles carefully.** Give your child small harmless rebellions. Teach your child to follow his instincts (his 'gut' feeling, or his 'spidey' senses).

7. **Honor your child to say "no" if he and you feel it's appropriate.** For example: sharing toys, accepting rides, participating at an event. Teach your child to be politely assertive with peers, siblings, other adults, and you. Other adults do not always have your child's best interests at heart. You don't want to raise a doormat.

8. **Keep communication lines open.** Listen, listen, and listen some more. Be non-judgmental and acknowledge feelings behind your child's words and actions. Seek to understand why your child wants the negative peer relationship. When a friend is a negative influence, ask "Tell me how Mike is important to you? What do you like about being with him? What risks might there be hanging out with him? What are your plans to deal with the risk? What role do you want me to play in helping you deal with those risks?"

9. **Increase your child's decision-making.** Limit rules to ones that are necessary for safety and get your child's input on them. They need autonomy and control over their lives as much as adults, even though they are lacking in experience. Children need practice in making good choices and decisions. They learn best by experiencing the consequences of those choices when the results are not yet so serious. They have you around to guide them. Ask "What did you learn about this? What can you do instead next time?"

10. **Build your child's confidence**. When your child seeks out his opposite-personality in a friend that's a negative influence, help your child find those unrealized parts of himself, so the need to seek them out in others is lessened. For example, get him into supervised rock climbing if he likes to hang around a peer that thrives on danger in destructive ways.

11. **Model handling peer pressure yourself**. Point out when you speak up in a group or in front of your friends. Role play what you said when describing those times you speak up at work or social situations. Discuss your feelings. Children need to know that it's hard for you too, but so necessary to do.

We have to remember that "we can't adjust the wind, but we can adjust the sails." Our children will inevitably meet up with negative influences. While we can't control how much or what type these influences are, we can control the quality of our parent-child relationship. In turn, it will greatly influence the type of people they are and the type of people they choose as friends. We still have the most influence over our children and can teach them how to seek and maintain healthy peer relationships.

HANDLING BULLIES

 What you permit is what you promote.   ~ Unknown

Often, bullies are considered to be the coolest children in the class. Bullies learn they can acquire power and status by repeatedly using aggression to control or cause distress to others. To acquire status, though, one needs an audience. Unfortunately, children want to be on the preferred side of affiliations, with the power source, not with the underdog victim, so they either remain silent or egg on the aggressor. They don't want to be the next victim, by standing up to the bully. However, this silent majority of bystanders are the key in delineating the effects. They must be encouraged to speak out in the safety of numbers and stand up for what is wrong. Bullying continues in silence. When bullying is exposed, and not tolerated by the majority and viewed as uncool, it will cease.

 Children must be encouraged to speak out to adults for help.

The qualities of respect, responsibility, honesty, integrity, empathy, fairness, initiative, perseverance, courage, and optimism are not taught to children through character education, although the parents and schools try very hard to do so. Cute little posters and slogans will not affect children that have been shown bad modeling from their parents, peers, and teachers.

We must change the culture of how adults relate to children. The essence of character education must be modeled to children from their parents and teachers to be truly effective. Teachers and parents must be the moral compass. They need to treat children with respect, as they would want to be treated. Instead of character education posters, kindness tickets, and slogans, time and money needs to be directed towards teaching children problem-solving, empathy, and communication skills. Teach them how to interact with others in conflict, respectfully.

As Will Smith, actor, talks about democratic parenting, "If you get them used to a master-slave relationship, when they leave your home, they're going to be looking for a master. We want them to be looking for partners."

In our high tech world, a lot of bullying is done not face-to-face, but behind the scenes in email, text messaging, blogs, internet bulletin boards, and social networking websites. Much is anonymous and pre-meditated. There are no simple answers to end bullying, but I believe that acknowledging that the problem exists is a huge step forward then 30 years ago when bullying was accepted as normal and necessary.

Tips to handle cyber-bullying:

Teach the children to keep calm. Get in the habit of writing a response and save it into drafts to sit on and think about for a few hours. Then decide to send it or alter it.

Teach the children to not open mail or messages that look abusive or threatening. Keep them on the computer to report.

Report the bullying to your internet Service Provider and the police.

Teach the children to never give out personal identifying characteristics such as real name, address, phone number, school name, sports teams, siblings, etc.

Teach the children to never meet anyone from the internet without a parent present.

Don't pull the plug on the computer or even threaten it. Most children do not report bullying to their parents because of the fear that they will shut down their communication and entertainment source. Better to keep communication lines open and teach the children how to solve the problem, rather then to punish them by taking it away.

Have discussions about how to critically interpret information on the internet and separate fact from fiction.

If bullying continues in a school situation, consider online schooling, home education (parent teaches or child self teaches), or home-based education (print or online delivery from a teacher). As all three options are becoming more common, increased social supports are being put into place for parents and children.

If bullying continues in sports, art, or other activities, consider pulling your child out and finding a replacement. There will be enough negative situations for your child to deal with when he is an adult and has a better sense of himself and more confidence. Shelter his self-esteem and confidence while he is young. Teach him that his self-respect and safety are paramount. Like a young sapling that has been shielded from the wind, he will grow straight, tall, strong, and able to withstand the hardest gales as a mature tree. Don't let him grow into a twisted, knarled tree that is bent from the wind from lack of shelter.

WHAT IS YOUR IQ? (INTEGRITY QUOTIENT)

We were on holidays with a rented van. As my husband signed the papers to acquire the vehicle, the skies opened up, and it started pouring rain. The rental clerk decided to forego the pre-customer condition check and wrote on the form that it was raining hard and the customer didn't inspect the van. We occupied ourselves by shoving children and bags in the van to escape the belting rain. All was well, until halfway through the vacation, another man swung open his car door at a gas station and banged our van door with his car door, hard enough to make a scrape the size of a quarter. When my husband turned in the van at the airport, I asked him if the rental clerk noticed the dent. My husband said he did, and my husband admitted doing it. "What? Why?" I retorted with surprise. There was no way the van company could prove we did it, especially with no pre-rental inspection report. My husband replied, "Yes, there was no proof, but we were responsible for it. I would feel better admitting it, rather than lying about it." During the plane ride home, I was a bit angry about his response but could gradually see the point in his argument. It didn't matter what other people knew or thought. He needed to do the right thing, for his own sense of self-respect and integrity.

Integrity is about doing the right thing when it's not always convenient, cheap, or easy to do so, and even when no one is looking or there is no way to get caught. It's about whether one can face themselves in the mirror and feel good about their actions. It's about being honest and integral to the self-image of who they are.

Parents want their children to have honesty and integrity, but they don't always model it themselves. When children see their parents preaching honesty, yet acting in ways that aren't honest, they may lose respect for them as role models and see them as hypocrites. And even worse, children copy the actions they see their parents do. They often don't have a clue that their behavior is dishonest or irresponsible.

Most of us are law abiding, good citizens. But there are times we have to admit, when the area is a bit gray in the integrity department!

What is your parenting Integrity Quotient? Take this simple test:

1. Do I try to always be truthful? Do I tell my children who answer the phone and door to tell the caller that I'm not home, when I really am?
2. Do I honor my commitments to people and organizations, even when it's inconvenient or costly to do so?
3. Do I honor my children's real ages when entering facilities, or do I lie about their ages to get a discount? Do I bring their friends in the facilities at the "family rate" or do I tell the cashier they are separate from family?
4. Do I obey signs in parks, zoos, playgrounds, and fields, or do I ignore them? Do I expect my children to obey the law when they are not with me, if I disregard laws while out with my children?
5. Do I honor "no outside food" rules at movie theatres, concert halls, and indoor playgrounds? Or do I sneak food in order to save money and time?
6. Do I copy CDs, movies, and games for my children, friends, or my child's friends?
7. Do I buy items at the store, fully intending to use them, and return them for a full refund when no longer needed?
8. Do I take more than my share when stores and organizations are giving items away for free?
9. Do I use business expenses and income tax deductions ethically, or do I stretch the meaning and intent of the privilege, to benefit my family and friends?
10. Do I point out to cashiers when they give me incorrect change in my favor?
11. Do I disregard the law by doubling up two children using one seat belt, putting both in danger of injury?
12. If I say that I'm going to take action, do I honor my word?

Your child's eyes are watching you. Be the person you want them to be: honest, responsible, law-abiding, and a good citizen. Above all, you want them to feel good about themselves. It's not about beating a big corporation, getting your due worth from "the system," or even getting something for free. It's about honorable parenting. Because ultimately, the costs incurred by dishonesty and irresponsibility is being passed on to the consumer: that's you, me, and our children.

In the end, the scrape on the van door cost us an extra $73, a small price to pay for my husband's self-respect and integrity. But the lesson taught to our children was priceless.

IT'S ALL ABOUT ME - DIFFICULTY WITH CLEANING UP

Children just don't see what has to be done around the house.

- Acknowledge and appreciate when they do something thoughtful. "I like the way this looks."

- Explain your needs in positive terms. "I need this room cleaned up before dinner."
- Problem-solve. "How can we get this place cleaned up?"
- Be patient.
- Don't look for maliciousness. Your son doesn't see how his actions create more work for you.
- Teach them how to do chores.
- Preteens are more apt to get chores done before sleepovers or hosting parties. Who among us waits to host company before cleaning our house? Just like adults, they are more motivated to clean up before friends come over then after.

PARENTAL AUTHORITY: CONTROL VERSUS INFLUENCE

Influence is the power to motivate people based on the connection in your relationship. It's invisible, fragile, and respectful.

 Nudge! Don't force!

"She's out of control." "My son won't listen to me anymore." "I've lost my parental authority." Sound familiar? These are common statements from parents in my classes that have preteen and teenage children. They want their children to grow up and express their own opinions, and beliefs, and make decisions for themselves. However, that process involves gradually letting go of control, and it can be a pretty hard thing for parents to do when they are used to controlling their children through bribes and punishments.

As children grow up, parents naturally lose their control over their children. When a baby is born, parents have 100 percent control over the baby's life, except for basic functions such as hunger, sleeping, and elimination. A parent still has about 90 percent control over a toddler, but now, more issues are beyond their control, such as a toddler's curiosity, temper tantrums, and picky eating habits. When the baby grows to be an eighteen-year-old adult, the parent has zero percent control over the child's life. The child is officially recognized as an adult, and our society affords them the right to decide all issues of their lives. Ideally, somewhere around aged nine, the parent should retain control over 50 percent of the issues that affect a child's life and let the child have control over the other 50 percent.

So if a parent is losing control of a child, what are they gaining? If the parent-child relationship is nurturing, open, respectful, and warm, the parents will build influence. As Dr. Thomas Gordon, author of *Parent Effectiveness Training* says, "Influence is the inverse of control. It's a paradox that the more control a person exercises in a relationship, the less influence they will have over the other person."

Parent Authority

Parent **Control** 9

Decreases

Parent **Influence** Increases

Lessens with Age

Grows with Age and Respect

0 Birth   **Age of Child**   **18** Years

Influence is what keeps children behaving even when their parents are not present. As children grow and become more capable, they don't need bribes anymore. They can obtain and buy almost anything they want without parents help. They don't fear punishments anymore because they are bigger, can escape easier, and fear them less. Yelling at a small child is much scarier to the child, than yelling at a 14-year-old. Although bribes are the carrot and punishments are the stick, they are both tools used to control another person.

Another consideration is that preteens and teens are around parents a lot less and around peers a whole lot more. Parental control works only if parents are around to monitor it. As the technological knowledge gap grows, between parents and children, parents are increasingly left out of control of a child's life. More children spend time on computers and cell phones then ever before, a world where their parents don't follow. In contrast to control, influence is parental trust that the child will consider what the parent says, even when the parent is not around. Influence does not include forcing or pushing the child to comply.

The child will make their own decisions based on valuable knowledge and experience previously imparted by the parent. A parent's role becomes that of mentor, coach, and consultant, rather than the role of police officer. In effect, the parent's control of the child may give way to the control wielded by the peer group, but the parent's influence will never, ever leave the child.

It's much easier to let go of control and build respectful trust if a parent has never resorted to bribes or punishments from the very beginning. To build a good parenting relationship, start by using influence from the toddler years on. It's still okay to control the toddler, but if he balks, then try using the tools of influence. The tools of influence are: open, honest, communication using I-statements, active listening; instead of lecturing, spending vast amounts of time together, sharing experiences. You're modeling the behavior and values you want to share. Children don't respect inconsistencies. Be available for discussions and gain the older child's consent for consultations on issues, but also be willing to leave decision-making to the child on their issues.

A child that doesn't feel pushed will be more likely to consult their parents on issues of concern to them than a child who thinks their parents will nag, lecture, intervene, force or threaten their viewpoints.

Get a child's input on family rule formation. If the child breaks the rule, discuss it, and mutually problem-solve with them, instead of punishment. Aim for a mutually satisfying solution that leaves everyone with good feelings toward each other. All of these strategies build the influence the parent has. It's a kid glove approach, rather then a hammer approach.

A child whose parents nag, lecture, or force their viewpoints and decisions, and use punishments, is the child who will "fire" their parents in the preteen and teen years. They tune out, ignore, and avoid them. They cut off communication. A child will listen to someone they respect and whom respects them. They won't open up to someone they fear or feel manipulated by.

"Children don't necessarily want more boundaries, limits, and rules. They want more parental involvement in their lives." said Linda, a mom of two children.

CHANGE ENVIRONMENT - MORE THAN JUST CHILDPROOFING

There are many ways to change the environment besides just putting away the breakables and putting plastic plugs in sockets. Changing the environment, or childproofing, can continue into the school-aged years, too.

Add to the environment

Enrich – make things more stimulating. Add toys, games, and activities to provide something to do. Children who are engaged have their needs met.
Enlarge – add space. Take the children out to the park, zoo, or playground. Make an enclosed backyard. Arrange a dedicated play space in the house or certain rooms, such as a play area in the kitchen, bathroom, and master bedroom.

Subtract from the environment

Reduce – take away stimulation at bedtime if you want them to go to sleep. Turn off TV or noise. Put away art materials. Put away anything you don't want to capture their attention if you want to go out.

Restrict – put limits on activities or areas. No balls in the house, but they're okay in the basement. Eat only at the table. Play dough in the kitchen. Water play outside.

Change things around

Simplify – make it easier for the child to do things himself. Put buckets and totes out for toy storage. Hang coat hooks at child level. Put cereal and bowls and plastic ware on a bottom cupboard. Pour milk from four-liter jugs to one-liter creamers that make it easier to pour.

Have step stools in the kitchen and bathroom. Have a basket for mitts, hats, and glasses for each child. Have a sock bucket by the door to catch those pesky socks that children remove as soon as they come in the house.

Rearrange – store things to encourage or discourage behavior. Activities such as paints and permanent markers that need to be supervised are stored up high, and out of sight.

GIFT GIVING FROM THE HEART AND HANDS, NOT THE WALLET

Christmas, birthday, and all-occasion gifts are items that children should be encouraged to make and give; it builds generosity of spirit, creativity, and true thinking of the other person. It's much better than going to the shopping mall and handing over the credit card. Be sure to supervise some of these activities such as sewing and woodworking.

Gift ideas for ages seven and up to make:

- Bake cookies and cakes
- Draw pictures
- Make and paint ceramics at clay studios
- Sew or knit scarves and clothes
- Saw wood toys and other items
- Give coupons for doing chores
- Record music
- Make bead pieces
- Paint wood photo frames
- Write a poem
- Make "production line" shirts
- Make candle holders

The school-aged years are a fun and rewarding period of childhood. They can take care of most of their physical needs but still think you know everything. Enjoy! They grow up so fast.

11

Discipline Tools for Teenagers 13 - 19 Years:
Negotiate

If you're complaining about your horse
pulling against your hand, you have a horse who is
complaining about his rider pulling on his mouth. ~ Unknown

Mention the word "teenagers" and roll your eyes in the midst of a group of parents, and you'll get the same moans and groans of sympathy as you would in the toddler phase. There is plenty of anecdotal evidence from parents that if you can survive the moody, rebellious, argumentative, door-slamming behaviors of your teenager, then you can survive anything!

I believe most rebellion and power struggles among teenagers and their parents result from the lack of change of discipline techniques that should occur when children grow, particularly the use of non-punitive discipline from the time children are born.

Some tools used with a toddler can be inappropriate with teens. Although, some tools are appropriate all through the ages, some do work better with certain ages than others. For example, have you ever tried to distract a teenager? It's more difficult! If the parent uses respectful techniques, like the ones in this book from toddlerhood on, they are more likely to have teens that don't need to rebel or engage in power struggles. The problem occurs when parents use punishments and bribes liberally through the school-aged years, and then find out those methods aren't working anymore with the children who are more resourceful and bigger than they.

There is plenty of research that shows a warm and nurturing parenting style is linked to better outcomes for children, such as school achievement, self-esteem, and peer relationship connections. The existing research also shows that democratic, nurturing, and non-punitive parenting supports close parent-child relationships. I personally have found that children whose parents rely mostly on negotiation, problem-solving, and modeling tools seldom have rebellious children.

The lack of research on teenagers is probably due to the ingrained use of punishments in our society. It would be quite difficult to find parents that never, ever used punishments in the raising of their children, unless we look outside Western culture. However, there are plenty of studies that also show teen rebellion, risk behavior, and crime are linked to harsh physical punishment and neglect.

Some anecdotal evidence comes from the home-schooling community. It's interesting to see the peer pressure that engulfs school teens is relegated to the sidelines in home-schooled teens. Family is still front and center in their lives. I've noticed the influence and warmth of family togetherness is still a priority in some home-schooled families' lives with teenagers. I'm hoping that someone will put together some studies someday to compare the differences. Even in families whose children attend school, I've seen close parent-child relationships if the parenting style was nurturing and democratic. It's even more important in non-home-schooling families due to increased amounts of peer pressure.

The problem is that it's very difficult for parents to change their parenting style in the school years. This is where most parents fall down. Parents are too embarrassed to attend courses and tend to go for counseling, which is a reactive approach when problems become too severe, rather than a proactive approach from taking classes. Books are always saying be consistent, yet, we wouldn't buy our children the same style, color, or size of clothing in the teen years as the toddler. We don't advocate consistency in clothes buying, why would we for discipline tools? Parents must change and be willing to be open to new ideas of parenting. Even better if it's before their children turn nine and stop communicating in the preteen/teen years. The teen years are so different in this generation.

Everything is connected in parenting.
You can't expect to be harsh and rigid in one area and not closed in another. These are the years, when you really need to know what's going on for your child and keep communication lines open.

~ Elizabeth Miles, Psychologist

Teens' hormones and emotional changes account for much of the moodiness, sensitivity, and distraction of the teen years. Rules work better when the child respects you and that respect comes back for them also. Harsh restrictions sometimes backfire, because teens become bigger, and more capable.

If you have been using the respectful discipline tools in this book up until the teen years, your teen should not have many special behavior concerns, such as drug use, eating disorders, sexual activity, school problems, suicide, or criminal behavior. It's important to remember that most teens experiment with those behaviors once or twice, but most do not make it a habit and quickly drop them or learn from them. If your teen has gone beyond experimentation and is engaging in those behaviors habitually, it's time to get professional help through government agencies, psychologists, counselors, and doctors.

> Anytime you think you have influence,
> try ordering around someone else's dog.
> ~ The Cockel Bur

All relationships are about give and take. Not about who wins and who loses. The parent-child relationship is no different. Compromise and negotiation is necessary more now then ever, yet many parents think that the teen years is the time to crack down and get more serious about rules.

YOUR TEENAGER'S DEVELOPMENTAL STAGE

Your teenager is in the Identity, Separation, and Sexuality developmental stage. It's a time of pulling away from parents and family and learning to shape their own lives.

Typical teenager behaviors
- The teenager's job is to experiment with sexuality and their changing body.
- They need to develop their own philosophy, values, and beliefs systems.
- They need to learn about work and life skills and prepare for entry in the adult world. They need to make mistakes and learn from them.
- They need to find out who they are.
- They need to separate from the family and emerge as a separate, but interdependent person, who takes responsibility for his own needs, feelings, and behaviors.

Teens can regress to behaviors of earlier stages. They will act very grown up one minute and very childish the next. This is totally normal!

For example:
- 13-year-old Brian is sometimes independent by not telling his parents where he is going and yet sometimes wants to be fed and cared for by having his lunch packed for him. (baby stage)
- 14-year-old Terry is sometimes very logical and reasonable and then suddenly bursts into a negative tantrum. (toddler stage)

- 15-year-old Joshua can engage in a thought provoking discussion of rights with his parents, and suddenly is arguing with his 11-year-old sister over very tiny detail of who has the larger piece of dessert. (preschooler stage)
- 16- to 19-year-old Derek is very responsible in attending his part time job, yet suddenly reverts back to irresponsible behavior such as climbing on the escalator handle for a quick ride at the mall! (school-aged stage)

DEVELOPMENTAL MILESTONES

Physical milestones

- They are naturally clumsy because their bodies are growing inconsistently. Their hands and feet are proportionally large to rest of their body parts and may be prone to tripping and dropping items.
- Girls develop breasts, armpit hair, pubic hair, hips and curves. Voices deepen. She begins to menstruate and ovulate. She will grow taller. Girls develop most from age 11-16.
- Boys develop muscle mass, grow taller, widen shoulders, and their genitals grow. They also grow body hair on their arms and legs, facial hair, pubic hair, armpit hair, and their voices deepen. They begin nocturnal emissions. Boys develop most from age 13 -17.
- Both have a voracious appetite for food.
- Boys and girls may develop acne.

Psychosocial milestones

- Teens are still growing their brains. The teen's physical, intellectual, and psychological changes affect their emotions. Anger outbursts may be part of this challenging time. The amygdala (part of the brain that controls emotions) is experiencing hormonal changes and is responsible for the mood swings. It's normal. The amygdala develops first in the preteen and young teen years. Therefore, they are very hot and cold toward you in the younger teen years. The rational part of the brain develops later in the older teen years. From age 18 – 25 is the last growth period of the pre-frontal cortex, the part of the brain that regulates logic, problem solving, and limits. As author Cheryl Erwin, states, "They are like big giant SUVs with a huge accelerator, massive engine, and brakes on back order."
- The teen may be critical of many things. Erratic moods, philosophical brooding, and periods of quietness are very normal. Reluctance to engage with family and siblings is also normal.
- Teens have intense energy, tiredness, reflection ability, and body preoccupation. Body hygiene becomes important. This is the most insecure time of their lives. They feel unsure about everything in their life.

**You may be the target, but it's not about you.
Don't take it personally!**

Cognitive milestones

- It's the beginning of formal operational thinking, where young people can think symbolically and hypothetically. Abstract thinking and concepts are now used. Teens can fully understand the gray areas of rules, opinions, values, and belief systems, which makes negotiation a wonderful relationship builder.
- They see themselves as immortal and may engage in high-risk behaviors that threaten safety.

PARENTS MATTER

Unhelpful parenting behaviors

- Anything opposite to the list below!

Helpful parenting behaviors
Communication

- Be sure your child knows that no topic is off limits. Any topic will be met with sensitivity, understanding, and knowledge from you. No "discussion closed" stance will be practiced.
- Listen attentively and try to understand their point of view, and restate it in your own words, before stating yours. Help your teen think through their ideas by putting forth your own.

- Share fun. Go to movies, play video games, eat out and shop together.
- Talk about your day: triumphs, disappointments, joys and problems may help to draw them out.
- Be comfortable with agreeing to disagree.
- Nurture your teen through touch, words, actions, and feelings.
- They may or may not need advice, but it's usually on their terms, when they ask. Don't patronize your teen by telling them your advice is the only way. Offer it as an option and let them choose.
- Use humor when appropriate.
- Get to know what concerns your teen has.
- Be ready to talk about difficult subjects with accurate information. Do your research beforehand. You want to know about crystal methamphetamine before your teen brings it up.
- Instead of telling them what they can't do, help them try to do what they can.
- Rehearse strategies with your teen to deal with unwanted peer pressures to have sex, smoke, shoplift, use alcohol or drugs, or any other risky behavior.

Development

- Realize that teens will temporarily recycle back through the stages of childhood.
- Admire and enjoy their emerging sexuality without being seductive towards them or allowing them to behave seductively.
- Be ready to affirm their independence.
- Recognize that their body clock supports sleeping late and staying up late.
- Don't make an issue about eating, weight, physical size, or shape. Model good eating and exercise habits. Model the lifestyle you want your child to live.
- Openly listen to all expressions of feelings. Help your teen understand the challenges of the intense feelings that arise. Accept that your teen's physical, intellectual, and psychological changes affect emotions. Anger outbursts may be part of the transition. **Avoid taking personally any teenage criticism or embarrassment of anything to do with you.** Remind yourself that it's their growing brain that does it. They are not rejecting you as much as they are trying to find themselves.
- Be free to admit your weaknesses. Your teen will see it's okay to admit to weaknesses.
- Communicate unconditional love and appreciation daily when they succeed and when they fail.

Living together issues

- Accept that their separation may be slower or faster than their peers.
- Do not pry with multiple questions into your teen's life. Respect their need for privacy. Realize that teens need more privacy and spend more time on the

phone, computer, in their room, and listening to music. Realize that room sharing with siblings is probably not a desirable thing for the teen's craving for separation and independence.

- Watch your stress level. Do you need more time, self care, anger management?
- They need non-interference in friendship issues. A parent's role is to be a sounding board and an advice giver, when asked.
- Teens need a safe place to hang out with friends. Welcome your teen's friends into your home.
- Believe that your teen wants to stay connected with you, but on their terms, so don't give up. The longer you put it off, the harder it is to build bridges.
- Have regular family conferences to solve family problems. Leave individual problems for solving between you and your teen.
- Give duties with choices.
- Quantity time together is important. One-on-one time more important then family time to your teen right now.
- Allow a balance of activities: some physical activity, some computer time, some daydreaming, and some homework.
- Give them spending money.
- Stay out of your teen's homework.
- Have clear limits around movies, music, video games, TV, and swearing. If those limits are pushed, seek a win-win solution with your teen.

Values collisions

- Use open-ended and reflective questions to support problem-solving.
- Share appropriate information with your teen about your life. Respect their boundaries of "too much" information.
- Avoid parentifying your teen. Deal with your adult problems as your own. Don't make your teen parent you.
- Ask for opinions on movies, music, technology, books, TV, people, and everything you can think of.
- Create a connection with your teen's friends' parents, and check in on the group's activity. Be comfortable with teens choosing their own friends.
- Continue meaningful family rituals and celebrations. Nudge, but don't force teen to participate.
- Teens need nudges to perform at peak, but too much pressure can be off-putting.
- Don't pretend that the teen's mistakes and failures are insignificant. Teach them how to cope with them and improve.
- Make your opinion of pre-marital sex, drug use, crime, and education clear and explain your decisions using your declarative I-statements.
- Understand that many teens are sexually active.

- Be comfortable talking about healthy relationships, intercourse, masturbation, menstruation, and sexually transmitted infections.
- Be comfortable talking about drug use, including coffee, smoking, prescription drugs, and illegal drugs. Be aware that your use is a powerful model.
- Be prepared to seek community support and information should sexual activity, drug use, or other risk taking behaviors go beyond teen experimentation.
- Actively support your teen's interests, even if they are not what you would choose. Watch, cheer and attend!
- Use all helpful parenting behaviors for previous age groups.

Discipline for teenagers should be very easy, if you've been following a non-punitive approach all along, and used many of the tools that have been presented for the other age groups. You and your child will be used to negotiation and problem-solving. You have been modeling the adult you would like them to grow to and your communication and relationship has been pretty good.

If you haven't done so yet, think of discipline issues between you and your teen as conflicts to be resolved. Conflicts are everywhere in our lives, between people who love each other and those that don't. Conflicts can be from going to church to conflict between religions; from who gets the preferred side of the bed to who sits at the chair of the boardroom table; from who picks up the toys to who cleans up the environment; from negotiating family rules to negotiating courtroom settlements; from neighbor parking habits to the country's immigration policies; from PTA decisions to United Nation Convention ratifications. Conflicts are everywhere, and the teenage years are the best time to practice positive resolution.

However, still being a child, your teen will most likely engage in experimental risky behavior, normal teen pranks and other parenting issues. Here are some of the best tools for handling respectfully.

DISCIPLINE TOOLS FOR TEENAGERS

Negotiate your "no"
Focus on the child's strengths
Speak respectfully
Offer a one-time consultation
Reflective questions
Keep communication lines open
Reconsider the situation with new information
Have a few clear rules
Decide what you will do
Parent time-out
Separate big issues from small issues
Reduce the reasons for rebellion
Respect privacy
Change environment
Stimulation
Model
Decide on problem ownership
Connect, then direct
Problem-solve
I-statements
Active listening
Spend time together
Natural consequences
Encourage capability
Contracts
Welcome their friends
Develop the "acceptance" bone
Holding, hugs, and cuddles

Negotiate your "no"

Your teenager will have lots of practice in setting limits and understanding the reasons behind them. They would be able to set their own limits now. For example, my children understand the effects of not using sunscreen through natural consequences (of getting sunburned) and a one-time consultation. They are now free to accept responsibility for their own bodies and choose to use it or not.

If your teen wants to attend a party, and you have reservations about it, tell him your needs and reservations. Listen to why he wants to go. Instead of saying "no", give him that information that would allow your needs to be met and let him decide how to meet your needs and still attend.

There is a difference between teaching teens what limits are, and forcing limits on them. Telling a teen that a shirt would be appropriate to wear to church because people judge you by the way you dress is much different than forcing a teen to wear a shirt. Children don't like to be told what to do, anymore than adults do. They rebel when ordered. However, if they were given a set of information and the decision about what to do, based on that information, was up to them, I truly believe, they would make the best choice, especially when they trust and value the information giver: the parent. The more force you use in the relationship, the less credibility and influence you have. Even if you have all the right answers!

> Often, our child's first experience of negotiation is when their employer gives them training courses as adults. It's a lifeskill that needs practice.

Focus on the child's strengths

Every child does something well. By commenting, acknowledging, and encouraging the positives of a child, you are highlighting those things you appreciate in him. This will build your relationship and his respect and appreciation of you. He knows what it is you don't approve of and the things you don't appreciate. You don't have to tell him. In fact, you may have told him a thousand times before. Focus, notice, and comment on the positive. Don't say anything about the negative, and he might just decide to work on the negative stuff by himself. If you are having trouble finding positives about your teen, see Chapter 9, "I like and appreciate about you."

Speak respectfully (and insist on being spoken to respectfully)

Your teen is angry and comes to you saying, "Can't you friggin' cook something good for a change?" Say, "I understand you are feeling angry about this. I would like to hear your opinion starting with 'I'm bored when we are always served macaroni and cheese.' I can hear your concerns better when I'm spoken to with respect." Attitude and disrespect are aggressive assertiveness. The same is true with sarcasm. Model respect, politeness, and non-sarcasm in your speaking voice. Funny or not, teens fail to see the humor if we use sarcasm because if we use it, they think they can use it on us.

Give teens practice and opportunities to express their ideas and opinions orally to an audience (large or small): dinner table conversations, family reunions, meetings, birthday parties, anniversary celebrations, and family meetings. Consider enrolling them in public speaking and interpersonal communication classes. Speaking can build a young person's confidence, oral articulation, and opinions. Our society doesn't give teens much of a voice and learning to speak effectively, and get along with people is a much more useful skill then learning equations.

Offer a one-time consultation

This is one of the best discipline tools for teenagers. It respects their growing ability to make decisions, to take in information that is not nagging, and to understand how their behavior effects themselves and others.

A professional consultation is when you hire someone to research and present their findings on some issue, then they report it to you, so that you can make a decision. You are left with knowledge, facts, opinions, and research on the issue, but the decision is left up to you. This is a great tool from Dr. Thomas Gordon's *Parent Effectiveness Training*.

In parenting, you can be "hired" as a consultant by your child. Let's say that your child is smoking, and you wish to consult to him:

- You approach him and ask if you can provide a one-time consultation about smoking.
- If he agrees, then arm yourself with facts, statistics, expert's opinions, photographs, and videos that support your point of view of the issue. In the smoking example, you get the health information, cost analysis, websites, death rates, and photographs of smoker lungs, ready to present.
- If he doesn't agree to hear you, you will build the relationship by letting it go. Don't revert back to nagging to get heard. Work on listening and building the relationship and then ask again in a few weeks or months.
- After presenting all the information, you leave the decision to smoke or not to smoke up to him. It's sort of like "informed consent." He has the information he needs to make a decision, and he knows your views on it. The key is to stop there. No more nagging, harassing, reminding, or even mentioning it. He will make his own decision.

A child will never hire you as consultant if he knows that the "consultation" will last forever!

Reflective questions

Asking careful, thought out questions to encourage your son's thinking can help him figure out solutions to his problems. Start the questions with "how or what," and they will require more thought than a simple "yes" or "no" answer to a "did you" type of question. "Have you thought about renting a car?" "What would happen if you partied in the street and the neighbors were angry and came out to yell at you?" "What if...?"

Keep communication lines open

Regular, healthy communication helps smooth the way when there are problems. It's the key to healthy parenting. However, forcing it will drive children away, too. One has to know when and how, based on cues from children. Get to know what they're into so you can comment and ask questions. Get to know their friends. "Tell me what you think…" is a great communication opener. Talk while doing dishes, making meals, over dinner, in the car, whenever you are together. Talking during chores, transportation, and before bedtime seems to be the best times for teens and parents. Often, my teens would open up more in the evening. The younger sibs were in bed and they had us all to themselves. They would be wide awake and in the mood for company just as I was falling asleep. But I realized the importance of this valuable connection time and made myself available for conversation.

On the other hand, respect their need for silence if they don't wish to talk. Look for behavioral communication clues. When a child says, "My friend did this…" or asks "What did you do when you were my age?" or "What would happen if someone…" they are most likely talking about themselves. Sometimes, it's easier for them to pose questions in the third person point of view.

Reconsider the situation with new information

Sometimes, new information comes to light that changes the whole situation. The key is listening well and with an open mind. Always listen to the whole situation before you make a statement or an evaluation and decide what to do.

Have a few clear rules

Keep your end of the agreements by following through. Help them to honor their end of the bargain by problem solving.

Decide what you will do

If your child comes home drunk from the party, decide that you will not drive him to the next one. Make it clear with your child the next day when he has his hangover. When he is sober, problem-solve what to do next time. Be clear about what you are willing and not willing to do. As parents of teens, you still have control over a lot of things: your feelings, your actions, and your values. If your teen's actions violate those, you have the right to feel the way you do, do what you do, and think how you do. Your teen will learn that the world is made up of different kinds of people and everyone, including their parents, deserves respect!

Parent time-out

Take good care of yourself. Have a social life and hobbies. Make time for yourself. Eat, sleep, and address your feelings. On an airplane, the flight attendants ask the parents to put on their oxygen mask first and then attend to the masks of their children. The airplane rule applies as much to you now as when your child was a baby. Designate one chair or room as your "worry place", go there, worry, then let it go! This is critically important if you are going through an especially hard time with your teen. You need work, hobbies, friends, volunteering, or activities that help you to feel good about yourself.

Separate the big issues from the small issues

This is key for teenagers. How important is the issue? Is it your problem or is it the child's problem? Will his behavior cause irreparable damage?

Small issues
Some issues that are open for negotiation are money, grades, transportation, recreation, conveniences, clothing, chores, and social manners.

Big issues
What are three that you will uphold no matter what? Purple hair? Drug use? They must empty the dishwasher? These are what you must decide. Establish connected and quiet times to have important talks about the big issues.

Reduce the reasons for rebellion

Don't treat them as if they are incapable of making their own decisions. Allow most decisions to be theirs with your experience-laden advice if they seek it. Let them express themselves as individuals. Let them know your love and support is unconditional whatever they decide.

Respect privacy

Knock first before entering their private space. Don't take a closed door personally. They want to be alone, to be private, and on their own territory. It's one step to moving out on their own. Try not to snoop through their stuff: email, instant messages, diaries. You wouldn't want it done to you, so snooping is not mutually respectful.

If problem behavior is happening, like drugs, crime and sex, you will see other signs in their behavior to watch for. If you suspect problems, ask them directly in a respectful, non-confrontational, caring way. Don't go looking for evidence in their stuff. That's the non-communicative, indirect way to approach problems. To look for warning signals in them, you have to have a good knowledge of your child, which you probably have if you've enjoyed an open relationship with them. Be aware and observant. As Dr. Scott C. Wooding says, "Hey, where are you going with that can of paint?" Parents need to know what their children are up to. Ask!

Change environment

Childproofing for teenagers? You bet! It's easier to change the environment then to change another person. It might be as simple as packing away most of the glasses for teens that dirty 30 glasses in a day, or as major as changing schools to stop bullying.

Stimulation

Toys for teens tend to be smaller and more expensive! Teens love electronics and technological gadgets. Music, table games; such as air hockey and pool, and computer and video games are popular. Also basketball nets, sports equipment, bikes, fashion items, crafts, videos, karaoke, fiction, and non-fiction books are desirable. Arts, crafts, sports, and drama items are only popular if there is a strong interest. Adult conversations are popular to listen in to. Don't forget the value of spending time engaging in conversation with you. Email, MSN, and phone are important parts of teens' lives, hence a computer and cell phone are increasingly desirable items. Make your home inviting and exciting to your teen. You will at least know where they are most of the time!

Model

Live the behavior and values you want to see. This one is pretty obvious, but so hard to do. If you want a child that doesn't back talk, watch how you talk. If you want your child to read more, read more yourself. If you want your child to not take drugs, watch your coffee, alcohol, and aspirin consumption. If you want your child to attend church, go yourself. Children are adept at spotting hypocrisy. The old saying, "Do as I say, rather than as I do" doesn't wash with today's children. They don't respect parents who don't walk the talk.

> Children are much more likely to learn from parental modeling if their relationship with the parent is a good one. Children seldom model after adults they fear, dislike, or resent. They adopt the values of people they admire, respect, and love.
>
> ~ Thomas Gordon, Psychologist

This is the best way to convey values. Speak and act your values on issues of underage drinking, skipping school, and lying. Make sure you don't do those things and don't condone them in your friends, either. If your friend offers you a burned CD of music, and you are against piracy, make sure your teen knows you have resisted peer pressure and refused to accept it. Those are the quiet teaching moments that go a long way in impressing teens.

Decide on problem ownership

Many parents take on their child's problems as their own. Areas such as friends, homework, dates, and sports are some examples when parents step and try to solve their child's problems. Ask yourself the following questions:

- Who is making the complaint? If it's not you, it's not your problem. Actively listen to the complainer.
- Whose goals are not being met?
- Who is the behavior interfering with <u>directly</u>?
- Who is having the most uncomfortable feelings about it?

If you answer "me" to most of the above, you are the person with the problem and need to take action to assert your needs. If you answer "no", then it's your child's problem to deal with. Empathy for our child is not the same as his direct feelings. Your role is not that of problem-solver. Your role is to actively listen to your child's feelings, point of view and be a sounding board. If he consents, you may also guide him in the process of problem-solving and then unconditionally support him in his decisions of how to solve them, even if you disagree that he didn't take your advice!

Education is a big "who owns the problem" issue. Put your teen in charge of his education. At some point, around age 12 or 13, school must become more important to him and his future, than it is to you.

Connect, then direct

When we are phoning up a friend and need to ask a favor, we would never say, "Marge, I want you to baby-sit tomorrow afternoon at 1:00 pm. Be here or else." It sounds too commanding and demanding. Marge may just respond with, "I don't think so!" However, if we worded it with "Marge, I know you are really busy these days, and your time is limited, but I really need a babysitter tomorrow at 1:00 pm. Could you help me out, please?" I'll bet Marge would do it, even if it were inconvenient for her. It's all in the way of asking. Children (and adults) do not like to be commanded. They like to be asked, politely. If you are going to ask your child to do something, go up to them and put your arm around them, give them a hug, touch them, or tousle their hair, and make the request. Acknowledge their feelings of not wanting to be interrupted. Find some way of connecting with them and then make the direction.

My son, 14, broke a glass and ignored me when I asked him to clean it up. I didn't realize he was in the middle of a computer game. I waited five minutes, went up to him, and rubbed his shoulder. "I know you are engrossed in this, but there is still glass on the floor, and I'm worried someone will step on it and get hurt." He cleaned it up as soon as he paused in the next game level.

Problem-solve

Most teenager behavior issues can be problem-solved. This is the other most important discipline tool for this age. It's respectful and an adult life skill. When there is nothing left but a few threads of communication, you will be glad the threads are there. Problem-solving requires those threads of communication.

My son was not turning in online assignments. Instead of taking away his favorite online game, I scheduled a teacher-parent interview. We discovered, through problem-solving, why he was not turning in assignments. It turned out he needed more organizational skills. We worked on them together, and he became more diligent about turning in assignments. This got at the real issue of the problem better then taking away his game.

Continue problem-solving issues between you, your child, and your family. Stay out of issues between your child and their friends, bosses, and teachers. If you are tempted to give problem-solving advice, ask them first if they would like it. "Would you like me to help guide you through the process of solving this problem or stay out of it?" Make it safe for them to talk openly about issues and give honest information when they want it.

> Children crave teaching, direction and advice, not punishment.
> They want to know how to do the right thing,
> but not be forced to do it.

I-statements
Use positive, preventative, declarative, and confronting ones. Declarative I-statements are very valuable for conveying values to your teen.

Active listening
Conversations with teenagers can be the most difficult when trying to relate and build a relationship with them. If you do more listening then talking, the teens will open up more. Especially if you just validate their experience. Don't criticize, interrupt, advise, nag, or lecture! Just listen!

Spend time together
Many studies show that teenagers still want to spend unstructured time together with their parents. By spending time with your teen, you enhance conversation, build relationships, and communication. One day, my son, 12, came up to me and asked, "How do you ingest cocaine?" I answered matter of fact. "Oh!" He said. He told me what he saw on the internet. He needed help understanding the "joke." He showed me the site, and I was better able to discuss cocaine along with what I knew and with my values slipped in there. I had a wonderful opportunity to express my beliefs and values in a moment when he was definitely open for it. This would not have been possible if we had a closed relationship, where communication was broken down. He trusted me not to lecture him, but simply state what I knew about cocaine, and leave him to form his own knowledge. I got an insight into what he knew and what info he was lacking.

Natural consequences

More teens learn from natural consequences if you do not jump in to rescue them or bail them out. Your job is to actively listen to their distress and be a person for them to bounce problem-solving ideas off you. But their job is to deal with the consequences of their actions. It's not your job or your problem.

My son, 15, hacked into a computer at school. The school was unhappy, and I got a call the next day from the principal. The principal told me that what my son did was not allowed in the school system, and he would be suspended from internet privileges if he continued. I asked the principal to speak with my son directly and handed the phone over. The principal was nice and preceded the conversation with a compliment (connect, then direct) in that my son had a gift in computers and science and that he needs to use that gift for something productive. He asked him to not use DOS programming with the computers, as it could break into the system. My son agreed, and he never did it again.

Encourage capability

Let them do what they can do for themselves. That means to back off of homework, work and chores. My friend, Patricia Morgan, author of *Love Her As She Is*, wrote a wonderful letter as a template for removing yourself from your child's school work:

"Dear Joey: For too long, I have accepted more responsibility for your homework than you. I want to apologize for taking over and giving you the message that you are not competent. Actually, you are a bright and capable young man. I hope you believe that. To prove that I mean what I am writing, I am resigning from involvement with your homework. I am available if you would like help with it. Anytime. Being there for you will never change. But, from now on, you are in charge. Maybe, you're thinking, "I'm so used to Mom nagging me about my homework and study; it will be hard." It might be. I'd be glad to help you figure out a plan, but that is up to you. I will be okay with you attending summer school. I trust you to make the best decision for you. Love, Mom."

Contracts

When you agree on a rule and responsibilities, it's good to have them written down and have the child sign them and the parent sign. They need to get used to the formality and importance of honoring a commitment that your signature bears.

Welcome their friends

Make your home inviting to your child and his friends. Give them a comfortable space and stimulation. Every hour or so, drop in the room unannounced with drinks and snacks. That subtle "hovering" helps keep things from getting out of hand and lets the teens know that you are around and "available if needed."

For young teens, give them something structured to do. They often just hang around, not coming up with any ideas, and need an adult ice-breaker to get the social waters flowing. When children don't know each other well, and it's a social event at your home, give them an organized craft, project, game or activity to do. Just make sure it's not too hokey. Then ease yourself out of the room and let them socialize in privacy.

Develop the "acceptance" bone

This is the one bone we don't have in our bodies, but should have. It's also connected to the "funny bone." Laughter makes things easier to accept.

> There is ample evidence that a necessary condition for helping others change is accepting them the way they are. 'Correction' does not inspire change. 'Acceptance' does.
>
> ~ Thomas Gordon, Author

This one is really hard to do. It works on the assumption that it's easier to change oneself rather than another person. Sometimes, in love relationships and especially as teenagers are on the verge of increasing independence, we must learn to accept certain behaviors of people as "part of the total package." Just as our partner has quirks that we have to learn to live with, our children do, too, and no amount of nagging will change them. It detracts from the relationship. Learning to live with it might just inspire that person to change when the desire comes from them.

Books and the self-help industry are full of ideas on how to change, reach goals, and forge ahead. We don't often give ourselves permission to just say "I can't change this. I have to accept it, and live with it for now." "And that's okay." So much of parenting (and marriage) is doing just that. It doesn't sell a lot of books, but it probably saves a lot of relationships.

Holding, hugs, and cuddles

It's as important as ever. Some teens may wish to be asked for a hug, especially during moody times. Respect their wishes if you ask for a hug and they refuse. Keep asking though!

SPECIAL TEENAGER BEHAVIOR CONCERNS
TEENS WANT TO CONNECT WITH YOU!

Not all teens want to disengage, rebel, and argue. Teens still need and want their parents very much but in different ways than the past. Teens that have respectful democratic parents really have nothing to rebel against, especially if their needs, feeling, and issues are mutually discussed, their needs are met, and problems are solved in a win-win fashion.

Teens go through a natural separation but don't want to slice the connection. Teens still crave connection but parents tend to push them away. Lots of teens say, "they were testing their parents to see if they cared." If a parent communicates love and confidence, then the teens don't really need to test their parent's love. But keep talking to them and offering love, hugs, attention, and a listening ear, even if they seem to push you away. A secure attachment can continue right through adulthood, even if the conflicts through the teen years escalate. We are growing from an independence valued society of 1950 to a more interdependent society, where young adults are not pushed out of the nest at 18 or even out of the family bed at five.

As one mom of a teen said, "I'm finding it better to not take anything personally. They are going through tons of changes and need to separate a bit from us as parents and the whole family thing. However, they don't want to sever the connections. They just want to define them their way. That's okay. Keep the lines of communication going. Find quiet opportunities to talk or just to hang out. My son is going to high school next year. I'm still going to carve out time we can be together."

Teens still want two critical elements of attachment theory: freedom to explore and a secure base. Many parents equate the teen years to the intense separation years of toddlerhood, where attachment is the balance between exploring the world and returning to the secure base of home, comfort and help. As a parent, your job is to provide both.

Foster open communication and problem-solving. It's one of your best discipline tools for this age. Have respect for their feelings and give them the acknowledgment that you will help them solve problems and not punish them for their mistakes. Be available when they want to talk and open up. Be committed to your relationship even in the midst of conflict. When your teen decides not to talk for awhile, it's about being available when he does and not taking offence or taking anything personally. Don't reject them, even if you feel rejected. You don't always need heart to heart talks. Just spending time together helps. When they want to talk, be available to them. At 14, my son went through periods where he didn't want to talk to me. We would sit in silence when we drove to lessons. It was very hard for me because I had always had a close chatty relationship with him. Yet, I knew I had to back off and respect his communication privacy. I kept trying to open topics for conversation, but when they were rejected (notice I said the conversation was rejected, not me personally!), I let it go.

Conflict is not a rejection of your values or a personal insult. It's so tempting to walk away and feel rejected. A teen's behavior is often thoughtless, illogical, and hurtful. Their frontal lobes in the brain are still developing. The part of the brain that governs planning and awareness of consequences is still under construction. They may be hurtful without intent. And it is so transitory. Here, this hour, but not the next. Often, teens come around to see their parent's side eventually.

A 2003 survey commissioned by the Vanier Institute of the Family in Ottawa found that teens' biggest influence is, by far, their parents. Not peers, not media, not teachers, not friends, or relatives. That figure goes up even more when the relationship is mutually respectful or at least respectful on the parent's side. Teens are still learning!

It's important to share values in times of neutrality. Teens need to know where you stand, even if they don't agree. Parents and teens need to nurture calm, nonjudgmental communication through frequent chats in captive places: cars, ski lift and restaurants. One good chat about the tough issues: homework, sex, alcohol, and driving is not enough. Frequent chats are preferable.

A parent's willingness to stay involved is only half the battle. Teens have different personalities. Some won't talk. Some children get very acidic and sarcastic. Some are very nice and polite. Parents can only control how they react to all this. Be available to talk. Don't take it personally. Find outside interests that bolster your self-esteem when your teen causes you to feel stupid and insignificant.

Some parents try to be their teen's best friend by hanging out with the teen's friends and engaging in teen behavior, such as watching lurid movies or smoking pot with them. The teen feels ridiculous and embarrassed, and the friends don't respect the parent. Other parents dispense with rules by stocking up the liquor and allowing free for all, no limit, parties. Teens are not adults yet. They need parents as mentors, guiders, sounding boards, and problem-solving facilitators. They have plenty of teen friends. Stay in your role as parent.

> Don't be a friend – be a friendly parent.
> ~ Wendy Froberg, Psychologist

HANDLING "ATTITUDE" RESPECTFULLY

Attitude is sarcastic anger. Sometimes, it's a snarky I-statement or You-statement. If you look underneath, often, it's a sign that your child is ready for more independence and feels thwarted in some way. Does she have reasonable choices? Can you give her more ability to make decisions? Or does she feel that she never has control over anything?

Children want their needs and wants taken care of, just like adults do.

Sarcastic statements that children use to communicate what they need or feel	What they really need or are feeling (NOF) restated in an I-statement
Whatevah!	I'm feeling nagged. Please leave me alone.
Just go away.	I need some time to myself.
That sucks.	I think this is unfair.
Who cares.	I don't feel listened to.
I hate you!	I don't want to hear what you said.
That's not fair.	I feel left out.
Get out of my life.	I need more control over my life.
No fair.	I feel victimized.
You can't stop/make me.	I need to do this.
You're not my boss.	I need more control over my life.
You're so out of it.	I don't feel understood. I dislike this.
Fine!	I don't have any choices.
I have rights, you know!	I feel victimized.
So!	I can't find a logical explanation right now.
Arrrgh!	I'm frustrated. I'm angry.
Yeah, yeah, yeah.	I'm tired of being nagged.
What do you care?	I don't feel understood.
Do I look like I care?	I can't handle this right now.
I'm not a kid anymore.	I need more control over my life.
I'm not your slave around here.	I feel the workload is unfair.
I don't give a s**t.	I'm angry because my needs are not being met.

One time, my son, 14, was playing a video game. I marched in with his sibling and demanded he give his sibling a time when the sibling could have the console. He looked at me and said, "Get lost." I'm not too sure if it was meant for me or the sibling, but my jaw dropped. I said, "I don't like to be spoken to that way. Can you rephrase what you really feel in an I-statement? You need to say, 'I'm busy with my game right now, and I feel ripped off if I have to get off before the next level.'" The sibling and I gave him a few minutes to calm down and we came back and asked again. He was more respectful, and we problem-solved to find a suitable computer transfer time for both.

I could have used a natural consequence in the above situation. When people are rude to you, you don't deal with them. One day, I was so mad, I couldn't talk. I think it took a day of not talking when he realized that something was up, then remembered on his own about the rude comment. He apologized sincerely, and things were right again.

When looking at sass from your child, try to identify what they are really trying to communicate based on their need or feeling (NOF), stripped of the sarcasm, and then feed it back to them. "You are upset because I'm interrupting your game?" Share your feelings. "When I hear your tone, I feel disrespected. I would like to talk about this. Can we try this again? Here is how you can say what you are feeling. Instead of saying, 'Whatevah!' say 'I'm feeling nagged. Please leave me alone.' Then I will really hear you. Can you try that please?" Sometimes, you really have to give them the exact words to use, or they don't know the respectful way to assert their needs. It's a critical life skill to speak up respectfully so people can know what's bothering you but still not feel attacked.

Or you could gently say, "Do you want a moment to rephrase that?" You could use humor in your response. You could also just walk away and your body language will reveal you don't want to be spoken to that way. Responding with anger or sarcasm doesn't teach them anything other than it's okay for them to continue that way.

Sarcastic statements parents use	NOF that parents are trying to communicate
That's it! I've had it!	Means I'm running out of patience.
I'm not your slave.	Means I think the work load is unfair.
Because I said so.	Means I have more experience in this matter and I'm too tired/busy/stressed to explain.
Fine! Do what you want,	Means I feel pushed to the limits.
I don't care.	Means I give up.
It's my house, my rules.	Means I don't think this issue is negotiable.
You are so...	Means I'm worried about this.

Be sure to model assertive politeness instead of "attitude" yourself. It's a hard trap to not fall into especially when family sarcasm is portrayed all over the media as cool and desirable. It's a false representation. If you said, "whatever" to your boss when she asked you why your project was late, I would bet that she wouldn't laugh.

VALUES COLLISIONS

Music choices, clothes, hairstyles, tattoos, piercing, friends, hobbies, food preferences, make-up, sports, homework, education, church attendance, movie and book choices, jobs, curfew, smoking, and swearing. These are all areas that teens and parents battle over. They are areas that don't DIRECTLY affect the parent. They are annoying to parents, but are pretty normal choices for teenagers.

If the child was 20 and living on their own and doing the behaviors above, the parent would worry about them, but really have no control over them.

There is no tangible effect on the parent. The parent is usually battling it out of the perceived protection and best wishes for the child, who is still living in their house – which is honorable but has the side effect of damaging the relationship. Parents can try their hardest to control the above, but the teen will find a way around it. Often, what happens is the teenager sneaks the behavior, totally ignores the parent, or moves out. Ultimately, the teen will be in control. The best ways to work out value collisions is to use the gentler side-door approaches, such as modeling, rather than a full front-door head on collision approach that will shut down communication.

HOW TO CHANGE ANOTHER PERSON

Happiness isn't found in things you possess, but in what you have the courage to release.
~ Nathaniel Hawthorne, Author

Say your partner or significant other came home one day and said to you, "Honey, you should go to Toastmasters. You need to learn public speaking. It would be good for you. I really value public speaking, so I'm going to sign you up for Tuesday nights." Or what if they came home and said, "Honey, I want to learn how to public speak. I think it's a valuable skill to learn, and it might be fun. I'm going to check out a meeting on Tuesday. Want to come and check it out with me?"

Which approach would motivate you to go to Toastmasters? Most people would probably go with the second approach. It's not a command to change but an invitation.

We often want to change other people: our partners, our children, our bosses, our co-workers, our friends. We want to change their annoying habits and behaviors: leaving wet towels on the bed, not picking up their toys, leaving the toilet seat up. We want them to quit smoking, clean up their language, pick up their cups, lose weight, and stop drinking.

We want to change their values, attitudes, and beliefs. We want them to get A's in school, get their black belt in karate and value learning to play piano.

Can we change another person? Yes! We can. But not in the usual ways we resort to. We nag. We lecture. We harass. We preach. We induce guilt, and the other person, far from being motivated to change, digs in their heels, and remains the same. Or they rebel or retaliate. We destroy relationships in the process of trying to make them a better person. But there is a better way.

When we nag and harass, we are intending to control. A key concept in this better way is called influence. Both will change another person, but one can destroy the relationship. Let's examine influence versus control. The more power and control you use in a relationship, the less influence you wield.

How to influence a behavior change rather than force it:
- Be ready to change yourself. Often, when we accept a certain type of music that our teens listen to, we are telling them we are open to change, and often, they will be open to change to our preferences. Maybe.
- Model.
- Confront the behavioral effect on you with an I-statement that tells your feelings if there truly is one. Listen to them. Problem-solve the effect on you, not the behavior itself.
- Do a one-time consultation.
- Appreciate the behavior and values you like.
- Use a declarative I-statement when the issue comes up. Once is enough. More than that is a nag.
- Acceptance. Often, letting go and leaving change up to the person is what they need to change.

Do not:
- Threaten to use power and control to get your teen to change.
- Use punishments and bribes to control them.

DATING

When should dating begin? When they are ready cognitively and emotionally. Ask reflective questions to see where they are in those areas. Every child is different and there is no one right age for dating.

DRIVING

Teens' inexperience, bad habits, and desire for partying makes for a dangerous mix when they begin to drive. Provide lessons for your teenager. Driving is a time of shared fun when you are supervising them. Be positive when they are learning and you have to ride with them. Have a zero tolerance (permanent marker) rule for drinking and driving, which is one of the highest reasons for teen collisions and deaths. Model good driving habits yourself including taking the bus or taxi home when you have been drinking. Role-play what to say when they are faced with peer pressure.

SCHOOL PROBLEMS

A teenager is in the driver's seat of his education. He is totally responsible for making decisions about his education. The parent's job is done. The more the parent takes on the child's educational responsibilities, the more the child will let him and the problem becomes the parents, not the child's.

The more you push education as a parent, the more your teen will push back, and you will erupt into more power struggles. You are the adult – step out of it. I understand your worry. But that won't make her study. If her motivation is not intrinsic, she is not storing anything, even when she is forced to learn. Until she finds that internal motivation, don't wreck your relationship with her over power struggles with schoolwork. The worse your relationship with her becomes, the less likely she will take on your values, which is education.

If conventional school is not working for your child, consider the many options available today. Teenagers don't need the same level of supervision as younger children from six to 12 years, so parents can go back to full time work and teens can take their education online or correspondence at home. There is also private school, charter schools, and tutoring to consider. Choice in education is much more plentiful today.

TEEN PRANKS

When teens are with a peer group, they need some fun, and stimulation in their lives and lack adult judgment, impulse control, and logic that comes with a developed frontal cortex; that means they often do things that are harmless in the present context, but not morally right, and could be potentially hurtful to someone in the future context, which teens don't really think through.

Egging houses, turning lights out in public washrooms, putting dish soap in public water fountains, etc., are all ways teens have fun. When the parents find out about these pranks, through their teens admission or being told by others, a permissive parent would ignore it and not take any action. That's not good. The issue needs to be addressed. Turning a blind eye will not help your teen develop or learn appropriate behavior. But don't overreact either!

The best discipline methods for teen pranks is <u>one-time consultation.</u> They need to know what could have happened even if everything went okay this time. What are the possible consequences of their actions?

Who could be hurt?
How could they be hurt?
What the law would call it.
Possible consequences from the law and society.
Problem-solving: what can they do to fix the situation now? Does it need fixing? What do they think is in order?

TEEN PEER GROUPS

Teens need a secondary peer group. It's important that the primary peer group, usually the school crowd, are not the only influence in a teen's life. Try to insist (as much as they will let you) on a secondary peer group for your teen. Get them involved in at least one other group that is apart from school. Band, sports, church, art, volunteering, Girl Guides, and Scouts are excellent groups to develop new friends, identities, and social contacts.

HIGH-RISK BEHAVIOR

Many teens think they are invincible. They are curious and peer pressure encourages them to try high-risk behavior such as sexual activity, drug use, criminal acts, and self-harm behaviors such as suicide, eating disorders, cutting, car racing, shoplifting, vandalism, overeating, aggression, and bullying. The danger of high-risk behavior is that it can cause temporary or permanent harm to your teen's physical or emotional health.

> We need to look beyond the actual high-risk behavior and find the needs behind the parent-child battles over the issues. That's the key to successful education programs.

Our needs as parents:
- Our teens need to have our moral base from us, community, and society.
- Our religious beliefs need to be passed on to them.
- Our need is to keep them safe, physically, mentally, and spiritually.
- Our need is for them to respect themselves and others.
- Our need is for them to feel successful in their relationships, school, work, and community.
- Our need is for them to meet all their needs in Maslow's hierarchy.

Teen needs for trying high-risk behaviors:
- Curiosity builds about what drugs, crime, and sex are like.
- Passion and sexual feelings for someone special become strong.
- Wanting to be close to someone.
- Has an unhealthy sense of self-esteem and wants to feel good about themselves.
- Has a lack of coping skills to deal with their problems; needing to escape from dealing with problems in their lives.
- Feeling a sense of obligation or pressure from peers or partner and not understanding their right to say "no".
- Needing to feel grown up and have more control over their life.
- Needing to rebel against parents, adult authority, teachers, and society.
- Needing to fit in and win approval of the peer group they are in or being "people pleasers" to others.
- Not understanding the risks, benefits, consequences, and issues involved in the behavior.
- Needing to escape feeling the uncomfortable feelings they are experiencing and unable to express and talk about their feelings, beliefs, and needs.

Prevention:
- Look out for a combination of high-risk behaviors. There is a strong link between smoking, alcohol use, and early sex.
- Seek out education programs on the issues.
- Emphasize healthy love relationships by modeling it with your partner and talking about it.
- Keep communication lines open.
- Self-esteem is critical towards delaying sexual activity and drug use. A child that feels loved and respected will delay both.
- Help your child work toward goals and a hopeful future. A child who has a life with meaning and purpose will delay or ignore risk behavior.
- Help your child express his full range of feelings in socially appropriate ways.
- Help your child learn how to solve his problems.
- Encourage a healthy body and sports participation. Teens who value their bodies' health will look at drugs, eating disorder behaviors, and sexual activity critically.
- Use lots of healthy touch, and encourage your partner to still hug and touch appropriately, especially daughters in preteen and teen years.
- Practice most of the behaviors under Parent's Helpful Behaviors in the beginning of the chapter.

How to discuss high-risk behavior

Children who don't want to talk can be reached by:

- Give him a book or leave the books lying around the table, in the bathroom. Casually ask, "Did you get a chance to look through that book?" This often works better with younger children.
- When watching movies, ads, internet, or listening to radio ads or songs, start a conversation. Talk about other people, you, movie heroes, your friends, and their friends.
- Talk about it in general terms. Use declarative I-statements, "I think that people should be in love before sex." "I think marijuana can cause depression and shouldn't be legalized."
- Give a one-time consultation about the risks. Keep it brief and get consent first.
- Ask what has been covered at school.
- Ask someone trusted to talk to your teen.
- Keep encouraging a positive self-concept in your children if they are sexually active or experimenting.
- Your teen will appreciate your efforts, and even if they don't talk, they will know they can come to you if they need to.
- Use a sense of humor.
- Never, never, ever punish your child for opening up and offering information for you. The fastest way to shut them down is to pass judgment, nag, order, command, and try to control them.
- Acknowledge that you may be embarrassed, and it's okay to feel that way. Be honest and tell your teen that this is uncomfortable for you but you want to be open for discussion. This lets your teen know that you are human and trying.

What to talk about:

Anatomy, responsible behavior, body image, love and passion, hormones and sex drive, sexually transmitted infections, pregnancy myths, and contraception, health and risks, values and beliefs, what is sex and what is it for, how to say "no", advantages of abstinence, contraception, sexual abuse and date rape, peer pressure and how to handle, different kinds of drugs, how drugs can be addictive, how drugs affect the body, where drugs are sold, what is prostitution, homosexuality, and heterosexuality, how crime affects people and how the laws affect young people, what is suicide and how it affects people. Once you start, keep going!

SEXUAL BEHAVIOR

Children learn about sex, whether we teach them or not, from the media, TV, internet, music, and their friends. Our society shows sex, but doesn't want to talk about it. Studies show that teens want to talk about sex with their parents but feel their parents don't have the information, and don't want to talk, and just don't want to know.

Some children don't ask at all. They never will. The parent must set the climate by giving more information than they can take in. That gives the appearance that any subject is okay to bring up. Don't worry about giving them too much information. Starting at age two, children will only take in what they can understand. You will not be putting ideas into their heads; the ideas are already there. You're just giving them permission to explore those ideas.

I was explaining to one seven-year-old son just how the sperm and the egg meet, and while I was doing so, my other son (the one who never asks questions) piped up with "Oh, so that's how it works!" He had been thinking about the mechanics of sex but was way too shy to ask me. Even more than giving him the specific answer, the main message he got was that he could talk to me about anything he wanted. That's important for any child to know. When he was 15, he asked even more questions. Don't wait for them to ask. Keep talking.

Take opportunities to discuss information, your morals, and values. Use the time available in captive situations! Children who feel they can talk to their parents delay sexual activity until a later age and are more likely to use protection.

Warning signs that your child may be sexually active:
- Your teen has birth control paraphernalia.
- Your teen is interested in books about sexuality, pregnancy, menstruation, or magazines about how to please a partner sexually.
- Your teen has a regular partner who they express feelings of love and affection with.

How to deal with your teen's sexual activity:
- Set limits (perhaps no sex, drugs or criminal behavior in your family house) but remember you can't control their behavior and that being too strict may backfire.
- Show that they can start saying "no" anytime they wish. Once they are sexually active doesn't mean always sexually active. Role-play how to say "no".
- Don't judge them or become angry with them, as it shuts down communication.
- Discuss safer sex.
- Discuss oral sex and the risks involved especially for girls. Oral sex is often perceived by teens to not be "real sex" and therefore has no risks of STIs (sexually transmitted infections). Not true.
- Talk about why it is important for them, if they want to continue.
- Rehearse strategies with your teen to deal with unwanted peer pressures to have sex, smoke, shoplift, use alcohol or drugs, or any other risky behavior.

DRUGS

Teenagers have a variety of drugs available for their use. Drugs that are legal are alcohol, prescription drugs and over the counter drugs, such as cough, cold, sleep aids, and diet medicines. Inhalants are drugs that are fumes from glue, aerosols, and solvents. Illegal drugs are marijuana (pot), stimulants (crack, cocaine, speed), LSD, opiates, heroin, PCP, and specifically designer drugs, such as ecstasy and crystal methamphetamine, which is pretty popular these days. Possibly due to the affluence of North American teenagers, the use of illegal drugs is increasing, especially among younger teens. The average age of first marijuana use in the U.S. is age 14, and many teens abuse alcohol by age 12.

Drug use has several complications. It can affect teen's developing brain and their mental health. It increases serious drug use later as they get older and affects their school performance and relationships. It can also affect a teen's judgment, which puts them at risk for other high-risk behaviors, such as sexual activity, crime, car and pedestrian collisions, and depression and suicide.

Warning signs that your child may be on drugs

Physical symptoms: tiredness, repeated health complaints, constant red and glazed eyes, and a nagging cough.

Emotional symptoms: personality changes, sudden mood swings, irritability, irresponsible behavior, low self-esteem, poor decision making skills, depression, and a general lack of interest in life.

Family: constant arguing, secretiveness, and withdrawing from the family most of the time.

School: decreased interest, negative attitude, drop in grades, many absences, truancy, and discipline problems.

Social problems: new friends who are less interested in their usual home and school activities, getting into trouble with the law, and big changes in dress and music.

Together, several of these symptoms can indicate problems of drug use or other issues. It's best to have a doctor check out your teen if you are concerned.

How to deal with one time experimentation

One-time drug use includes prescription drugs, over the counter drugs, coffee, tea and caffeinated beverages, nicotine and smoking, as well as marijuana and some illegal drugs. Most teenagers are curious, and when egged on by their peers, they tend to try out the drugs to see what happens. If the reaction is an unpleasant one and they have a good sense of self-esteem and problem-solving abilities, the teenager will likely refuse to try again.

Discipline for one-time experimentation could include:

- Problem-solving while looking at the teen's needs list.
- One-time consultation.
- Declarative I-statements outlining your worries.
- Examine enabling behaviors from you. Do I help my teen or make it easy for him to continue this behavior?
- Referring teen to professional help.

Habitual high-risk behavior

Is it a habitual problem?
Does the teen feel they have a problem?
Have people annoyed your teen by criticizing their drinking or drug use?
Is the use affecting their health, work, school, or relationships?

Get help! You can't solve this on your own and owe it to you and your child to seek help from:

- Parent support groups and other parents going through similar experiences.
- Professionals: family doctor, psychologists, psychiatrists, and social workers.
- Family counselors and therapists.

Be sure to find help that addresses the teen's motivating needs, not just the problem behavior. Tough love groups don't reach far enough below the surface to find out the reasons for the behavior.

SUICIDE

In the U.S., U.K., and Canada, suicide is in the top three leading causes of death for 14 to 19-year-olds. Statistics Canada (1999) puts it in the number one place because many auto collisions could be suicides in a vehicle. Suicide is even more prevalent among gay teenagers than heterosexual teens.

Warning signs of possible suicide intentions:

- Changes in eating and sleeping habits.
- Previous attempt at suicide can increase risk again.
- Withdrawal from friends, family, and regular activities.
- Violent actions, rebellious behavior, or running away.
- Drug and alcohol use.
- Talks about death and what it might feel like.

- May engage in thrill seeking, high-risk behavior such as street racing.
- Unusual neglect of personal appearance.
- Marked personality change.
- Persistent boredom, difficulty concentrating, or a decline in the quality of schoolwork.
- Frequent complaints about physical symptoms, often related to emotions, such as stomach aches, headaches, and fatigue.
- Loss of interest in pleasurable activities
- Refuses appreciations and compliments from others. Complains of being a bad person.
- Gives verbal hints with statements such as: "I won't be a problem for this family much longer. Nothing matters. It's no use. Take my guitar, I probably won't need it anymore."
- Puts his or her affairs in order, for example, gives away favorite possessions, cleans his or her room, and throws away important belongings.
- Becomes suddenly cheerful after a period of depression.
- Has signs of psychosis (hallucinations or bizarre thoughts).

Talk to them. Ask how they are feeling about life? Ask them if they are suicidal. Say "Are you thinking of hurting or killing yourself." Don't worry about putting the thought about it in their heads. If they are suicidal, they are already thinking about it. They will be very glad that someone has opened up the discussion. Try to stay calm and really hear what you might not want to hear.

Your teen may have many reasons for exploring suicide. Yes, it may be a "cry for attention." Give it to them! They need attention! Their reasons may seem trite or superficial to us, such as a recent sweetheart break-up, yet, it's important to keep in mind that their perceptions are very real and hurting to them. How they feel about things matter more than what we think they should feel. A teenage break-up doesn't seem so big in light of adult problems, but it's a huge deal to a teenager.

Your teen is also coping with huge pressure to fit in with peers and to maintain being a great child at home in a time of their lives that they are most self-conscious. Perhaps keeping up socially and academically can be too overwhelming for them. Add to the mix, changing hormones during puberty and many mental illnesses emerge during adolescence and it's no wonder that suicide is so high for the teen years. Many teens feel invincible during this time and often, they don't grasp the finality of suicide. Even many adults don't. They need to know that the teen years are temporary, the awkwardness and the worst of those years will pass and that all problems can lesson their effect or be solved. Suicide is a permanent solution to temporary problems. Everything will pass.

If there is ever a time that you need open communication with your child, the teen years are it. Hopefully, you have been working on it since toddlerhood, when the trust is built. Even then, it can be a challenge when you have had a great open relationship and your teen shuts down on you.

If you suspect suicide, seek professional help for you and your child immediately.

CRIME

According to Statistics Canada, the rate of violent youth crime has remained stable until 2000, then has gradually increased for homicide, sexual assault, assault, and robbery, mostly in the age group of 12 to 20.

Two new kinds of crowd criminal behavior are called swarming and taxing. When a group of teens gather around a target teen to be hurt, it's called swarming. Taxing is the same as swarming but with the purpose of robbery and taking the target's possessions.

The anonymity of the group makes it easier to bully someone, and as a crowd watches, the aggression can escalate. Group crimes tend to be on the rise, although it's not normative teenage behavior. Gang crime and female perpetuated crime are also on the rise.

Warning signs your child might be engaging in criminal behavior:
- He has items that you haven't bought or helped him obtain.
- He has extra money but no job.
- He has secretive outings at different, unusual times during the day or night.
- He is on drugs or has a past history with drugs.
- His marks at school are dropping due to missed assignments.
- He doesn't bring friends home anymore.
- He has dramatic changes in clothing and an identity with a group or gang.
- Your friends and neighbors are dropping hints to you.
- A police officer knocks on your door.

Get immediate professional mental health couselling and also legal help.

WEAPONS POSSESSION

Many teens carry weapons for their personal security and safety. This is becoming more common in schools and social events now. Small knives are the most common. Teens need to understand that weapons have high risks. Crimes, even self defense with weapons involved, escalates the event for both victim and perpetrators. As a parent, you need a frank discussion with your teen about the risks of weapons and your feelings about their use. This is a good time for a one-time consultation and your declarative I-statements on your values. Natural consequences are also in order, if your teen displays a weapon in a place they are not supposed to and the police, teachers, or friend's parents are taking action. Let them learn what they need to learn about weapon use.

EATING DISORDERS

They are most common in girls but eating disorders are also increasing in boys.

Warning signs your child may have an eating disorder:
- Shows a drastic loss of weight (Anorexia).
- No loss of weight, but has sores on her hands (Bulimia).
- Picks and moves food around her plate without eating.
- Avoids meals and snacks or heads to the bathroom to purge (vomit or take laxatives) after food intake.
- Wears bulky clothes because she is cold all the time.
- Stops menstruating and grows more body hair.

Seek professional help.

The teen years are a wonderful time of growth and enjoyment for you both. They are developing into lifelong friends, and as a parent, it's wonderful to witness the transformation. Enjoy and accept who they are becoming.

 If parents only had one discipline tool to use for
all the ages of their children,
modeling would be the most effective.

12

Technology Without Distress:
Educate, not ban

 The biggest technological advances in the last 20 years has been in communications, and yet, our biggest hurdle in our relationships has been in interpersonal communication.

The generation gap

In the past 20 years, our lives have changed so much in the way we live, work, communicate, and have fun. The huge leap in technology has put parents way behind children in terms of their ability to use it and have it benefit their lives. Never has there been such a generation gap in so many areas of their lives as the canyon between parents who are computer illiterate and children who are technologically savvy. Here is the medium that we parents are familiar with and here is today's equivalent. Often, parents of an older generation find it hard to change and accept what the children are now embracing to enhance their lives.

Today's equivalent	Thirty years ago
Instant messaging	Book discussions
Newsgroups	Phone
Internet	Encyclopedias, books, microfiche, magazines
IPods	Walkmans, portable boom boxes
Social websites	Pen pals
Websites	Books, pamphlets
Forums	Message boards, party line, phones, book discussions, coffee klatches, study groups
Chat rooms	Parties

Today's equivalent	Thirty years ago
Email	Pen pals, ads, phone, letters
Computer and video games	Quilting bees, card nights, bridge nights, scrap-booking, board games, craft groups, solitaire, watching TV sports
Handheld games and portable DVD players	Books, music players, solitaire
Classrooms	Synchronous classrooms online
Text messaging	Writing notes, signing, phone
Palm Pilots	Calendars and address books

Of all the electronic devices designed to make adult and children's lives easier, computer and video games, as well as instant messaging and the internet, are the major concerns of parenting and discipline.

INSTANT MESSAGING, EMAIL, AND INTERNET USE

Instant messaging is like the good old fashioned telephone, however, the likelihood of your daughter talking to strangers across the world is much higher when there is absolutely no cost in doing so, as with instant messaging. When long distance telephone was the only way children could talk, parents would have a charge to the phone bill and a number to trace who was calling and who was receiving. Therefore, rules surrounding instant messaging use must be agreed to by parent and child.

The internet is of major concern to parents. Social websites allow a child to have thousands of "friends" that the parent will never meet. The major danger of the internet is when your child's identity is traceable and strangers show up uninvited, face-to-face in your child's life, either at school, the mall, sporting events, or other places. The other danger is if the stranger wants to meet your child face-to-face and has set up a visit.

Parents need to discuss internet family rules with their children. Basically, three rules would help to keep them safe:

1. Never give out personal information on the internet, even while writing to a "friend." This includes name of school, last names of friends, sports teams,

clubs, etc. When purchasing online games or items, check with parents first about divulging personal information.

2. Never meet with anyone from anywhere in the internet, without parent notification and approval.

3. Always feel free to come and ask questions if you are not sure of anything. This is the rule that good communication with your child will enable to be followed. Parents, you have to promise not to take away their computer privileges!

Parents need to have many discussions, (one is not enough) about the permanency of email and text messaging. Anything said that is written on computer can be copied and sent to anyone. This includes photographs and video. Even if your child sends an email to a friend and she is sworn to keep it confident, your child must know that it can be forwarded unintentionally to someone else. I discuss this with my children by showing them a tube of toothpaste to illustrate a point. Words and photographs written on computer are like toothpaste. Once it's out of the tube, it's impossible to get it back in! Always, always write on computer like the whole world is going to read it, and you will never regret a sent message. If it's that confidential, use the phone!

It's helpful to buy an updated book on technology etiquette to help your children learn the social rules and manners to go with our new communication tools. Parents know it's rude to talk on the phone in the middle of a movie theatre, but many children don't know. To prepare them for the adult world, they need to know it's not okay to answer a phone call in the middle of a job interview or text message a friend during a class lecture.

Children will never go wrong by acting according to the golden rule of getting permission first. If they want to photograph their friends with a cell phone, they should ask their friends first. Especially with the ease nowadays that photos can be uploaded to the internet. Asking permission before forwarding messages and email has saved many a friendship.

GAMES, GAMES, GAMES...WHAT'S THE DIFFERENCE?

Moms, imagine that a stranger gives you a package full of scrap-booking materials. You look into the box full of beautiful papers, trimmers, textured pages, and sparkly pens and think of all the wonderful photographs that you could turn into a masterpiece album. You are excited with the limitless possibilities ahead. Now, the stranger says you can only scrapbook for one hour at a time and only on Saturdays. It doesn't matter how much you have to do or how far you can create.

Dads, imagine that you have just received a new bag of golf clubs and a year membership in the most ritzy golf club in the city. You have access to so many greens and the best equipment ever. You can't wait until you can smell that green grass and soak up the warm sunshine and have your senses overwhelmed by the energy in the air. Now, you've just been told by the club manager that although the club provides 18 holes, you can only play for one hour on Sunday, and that's it.

You are probably feeling disappointed, angry, and frustrated at the limitation, especially in spite of this whole new world opened up to you. This is probably how a child feels the first time she experiences a computer or video game. It's new, exciting, colorful, intriguing, and enticing. She can't wait to dive in and explore.

Video games, handheld games, internet online games, and computer games are today's parent's new nemesis. Parents observe how much time, money, and energy is used on gaming by their children, and many parents worry "Is gaming harmful and how much is too much?"

To ration time or not to ration

Among the home-schooling community, this topic is hotly debated. Home-schooled children have more free time than anyone because their school portion takes up a very small portion of their day. Do they spend their free time (about 10 hours a day) on gaming or doing other activities? Many home-schoolers, like any parent, will strictly ration time, and many home-schoolers will not ration at all.

From a parent educator

The professional parent educator in me reads the minimal research on internet addiction, the risks of gaming, and the effect on children's mental, social, and physical health and listens to the massive recommendations, based on heavy bias and not much evidence. "Screen time" refers to all forms of entertainment that involves a screen: TV, DVDs, computer games, video games, portable DVD players, handheld games, cell phone text messaging, children's "educational" screen toys, and palm piloting. Anything that involves an electronic device and a screen is referred to as "screen time."

Unfortunately, the emergence of gaming as a leisure activity is so new that not enough credible studies have been done with a wide enough sample to determine if gaming (I'm talking mostly about computer games, video games, and handheld games) is beneficial or detrimental to a child's development. In surveys, many parents don't openly admit to exactly how much screen time their children are actually getting. Screen time does make a parent's life easier. It engages the child and keeps them busy so parents can work, nap, or catch up on chores. It's easy for the parents to let the children slide into more screen time than intended.

When I tell parents about the one hour a day screen time (includes movies, computer, and TV) preschool recommendation from the Canadian Paediatric Society, they sheepishly admit they have never ever followed it. Even a Disney™ movie comes in a 1.5 hour form. What parent is going to turn off the movie right when Cinderella goes to the ball?

Recommendations of screen time for school-aged and teenagers are trickier, as there are none. Each parenting expert devises their recommendations based on their own biases about the new technology. Many experts have never played games or understand the complexity of them. I was recently at a talk by a local parenting expert, who suggested parents of teenagers should pull the computer game power plug after an hour a day. I came home and told my teens. Their reaction was "What? An hour? It takes at least an hour to set up the hardware of laptops, decide what game to play, set up and load the game, get connected with the buddies, discuss what domain to start, get some items, set up snacks, and start playing!" Sounds like a good old-fashioned game of Monopoly™ to me. Takes at least an hour to set up and longer to play!

From a mom

The mom in me has three teenagers, a preteen, and a preschooler who was moving a mouse before toilet training, and all who love gaming. What I see at home is purely anecdotal evidence, and no one has knocked on my door asking to use our family as research, so I'm a bit skeptical of the minimal research findings out there so far. Gaming at our house tends to dismiss many of the concerns of the "experts."

Let's look at some statistics

Gaming is the second leading leisure activity behind movies, so its popularity cannot be discounted. Video and computer game software sales hit a record 7.3 billion dollars in 2004. The industry took in 30 billion dollars worldwide in 2006. Clearly, the sales and use of such products are not waning. The average gamer age is 30, which translates into a much larger customer base than when games were marketed solely to teenagers. According to a new AP-AOL games poll, 40 percent of American adults play games on a computer or console. Of those, 45 percent play over the internet. Doug Lowenstein, president of the Entertainment Software Association of U.S., said there will soon be 75 million Americans who are 10 – 30 years old – an age bracket that has grown up on gaming. They will be looking at gaming applications beyond just mere leisure pursuits. They will probably be more comfortable bringing gaming into the educational realm of schools and learning centers. Gaming is not going to go away!

THE CONCERNS OF GAMING

Experts and parents are wary of video and computer games for several reasons and want to ban gaming or ration time spent playing because of the following concerns:

Too much sedentary activity

A valid concern, but let's explore this. A parent would never tell a child who is reading, to put the book down and go outside and play. Yet, reading books is also a sedentary activity. The Canadian Paediatric Society would probably never recommend preschoolers limit reading to one hour a day. There is a definite societal bias against screen reading (website reading) that is not directed to book reading. That being said, time spent playing games that would replace time spent doing sports is a valid concern.

But rather than discriminate against one form of sedentary activity, parents need to look at the overall picture of total sitting time for their children and replace that with activity time. Adults who spend 10 hours at a time scrap-booking, knitting, or watching movie fests tell their children to get outside and play. If we are truly going to address the lack of physical stimulation of children, we must look at the whole picture: our penchant for driving children everywhere instead of letting them walk or bike ride, and seldom going to the playground. Stranger danger is no worse today then when we were children. Vending machines in schools, less physical education, the frequency we eat out, parental modeling, and genes all play a part in our children's increasing waistline tendencies. Sure, talking forever on instant messaging is not physical, but neither were we when we were teens and burning up the phone lines for hours at a time. Many young people are foregoing TV for the internet. This is more like trading one activity that we used as children for another activity that is used now. The sedentariness hasn't changed, just the medium.

Gaming is anti-social

Video games are a solitary activity and take time away from socializing. The new reality of socialization and technology is that children and adults socialize, not face-to-face, but through online email, telephone transmission, text messaging, and in the field of gaming, through web-linked games in a LAN (local area network) party. You can find your friends, you can talk, you can see who's the best, and you can have contests. With the advancement of technology, games are making people become more social. The popularity of online and multiplayer games is soaring. Video game palaces are sprouting up all over. I have children who love the local video game palace, in spite of having the same games at home, because of the social nature of connecting, interacting, and playing with other gamers on much more powerful machines than available at home.

Many households have more than one computer now, and the popularity of wireless networks provide players and gamers with access to play the same game with more then one person in the house.

In our house, we have five networked computers, mainly because my 15 and 14-year-old sons saved up for their own gaming computers. They have LAN (local area network) parties, where the teens all come over, gather in the tech room (was the dining room), and play the same game on all five computers with a table of snacks in the middle. LAN parties are like board games on computer screens. What I have to chuckle about is that they both moved downstairs with their computers to join the family tech room, because they felt so isolated in their rooms!

Even in homes with one computer, one player, and several children over for a play date, I see socialization happening. The children are all huddled around the one player, some playing, some watching, some commenting, cheering and shouting directions. It reminds me of an old-fashioned baseball game on TV. Some are players, some are commentators, and some are spectators. Yet, all are involved in the game and are mutually sharing the experience. No different from going to the movies with a gang of friends either.

Gaming can be addictive for some children
The nature of video and computer games is that they take vast quantity of time to

play – time that could be better spent studying or other recreational activities. Just like a soap opera television show, many online games are designed to never end. The average non-online computer game takes about 40 hours to finish. That can be pretty hard to concentrate and play in 20 minute rations of time. What parents see as addictive desire to continue playing, is in reality, a concentrated effort to get somewhere in the game. Games are very complex, and many things need to be done in correct order to reach the next level. Not all levels are attained or success guaranteed. It takes a huge amount of time in order to succeed.

Many parents don't understand gaming. Moms tend to be more concerned than Dads because statistically, there are more male gamers then female. Dads who play games with their children actually understand the demanding nature of the games and may be more relaxed in allowing game time. Many people who are wary of games have never played them or haven't observed their children playing.

Video and computer games don't tax the imagination of children like books do

Yes, but they can be the catalysts for further expansion of the imagination. For example, when my children played the Mario™ and Kirby™ games, they would create sewn Kirby™ stuffies and wooden Yoshi™ characters and Pokemon™ figures out of play dough. They would write stories based on the characters but create their own storylines. That requires imagination. Gaming is wonderful, but have art supplies on hand and encourage artistic and literary expression of the games, which will help a child have a more balanced life and expand their imagination.

Children become wild after too much playing

Children become more aggressive, active, and ballistic after several hours of playing a game. But the same behavior occurs after too much sitting of any kind. This is hard to differentiate between any sedentary activity or the game playing itself. Again, not enough studies have been done to isolate this difference. Six hours of sitting in school will also cause children to let loose. That's why many parents linger after school and let their elementary children blow off steam at the playground. The same children need an energy outlet after any quiet period, whether being in church or after watching a two-hour video.

Some parents report that their child's personality can be more argumentative after playing than before. And are children snarky because of the game content and modeling, or because of the child's frustration of having an enjoyable activity curtailed?

We do know that video games raise the arousal of the brain. They reawaken the flight or fight response, which stimulates the brain chemicals. Games are not the best activity for winding down for sleep, probably due to the complex brain processes required for playing. Again, moderation is the key. It might be helpful to have an hour before bed, a game-free time to allow the brain to relax and de-stress before sleep.

Video games can be quite violent

According to the Social Learning Theory of child development, children can copy what they see on the screen and learn to think that the violent behavior is acceptable and condoned in real life.

This topic needs a bit of exploration. Many parents believe that the more children play and watch violence, the more desensitized they become to it. Many of us grew up with whole childhoods filled with violent video games, books, movies, and role playing games and it hasn't desensitized us or made us more prone to violence in any way. I know it's popular to think that violent movies and games are bad for children (it was comic books a few decades ago, novels before that, playing cowboys and Indians before that), but in my experience, it just isn't true.

Violent play is just another tool that children use to work through, express, and understand their emotions. Toys and play are and always have been children's means of expressing their developmental tasks and inner feelings. Video games are no different than playing with toy guns, arrows, and knives like we did when we were kids. If anything, video games may be a healthy outlet for role-playing out feelings of violence, anger and frustration. As my 14-year-old son says, "I can do things in the game that I would never do in real life. It's fantasy and I know the difference between that and reality." I see this when my other 15-year-old son will "blow away 25 people" in a particularly violent game, and yet, won't go fishing because "you have to kill the fish to take it home." Better a screen than a real person.

That being said, a parent has to remember that developmentally, children up to the ages of seven are still in the murky power-fantasy-reality jumble and have a hard time distinguishing between reality and fantasy. Teen's know the difference. Younger children may not. For this reason, violent games are not recommended for anyone younger than 14. Parents should familiarize themselves with the gaming industry rating system and use those guidelines to make good game choices for their children.

It's interesting to note that the most violent age of children is toddlerhood. They push, hit, and shove the most in that age group and 95 percent of children grow out of it by the teen years. Yet, not too many toddlers are playing violent video games! They are not the gaming demographic. Toddlers grow out of physical aggression because they become more verbal and can articulate their feelings in other ways. Gaming might just help teens and adults express their feelings on a screen.

Even the gaming statistics don't match the crime demographics. Video games are the fastest growing technology and a 30 billion dollar a year industry. That's a whole lot of consumers playing those games. Our society's violence has not increased in the same way. In fact, studies show that North American society's acceptance of real life violence is waning. Adult males in the 18 to 30 age range is the biggest demographic of gaming and the numbers are growing. Yet, crime rates in that age group has dropped dramatically. Crimes committed by young teenagers in the 13 to 16 age is increasing. The correlation doesn't fit.

Even the most graphically violent of games (Counterstrike™, Grand Theft Auto™, Half Life™) are nowhere near as violent as what children see in many societies and cultures. Our children don't go down to watch the weekly beheadings and appendage removal like certain countries in the Middle East. Our children don't have to witness public hangings, ritual sacrifices, war ambushes, and executions like they did 100 years ago and still do today in many parts of the world. Many, many cultures are much more violent. I took out a book from the library last week called *Horrible Histories: The Wicked History of the World*™ and I couldn't believe what they used to do to children and what the children were exposed to.

The key here is balance. Too much of anything is not good. Violent games have to be tempered with non-violent, respectful relationships in real life. Morals are taught by parents, not video games. Good, solid relationships do a lot to counter the effects of violent games.

Studies definitely show a link between video games and aggressive behavior is not conclusive. But there are many definite studies showing links between punitive parenting styles and aggressive behavior! Thus, parents have more effect on children's behavior than video games. What children witness in the home has a far greater effect on a child, than what's on a screen. It's the total package that may have greater effect. A child raised in a loving respectful home with plenty of communication that plays violent video and computer games is not likely going to be a mass murderer. Parenting style and connection speaks louder then toy choices.

Here's my little bit of anecdotal evidence. My 14-year-old son who LOVES first person shooter games is the most gentle, caring person in real life. He is the first in the family to hug the two-year-old when he's upset at home or gets knocked over at the playground.

When I first became a parent, we banned all guns from the house. Now we have four boys and various K'NEX™, Lego™, stick, wood, clay, water, cap, and plastic guns and rifles of all shapes and sizes. It's strange how your children make you humble in parenting.

THE BENEFITS OF GAMING

Academic benefits

Video and computer games are educational. NO doubt about it. They engage children for huge amounts of time, and very few books, classes, or teachers have the same effect. The anecdotal evidence shows that many children learn to read, write, spell, and do math, and learn social studies and science through videos, computer games, and video games. And it reaches the children in a way that spelling or grammar workbooks could never do. When I sit and watch the problem-solving skills being attempted by my three-year-old, he's onto something good! One son even learned integers from his favorite online game. My daughter and two sons all learned how to read from computer gaming.

Specifically, games develop critical thinking, analytical thinking, and problem-solving skills. Think about the scientific method. Most games give clues but not directions. So a player has to use hypothesis in order to find a strategy that might work. The game developers withhold critical information, so the players have to use trial and error to find it out. No parent would dare ration a child doing geometric puzzles on a piece of paper, yet when the same child does them onscreen, somehow parents are biased against it. Even better, gaming teaches problem-solving under duress because many of the tasks they have to figure out have time limits!

Players learn to manage tons of information and options. Gaming helps their multitasking skills. Just to memorize the number of items one can get in a game is amazing.

<u>The games build reading skills.</u> Children are reading game manuals, which are often written at a high school level and tell players how to play and offer insights to get over rough spots. Children who can't read certainly try to learn!

<u>Players have to juggle competing interests</u>. Some games make a player battle in order to keep alive, which is great training ground for the workplace! When juggling competing interests, players need to learn time management and setting priorities.

<u>Games develop pattern recognition.</u> Players have to figure out a pattern in order to climb a level and replicate a move.

<u>Games enhance creativity.</u> Once children reach school-age, parents get rid of traditional creative outlets, such as arts and craft supplies, painting, dress-up clothes, and drama props because "the schools can deal with the mess." However, the schools tend to become more academic in the later grades, grades four and up, so very few children have creative outlets at home or school. Hence, the appeal of being creative on the computer, with games like the Sims™, Sim Theme Park™, and Animal Crossing™, where children can create their own worlds. The child's need for creativity is still there, but the medium has changed.

If you treat screen time just like any other educational tool, it won't be elevated to "treat" status in the eyes of the children, and they will find other things to do. Forbidden fruit has the best appeal! Just leave lots of other play options lying around, too. Everything kids are curious about is educational and adds some way to their development.

Life skill benefits

<u>Gaming helps players zone out and relax.</u> My friend is 45 years old and works as a realtor. To de-stress, she comes home and plays computer games with her daughter.

<u>Gaming teaches delayed gratification</u>, another skill useful for real life. Studies show that children who demonstrate delayed gratification at an early age tend to do better in life.

<u>The games demand total focused concentration</u>. This is a useful skill for many children. Often, children are diagnosed with improper attention in school, yet, can focus for hours on gaming.

<u>The games build self-esteem and confidence.</u> They give children who are not athletic, artistic or academic a chance to succeed at something that their friends admire. Being accepted for a particular skill can build confidence in other areas of their lives.

<u>Games give children practice in handling strong emotions</u>, such as anger, frustration, and setbacks (especially when they lose an acquired level because they forgot to save). It even teaches natural consequences and how to fix the situation. Of course, children will need an adult around to help them deal with those strong emotions, or else a controller will go flying against the wall!

And, they're fun!

Socialization benefits

Contrary to being considered a solitary endeavor, games teach children social skills.

<u>Many games lend themselves well to team building</u>, where players have to work together to develop a plan, achieve results, and cover each other's backs.

<u>Provides opportunity for negotiation, cooperation and problem-solving</u>. The lack of expensive equipment, such as computers, controllers, and consoles means that much time is spent in negotiating screen time between children. In our house and many houses, one system and many children means complex negotiation skills and learning time management. There were times there were so many squabbles over game-time, I was tempted to throw all the gaming equipment out the window. And shut off the power! But I realized how they learned valuable lessons of compromise, fair play, and negotiation. They were motivated to learn how to tell time. They wanted to know exactly how long a half an hour was and how many more minutes until Johnny gets off and they get their turn. As well, when one child plays and one watches, they learn how to encourage each other to take a risk, try another solution, and to keep going. It's wonderful to watch "their team approach," even if one child is only playing the controls.

<u>Games give children a secret world, which bonds them together away from adults.</u> They spend non-gaming time engrossed in conversations, bragging about items they have, and which ones to go for next, which character they want to play, and what level they achieved. Much like we used to discuss hockey stats, car enhancements, and movie stars. Teens especially like to separate from adults in dress, hair, music, and activities. Gaming is one more avenue to separate them.

<u>Games connect children and adults.</u> In a U.S. survey released in January, 2006, 35 percent of 501 parents living with children ages two to 17 said they played computer or video games together, according to the Entertainment Software Association. Of those, 80 percent also played with their children. On average, these moms and dads spent 9.1 hours a month gaming with their children. I personally found that taking an interest in my children's gaming, sitting and watching them, and listening to their descriptive adventures in the game, has brought us closer in communicating and sharing fun times.

Implications for discipline

Taking away technology is one of the most popular punishments parents use in controlling their children's behavior. Children love their technology and parents know it. When banning is used as a punishment, then we can't very easily impose limits on screen time use, because then it's seen as a punishment by children. If you want to build a good relationship, don't take away technology as a punishment.

> Children do not easily share feelings and thoughts
> with parents they fear.
> ~ Thomas Gordon, Author

Many parents fall into two camps: pro-gamers and anti-gamers. I must admit, if you haven't guessed by now, I fall into the first camp. Raising four boys and a girl has definitely brought the games into our house. I regretted it for the first two years when I thought these children would never self-regulate themselves. Many times, I thought I should draw some limits and put my foot down. Then I saw another positive aspect of the game and relented. I've never rationed time, and six years later, the gaming systems and computers can sit unattended for months at a time by the children's own desires. They have too many other interests now. I've always believed in the theory that forbidden fruit is more succulent and the children have proved me right. They have gotten over the gaming genre and now are into other things. Even my 12-year-old game addict quit playing for a summer on his own accord and has spent his time reading chemistry and physics text books for fun.

Moderation and a balanced life

Moderation seems to be the key. Initially, when a child receives a system and a few games, they will naturally be drawn into the novelty and want to play all the time. Maybe even 16 hours a day, if you let them. But after a year or two (if you have the stamina), most children will get used to the genre and the typical game formula that doesn't change much from title to title, and they will ease off the games and more into other activities.

After two years of unrestricted gaming, here is what my children spent the summer holidays doing: one son (15) spent two hours a day reading. He read 45 novels in that year, in between breaks of computer gaming. My other teen son (14) the computer addict, was reading books daily about social issues and working on problems out of a high school physics and chemistry textbook. He has also checked out every electronics book out of the library and read them at the beach with us. My daughter (12) was reading a 200-book series and was writing her first novel and attempted a grade seven math workbook. She also came to me one day and requested starting piano lessons again. She has been knitting, painting rocks, doing chemistry experiments, and baking. One time, she was hired by us to baby-sit her little brothers so we could have a romantic dinner out. We came home to a clean house, because she vacuumed, scrubbed the floors, and cleared the counters of dishes while we were away, without even being asked. The children could have all been playing computer games, but they chose not to. Instead, they pestered me to go to the library to get more books.

As long as a child is doing other activities, such as reading books, internet socializing, face-to-face socializing with friends and family, crafts, hobbies, sports, exercise, and academic work, then they are probably living a balanced life, and gaming is definitely a part of that lifestyle.

When I complain that my children are not being productive enough, my son, 14, questions "productivity." He wonders how anyone can judge what another person does with leisure time is productive. He asks, "Is gardening or golfing more productive than playing a computer game? Who judges that?" He does have a point!

 Talk to your children. Instead of banning screen time, educate them.

Tell them your values and concerns when you are in a good space with them. Listen to why they like something. Avoid lecturing and stay cool! Be aware of what your child is playing and be available for them to ask questions. Live your values. Keeping those lines of communication open is more important than banning or rationing time. After all, would you speak to someone who presented you with a beautiful scrap-booking kit and pulled it away from under your nose? I wouldn't.

NON-PUNITIVE DISCIPLINE TOOLS FOR LIMITING SCREEN TIME

Despite the benefits of gaming, parents still are very uncomfortable with the amounts of time spent on the activity. That's okay. We all have our own comfort levels, and they fluctuate week to week. I realize that not many parents can tolerate their children's unrestricted game playing. A parent might feel perfectly okay with letting their child zone out all day on Sunday playing games, because they've had a week full of chores, sports, and school. Yet, the same parent will want all electronics off when there has been a week of no school and nothing getting done around the house. As was outlined in the earlier chapters, it's hard to have strict rules when life is not consistent!

Babies

Spend time together

Babies don't need technology. Not even those "educational" videos of color and shape. They need your touch, voice, and face. They need to see the real world.

Toddlers and preschoolers

Fulfill needs

Stimulation

Toddlers need experiential learning: real touch, taste, hearing, and seeing. Toddlers and preschoolers don't need computers, hand-held games, educational electronics, or video games. They are building hands-on experiences to layer their knowledge of the world for abstract learning later in the pre-teen and teen years. They need to be active and engaged in hands-on, real tangible toys and items. They need to visit parks and see trees in the world rather than on a screen or on flash cards or in a book. Preschoolers need to paint on paper and build real blocks, not on-screen. They both need to develop fine motor and large motor skills actually doing activities.

Redirection

Toddlerhood is a time that children love repetition. Toddlers will want to watch the same video and read the same stories over and over again, up to 12 times a day. That much video viewing is not good for their cognitive and social development! Engage them in another activity even if it's tempting to keep the video on because you get more done around the house!

School-aged children

School-aged children do best with hands-on learning, but it's harder to compete with the appeal of technology when peers are using it.

Stimulation

Have lots of creative supplies around the house, even if they attend school. Books, board games, craft supplies, workshop tools, garden tools, building toys, sewing machines, etc. These are great items to compete with screen time.

Reduce the reasons for rebellion

Never divide games into A) educational games and B) eye candy. Children don't know the difference unless you elevate the status of one and not the other. Then they will always play the ones you don't think are valued. All games teach children. All have some redeeming merits. If you treat games as a game, then they will see no difference and value the "educational" ones, too.

Re-evaluate limits

Acknowledge that the minute a new game is played or a console or computer is received, that children are going to spend every waking minute on it. It's new, a novelty, and totally consuming. They will behave like that for the first year of owning a system. It will, guaranteed, wear off. Games are not unlike movies, where there are only about 20 really different plot lines. All movies, books, and games are just minor variations on the same plot. The novelty will wear thin and other events will become more appealing, but not if time is rationed too strictly. Addictions are often the result of forbidden items withheld too long. Studies show that when children are allowed moderate amounts of candies and sweets, their incidence of eating disorders and weight gain goes down rather than up. It's the same with gaming. Moderation is the key.

Plan ahead

Plan outings and activities to compete with screen time. Spend time together. Play board games with your children. Communicate with text messaging and email. Create a family website together.

The key to this is, when the gaming has to stop, to get ready for an activity, dinner, chores, or family outing, be reasonable and don't insist on immediate cessation. Often, the games are designed so that players can't just stop; they have to get to another level or lose all their progress or go to a safe place, etc., which may take a few more minutes.

Say, "At the next saving place, could you quit and come to dinner please?" With that kind of consideration for their needs, you will find they will be more considerate for your needs.

Never just go and turn off the screen or tower button. It's very disrespectful and you wouldn't do it to an adult.

Model

Show, discuss, and live a balanced lifestyle over a week.
Everyone in the family should have some time in seven areas for health:

- Social time with others outside the family. This could include gaming time.
- Family time with siblings and parents.
- Spiritual time in organized church, meditation, solitude, unstructured play, study, reflection, or volunteering.
- Physical time, such as sports, exercise, heavy activity or active play.
- Mental exercise time learning reading, puzzles, and doing homework.
- Financial time earning money.
- Hobby time, projects and leisure pursuits.

Look at time over the week. A one hour a day rule doesn't work if on Monday, a child has heavy homework commitments and no time for gaming, but has lots of free time on Sunday and can play for five hours straight. Rather then make a one-size-fits-all rule, be flexible. Use a ticket system to budget game time over a week long period.

Change environment

If you know that you may have a gaming addict in the house, delay getting a system as long as possible. Avoid satellite and cable TV that is going to present a problem. Limit the computer to one per house (which naturally limits screen time per person) or get several computers and a LAN (local area network) connection to encourage group play. Avoid placing screens in bedrooms to encourage social activity in the main family areas. Also, it's easier for children to ask parents questions if they are in close proximity.

Schedule daily downtime

Encourage children to wrap up gaming at least an hour before bed, so they can wind down before sleep.

Family conferences

Discussion creates rules that work for everyone.

Problem-solving

As a parent, you have the most power in cooperation and negotiation before the machines are turned on! Decide how each child can schedule screen time based on that child's commitments for the week and availability of screens between siblings. This teaches children self-discipline by educating them on planning their activities and commitments (to job, school, social events, volunteerism) and planning their gaming time around them. A blanket rule of time doesn't work for everybody all the time.

Contracts

If you have a gaming addict in your house, this tool helps. Sit down, talk, and agree on some time limits that you both could live with and write up a contract. Helps the child with limits that he set, when it's in the moment and he doesn't want to stop.

Teenagers

One-time consultation

When you feel the child has not enough balance in their lives, have a talk. See what their values are and educate on the health aspects of not enough balance. Continue to share your values in the harmonious times.

Separate big issues from small

Is too much gaming time really a big issue in the face of drugs, suicide, and other biggies?

Connect, then direct
"I can see that you have made another level! Great job! I need you to go to the store with me and help with groceries."

Contracts and Problem-Solving
These are also effective in the school-aged and teen years.

Welcome their friends
Having a gaming-friendly house encourages them to bring friends over. You get to know who they are and what they are like. It builds a connection with your child and you.

Spend time together
Play games with your child. Sometimes, if you can't beat them, you join them. Gaming together can help you communicate over common ground.

Text message, email them, and communicate on their terms. Watch interesting websites and things they show you. Laugh with them. Take an interest in what they find funny.

Respect privacy
Don't log on in their name and see what they write and to who. Trust them.

Decide on problem ownership
Educate them on a healthy lifestyle and hope they choose best decisions for themselves. You can't control them forever.

Model
Model and include them in your leisure choices.

Decide what you will do
When their computer breaks down and they have no money, don't offer to fix or finance new equipment. Let them figure out a way to do it.

Keep communication lines open
We often push teens to their peer group by spending less time with them as they grow older and then pull their peer connection out from them (no text messaging and grounding them) when we want to punish. It's hard to build communication with children, when we take away theirs.

 The surest way to cut off your parent-child communication lines is to cut off their peer communication line.

Change is new and frightening for parents. The huge impact of technology will affect all of us, and no one is sure how to handle it. However, you can't go wrong keeping the communication open between you and your child. Do you have to know everything about what your child is into on the internet? No! If you have trust and communication and as long as your child knows that anytime he needs help, he will have it from you, and he can communicate to you without the fear of punishment or his technology being taken away, then he will be safe.

Lose the guilt. It's okay to admit that your children play games. With a billion dollar industry, games are here to stay. They will grow beyond the living room and will probably be a major influence in the classroom in the next 20 years when our children become teachers, curriculum developers and educational administrators! Until we have conclusive, long-term, large sample studies of the effects on children, no one can tell you if and how much is good for your children. Just strive for a balanced life.

A FINAL WORD

 You must be the change you want to see in the world.
~ Gandhi, Leader

Today is a new day. Whatever you have done before in your parenting journey is now behind you. You are now armed with new information and tools. You can make changes in your relationship, beginning now! Every parent begins along a point on a continuum. We all start from different places. Don't compare yourself with other parents. Just focus on what small change you can make today. Research shows that when parents change their parenting style to one that is more democratic and nurturing, their children exhibit less aggression and more favorable outcomes.

Discipline does not have to be distressful to you or your children. Teach, talk, comfort, and love. You both will benefit.

Excellent parents have children who get into trouble, tantrum and rebel. Excellent parents are willing to learn, change and grow. Regardless of what parenting style you follow and how many books you have read, the parent-child relationship is still much like any other love relationship. There will be bad days and good days. Hopefully, after reading this book, there will be more good days! There are days when one or more people are extra cranky and days when they will be helpful, cheery, and fun. There will be times when the children have more conflict than usual and times when they get along famously; times when problems are easily solvable and times when problems don't get solved. They may snowball or they may fade over time. You may have more expressive children, who are in touch with their feelings, and sometimes that can be hard for you to listen to, but it will be healthier for them and your relationship in the long run.

All parents second-guess themselves. That includes psychologists, social workers, psychiatrists, doctors, nurses, teachers, and parent educators that are parents. Even authors of popular parenting books probably had times when it "didn't work." We all make mistakes. There are times when every parent wonders "what if" and "should I" and there are times we just don't know what to do. If they didn't have times like those, there wouldn't be thousands of new parenting books and classes every year. Just like the diet industry, parenting is a lot of work and fumbling for answers. Get support. Talk to family, friends, and professionals. Be open to new information and make the best choice for the time. It's all anyone could do. You will survive and your children will thrive!

Just remember Newton's law: for every action, there is an equal and opposite reaction. There are two people in your relationship, you and your child, and at the end of the day, your relationship is all you have. Just remember: two.

Discipline Tool Summary for Common Behaviors

Feelings guide: These are common feelings in children that are under the behavior.

Confused: Doesn't know how or understand why.

Indifferent: Not important to them. Not sure how or if their actions affect others. It's not malicious but just clueless!

Curious: Needs to explore and watch before learning.

Uncomfortable: Physically impedes them in some way.

Insecure/ inadequate: Not sure if they belong. Doesn't feel valued for contributions or as a person.

Invaded/confined: Feels a personal boundary has been ignored.

Distracted: Too busy with the excitement of life or what's engaging them at the moment.

Wants to fit in: Wants to belong to family or peer group.

Desperate: Has overwhelming need to have something or somebody and sees no other way to get it. Their desire exceeds their self-control ability.

Unfair/victimized: They perceive being wronged in some way.

Bored: Can't see any value to them in doing request.

Needs power/ competency: Needs to feel they are in control of their own lives and have autonomy in action and decision-making.

Scared/fear: Frightened of body harm or emotional harm.

Needs exercise: Body needs to expand energy.

Poor self-control: Can't stop themselves.

Content: Sees no need to change. Their needs are being met.

Problem	Child Feeling	Tool	Details
Crying	Upset	Fulfill needs. Holding, hugs, and cuddles.	Pick up, feed, check, hold, and rock baby.
Won't go to sleep	Awake	Fulfill needs. Holding, hugs, and cuddles.	Feed, change, hold baby. Trade sleep with partner. Sleep when baby sleeps. Use white noise: ticking clock, tape recording, aquarium. *More in Chapter 7.*
Fussing	Upset	Fulfill needs.	Pick up, hug, and cuddle.
Touches everything	Curious	Change environment. Substitution. Prevention. Redirection. Spend time together.	Move things out of reach. Leave unbreakable items out. When visiting, move items. Move child to more interesting focus. Stay with child and show how to touch gently.
Doesn't appear to listen	Confused Distracted	Learn child development. Change environment. Prevention.	Accept that it's normal. Make surroundings safe. Stay with child to prevent accidents.
Hates diaper change	Uncomfortable	Distraction. Active listening.	Have a basket of toys they can play with in their hands. Hang a mobile. Say "You don't like diaper changes, do you?"
Inconsolable crying	Upset Uncomfortable	Parent time-out. Fulfill needs. Holding, hugs, and cuddles. Active listening.	Put baby down if you are feeling frustrated or give to another caregiver. Look for a cause. Hold and rock. Say "You are really upset, aren't you!" *More in Chapter 7.*
Won't accept bottle	Unfamiliar Scared	Parent problem-solving.	Try wearing partner's shirt or partner give bottle. Try upright feeding position. Try newborn nipples, as they flow slower. Try sippy cup. Try giving juice (after six months).

Problem	Child Feeling	Tool	Details
Won't accept soother	Uncomfortable	Fulfill needs. Parent problem-solving.	Accept and don't force. Put in nursing position and give a soother in breastfeeding position. Let partner give it.
Hates car seat	Uncomfortable Confined	Holding, hugs, and cuddles. Change environment. Distraction. Parent problem-solving. Active listening. Prevention.	Hold their hand or stroke their forehead. Hang plastic chain links from roof hooks to hang items on them to entertain baby. Put big black and white pictures printed from the computer taped on a towel for the back seat. Hang a mirror. Keep a box of toys on seat beside you to hand to baby. Turn on fan or open window for white noise to lull baby to sleep. Keep a special music tape or pacifier only for car trips. Say "I know that you feel upset." Consider walking or transit where you can hold baby.
Screeches	Curious	Learn child development.	Ignore. Only a brief stage of discovering vocal variety.
Hates getting dressed	Uncomfortable	Substitution. Distraction. Active listening. Prevention.	Distract with toys or favorite video. Talk or sing so he focuses on your face. Give a toothbrush or have a stack of toys to chew or hold. Change clothes less often. Use clothes that don't go over the head.
Pulls off hats and mitts	Uncomfortable	Change environment. Substitution.	Use socks as mitts. Use a wide string Velcro hat or balaclava.
Won't keep clothes on	Uncomfortable	Change environment. Substitution.	Use overalls or one piece sleepers.
Hates hair cut/wash	Scared Bored Invaded	Distraction. Active listening.	Do it while sleeping. Let grow long. Let baby watch a video in the high chair. Say, "You are scared about the haircut?"
Hates nail clipping	Scared Invaded	Distraction. Active listening.	Same as haircut. Use nail file instead.
Bites while breastfeeding	Curious In pain from teething	I-statement. Parental problem-solving.	Say, "Ouch! No! I hurt!" Remove from breast when bites. Break suction first!

Problem	Child Feeling	Tool	Details
Won't go to bed/sleep or stay in bed	Insecure Separation anxious Scared Not tired	Routines. Give attention. Fulfill need. Time-in. Parent time-out. Active listening. Parent problem-solving. Change environment.	Have a regular bath/teeth/pajamas/book/talk routine. Have time for you before starting the bedtime routine – enjoy their bedtime more. Find sleep arrangement that works for everyone. Provide books for reading in bed. *More in Chapter 8.*
Won't nap	Same as above	Same as above.	Make a nap nest. Use a box or corner of the living room and set up blankets, pillows, stuffies, and books. Set up a nap routine. Call it quiet or downtime. Let them read or watch a movie. Go for a drive and you read, sleep in car when they are asleep and car is parked. Give them a back or foot massage.
Won't brush teeth	Scared Invaded	Routines. Plan ahead. Make request a game. Pretend that you need help.	Brush teeth in same time and place everyday. Give choice in toothbrush colors and characters. Let play in the sink. Use sand timer or battery lighted brushes. Ask "Who is going to get to see your teeth today?" Have everyone brush another's teeth. Get them to brush your teeth at the same time. Let them chew a toothbrush.
Won't tolerate diaper changes	Distracted	Make request a game. Distract. Change environment.	Change pee diapers standing up or on the run: have toddler face mirror, use your chest to hold diaper to bum, and put tabs on in front. Give book or toys. Sing to distract. Pull pants half down to stabilize legs. Let them help to pull tabs down. Give them a lump of play dough to manipulate. Move change mat in front of movie.

Problem	Child Feeling	Tool	Details
Won't wear hat	Invaded	Routines. Plan ahead. Pretend you need help.	Always wear a hat when outside. Buy six and let them choose, then compliment choice. Use Velcro straps. Let them pick out yours, too.
Won't wear sunscreen	Invaded	Routine. Pretend you need help. Plan ahead.	Always put on in winter and summer. Let them smother it on you and themselves. Take turns doing each other. Do it at night while sleeping. Use a sprayer.
Throws food from high chair	Curious Bored	Learn child development. Supervision. Change environment. Remove child from environment.	Accept that it's normal exploration. Watch for when child is done eating and doing more playing. Have shower curtain under chair. Remove from chair. Have a naked lunch, so food is not smeared on clothes.
Throws water from the bathtub	Curious	Supervision. Change environment.	Always stay with toddler. Remove water. Take child out of bath. Tell her water goes down the register and floods downstairs.
"I do it!" Demands	Needs power/ competency	Help child complete the task. Change environment.	Offer help, but don't rush in. Set up for success – buy easy to accomplish-reach for-put away items. Encourage effort. Practice patience. Wait. Say, "Take your time," instead of "Hurry up." Do a bit and leave the last for them.
Runs into the road	Excitement from playing "chase me" Distracted	Pretend you need help. Supervision.	Ask for them to lead you by hand. Put in shopping cart so they can ride with baby car seat in there too. Always keep within arms reach. Ask them to hold your coat if you have more than two children.
Runs away in shopping mall	Curious Distracted Bored	Pretend you need help. Supervision. Routines. Plan ahead.	Give them a job to do or toy to hold. Get a leash so they can walk and tie it to the stroller. Keep at home or avoid shopping malls until preschooler age. Shop at night alone. Carry in a backpack. Online shopping.

Problem	Child Feeling	Tool	Details
Won't sit in high chair in restaurant	Curious Confined	Plan ahead, Stimulation. Childproof.	Go early so service is fast. Pre-feed baby so not too cranky. Let them play with ice cubes or straws. Bring snacks and small toys from home. Bring a roll of masking tape. Choose seats so they can see out the window or kitchen. Take outside and eat in shifts with partner if tantrum develops. Childproof the table. Tie toys with string on to high chair table. Leave a huge tip.
Won't stay in car seat	Confined Anxious	I-statement. Routines. Active listening. Plan ahead.	"I love you and want you safe." Always use seat every time. Move him into seat and acknowledge feelings. Let him choose a toy to bring.
Toilet accidents	Embarrassed Confused	Natural consequences. Plan ahead. Give encouragement. Change environment. Help child complete task.	Treat matter-of-factly, "Oops, let's clean up. Can you help?" Consider whether really ready. "We can try again." Make easier to pull up pants, easy to reach step stool, pump soap, towel to reach. Go camping naked so they can connect body sensations with the output. Stickers on a calendar for dry days. Show other children doing it. Make a big deal of it. Have a potty fort by making a huge fort, house, or castle out of an appliance box and set around the toilet. Bring a change of clothes everywhere. *More in Chapter 8.*
Gets frustrated when parent doesn't understand	Frustrated	Active listening. Give Information. Holding, hugs, and cuddles.	Say, "I don't understand but I really want to." Learn and teach sign language. Hug. Really try to understand.
Climbs	Curious	Change environment. Supervision.	Childproof: fasten anything big to the wall. Remove or block enticements. Remove chairs from the kitchen when not in use for eating. Put a stick into drawer handles so they can't be opened and used to climb.

Problem	Child Feeling	Tool	Details
Runs around while eating	Poor self-control Excited	Supervision. Give information. Routines. Change environment.	Say, "You must sit while eating or you could choke." Serve food only at table. Remove food if he leaves. Have a floor picnic.
Jumps on bed	Needs exercise	Give information. Change environment.	Show where it's okay to jump. Provide sofa cushions or a chair for jumping. Provide physical activity.
Throws toys	Angry Frustrated	Holding, hugs, and cuddles. Give information. Active listening. I-statement. Redirect.	Teach calm-down tools. Acknowledge feelings of anger. "You are angry! That's okay. However, I don't like toys thrown. Here, try this." "Let's go do something else."
Makes mess	Curious	Learn child development. Give information. Pretend you need help. Supervise. Plan ahead.	Toddlers are messy. They don't know how to clean up. Show how to and work with them to clean up. Contain mess by clean up as you go. Eat Popsicles and messy foods outside. Paint with plastic tablecloths. Supervise to monitor mess containment.
Draws on walls	Curious	Plan ahead. I-statement. Substitute. Natural consequences.	Hide markers if can't supervise. "I don't like drawings on walls." "We draw on paper only." Have them help you clean up.
Doesn't follow directions	Curious Distracted Confused	Use positive commands. Learn child development.	It's normal not to listen. Accept. Use one or two word positive commands. "Get your coat." "Drink juice." If they don't comply, do it for them.
Bugs parents while on the phone	Ignored Confused	Give attention. Give information. Change environment. Parent time-out. Substitute.	Take the time to hug, hold, and carry while talking. Show that there is a voice on the other end. If you are in the kitchen, get out play dough and or set up water in the sink they can play in. (You probably needed to clean the floor anyway!) Keep a special

Problem	Child Feeling	Tool	Details
			box of "telephone toys" hidden in a cupboard by the phone for pulling out during calls. Make calls at naptime. Request return calls later in evening. Leave email address with request instead of a phone number. That way, your request is responded to on your time, not theirs. Get your child a real phone to pretend with. Avoid letting child say hello at this age. They will want to for all calls and are too young to reason with why they can for some calls and not others.
Throws tantrums	Frustrated Angry Upset	Allow ownership of feelings.	*More in Chapter 8 and 5.*
Wants to be carried all the time	Insecure Desperate Scared Fearful	Give attention. Time-in. Holding, hugs, and cuddles. Parent time-out.	Spend lots of cuddle time in a chair, get on floor, and cuddle or get a sling to carry toddler around. Don't push away. Meet your needs so you can give to her.
Dawdles	Curious Distracted	Plan ahead. Learn child development. Change environment. Hold, carry, restrain, and remove.	Build in dawdle time in other parts of the day. Accept that toddlers have no clue of time. Change your own schedule. Have door bins to keep next day stuff. Get organized. Scoop them up and out the door as you dress them.
Won't share	Scared/fearful	Allow ownership of feelings. Change environment. Substitution.	Allow space and share-free possessions. Put away non-sharing toys. Make other toys available for friends.
Hits, pushes, shoves, bites	Invaded Angry Frustrated Curious Desperate Scared	Learn child development. I-statement. Supervision. Hold, carry, restrain, and remove. Allow own space. Time-in. Teach calm-down tools. Teach personal boundaries. Substitution.	Normal behavior for this age. *More in Chapter 8.*

Problem	Child Feeling	Tool	Details
Hits, pushes, shoves, bites	Invaded Angry Frustrated Curious Desperate Scared Poor self-control	Learn child development. I-statement. Supervision. Hold, carry, restrain, and remove. Allow own space. Time-in. Teach calm-down tools. Teach personal boundaries. Substitution.	Normal behavior for this age. *More in Chapter 8.*
Hates bath	Scared Confined	Pretend you need help.	Respect is key. If fear is the problem, cajoling, forcing, or belittling the child is not helpful. Go swimming instead. Showers are an option. Baby bathtubs are less intimidating. Take a bath with him. Run bath water before he gets there and drain after he leaves.
Whines	Insecure Frustrated Ignored Desperate	Say "no" another way. Selective ignoring. Give information. Distract. Stay with your "no". Parent time-out.	Teach emotion words. Teach how to say properly. Give item as soon as proper tone is heard. Get eye contact. Don't give item when whining. Take a break for you. *More in Chapter 8.*
Swears	Needs power/ Competency Curious Eager to mimic	Selective ignoring. Parent time-out.	If the word is not reinforced or acknowledged, it loses its power. Child can find another way to feel powerful. Pretend not to notice.
Touches everything	Curious Bored Poor self-control	Redirect. Substitute. Change environment. Say "no" another way. Supervise. Stimulation.	Point out another focus. Give toys or safe objects to touch. Consider not going to "problem areas" during toddlerhood. Childproof while visiting or in hotels: use duct tape to tape socks to table corners, tape over outlets, tape fridge, and toilet doors closed, etc.

Problem	Child Feeling	Tool	Details
Wakes up too early in the family bed	Awake Eager to play Needs exercise Curious	Parent problem-solving. Change environment.	Have a basket of small toys for him to discover in the morning. Have a TV in the room and remote close, so you can flick on TV to cartoons and catch a few extra zzz's. Have a small snack handy for him to eat.
Fears	Scared	Allow ownership of feelings. Holding, hugs, and cuddles. Learn child development. Change environment.	Accept and validate at this age. Say, "It's okay to feel scared." Too young to reason. Avoid triggers. *More in Chapter 8.*
Hates hair cut/wash	Confined Invaded Scared	Allow ownership of feelings. Change environment. Pretend you need help. Distract.	Acknowledge feelings. "I know you hate your hair being touched." Work fast. Let child wear a sun visor goggles or divers mask so hair doesn't fall on his eyes. Distract with a movie. Do it while asleep. Go swimming. Put shampoo in their hand and let them do it. Hold dry washcloth over their eyes or let them look up (have a decal or picture on the ceiling) while you carefully pour rinse water from a bottle on their head. Let him shampoo a doll or stuffy while you do him. Try a booster seat or high chair for cuts. Let them play in bathroom or kitchen sink. Let them face paint at the same time. Let them sit on your lap. Call it hair "style" not cut! (they may be scared at "cut") Take them with you when you go. Have partner or friend take them home after five minutes.
Won't get dressed	Distracted	Routines. Change environment.	Get dressed together. Sing 'hokey pokey.' Sleep in next day clean clothes instead of pajamas.

Problem	Child Feeling	Tool	Details
Child pulls books/items from the bookshelves, cupboards and drawers	Curious	Learn child development. Change environment.	Accept and put in a few sturdy books you don't mind pulled out and put back only once a day. Same with baking pans and other items in a cupboard. Skip folding clothes for a year.
Takes apart everything	Curious	Change environment. Fulfill needs.	It's normal! Put away off limits stuff. Hide it and barricade as much as possible. Provide lots of toys and interesting safe items.
Gets out of toddler bed	Eager to start day Poor self-control	Give attention. Change environment.	Make night cozy by inviting him in bed with you. Provide playthings near his bed (on your floor or in them). Lock your room and childproof if you are sleeping with him, so he doesn't wander out. Keep room dark. Don't play with him. Be boring and pretend to be asleep.
Won't eat	Not hungry Distracted	Teach personal boundaries. Learn child development.	Let him decide when full. Accept. More interested in exploring than eating. Put small amounts of food on high chair tray and give a spoon and don't watch. Take down if food begins to fly. Serve again in two hours. Make sure snacks are nutritious too. Don't serve same meal at next meal. Serve snack tray with compartments instead of a full meal. *More in Chapter 8.*
Says "no"	Needs power/ competency	Give choices. Active listening. Make request a game. Allow ownership of feelings. Teach personal boundaries.	Offer two choices. Say, "You are not happy about that?" Say, "Let's do this and see if we can clean up before the timer." Limit use of your "no." If it's not important, let them insist on "no." Respect their "no" on issues related to their body: tickles, hugs, holding, kisses. *More in Chapter 8.*

Problem	Child Feeling	Tool	Details
Separation anxiety Clings to parent Demands attention	Scared Insecure	Give attention. Time-in. Active listening. Holding, hugs, and cuddles. Spend time together. Fulfill needs.	Spend time together. If they are craving attention, take 10 minutes and give focused attention. Limit separations. Try to work at home – go out front door and come in the back. Say, "You are sad that mommy is leaving you again." Have cuddle time before you leave. Get the sitter to come half hour early so they can engage in an activity before you leave. Say a firm, definite goodbye to reinforce trust. Try not to rush off hurriedly. Leave something that smells of you for them to hold. Have a goodbye ritual. Limit amount of separation.
Steals things	Desperate Curious Poor self-control	Natural consequences. Give information. Distract.	Take the object and say, "That's not ours. Let's put it back." Distract with a snack or toy if they persist. Stealing is abstract at this age. They don't understand ownership.
Won't clean up toys	Distracted Confused	Pretend you need help. Use positive commands. Change environment. Model. Help child complete task.	Have them help you as you do it. "Let's pick up the blocks." Pack away 90 percent of toys so they won't be overwhelmed. Have buckets available so they can easily throw items in. Keep your areas tidy. Do it together.
Hates waiting	Restless Bored	Distract. Plan ahead. Stimulation.	Give a roll of masking tape or carry bubbles or a pen and paper. Sing. Read books. Play finger games.
Won't sit in circle time	Restless Bored Distracted Curious Confined	Remove child from environment. Fulfill need. Stimulation. Learn child development.	Children learn best when they are active and interested. Keep them home or take them out, if it's not working. Give them something else to do. Accept that it's very hard for toddlers to sit still for more then a few minutes.

Problem	Child Feeling	Tool	Details
Hates getting out of bath	Content	Change environment. Distract.	Discreetly pull plug and all water runs out. Offer a snack or book to entice out.
Wanders out the door	Curious	Change environment. Supervision.	Put bell on door. Socks on doorknobs. Use duct tape (the great all purpose childproof item) to put a strip over high door. Great for keeping fridge and toilets closed. Always know what child is doing.
Interrupts when talking to people	Ignored Insecure Distracted Poor self-control	Use positive commands rather then negative. Fulfill needs. Give attention. Stimulation. Learn child development.	"Mommy needs to talk for one minute." Give hugs and something for them to do. Get them involved in an activity and then resume talking. You may have to stay with them as they want you near. They are too young to teach not to interrupt at this age. It's hard for toddlers to wait.
Only prefers one parent	Scared Insecure	Learn child development. Allow ownership of feelings. Holding, hugs, and cuddles of non-preferred parent.	Accept that it's a very normal stage. Don't take personally. Have non-preferred parent respond when child is sick, hurt, or upset, and to handle bedtime routines, to build attachment. Indulge preference and let preferred parent do it if possible.
Crying and screaming	Upset Sad Frustrated Angry	Holding, hugs, and cuddles. Give attention. Parent guided problem-solving. Allow ownership of feelings.	Hold and hug if they allow you. When calm, ask if you can help. Try to figure out the problem. Say, "It's okay to feel angry" so they develop a feeling vocabulary. Use assuring words, "That's okay," over and over again.
Doesn't like to change activity or leave places	Content Distracted	Distract. Use positive commands. Plan ahead. Learn child development.	Offer snack in new situation. "Let's get our coat on." Pick up and remove child. Accept that you can't go anywhere fun for just 20 minutes with toddlers.

Problem	Child Feeling	Tool	Details
Dawdles	Distracted Indifferent Content	Give a choice in time or place. Get eye contact. Use a timer. Clock or calendar to set time limits. Use when/then. Change environment. Learn child development.	"Would you like to get your coat on first or your boots?" "Let's get dressed. Shall we go to Grandma's first or the store?" Go up to him and speak. Set a timer and make a game to see if he can beat it. Say, "When you get dressed, then you can have breakfast and watch TV." Keep distractions to a minimum. Build in dawdle time. Physically move them through. Help put their coat on or carry them out to car and bring shoes, hats, coats in bag to get dressed later. Accept that small children take longer to do things. Change your schedule and stress level. Keep games and books, especially for the car.
Disruptive when has to wait	Bored Restless Needs exercise	Honor promises. Stimulation. Clarify expectations. Give attention. Change environment. Give positive feedback. Time-in. Show and tell correct behavior. Parental problem-solving.	Honor your word. Keep waiting times to a minimum. Provide toys, snacks, and diversions. Tell the child what will happen and for how long. Use waiting time for one-on-one play or reading time. Childproof waiting area so they can play safely. Bring a DVD player to keep busy. Reinforce every little effort to wait. "Thank you for not disturbing me on the phone. I have some extra time now and would like to play a game with you, or read a book with you." Also works with sibling fighting. "Thank you for not disturbing me with fights. Can we bake now or read a book together?" Go to balcony and talk on phone while your child can see you through glass. Teach that when you put your hand out or some other signal that the call may not be

Problem	Child Feeling	Tool	Details
			interrupted. Show a sign for calls that can be interrupted. Or wear a special red hat for uninterrupted calls and no hat for calls that are interruptible. Don't interrupt them when they are doing something important. It's hard for little ones to hold on to their thoughts while they wait for you to finish talking. They need constant reminding. Ask them to wait a minute while someone else is finished talking. Ask them to hold your hand when they want to interrupt to tell you something.
Teases	Needs power Insecure Wants to fit in	I-statements. Model. Be polite, kind, and firm. Tell a story with an appropriate moral. Reflective questions.	Say, "I don't appreciate teasing. It hurts feelings." Avoid teasing them. Use all words with politeness. Read books about children teasing. Ask, "How would that child feel if he were teased? How would you feel about that?"
Won't play in the basement alone/won't play alone anywhere	Scared Insecure	Learn child development. Stimulation. Change environment. Time-in.	Normal for young children to not play in separate rooms away from parents. Have a corner in the kitchen or special basket of toys in each room. Most children want parent attention and involvement or presence nearby. Sit and play for 15 minutes then lead in to another activity. Schedule play dates. Children will often play with others. Help set up an activity that involves them for awhile.
Wake-up at night	Scared/fearful Lonely Insecure	Time-in. Fulfill needs.	Same as toddlers. Have bedtime rituals, problem-solve, sleep with child in family bed.
Won't brush Teeth	Distracted Invaded	Distraction. Give choices between three things.	Same as toddlers. Plus provide choice of toothpaste and brush in colors and styles. Use an egg timer or sand timer from a board

Problem	Child Feeling	Tool	Details
		Make the opposite request. Get eye contact.	game. Let brush in tub while bathing and distracted. Let play in water in sink. Pick a favorite song to sing while brushing. Compete, "I'm going to brush my teeth before you!"
Won't get dressed	Bored Engaged Distracted Insecure	Pick your battles. Give choices between three things. Make the opposite request. When/then. Get eye contact. Time-in. Distract. Fulfill needs.	Sleep in next day's clean clothes instead of pajamas. Let them go to their activities in pajamas. Let them choose which ones. Say, "You are NOT allowed to wear pajamas/those clothes!" Smile. Say, "When you get dressed, then we can have breakfast." Go right up to them and make request. Put an easel by the door to distract them with coloring while you put on shoes, coat, mitts, etc. Many preschoolers want the extra attention given when Mom dresses them. Give more attention in other ways.
Won't brush hair	Scared Invaded	Make the opposite request. Parental problem-solving. Give a choice in time and place.	Say, "You may NOT brush your hair." Smile. Consider a short cut or braids. Show them how to brush. Say, "Do you want your hair done while watching the movie or after supper?"
Won't eat breakfast	Distracted	Same as toddlers.	Pack a portable one.
Won't gather stuff to go	Distracted Confused	Give warnings of transitions. Use the when/then rule. Use a timer, clock, or calendar to set limits. Change environment.	Say, "After the show is done, we have to leave." "When the movie is over, we need to go." "When the timer goes off, we have to leave." Have special bins by the door with the day's necessities (socks, hats, juice boxes, pre-packaged snacks, water bottles). Hang jackets on small hooks so they can reach. Have a photograph checklist as a visual reminder of what to bring.

Problem	Child Feeling	Tool	Details
Accidentally breaks furniture or electronic equipment	Confused Indifferent Distracted Poor self-control	Give information. Reflective questions. Learn child development. Parent time-out. Parental problem-solving.	Say, "What did we learn about this?" "What happens when we put coins into the CD drive?" Realize that young children don't know how delicate machines can break. It's normal for children to be careless without being malicious. People's feelings are more important than items. Calm down and problem-solve what to do: fix, or replace. Encourage any help or restitution child can offer.
Fears	Scared Confused	Give attention. Active listening. Time-in. Holding, hugs, and cuddles.	Don't belittle or patronize. Take fears seriously. Say, "It's okay to feel scared. I used to be scared of dogs too." Don't take away any security items. The secure child gets over fears faster. Vacuum fears: Use backpack. Let them vacuum and use the on/off switch. Get partner to take them out. Monster fears: Acknowledge fear, but not monsters. Say, "It's okay to feel scared, but we have no monsters in our house." Leave night or overhead light on. Get a fish tank. Leave taped music on, books on tape, or put on a video (same one every night so they get bored). Dark: Go on regular night hikes or walks and point out moon and stars. Celebrate night with candles outside and sparkly stardust. Avoid scary movies or books that reinforce scary darkness. Dog fears: Avoid introducing at this age. Events fears: Rehearse with "what if?" Car wash, movie theatre fears: Take child out. Give plenty of cuddle time. Return if child consents.

Problem	Child Feeling	Tool	Details
Tattles	Victimized Angry Frustrated Jealous	Tell a story with an appropriate moral. Reflective questions. Give information. Parent guided problem-solving.	Don't set up to trap into lying. Say, "Would you like to tell me where the cake went?" Teach difference between tattle (to get someone in trouble) or telling (to get someone out of trouble). Read books about the differences. Deal with problem without bringing attention to the tattle. If the tattle is to get someone in trouble, ask if they can work it out themselves? When they come back, ask if they need an adult to help. Go in and help problem-solve if they need adult.
Destroys property	Angry Frustrated Curious Poor self-control	Reflective questions. Model. Natural consequences. Change environment. Supervise.	Give information about proper care. Show how to use gently. Show how to use calm-down tools when angry. Show how to fix broken items. Have them attend with you. Leave out non-destructibles. If you know they will break (like delicate toys) then pack away until older. In a few months – try again. Supervise play. Get help cleaning up so they know how long it takes to make messes and clean up.
Too hyper – is loud and boisterous	Energetic Poor self-control Excited Happy Joyous	Change environment. Parental problem-solving. Learn child development. Show and tell correct behavior.	Take to park or playground. Provide physical diversions: safe sofa cushions or old mattress to jump on if weather is bad. Go out once per day to park, swimming, play-tot groups, etc. Preschoolers need a physical burst every 1.5 hours. Provide an outlet. Fresh air and exercise are really beneficial just before dinner or bedtime. A child under 10 can't lower her voice without being reminded. They need to practice different voices. Tell them to pretend to be mice or fish when you need them to be quiet.

Problem	Child Feeling	Tool	Details
Bathroom language/ swearing	Needs power/ competency Curious Bored	Parent time-out. Model.	Ignore it. If the word is not reinforced, it loses its specialness. Tell friends you are aware of the swearing and are working on a new strategy. Watch your own language!
Wants own way all the time	Needs power/ competency Unfair/ victimized Inadequate	Fulfill needs. Pick your battles. Parental problem-solving. Reflective question. Give a choice in time or place. Use when/then. Show how to use words.	A spirited child will probably need and want their own way most of time – if it meets your needs and doesn't conflict with what you want, no problem. When it conflicts, problem-solve. Is there another way to meet both needs? Word your answer in some kind of choice, so the child feels that he has power. If you decide to give him his own way, don't do it immediately so he connects whining and tantrums with getting it. Wait until he is calm and asks in a calm voice. Show him how to ask politely and assertively and give the desired result immediately.
Doesn't follow directions	Indifferent Distracted Confused	Give positive feedback when they do listen. Learn child development. Show and tell correct behavior.	Gush when child does follow directions. Use a simple sentence. One direction at a time. Get eye contact. Expect 40 percent compliance rate for children under five. It's normal. Take their hand and gently lead them and show what needs to be done. Avoid power struggles if they refuse. Connect with them and try again. Try in a few minutes, hours or days.
Makes messes and won't clean up	Distracted Confused Bored Indifferent	Use a timer, clock or calendar to set limits. Give positive feedback. Give transition warnings. When/then rule.	Play a five minute song and race to clean up before song ends. Use a timer. Teach to clean up before next activitygets spread out. Help them clean up and make it connection and pleasant time. Sing and talk while doing it. Say appreciation for any help. Give

Problem	Child Feeling	Tool	Details
		Change environment. Keep routines. Give choices in place and time.	warning of when clean up will happen. Say, "When we clean this up, we can have a snack." Be specific – assign one item per child (can sort about age five). Say, "You pick up all the blocks and put in this container. I'll pick up the rest." Don't expect perfection. Keep a "clean toys only" dustpan to help pick up small toys like plastic blocks easily. Have a sheet that small pieces can be played in and picked up easier. Offer to do it occasionally yourself, if they do a job for you. Have visiting friends help in pick up. Keep it routine. Have open shelves with photos of items so they know how and where things go. Horizontal storage is better than vertical buckets because small items get lost at the bottom. You pick up and hand to them to be mailperson so they deliver to proper room. Works when things are all over the house and need to go to proper rooms. Give each child a basket and toss everything in. Then, you and he go to the rooms of the house and deliver the items to the rooms. They learn where things go. And when they are older, you can just say, "Put this away please."
Won't be quiet at church, concerts, adult events.	Poor self-control Happy, joyous Confused Needs exercise Bored	Give positive feedback. Stimulation. Fulfill needs. Learn child development.	Appreciate every minute that they are quiet. Bring quiet toys like markers and paper, magnetic boards, and quiet food that take a long time to eat: raisins, cheerios, juice boxes. Find little jobs for them: count the blue hats or how many times the minister says "we." Practice whispering on a

Problem	Child Feeling	Tool	Details
			tape recorder so they can hear what being quiet sounds like. Sit in the back for quick get-aways. Sit in the front so they can see if it's big graphics or a child-friendly show. Sit between siblings so they don't fight when they are bored. Have an active activity right before they are supposed to sit quietly. (Go to a playground before a wedding.) Children can't be inactive or quiet for more than a half hour at this age. Accept and go home.
Lies	Confused Curious Desperate Poor self-control Scared	Learn child development. Tell a story with an appropriate moral. Honor promises. Reflective questions.	Still in age of fantasy/reality blur. Often tells wishes rather than reality. Describe what you see rather then trap them into a lie. Say "I see that you have the toy from Jimmy's house. We need to give it back." Instead of "Did you take that from Jimmy's?" Read books about lying. Help them find a way to get their needs met without lying.
Name calls	Inadequate Frustrated Angry Jealous Unfair/victimized	Parent time-out. Tell a story with an appropriate moral. I-statement. Give information. Clarify expectations.	Ignore. Say I-statement "Ouch, I feel hurt!" "That hurts peoples' feelings." Avoid nicknames. Teach child how to respond to name calling. Teach to say, "I don't like that" and walk away. Educate on slang names, bad names, and really bad names and swear words. Recite family rules: "In our family we don't call people that." Say it over and over again!
Talks back/gives attitude	Curious Desperate Needs power	I-statements. Selective ignoring. Model. Show how to use "their words."	"I don't like that." Ask me this way, "I would like a drink please." Don't respond until they say it politely. Avoid sarcasm and "attitude" yourself. Show how to ask for things assertively, with respect and meet their needs as soon as they do.

Problem	Child Feeling	Tool	Details
Interrupts	Indifferent Desperate Poor self-control Excited	Show how to use "their words." Change environment. Stimulation. Model.	Teach them to wait for a pause in the conversation. Then teach to say "excuse me" or to hold or squeeze your hand if they want to say something or need you. Introduce children to people so they know you are visiting. Limit conversation time. Involve in conversation. Set up play activity.
Steals	Desperate Confused Poor self-control	Tell a story with an appropriate moral. Learn child development. Natural consequences. Reflective questions. Routines.	Read books about stealing. They know its wrong but struggle with self-control. Coach through the process of taking the item back, saying sorry, and making restitution. Phone the victim ahead to discuss strategy. Emphasize empathy. How would they feel if their treasures were taken? Ask what they think if everyone stole everything – where would we get items? Avoid letting a child take home toys from others homes if it's not a gift. Avoid borrowing. Say, "That toy doesn't belong to us. We can leave it here to play with next time." Say, "See you later" to the toy. In stores, don't let child have item until they give the money to the store clerk. Toddlers don't have the cognitive power to handle this but preschoolers do. Teach how to ask for things without stealing. Give permission as much as possible, so they know that asking will meet their needs. Avoid labels. Always ask permission before you take something from your child. Good habit to get into and models respect.

Problem	Child Feeling	Tool	Details
Wakes parents too early	Joyous Excited Happy	Use a timer, clock or calendar to set limits.	Draw a line on the clock so he can tell when to wake you. Or draw a picture of where the hands will be. When the clock matches the picture, it's time to get up. Provide toys or books to read until its time to get up.
Doesn't do as parents ask	Distracted Confused Indifferent Poor self-control	Give positive feedback. Clarify expectations. Connect, then direct. Stay with your "no". Pick your battles. Learn child development.	Wait until distraction ends and then make request. Be sure they understand what you want. Try a humorous approach: Tell them they can't do something you want them to do. "No, you can't brush your teeth! Don't go near that toothbrush...Oh no!" Say it with a smile. Children love dichotomies. Get eye contact, smile, and say, "I need you to put your boots on." Then help them get them on. When they do something, say, "Thanks! I appreciate it so much!" When you say "no," be firm and kind. Get them to help you do it. Preschoolers comply less than 40 percent of the time and that's normal.
Won't use toilet	Scared Distracted	Give choices between three things. Give positive feedback. Active listening.	Provide choice in toilets, paper, underwear, etc. Celebrate successes. Have a toilet party! Investigate reasons for fear. Say, "You seem to be scared of the toilet?"
Won't take medication	Scared Dislikes taste	Change environment. Active listening. Give information.	Put in a teaspoon of applesauce or pour into a bottle nipple and they can suck it out. Make a Popsicle of it (check with doctor) or put in an eyedropper. Acknowledge feelings with "You are scared of the medicine?" Explain the need.

Preschooler 3 - 5

Problem	Child Feeling	Tool	Details
Won't get in car seat	Distracted Invaded	Routines. Make the opposite request. Distraction. Stimulation. When/then.	Make a rule that the car doesn't move until all belts are fastened. This is one that requires routine habit. Hand them a toy or snack as you gently move them into seat. When they get into seat, then they can have toy or book.
Wanders away while shopping	Curious Distracted Bored	Stimulation. Change environment.	Give a task to do or items to find in the same aisle. Make a list on a clipboard with pictures to help them find things or match box cutouts to the product so they can recognize. They can check off or draw. Go early in the day when less crowded. Bring snacks. Consider store daycare. Shop online or leave at home with partner.
Wets bed	Embarrassed Scared	Give positive feedback. Parental problem-solving.	Clean up matter of fact. Give appreciation for dry days. Get child up before you go to bed and help them to bathroom while they are half asleep. Put diaper or padding on at night. Have padded bedding.
Won't sleep alone	Scared Lonely Insecure Separation anxious	Give attention. Time-in. Fulfill needs.	Use baby steps out the door: lie with, than sit on bed, than sit in room. (takes about 10 days). Let fall asleep on sofa and move to bed later. Co-sleep. Have small bed next to yours on floor. Incentive charts work for some children. Spend time together before bed. Put on a movie, music, or book tape that they can fall asleep to. Say, "I need to leave the room to go to the bathroom, or get a drink," and take increasing amounts of time to do it before coming back to them. Let siblings sleep together. They will be giggly at first, but will settle down. Consider two bedtimes: one for "in room" with quiet reading in bed, and one for "lights out."

Problem	Child Feeling	Tool	Details
Whines	Desperate Confused	Show how to use "their words."	"I need you to... (Use words)." Leave at home if shopping is a major problem. Tell them if they whine, they definitely won't get what they want, but if they use a normal voice, then they will get it. Model different tones. Give immediately if they don't whine.
Wants everything in store	Desperate Poor self-control	Clarify expectations. Active listening. Holding, hugs, and cuddles. Distract. Change environment. Stay with your "no." Honor promises. Parent problem-solving. Give a choice between three things.	Make sure they know that you are only shopping for a present for their friend today. Say, "I see that you are upset about not getting that toy. It's okay to feel upset." Say, "You really loved that truck, but we have no money for that today." Stockpile things that you don't want but child has thrown in cart. Leave items with cashier. Have child carry pad and pen and mark it down for birthdays and Christmas. Leave at home with caregiver if a big problem. Carry snacks. If you promise one treat, stay with it. Say, "I hear you. But I can only get you one treat." When they protest, try one parent shops, one takes children somewhere else. If you promise a treat, give a choice between three acceptable items.
Jealous of friend or sibling	Jealous Victimized	Holding, hugs, and cuddles. Give positive feedback. Time-in. Give attention.	Encourage and appreciate uniqueness. Give extra hugs and touches. Show empathy. Don't compare. Spend time alone together. Time is love.
Won't wash hands	Distracted Indifferent	Make the opposite request. Change environment. Give information.	Buy special soap dispenser and have a stool and hand towels at his level. Make it routine. Tell about germs and importance of washing.

Problem	Child Feeling	Tool	Details
Nags for vending treats and throws tantrums when you say "no"	Desperate Poor self-control	Show how to use "their words." Stay with your "no". Give a choice in time or place or item.	Never buy a treat when they nag. Consider buying a treat when they ask politely! Clarify expectations. If you say, "yes," then give a choice. Ignore the tantrum when you stay with your "no." Scoop them up and leave calmly.
Too aggressive weapon play	Boisterous Excited Happy Curious Needs power/competency Poor self-control	Model. Change environment. Stimulation. Parental problem-solving. I-statement.	Make "caring" a family rule. No hitting with weapons. Model kindness and resolving problems without violence. Eliminate violent games, movies, TV shows for this age. Change activity to sport-type physical expression. Teach compromise and problem-solving skills. Say, "I'm worried that someone will get hurt."
Picky eating/won't stay at table	Full Distracted Excited Indifferent	Learn child development. Routines. Pick your battles. Change environment.	Food jags (eating same food for months) and picky eating normal. Make it routine to come to table for social talk even if they are not hungry. Have a floor picnic. Let them assemble snack dinners. Limit juice and milk. Serve only water between meals and snacks. Be sure all snacks are healthy. Hide the junk food or don't buy it.
Hates tying shoes	Confused Bored	Give information. Parent problem-solving.	Teach by using long strings of black and purple licorice. They can practice. Buy Velcro. Tie loosely so that shoes can go on and off without affecting laces.
Socks all over house	Bored Distracted	Change environment. Routines.	Buy socks all one color for one child. Or, if several children, the same size, buy all one color. Have a big bin of clean socks by the door. Let child search for pairs. Have child pick up socks from house once a week as a chore. Have a special cubby or basket for each child's socks, mitts, hats and coats by the door.

Problem	Child Feeling	Tool	Details
Clothes all over house	Bored Distracted	Change environment. Routines.	Hang a basketball hoop over a laundry basket in their rooms. Or hang a colorful pillowcase they can use for throwing practice. Make routine for hanging jacket as soon as home. Appoint one item as the "magic" one they have to find.
Separation anxiety	Insecure Scared	Give attention. Honor promises. Give information. Active listening.	Same as toddlers. Limit separations as much as possible until more secure. Talk about where and when you will be back. Come back at promised time. Leave an item of yours for them to hold. Give a locket of hugs and kisses from Mom. Mark on their fingers or hand a happy face of Mom. Have matching stuffys: one for Mom and child. (Identical clothes, scarves, or blankets also work.) Leave a mini photo album or photo frame of you. Say, "You are sad that Mommy is leaving? You want me to stay with you?"
Masturbates	Content	Give information.	Say, "I know that feels good, but that is a private action, and you need to do that in private."
Won't carry their items	Indifferent Distracted	Routines. Make the opposite request.	Pack small backpack for them. Get them used to carrying their own swim/snow gear. Have them bring in items from car to house. Use a wagon or sled at the beach (wagon wheels get stuck in the sand) when they are past stroller age and you have a lot to carry.
Shy	Scared Insecure	Give positive feedback. Show how to use "their words." Show and tell correct behavior.	Accept their shyness. Nudge to social activities but don't force. Stay with them as they wish. Acknowledge small steps. Practice social skills.

Problem	Child Feeling	Tool	Details
Too friendly with strangers	Happy Joyous Exuberant	Supervision. Give information.	Preschoolers need 24-hour supervision! Give info about "funny" feelings or "tornado" in tummy. Enroll in stranger danger classes. Don't instill fear of people. Teach basic rules – go to a mommy with children when lost, ask for help, run and scream if scared.
Won't share	Scared	Connect, then direct. Natural consequences. Show and tell correct behavior.	Same as toddlers. Assure you will replace if item gets broken. Put away items that they absolutely don't want to share. If possible limit play dates to playroom and make bedrooms off limits. Show how you enjoy sharing with your friends. Point out how sharing is reciprocal and benefits them. Role play how to give up a toy when someone asks and how to ask for it back.
Won't give back play item to friend or playgroup	Scared Poor self-control	Honor promises. When/then. Learn child development.	Ask permission first to take home and give back the next day. Honor promises to bring back. Say, "When we leave, the toy stays here, and we can stop at the park on the way home." Say that the item misses its family back at the group. It's normal to find it hard to let go of toys at this age.
Won't play alone when you are busy	Bored Insecure	Give attention. Stimulation.	Play with them for some focused time (15 minutes). Bring out rotating toy bucket. Schedule a play date.
Won't go to doctor or dentist	Scared Invaded and confined	Give positive feedback. Holding, hugs, and cuddles. Model.	Appreciate any little steps, even letting dentist look in their mouth. Hold them on your lap. Take a few times on your visits. Model the fun!
Won't wear hat or sunscreen	Invaded and confined Uncomfortable	Parent problem-solving.	Same as toddlers.

Problem	Child Feeling	Tool	Details
Won't accept transitions	Content Focused	When/then. Give warnings of transitions. Change environment. Stimulation.	Make the "then" part extra enticing! Snacks work well. Show how much time is left with your hands. Pick up child and carry. Acknowledge feelings. Have a good-bye routine; "See you later, Alligator." "We are going to Rock and Roll" (On "Roll" you go!) "Last time!" (Really must mean, "Last time.")
Loses things	Distracted Poor self-control	Learn child development. Give attention. Routines.	Pin stuff together. Be on the lookout for special items. You have to remember at this age. Preschoolers don't. Make it routine that special toys don't go out or they stay in car.

Problem	Child Feeling	Tool	Details
Won't clean room	Indifferent Content	Change environment. Show child benefit of behavior change. When/then. Connect then direct. Problem-solve. Gentle reminders in preferred learning style. Walk away from power struggles. Use humor.	Minimize clutter. Make bins and storage available. Use storage under the bed. Model a clean room. Institute a one in-one out rule. Promise a bouquet of flowers or sleepover when clean! How many of us invite company so we will be motivated to clean up? Say, "How about we organize your room together?" Remind with photos of messy room. Post on fridge so they see it. Accept that it is their room and a wee bit of space that they can have control over. Play "chore bingo" – first line of tasks done wins.
Won't eat	Distracted	Change environment.	School-aged children eat better after exercise and fresh air.
Won't sleep	Content	Re-evaluate limits.	Every child has different sleep needs. Provide activities to do in room or bed if not sleepy.
Won't carry their stuff	Unfair Content	Clarify expectations. Use humor. Problem-solve.	Refuse to do it. Show them how to pack lighter. Say, "I know a big, strong guy like you can carry that."
Won't do chores	Unfair Tired Distracted Confused Indifferent	Skills chart. Give input into rule-setting. Family conferences. Use humor. Give gentle reminders in preferred learning style.	A skills chart provides routine and gives a progress record of what has been learned. Give choices in time, place, and job. Put a time limit on family chores such as 10 am – noon on Saturday. Emphasize team spirit. Build in fun aspects of the job. Let them play a bit while cleaning the sink or smash the glass while at the recycle depot. Play music and dance while vacuuming. Post photos of what needs to be done.
Won't do homework	Unfair Tired Distracted	Change environment. Give gentle	Set aside a family time to do quiet things: pay bills, read, paperwork, or do

Problem	Child Feeling	Tool	Details
	Confused Indifferent Inadequate Bored	reminders in learning style. Clarify expectations. Schedule daily downtime. Show child benefit of behavior change. Give choices. Model. Natural consequences. Problem-solve. Contract.	homework. It's less distracting if one sibling is playing video games and the other has to do homework. Give one reminder. Let him decide when and where. Offer a hand. Show how work affects job employment. Let them choose: summer school or repeat grade or do homework. Don't rescue from teachers wrath when it's not done. Have snacks. Make it fun. Help set goals. Let them take breaks. Talk to teacher and problem-solve with child actively participating. Look for need: is work too boring, too hard, undiagnosed learning disability? Write up a mutually acceptable contract and have you and child agree to it. *More in Chapter 10.*
Uses weapons for play	Excited Powerful Curious	Stimulation. Model. I-statements. Re-evaluate limits. Substitution. Problem-solve.	Redirect to other forms of stimulation and play. Live your values. Don't give as gifts or use yourself. Say, "I don't like guns and prefer not to watch this." You may decide to allow weapon play at friends' houses but not at home. Substitute with board games or cooperative games.
Wants to quit lessons	Bored Inadequate Scared	Give choices. Re-evaluate limits. Skills chart. Stay with "no". Problem-solve. Schedule daily downtime.	Show a calendar and how many times a week they have to go. Let them pick the days. Hang it by the door so they know they've committed to it. Did they sign up or you? If after two lessons, it's not working for them, consider letting them quit. Make a chart of skills learned so they can see accomplishments. Find balance between pushing and protecting. Sometimes a bad experience can set them back or turn them off.

Problem	Child Feeling	Tool	Details
Siblings fight while driving	Bored Victimized	Stimulation. Clarify expectations. Show child benefit of behavior change. Plan ahead. Problem-solve.	Provide a distraction. Teach how a distracted driver can be dangerous. Pull over until they stop or work something out. Bring diversions for next time. Have a supply of ear plugs for the car.
Behavior problems in school	Bored Scared Inadequate Confused	Clarify expectations. Active listening. Problem-solve.	Ask teacher to go over behavior expectations – perhaps child doesn't know. Say, "Sounds like you are feeling anxious at school and can't sit still. Want to talk about it?" Mutually come up with some solutions.
Secretive about outings	Scared Wants to fit in	Clarify expectations. Family conference. Stimulation. Active listening. Problem-solve.	Family rule: someone needs to know where someone is at all times-parents included. Phone home whenever there is a change of venue or plans. Have a family meeting to clarify. Make sure your home is inviting to friends. Say, "You feel scared that you won't fit in if you say 'no'? What can you do instead?"
Dawdles before school	Distracted Scared	Routines. Change environment. Family conference.	Have the same plan every school day. Have a "next day" bucket with all items needed for school and activities. Set a timer. Turn off TV during the week. Give a paper towel tube to store homework and signed papers. Get partner involved in preparation. Have children lay out items, with a pre-printed checklist (words or pictures) and pack themselves. Teach them to make own lunch. Stock up on portable breakfasts and snacks.

Problem	Child Feeling	Tool	Details
Won't come to table for dinner	Distracted Not hungry	Clarify expectations. Re-evaluate limits. I-statement. Routines. Problem-solve.	Insist on table time even if not eating. More often or not, they will eat. Respect their need to finish quickly if in middle of a project or activity. Make table time pleasant. Say, "I feel disrespected when I call to the table and no one comes." Have meals and snacks at same time everyday.
Steals	Scared Curious Desperate Needs power/ competency Wants to fit in	Active listening to peer pressure. Natural consequences. Model. Reward truth and honesty. I-statement. Problem-solve. Tell story with appropriate moral. Show child benefit of behavior change.	Say, "I can see that you feel desperate to fit in." Coach through the process of returning the item and apologizing. Perhaps get them to write a letter. Ask reflective questions, "What would happen if everyone stole?" Give information: it's against the law and wrong. Discuss books and movies that portray stealing. Model honestly and not stealing. Role model how to handle peer pressure. Express your sadness and disappointment. "I'm sad that peer pressure has been hard for you. What do you need to equip yourself to handle it?" Find a way to help them get things they think they need, legally and honestly. Find a way to help child get a "rush" instead of stealing. Don't lecture, don't overreact; do address it.
Destroys property	Needs power Angry Frustrated	Natural consequences. Problem-solve. Teach calm-down tools. Reflective questions. Stay with your "no."	Help and show how to calm down in the moment of anger. Problem-solve how to make restitution to property and person. Ask, "How would you feel if someone kicked your bike over when angry?" Address the issue every time.

Problem	Child Feeling	Tool	Details
			Say, "I know that you are angry and that's okay. We can't kick bikes though, but we can stomp our feet."
Is surly and uses attitude	Victimized Angry Frustrated Needs power/ competency	I-statement. Model. Stay calm. Ignore provocations. Natural consequences. Use humor. Walk away from power struggles. Spend time together. Show benefit of behavior change. Model. Re-evaluate limits. Problem-solve. Walk away from attitude.	Say, "I don't wish to be spoken to in that tone." Walk away. Don't be surly back to them. Introduce them to your friends and visitors. Model respect: don't tell friends that they are "terrible teens" or "that stage." Remember the self-fulfilling prophecy! Children live up to their labels. Talk to child the way you want to be spoken to. Monitor their friends and media. Provide interesting competing activities to reduce their dependence on them. Point out to your child what is acceptable and when and with who, and what is not. Give encouragement when you hear politeness. Always speak politely, respectfully and assertively to others in front of your children- service people, partner, friends, people who you are in conflict with. Don't stay and be a target. *More in Chapter 11.*
Doesn't follow directions	Confused Distracted Poor self-control/time management Indifferent	Give gentle reminders in learning style. Connect, then direct. Clarify expectations. Problem-solve. When/then rule. I-statements. Give choice in time and place.	Teach. They may not know how you want things done. Get eye contact: ask what the problem is. Doesn't understand? Doesn't know how to do it? Use sticky notes as reminders. Ask for repeat of request: "What are you going to do by suppertime?" Express appreciation and hope they do it! Don't expect perfection and don't redo. Say, "When you take out the garbage, then we

Problem	Child Feeling	Tool	Details
			can drive to the mall." If they don't do it, keep problem-solving so they learn that avoidance doesn't mean they get out of it. It means there is still a problem to be solved. Say "I need the garbage to be taken out please."
Name calls	Angry Insecure Unfair/ victimized	I-statements. Model. Clarify expectations. Teach calm-down strategies. Problem-solve. Walk away from attitude.	Say, "I dislike name calling." Use respectful language. Teach strategies on how to handle anger. Teach them how to use I-statements. Say, "Here is the language to use instead of name calling: Say, 'I'm feeling angry when you mock me and I want you to stop now.' Can you try that?"
Throws or breaks toys	Angry Frustrated	Teach calm-down tools. Model. Natural consequences. Problem-solve.	Is frustrated with video games and throws them or jumps on them. Say, "The family rule is that if a game is frustrating, take a break!" Don't fix broken toys. Or fix them together to show how to make amends, after child has calmed down of course!
Swears	Angry Frustrated Needs power Wants to fit in	Clarify expectations. I-statement. Give input into rules. Re-evaluate limits. Model. Problem-solve.	Express your values. Coach children when it is appropriate and not. Ask questions. Teach to express anger and frustration with feeling words. "I'm angry. I'm really annoyed." Instead of "Sh**!" Teach how language affects how people view you. Have a family conference to set up rules of conduct in the home and outside. Accept that swearing will occur among peers. Watch your own expletives, especially when driving!

Problem	Child Feeling	Tool	Details
Experiments with bullying	Unhealthy self-esteem Wants to fit in Needs power/ competency Insecure	Reflective questions. Stimulation. Spend time together. I-statements. Show benefit of behavior change. Problem-solve with other parents/teachers.	Ask, "How does that person feel when you do that?" Provide alternate activities that the child can feel powerful about: volunteering, sports, etc. Do things together. Comment on his strengths. Say, "I abhor bullying and it's not acceptable." Show how people respect others who don't bully. If you suspect bullying, closely supervise your child. Get professional help if it persists. Bullying children grow into bullying adults.
Ignores parental advice/says "no"	Needs power Indifferent	Natural consequences. Model. Show child benefit of behavior change. Walk away from power struggles. Problem-solve.	Sometimes they just need to learn life's lessons – no shortcuts! Stay with your "no" as much as you can by changing what you do. Model your own advice. Give a minute for them to reconsider their "no" after you give them information. Let go if not a big issue.
Disregards hygiene	Distracted Indifferent	Show benefit of behavior change. Use humor. Give input into rule setting. Model. Natural consequences. Problem-solve.	Teach about hygiene. Make it fun. Let them choose soap, deodorant, shampoo, toothpaste. Play mad dog when tooth brushing: whoever can foam at the mouth the most wins! Show pictures of rotten teeth. Discreetly point out stinky people. Discuss how to keep hygiene healthy in the house.
Stays up late	Distracted Poor self-control	Natural consequences. Re-evaluate limits. Connect, then direct. Problem-solve.	Ensure that the next day commitments are attended, even if tired. Look at sleep needs. Perhaps the child doesn't need a lot of sleep. Say, "I know that you are excited about this game, but it's bedtime." Discuss how your child's late bedtime affects you and what to do about it.

Problem	Child Feeling	Tool	Details
Dress is inappropriate for weather/ dresses like a tramp, hobo, etc.,/wears too much make-up	Indifferent Wants to fit in Needs power/ competency	I-statements. Walk away from power struggles. Problem-solve. Show child benefit of behavior change.	Say, "I think it will be cold today. Perhaps a coat might be helpful?" Accept the different clothing standards – remember when you were young! Dress is a safe way for children to express individuality and power. See if they can carry a coat or socks in their backpack in case they are cold. Expose to strong role models that dress appropriately. Dress like they do and they will stop.
Surfs forbidden web sites	Wants to fit in Curious	Problem-solve. Give input into rule setting. Model. Clarify expectations. Reflective questions. Plan ahead. Stimulation. Spend time together.	Problem-solve your concerns and their curiosity. Decide on mutual rules for Internet use. Role-play handling peer pressure and how to deflect peer requests. Get creative: call a web designer to teach your child and you how to web build. You and the designer can talk and ask reflective questions about how to keep safe on the Internet. Narrow that cyber gap and take a web course together. Be sure they have face to-face social time, too. Routinely sit down with them while they surf and watch what they watch without comment. Keep discussions open. Don't ban computers or they won't open up about questionable sites or seek your advice.
Lies	Wants to fit in Scared (of consequences or punishment) Desperate	Problem-solve. Model. Clarify expectations. Plan ahead. Natural consequences. Active listening.	Help child get what he needs without lying. Model honesty. Describe specifically what you see, "I see a child that didn't wear a coat leaving the house." instead of saying, "You are lying. You didn't have a coat on." Say, "I like it when you

Problem	Child Feeling	Tool	Details
			tell the truth. Do you understand what the truth is?" Tell them if they have a problem, you can help them solve it. You will not punish for truth, no matter how bad. Cover-ups make the problem worse. Don't rescue but teach. Show how to handle peer induced lying. Appreciate the truth telling times. Show how lying hurts – read the story of the *Boy Who Cried Wolf.* Avoid trapping child into a lie. "Did you eat the last cookie?" Set up for honesty. "I hope the person who ate the last cookie, will put the plate in the sink." Don't label and don't overreact, but don't dismiss addressing it. Say, "I can see that you were scared of telling the truth, but I really appreciate it when you do."
Leaves messes in the kitchen	Distracted Indifferent	Connect, then direct. Give gentle reminders. Give input into family rules. Problem-solve. Show benefit of behavior change.	Say, "I see that you are busy with that computer game. I'd appreciate a kitchen clean up by 4:00 pm please." Problem-solve by making new clean up rules together with their input. Say, "Thanks for cleaning up. I can make dinner now."
Couch potato: Does no activity except T.V. or computer	Indifferent Bored Inadequate	Problem-solve. Stimulation. Spend time together. Plan ahead. Change environment.	Find a sport/physical activity they love. Problem-solve time limits on sedentary activities. Model an active lifestyle. Invite them on physical activities with you. Avoid getting high speed Internet, cable, satellite TV.
Doesn't take care of pets	Distracted Inadequate Indifferent	Connect, then direct. Reflective questions.	Gently remind of pet care. Ask how the pet might be feeling to remind them. Ask child how they can remember. Come up

Problem	Child Feeling	Tool	Details
		Skills chart. Plan ahead next time. Problem-solve. Learn child development.	with a plan together. Don't expect reliable care before age 12. Think twice before replacing a pet that dies. Do YOU want to take care of it?
Uses your clothes without asking	Scared	I-statements. Model. Problem-solve.	Say mostly "yes" when they do ask, so they learn that asking for permission does get them what they want. Say, "I am frustrated when I go to wear something and it's not clean. I have to take time and money to clean it." Ask to use everything of theirs.
Lends your items to her friends	Wants to fit in	I-statements. Model. Problem-solve.	Write a list of things loaned out and ask child to call and get them back. If the items don't come back, problem-solve restitution or how to recover items.
Leaves wet towels in the bathroom floor Leaves dirty dishes in the family room Socks and clothes all over	Distracted Indifferent	I-statement. Model. Gentle reminders. Family conferences.	Say, "I feel disrespected when I have to retrieve items from all over the house, because it eats up my time for doing things I enjoy. Please clean up after yourself." Give humorous reminders.
Demands more freedom	Wants to fit in Needs power/ competency	Re-evaluate limits. Problem-solve.	Give it with caveats addressing your concerns. Discuss needs and mutual new rules.
Sibling fighting	Bored. Unfair Desperate	Stimulation. Have a "yes" means "no" day. Have a "favorite kid day" and alternate days. Teach calm-down tools. Family conferences. Plan ahead.	Give them something to do. *More in Chapter 10.*

Problem	Child Feeling	Tool	Details
Bad table manners	Bored Indifferent Distracted	Spend time together. Model. Family conference. Give input into rule setting. I-statements.	Get them to help with meal preparation. Model good manners. Problem-solve it with all siblings. Say, "I feel upset when people talk with their mouth full because it looks so disgusting."
Won't get out of bed	Tired Bored	Natural consequences. Problem-solve.	Let them face the day late. Come up with ways for them to get more sleep.

Problem	Child Feeling	Tool	Details
Experiments with drugs, alcohol, smoking	Curious Wants to fit in Insecure Wants to feel grown up Needs power/ competency Confused about risks and information Wants to escape feelings or problems Insecure about belonging	One-time consultation. Model. Keep communication lines open. Have a few clear rules. When rules are broken, go to problem-solving. I-statements. Spend time together. Active listening. Problem-solve the behavior.	Listen to why they want to engage in behavior. Get consent for a one-time consultation about risks/benefits. Model a healthy lifestyle. Help to feel grown up in other ways: give more privileges and tie it in with responsibilities. Trust them. Keep listening more than talking, to build communication. Active listen to feelings without judgment so they continue talking. Problem-solve broken rules. As a last resort, work on the relationship first. If behavior becomes habitual, get professional help. *More in Chapter 11.*
Experiments with sex	Curious Insecure Wants to fit in Scared Confused Wants to feel grown up Confused about risks and information Wants to feel special and loved Has a perception of passion that is desirable	One-time consultation. Model. Keep communication lines open. Have a few clear rules. When broken, go to problem-solving. I-statements. Spend time together. Active listening. Problem-solve the behavior. Give information. Reflective questions.	Same as for drugs above. If you haven't given books about sexual health, get some fast! Use reflective questions to ask why scared of losing love interest if sexual activity doesn't happen. *More in Chapter 11.*
Experiments with crime	Curious Wants to fit in Insecure/Inadequate. Confused Wants to feel	One-time consultation. Model. Keep communication lines open. Have a few clear rules. When broken,	All the above. Don't rescue from natural consequences. *More in Chapter 11.*

Problem	Child Feeling	Tool	Details
	grown up Needs power Confused about risks Poor self-control Desperate for item	go to problem-solving. I-statements. Spend time together. Active listening. Natural consequences. Problem-solve the behavior.	
Uses inappropriate language	Insecure Wants to fit in Indifferent Needs power	Separate big issues from small issues. Reduce reasons for rebellion. One-time consultation. Develop the acceptance bone. Decide what you will do. Model. Speak respectfully to them. I-statement. Problem-solve the use of language in your presence.	Check if the words are truly offensive to you. Ignore them. Give a consultation on why swearing in certain situations is not correct. Accept that they will adopt the language of their peers. Walk away when they use that language. Avoid swearing yourself. Model appropriate language without sarcasm and "attitude." Use polite words to them. Say, "I feel disrespected when I hear all those F words in my presence." *More in Chapter 11.*
Cheating on school work	Inadequate Indifferent Desperate Scared	Natural consequences. I-statement. Problem-solve. Decide on problem ownership. Keep communication lines open.	If caught, don't rescue. Say, "I'm disappointed that you would cheat to gain a mark. How can you bring up your mark in an honest way?" Leave school matters to your child. Let your child know that you love him unconditionally regardless of academic achievement.
Won't do homework	Indifferent Bored Distracted	Natural consequences. Decide on problem ownership. Develop the "acceptance" bone. Problem-solve. Contracts.	Allow failure if necessary. Allow a low paying, low education job to teach the importance of doing coursework. Focus on your activities to take worry off them. Explore with them

Problem	Child Feeling	Tool	Details
			alternate ways to finish coursework (online, night school, etc.) Problem-solve distractions such as online gaming. Draw up a contract you both can agree on.
Wears inappropriate hair, make-up, and clothing	Insecure Wants to fit in Needs power/ competency Content Indifferent	Separate big issues from small issues. Reduce reasons for rebellion. One-time consultation. Develop the "acceptance" bone. Problem-solve.	Decide that what's on their body is their business. Appear that you don't care what they wear. Give information in case they don't know what appropriate dress is. Remember that how they dress is no reflection on you.
Wants a tattoo or piercing	Insecure Wants to fit in Needs power/ competency	Separate big issues from small issues. Reduce reasons for rebellion. One-time consultation. Develop the "acceptance" bone. Problem-solve.	All the above. Give information on risks/benefits of body piercing.
Disrespectful attitude/ speaks belligerently	Needs power/ competency Unfair/ victimized	Same as for "uses inappropriate language." Active listening. Problem-solve behavior.	Same as for "uses inappropriate language." Say, "I hear that you are very angry. What's up?" Don't take personally.
Room is a mess	Indifferent Needs power/ competency Poor self-control	Separate big issues from small issues. Reduce reasons for rebellion. One-time consultation. Develop the "acceptance" bone. Change yourself. Respect privacy. Problem-solve health issues.	Shut the door. Recognize that many things are under your child's power: dress, attitude, room organization, etc. Allow choice and decision making. Give a small consultation on health issues like food in room. Let it go.
Won't do chores	Indifferent Distracted Overwhelmed	Problem-solve. Reconsider the situation with new information. Connect,	Sit down and work out schedule of what gets done, when, and by whom.

Problem	Child Feeling	Tool	Details
		then direct. Contracts.	Consider their other obligations. Teach how to do them or do together as quality time. Say, "Hey, that game looks great. By the way, can you clear the table during the next time you can pause? Thanks!" Draw up an agreement on who does what and when.
Visits chat rooms or websites that are not appropriate	Curious Insecure Wants to fit in	Connect, then direct. Have a few clear rules. Spend time together. Change environment. Keep communication lines open. Problem-solve.	Say, "I know that you love that site, but I'm concerned about your photo on that social website." Set up rules with teen's input. Problem-solve when they are broken. Make it routine to sit and see with teen while they are surfing. Avoid computers in bedrooms. Listen to their reasoning for profiles or photos, without judgment. Learn web design together.
Lies	Scared Wants to fit in Insecure	I-statement. Avoid punishment for truth telling. Problem-solve original issue.	"I'm upset when I'm not told the truth. I find it hard to trust you."
Sneaks out of the house at night	Scared Wants to fit in	Welcome their friends. Stimulation. Re-consider situation with new information.	Make your home friendly for visitors. Consult teen on how to make it so. Provide games, music, and food and "invisible" supervision. Re-visit curfews – perhaps the child is ready for more time away.
Stays out late	Wants to fit in	Welcome their friends. Stimulation. Re-consider situation with new information. Problem-solve.	Re-visit curfews – perhaps the child is ready for more time away.

Problem	Child Feeling	Tool	Details
Leaves bike and sports equipment out on lawn	Distracted Forgetful	Natural consequences. Connect, then direct. Problem-solve. Decide on problem ownership.	Don't rescue by replacing or fixing damage. Say, "I'm glad that you were building that birdhouse. However, my saw was left in the rain and now it's rusty. Any ideas on how you can fix it?" If it's your equipment, it's your problem. If it's their equipment, it's their problem and don't replace.
Ties up the phone for hours	Wants to fit in Indifferent	Problem-solve. Respect privacy. Decide what you will do. Change environment.	Get Internet and instant messaging. Don't listen in. See how to facilitate normal teen connection with peers.
Phones long distance without asking	Scared	Problem-solve.	Help them find a way to make long distance calls without running up the phone bill.
Won't dress appropriately for certain occasions: photos, weddings, funerals	Wants to fit in Scared	One-time consultation. Develop the "acceptance" bone. Model. Decide on problem ownership.	Talk about why dress is important. Address issue of looking goofy and peer pressure. Accept they will wear what they want. Model appropriate dress.
Has undesirable friends	Insecure Inadequate Wants to fit in Needs power/competency Desperate	Reduce reasons for rebellion. One-time consultation. Develop the "acceptance" bone. Decide on problem ownership. Natural consequences. Welcome their friends.	Examine why those friends are desirable for teen and find other ways for teen to get what he is looking for. Give information of peer pressure and role play how to resist. Accept friends – the more you reject them, the more their appeal is. Don't rescue when friends get them into trouble. Allow socializing within family rules at your house. You will know what they are up to and it will open communication lines.

Problem	Child Feeling	Tool	Details
Violent	Confused Indifferent Curious Insecure Wants to fit in	Natural consequences. One-time consultation. Problem-solve.	Don't rescue from consequences. Give information on possible outcomes on future. Problem-solve how to make amends. Get professional help.
Has a much older girlfriend/ boyfriend	Content	Separate big issues from small issues. Reduce reasons for rebellion. Keep communication lines open. Develop the "acceptance" bone.	Is this their problem or yours? Can you accept this in the hopes of keeping communication lines open?
Watches too much TV, computer, video games, listens to too much music Uses too much Instant messaging	Needs solitude Poor self-control Content Indifferent Insecure/ inadequate	Separate big issues from small issues. Reduce reasons for rebellion. One-time consultation. Develop the "acceptance" bone. Contract. Welcome their friends.	If you look at the alternatives of gambling, drinking, vandalism, sex, and drugs, is this a big issue? Consider downsizing channels, Internet speed, etc. Give information on your concerns about: physical activity, violence, eye-strain, etc. Accept that this is now a big part of our culture and how teens socialize. Agree on time limits that meet everyone's needs. Make your home a social hotspot for their friends. *More in Chapter 12.*
Lies around all day doing nothing productive	Unmotivated Indifferent	Contract. Problem-solve. Focus on child's strengths.	Agree to expectations and time frames. Come to solutions for getting things done. Encourage developing strengths and talents.
Won't go to school	Bored Confused Scared Indifferent	Active listening. Contract. Problem-solve.	Consider if work is too hard, too easy, or too boring. Explore bullying or peer pressure. Problem-solve alternative ways to get education (new school or new format).

Problem	Child Feeling	Tool	Details
Brings friends home while you're gone without asking/ lets other children steal from you when they are in your house	Insecure Wants to fit in Desperate for friends	Problem-solve. Contracts. Active listening.	Get professional help.
Doesn't take baths/care about hygiene	Indifferent Invaded	Separate big issues from small issues. Reduce reasons for rebellion. One-time consultation. Develop the "acceptance" bone. Natural consequences.	Consider it might be depression and get professional help if persists.
Has tantrums and threats when they won't get their way	Angry Frustrated Desperate Poor self-control	Stay with your "no." Connect, then direct. Parent time-out. Problem-solve.	Say, "I understand you are angry about this. It's okay." After they calm down (five minutes or an hour later), stay with your "no." Keep your cool. Focus on your hobbies and what fulfills you. Teach them the problem-solving process. Get professional help if persists.
Runs away	Desperate Needs power/ Competency Unfair/ Victimized	Keep communication lines open. Focus on child's strength. Problem-solve.	Get professional help. Keep listening and listening. Avoid any punishment. It's time to rebuild relationship.
Fights with brothers and sisters	Victimized Invaded Bored Needs power/ Competency	Parent time-out. Decide on problem ownership. Model. Keep communication lines open. Active listening. Family conferences.	They should have had enough practice by now to solve it respectfully and without you. It's their problems, not yours. Keep modeling respectful conflict resolution with your partner, neighbors, friends,

Problem	Child Feeling	Tool	Details
			and workmates. Say, "I can see that you are feeling really angry about what your sister did to you. Want to tell me more?" Offer mediating if they agree and consent.
Does pranks	Bored Wants to fit in Desire for fun	One-time consultation. Stimulation.	Discuss possible outcomes and how to deal with the risks.
Say's you don't love them	Insecure Inadequate Desperate Scared	Active listening. Holding, hugs, and cuddles. Spend time together. Focus on strengths.	Don't defend. Say, "You feel sad that you think I love your sister more?" Listen without judgment. Give extra physical affection. Build the relationship.
Calls you names	Needs power Angry Unhealthy self-esteem	Active listening. Connect, then direct. Spend time together. Focus on strengths. I-statement. Keep communication lines open.	Say, "I hear you are angry about something. Want to talk? I need to be spoken to politely if we are going to talk." Do more things one-on-one with child. He may open up about resentments which lead to name calling.
Won't do things with the family	Bored Indifferent Needs power/ competency Invaded Content	Reduce reasons for rebellion. Develop the "acceptance" bone. Respect privacy. Keep communication lines open.	Accept that teens often reject family time. Encourage and invite; don't force. Accept if they decline. It's a phase. Don't sneak into their computer, journal, or drawers. Keep listening more then talking.
Wants to be by herself most of the time	Solitude Needs power/ competency Content	Develop the "acceptance" bone. Respect privacy. Keep communication lines open. Focus on strengths. Stimulation. Invite sharing one-on-one activities with you.	It's pretty normal for teens to spend a lot of time brooding on their own. Set up times to be with them on outings if possible. Set up unstructured time to talk if it comes. Encourage her hobbies and interests. If behavior becomes problematic, get professional help.

Problem	Child Feeling	Tool	Details
Demands money	Entitled Desperate	Have a few clear rules on money handling. Problem-solve if broken. Negotiate your "no".	Problem-solve together ways they can earn or get extra money for what they desperately need. Be sure your needs are met in the deal.
Tells others that you're a bad parent	Victimized Scared	Active listening. Problem-solve the behavior of speaking to others.	Seek to find out what they are thinking and feeling, without judgment. Don't defend yourself. Say, "I can tell you have strong feelings about this and I accept it. But, I would like your feelings to stay in this family. It's not respectful to complain to others, while not coming to me directly."
Threatens bodily harm to you or others or your house	Poor self-control	Decide what you will do. Model. I-statement. Have a few clear rules. One-time consultation of aggressive behavior.	Get professional help. Avoid threats you won't carry through on. Say, "Violence is not acceptable in this house." Give information on local assault laws and natural consequences for the future.
Got pregnant	Embarrassed Scared Grief of old life Excitement	Problem-solving. Keep communication lines open. Decide what you will do.	Depending on age, decide who owns the problem. 13 compared to 19 years is a big difference in how to handle. Get professional help.
Had an abortion and is now pregnant again	Fulfilled Scared	Problem-solving. Keep communication lines open.	As above.
Takes someone's car and goes joyriding. Breaks into others houses or stores and steals.	Insecure Wants to fit in Curious Excitement Poor self-control	One-time consultation. I-statements. Reflective questions. Natural consequences. Problem-solving.	Get professional help.

Problem	Child Feeling	Tool	Details
Steals and shoplifts	Insecure Wants to fit in Curious Excitement Desperate for item	One-time consultation. I-statements. Reflective questions. Natural consequences. Problem-solving.	Get professional help.
Threatens suicide	Hopeless Lonely Depressed Despair	Keep communication lines open. Active listen. Spend time together. Holding, hugs, and cuddles. Contract.	Encourage hope. Say, "Are you thinking of hurting yourself? Have you had any thoughts of suicide?" Assure love and things will get better. Get professional help immediately.
Rides in car with drunk drivers	Wants to fit in Insecure about assertion	One-time consultation. I-statements. Have a few clear rules. Contract. Reflective questions. Natural consequences. Problem-solving.	Offer unlimited rides, no questions asked, anytime. Draw up a "Contract for Life" that states you will drive them home no matter what.
Logs on to porn sites or engages in questionable Internet relationships	Curious Insecure Wants to feel loved Needs power/ competency	One-time consultation. I-statements. Reflective questions. Contracts. Problem-solving. Have a few clear rules. Connect then direct.	Get professional help if becomes habitual.

Index

References

Chapter 1

Goals of Discipline, adapted from the Canadian Paediatric Society, (n.d.) retrieved November 2004 from http://www.caringforkids.cps.ca/behaviour/EffectiveDiscipline.htm.

Short Run Goals and Long Run Goals, adapted from Discipline Dilemma Conference, Presented by Cheryl Erwin, Calgary, April 2005

Parenting Iceberg, adapted from Virginia Satir

Chapter 2

What does a respectful relationship look like? adapted from the booklet, *The Fact of Life: A guide for teens and their families*. Planned Parenthood. Jon Knowles, 2004

You and your parenting partner are modeling a bond, and "Does He Respect Me?" from "Will He Ever Change?" Questions by Karen Flint, M.Ed., Registered Psychologist, p.6 Women's Health Resources, Women's Newsletter, January/February 2006, www.gracewomenshealth.com, Volume 20, Issue 1

Share feelings, adapted from Toastmasters International Program, *Interpersonal Communication Manual*, ATM Program.

What do children and parents' need? adapted from "Maslow's Hierarchy of Needs" by Abraham Maslow.

Chapter 3

Praise Versus Encouragement, adapted from handout, *Teaching Parenting the Positive Discipline Way* by Bonnie Smith and Judy Dixon

Some Tips To Encourage, adapted from "Some Tips To Encourage": by Barb Elder, Parent Educator

Chapter 4

The Problems with Punishments and Bribery, adapted from *Teaching Children Self Discipline* By Dr. Thomas Gordon, 1989, p. 38-77

Disadvantages to Spanking, and Spanking statistics, adapted from Research from the Repeal 43 Committee, www.repeal43.org

Research on Outcomes of Physical Punishment. Elizabeth Gershoff 2002, Meta-analysis of 88 physical punishment studies. Presented by Dr. Joan Durrant at the Discipline Dilemma conference, Calgary, Alberta, April 2005

Spanking statistics, from *Parenting With Grace: The Catholic Parent's Guide to Raising (Almost) Perfect Kids* by Gregory K. Popcak, and Lisa Popcak. Our Sunday Visitor Publishing Division, 2000 Huntington, Indiana

The case against bribes, the case against punishments, benefits to children of using no punishments – adapted from *Teaching Children Self Discipline* by Dr. Thomas Gordon, 1989

Why Do Children "Misbehave"? adapted from "Why do Children Misbehave?" *Connections: The Threads That Strengthen Families* By Jean Illsley Clarke, Hazelton, 1999 and "Mistaken Goals" from *Children: The Challenge* by Rudolph Druikers, 1991

Children's coping behaviors to punishments, adapted from *Teaching Children Self Discipline* by Dr. Thomas Gordon p.82

Chapter 5

Calm-down Tools, adapted from Elizabeth Crary, *Dealing with Disappointment: Helping Kids Cope When Things Don't Go Their Way*, Parenting Press, 2003
De-clutter Your Life, adapted from Fujita, Journal of Personality and Social Psychology, 1995

Chapter 6

Developmental Milestones, adapted from Gesell Institute of Child Development.

Developmental Stages, adapted from Jean Illsley Clarke, *Self Esteem: A Family Affair* and *Help! For Parents*. Winston Press Inc, 1978

Learning Styles, adapted from www.usd.edu/trio/tut/ts/stylest.html

Multiple Intelligences, adapted from Thomas Armstrong's, *7 Kinds of Smarts*.

Gender differences

1. More males are enrolled in special education classes then females. Galley 2002

2. Boys learn best by moving around and manipulating objects. Grubbs 2001, Pollack, 1998, West 2001

3. Boys are 10 times more likely to be diagnosed with Attention Deficit Disorder and boys are also more likely to drop out of school. Pollack, 1998 "Real Boys: Rescuing our sons from the myths of boyhood."

4. Boys tend to score lower on standard tests in Language Arts. U.S. Dept of Education 1999, 2000

5. In an age of increasing majority of female enrollment in university education, only 28 percent of computer science degrees and 18 percent engineering degrees are earned by women. U.S. Department of Education 2001

6. Boys learn better through computer technology. Online courses may help to rescue boys from dropping out.

Points 1-6 from "Helping Girls Succeed" by Denise A. Jobe, "Helping Boys Succeed" by Deborah Taylor and Maureen Lorimer, *Educational Leadership*, Dec 2002 Jan 2003, p.64-70

Chapter 7

Babies can remember, from Infant mental health, Dr. Susan McDonough, Calgary Herald

Sleep Issues, Brain research, adapted from *Ghosts From The Nursery*, Robin Karr-Morse and Meredith S. Wiley, Atlantic Monthly Press, New York 1997 and *The First Years Last Forever*, Canadian Institute of Child Health, MacLean Hunter Publishing Limited and *Emotional Intelligence*, Dr. Daniel Goleman, Bantam Books, 1995

Reframe the situation, National Sleep Survey, *The No-Cry Sleep Solution for Toddlers and Preschoolers* by Elizabeth Pantley, p.123

All babies wake two to seven times a night, adapted from Infant Sleep Article, Wendy Hall, Associate Professor of Nursing at University of British Columbia, *Today's Parent*, July 2006

Chapter 8

The Feeding Relationship, copyright by and reprinted with permission from *Secrets of Feeding a Healthy Family*, by Ellyn Satter. Kelcy Press, Madison, WI 1999. For ordering information call 877-844-0857 or see www.EllynSatter.com

Chapter 9

Recent studies show that children don't develop the ability to multitask until the teen years, adapted from the McMaster University Study, Reported by Denise Davy, The Hamilton Spectator, October 20, 2006

I like and appreciate about you…, adapted from *In Their Own Way*, by Thomas Armstrong and adapted from *Playful Parenting*, by Denise Chapman Weston and Mark S. Weston

Young children under 5 follow rules less then half the time. A Simple Gift

Chapter 10

Walk away from attitude, adapted from "Cruelty is a Learned Response," reported by Calgary Herald, July 21, 2005, University of Montreal Study of 234 sets of twins

Problem solving sibling issues, adapted from Cheryl Erwin's chore process.

Will Smith, The Calgary Herald, Dec 13, 2006

Chapter 11

Teens can regress to earlier behaviors, adapted from *Self-esteem: A family affair*, 1978 and *Growing up Again*, Jean Illsley Clarke. Hazelton 1989

Helpful parenting behaviors: Communication, Development, Living Together Issues, adapted from handout material by Patricia Morgan, MA, Co-author of *Love Her As She Is* and speaker, www.LightHeartedConcepts.com

We are growing from an independence valued society of 1950 to a more interdependent society, where young adults are not pushed out of the nest at 18 or even out of the family bed at five. Marlene Moretti, Simon Fraser University, Burnaby BC, lead author of a 2004 review of studies on parent-child attachment

Warning signs that your child may be on drugs, adapted from www.aacap.org American Academy of Children and Adolescent Psychiatry, adapted from (Facts for Families, (n.d.) Retrieved October 2006 from http://www.aacap.org page.ww?name=Teens%3A+Alcohol+And+Other+Drugs&section=Facts+for+Families)

Warning signs of possible suicide intentions, adapted from Teen Suicide, (n.d.) retrieved October 2006 from http://www.aacap.org/page.ww?name=Teen+Suicide&section=Facts+for+Families

Chapter 12

Video and computer game software sales hit a record 7.3 billion dollars in 2004. The average gamer is 30, which translates into a much larger customer base than when games were marketed solely to teenagers. From Gaming article in Calgary Herald April 19, 2005

The video game industry is 30 billion worldwide, from Avenue Magazine article by Tyler C. Hellard, December 2006

A Final Word

"Parenting Styles Change Outcomes,?" from National Longitudinal Survey of Children and Youth, Statistics Canada, reported in The Daily, October 25, 2005

Permissions

Grateful acknowledgement is made to the following for permission to reprint previously published material.

Control versus influence rectangle
Benefits to children of using no punishments
Benefits of problem-solving
Excerpt from *Parent Effectiveness Training*, by Thomas Gordon. Copyright @ 1969, renewed @ 1980 by T. Gordon. Used by permission of Harper Collins Publishers.

Reasons not to spank
Excerpt from *The Catholic Parent's Guide to Raising Almost Perfect Kids*.
The permission to reproduce copyrighted materials for use was extended by Our Sunday Visitor, 200 Noll Plaza, Huntington, IN 46750. 1-800-348-2440. Website: www.osv.com. No other use of this material is authorized.

Division of Responsibility in Feeding
Excerpt from *Secrets of Feeding a Healthy Family*
p. 32, copyright by and reprinted with permission from *Secrets of Feeding a Healthy Family*, by Ellyn Satter, Kelcy Press, Madison, WI 1999. For ordering information call 877-844-0857 or see www.EllynSatter.com

Calm-down tools adapted from
Self Calming Tools
Excerpt from *Dealing with Disappointment*, by Elizabeth Crary, Parenting Press, 2003, p. 86 and 87

Will He Ever Change? Karen Flint, M.Ed., Registered Psychologist, p.6 Womens Health Resources, Women's Newsletter, January/February 2006, www.gracewomenshealth.com, Volume 20, issue 1

Helpful Teenager Parenting Behaviors: Communication, Development, Living Together Issues. Adapted and reprinted with permission from Patricia Morgan, MA, speaker and author of *Love Her As She Is*, www.LightHeartedConcepts.com

It takes 2 to tangle, Power Struggles Boxing Ring, Celia Osenton

Bibliography

Normal development

Your Two Year Old, Dr. Louise Bates Ames and Frances L. Ilg
(Also, Your Three, Four, Five and Six Year Old) Gesell Institute of Human Behavior,
Dell, 1979

Your Seven Year Old, Dr. Louise Bates Ames and Carol Chase Haber,
(Also, your Eight and Nine Year Old) Gesell Institute of Human Behavior,
Dell, 1990

Your One Year Old, Dr. Louise Bates Ames, and Frances L. Ilg, and
Carol Chase Haber, (Also, Your Ten to Fourteen Year Old) Gesell Institute of
Human Behavior, Dell, 1990

Between Parent and Teenager, Dr. Haim G. Ginott,
The MacMillan Company, 1969

Between Parent and Child, Dr. Haim G. Ginott, An Avon Book, 1965

The Gallagher Guide to the Baby Years, Stephanie Gallagher, 2005

The First Twelve Months of Life, Frank Caplan, Putnam Publishing Group, 1973

The First Three Years of Life, Burton L. White, Avon Books, 1975

Child Care and The Growth of Love, John Bowlby, Pelican, 1971

The Emotional Life of the Toddler, Alicia F. Lieberman, Ph.D, The Free Press,
1993

The Second Twelve Months of Life, Frank Caplan and Theresa Caplan, Bantam
Books, 1979

Early Childhood Development: Prenatal Through Age Eight, Sandra Anselmo,
Macmillan Publishing Company, 1987

The Psychology of the Child, Jean Piaget and Barbel Inhelder, Basic Books, 1969

Your Baby and Child, Penelope Leach, Dorling Kindersley, 1989

Why Love Matters, Sue Gerhardt, Brunner-Routledge, 2004

Emotional Intelligence, Daniel Goleman, Bantam Books, 1995

7 Kinds of Smarts, Thomas Armstrong, Penguin Books, 1993

In Their Own Way, Thomas Armstrong, Ph.D Tarcher Putnum Books, 2000

Boys and Girls Learn Differently! A Guide for Teachers and Parents by Michael Gurian, Patricia Henley, and Terry Trueman Jossey-Bass, 2001

The Mother of All Toddler Books, Ann Douglas, John Wiley, 2002

Parenting styles

Hold On To Your Kids: Why Parents Matter, Gordon Neufeld, Ph.D and Gabor Mate, M.D. Alfred A. Knopf Canada, 2004.

The Parent's Handbook, Dinkmeyer, McKay, American Guidance Centre, 1997

But Nobody Told Me That I Would Have To Leave Home, Kathy Lynn, Whitecap, 2006

Kids Are Worth It! Barbara Coloroso. Somerville House Publishing, 1995

Active Parenting Today, Michael H. Popkin, Ph.D Active Parent Publishers, 1993

Connections: The Threads That Strengthen Families, Jean Illsley Clarke, Hazeldon, 1999

Attachment Parenting, Katie Allison Granju, Pocket Books, 1999

Growing Up Again: Parenting Ourselves, Parenting Our Children, Jean Illsley Clarke and Connie Dawson, Hazelton, 1998

On Becoming a Person: A therapist's view of psychotherapy. Rogers, Carl and Peter Kramer, Houghton Mifflin Co. 1963

Behavior Modification: What it is and how to do it. Garry Martin/Joseph Pear, University of Manitoba, Prentice-Hall, Inc, 1978

Playful Parenting, Denise Chapman Weston and Mark S. Weston, Tarcher/Putnam, 1996

Why Parents Disagree, Dr. Ron Taffel, William Morrow and Company, 1994

Natural Childhood, John Thomson, Simon and Schuster Inc. 1994

Positive discipline

Punished By Rewards, Alfie Kohn, Houghton Mifflin, 1999

Raising Your Spirited Child, Mary Sheedy Kurcinka, Harper Collins, 1991

Effective Discipline: A Healthy Approach, Canadian Pediatric Society (Website)

Guidance for Effective Discipline, American Academy of Pediatrics (Website)

Siblings Without Rivalry, Adele Faber and Elaine Mazlish, Avon Books, 1998

Kids, Parents and Power Struggles, Mary Sheedy Kurcinka, Harper Collins Publishers Inc., 2001

Time-In Parenting, Otto Weininger, Ph.D, Rinascente Books Inc. 2002

Loving Each One Best, Nancy Samalin and Catherine Whitney, Bantam, 1995

Teaching Children Self Discipline, Dr. Thomas Gordon, Random House, 1989

Pick Up Your Socks, and Other Skills Growing Children Need, Elizabeth Crary, Parenting Press, 1990

Positive Discipline: The First Three Years, Jane Nelson, Ed.D, Cheryl Erwin, M.A. and Roslyn Duffy, Prima Publishing, 1998

Discipline Without Stress, Punishments or Bribes: How Teachers and Parents Promote Responsibility and Learning. Dr. Marvin Marshall, Piper Press, 2001

Parenting Without Punishment: Making Problem Behavior work for you. John W. Maag, The Charles Press, 1996

No More Tantrums, Diane Mason, Gayle Jensen, Carolyn Ryzewicz, Contemporary Books, 1997

Communication and self-esteem

Your Child's Self-Esteem, Dorothy Corkille Briggs, Doubleday, 1970

Self-Esteem, A Family Affair, Jean Illsley Clarke, Winston Press Inc. 1978

How To Talk So Kids Will Listen, and Listen So Kids Will Talk, Adele Faber and Elaine Mazlish. First Avon Books, 1995

How Children Fail. Holt, John C., Perseus Press, 1995

Love Her As She Is, Patricia Morgan, M.A. with Kelly Morgan, Light Hearted Concepts, 2000

Dealing with Disappointment, Helping Kids Cope When Things Don't Go Their Way. Elizabeth Crary, Parenting Press, 2003

Parent Effectiveness Training, Dr. Thomas Gordon, Three Rivers Press, 2000

Parents, Please Don't Sit On Your Kids: A Parent's Guide to Non-Punitive Discipline, by Clare Cherry, Fearon Teachers Aids, 1985

Love and Anger: The Parental Dilemma, Nancy Samalin with Catherine Whitney, Penguin Books, 1991

Elbows Off the Table, Napkin in the Lap, No Video Games During Dinner, Carol McD. Wallace, St. Martin's Press, 1996

Parenting With Grace: Catholic Parent's Guide to Raising (Almost) Perfect Kids, By Gregory K. Popcak and Lisa Popcak. Our Sunday Visitor Publishing Division, 2000

How To Deal With Your Acting Up Teenager. Robert T. Bayard and Jean Bayard, MD M. Evans and Co., 1981

Talking With Your Teenager, Ruth Bell, Random House, 1983

The Magic of Encouragement: Nurturing Your Child's Self Esteem, Stephanie Marston, Pocket Books, 1992

P.E.T. In Action, Dr. Thomas Gordon, Wyden Books, 1976

Parenting Concerns

Mom Management, Tracy Lyn Moland, TGOT, 2003

The Highly Sensitive Person, Elaine N. Aron, Ph.D, Broadway Books, 1996

The Birth Order Book, Dr. Kevin Leman, A Dell Book, 1985

More Speaking of Sex, Meg Hickling, R.N., Northstone Publishing, 1999

The No-Cry Sleep Solution, Elizabeth Pantley, McGraw-Hill, 2002

Parenting The Fussy Baby and High Need Child, William Sears, M.D. and Martha Sears R.N., Little, Brown and Co. 1996

Order Form

This is a caring gift for anyone who is interested in parent issues and personal development of their important relationships.

Send me _____ copies of **Discipline Without Distress**: 135 tools for raising caring, responsible children without time-out, spanking, punishment, or bribery @ $35.00 each. Includes GST, shipping and handling.

I have enclosed a check for $_____

Made payable to Professional Parenting Canada:
12018 Lake Erie Road S.E. Calgary, Alberta, Canada T2J 2L8

Name _____
Address _____
City_____
Province/State _____
Country _____
Postal/Zip code _____
Email _____

For groups, organizations, or businesses, please enquire about volume order discounts. Call (403) 714-6766

An Invitation

I would be interested in your experience in reading and applying this book. Please send a note if you wish to share any thoughts, feelings, or questions with me. I would also love to hear about your tips for handling difficult behavior with love and guidance instead of punishment.

Love and wonderful wishes to you,

Judy Arnall
jarnall@shaw.ca

Should you be interested in Parent Coaching, or booking a speaking engagement or workshop, please feel free to contact Judy at 403-714-6766, or visit www.professionalparenting.ca for Keynote and Workshop descriptions.

Conference Keynotes, Breakouts and Webinars Available

www.professionalparenting.ca

Keynotes:

Delete Your Distress: Mastering Work-Life Balance in the Digital Age
Creative Education: Play-based Learning is the Key to University
Plugged-In Parenting: Connecting with the Digital Generation for Health, Safety and Love
Eggs for Dinner Again? Holding Down the Fort When Your Parenting Partner
Works Away From Home
Discipline Without Distress: 10 Essential Tools for the New Millennium.

Interactive Breakouts, Seminars and Webinars:

Delete Your Distress: Mastering Work-Life Balance in the Digital Age
Plugged-In Parenting: Connecting with the Digital Generation for Health, Safety and Love
Discipline Without Distress: 10 Essential Tools for the New Millennium.
Eggs for Dinner Again? Holding Down the Fort When Your Parenting Partner
Works Away From Home
Creative Education: Play-based Learning is the Key to University
Communication Essentials: Conflict to Connection
Temperament Traits: Raising Your Spirited Child
Every child is gifted! Understanding Multiple Intelligences
Taming the Gaming: How to Encourage Digital Intelligence
Run for your life! Taming Parent Anger
123 Time-Out: The Pros, Cons, and Alternatives
Self Esteem For Building a Better World
Ages and Stages: What to Expect When
Sleep Without Distress: Solving Your Family Sleep Problems
Mealtimes Without Distress: How to Solve Picky Eating Issues
Sleeping, Eating and Toileting: Turn Battlegrounds into Bonding Zones.
Brain Building Play Ideas
Sibling Rivalry Remedies
Harnessing Homework Hassles
Home-Schooling: Navigating the Sea of Choices.
Taming Temper: Handling Your Angry Child
He Dared Me! Helping Children Manage Peer Pressure.
Parenting Your Tween
Attachment Parenting For Everyone
Peaceful Partnering with Differing Parenting Styles
And Baby Makes Four: Smoothing the Way for the Second Child's birth
When Consequences, Spanking and Time-Out Don't Work
Your Terrific Toddler (four-week class)
Your Promising Preschooler (four-week class)
Your Savvy School-aged Child (four-week class)
Your Tremendous Teenager (four-week class)
Dr. Thomas Gordon's Parent Effectiveness Training P.E.T. (six-week class)

Also By Judy Arnall

Canadian Association of Professional Speakers

Judy Arnall, BA, DTM

Conference Speaker, Trainer and Bestselling Author

Judy is an international award-winning professional speaker and a well-known Canadian education and parenting expert, who regularly appears on television interviews on CBC, CTV, and Global as well as publications including Chatelaine, Today's Parent, Canadian Living, Parents magazine, The Globe and Mail, Sun Media and Postmedia News.

She teaches family communication and parenting leadership at the University of Calgary, Continuing Education, Chinook Learning, and Alberta Health Services. Judy founded the non-profit organization, Attachment Parenting Canada, which offers public courses and webinars across Canada. Judy is an authorized facilitator of the Parent Effectiveness Training (P.E.T.) series, and the Terrific Toddlers program, which she assisted in developing for Alberta Health Services.

As a professional conference speaker, Judy engages audiences in interactive activities. Her keynote, *"Delete Your Distress: Mastering work-life balance in the digital age,"* is popular with corporations and associations. She is a professional member of CAPS (Canadian Association of Professional Speakers) and a DTM in Toastmasters.

Judy is the author of the worldwide bestseller, *"Discipline Without Distress: 135 Tools for raising caring, responsible children without time-out, spanking, punishment or bribery."* As a parent of five children, Judy has a broad understanding of the issues facing parents and the digital generation and has authored an educational DVD titled *"Plugged-In Parenting: Connecting with the digital generation for health, safety and love."* She is also the author of *"The Last Word on Parenting Advice," "The Unschooling Graduates"* and *"The Parenting Information Maze: How to find the advice that fits your family."*

www.professionalparenting.ca   www.attachmentparenting.ca
jarnall@shaw.ca   (403) 714-6766